Caribbean Tourism

Caribbean Tourism

Jean S. Holder

Canoe Press UWI
Jamaica • Barbados • Trinidad and Tobago

Caribbean Development Bank

Canoe Press
7A Gibraltar Hall Road, Mona
Kingston 7, Jamaica
www.uwipress.com

© 2013 by Jean S. Holder
All rights reserved. Published 2013

ISBN: 978-976-653-015-0

A catalogue record of this book is available from the National Library of Jamaica.

Front cover photographs, from top left:
© Jessica Bee, http://www.flickr.com/photos/jessicabee/357444095/;
© GoToVan, http://www.flickr.com/photos/gotovan/7674706682/;
© K. Alexander, http://www.flickr.com/photos/onourtravels/7874105626/;
© Derek Hatfield, http://www.flickr.com/photos/loimere/4559614202/.
Back cover photograph: © vgm8383, http://www.flickr.com/photos/vgm8383/2766980454/.

Cover design by Robert Harris.

Printed in the United States of America.

Contents

Foreword	ix
Preface	xi
Acknowledgements	xiii
List of Abbreviations	xvii
Introduction	xix

CHAPTER 1
Coming to Grips with the Complexity and Other Characteristics of Tourism — 1

CHAPTER 2
History, Race and Tourism in Bermuda, the Bahamas, Barbados, Jamaica and Cuba — 14

CHAPTER 3
Regional Integration in the Caribbean and the Birth and History of Regional Tourism Institutions — 71

CHAPTER 4
The Changing Face of Caribbean Tourism — 95

CHAPTER 5
CARIFTA: Views and Strategies Relating to Caribbean Tourism — 108

CHAPTER 6
Caribbean Tourism Expands to Europe — 131

CHAPTER 7
The Creation of the Caribbean Tourism Organization — 148

CHAPTER 8
The Role, Economic Contribution and Impact of Cruise Tourism on Caribbean Societies — 159

CHAPTER 9
Creating a Sustainable Tourism Strategic Plan for the Caribbean — 172

CHAPTER 10
Failed Attempts to Create the Regional Tourism Fund — 213

CHAPTER 11
Developing the Sports Tourism Niche Market — 226

CHAPTER 12
Developing the Culture/Heritage Tourism Niche Market — 244

CHAPTER 13
From Sugar to Tourism: The Shift to Services — 271

CHAPTER 14
The Major Factors Determining How Global Tourism Performs — 291

CHAPTER 15
The Second Decade: Whither Caribbean Tourism? — 318

APPENDIX 1
International and Caribbean Tourist Arrivals, 1970 to 2010 — 351

APPENDIX 2
Key Information on Various Aspects of the Cruise Industry: Caribbean Cruise Survey, 2000 — 355

APPENDIX 3
Tourism Taxes in Five Selected Caribbean Societies — 363

APPENDIX 4
Draft Inter-Governmental Agreement for the Regulation of Cruise Shipping in the Caribbean — 372

APPENDIX 5
Tourism Arrivals, 2008–2011   385

APPENDIX 6
Excerpts from a Speech by Sir Ronald Sanders in June 2007
at the Watershed Media Centre in Bristol, England   418

APPENDIX 7
LIAT Fares and Taxes Tables   424

INDEX   433

Foreword

I welcome the invitation to write a brief foreword for Jean Holder's book *Caribbean Tourism*, which traces the development of tourism in the wider Caribbean from its early beginnings in the mid-nineteenth century to its current status of major, or significant, industry in most countries within the Caribbean Basin. No one else is better qualified for this undertaking than Mr Holder, who served for fifteen years as founding CEO of the Caribbean Tourism Research and Development Centre, fifteen years at its successor, the Caribbean Tourism Organization, and as chairman for the last nine years of LIAT, the maidservant of Caribbean tourism. In these roles he interacted with prime ministers, ministers of tourism, hotel and airline executives, chairmen of regional tourism associations, and representatives of countries and international organizations such as the World Bank, the International Development Bank and the Organization of American States.

Holder seeks, in his own words, "to tell the story of why, when, how and where tourism, one of the world's oldest industries, came to the Caribbean region and why its journey has been so turbulent". He identifies the abolition of slavery in British Caribbean colonies in 1834, and the repeal by the British Parliament in 1845 of tariffs that protected West Indian sugar from foreign competition, as the root causes of the collapse of the sugar industry in the Caribbean leading, in the search for economic diversification, to the introduction of tourism, the most promising service industry at the time.

However, Holder does not limit himself to an exposition on the economic and business factors leading to the industry's transformation into the most important earner of foreign exchange for Caribbean countries not endowed with natural resources. Rather, he views tourism through a wide lens that displays the historical, political, social, ethnic and psychological factors which, for better or for worse, have affected this invasive industry, rendering it a complex and controversial activity capable of exciting extreme reactions from the local population. Several academic economists in the region considered tourism a volatile and fickle industry, while social scientists feared the visitors might corrupt the morals of the locals. Their fears were not totally unfounded, since the new industry would not only mimic the monocultural seasonality of the sugar industry but also "exhibited many of the negative socio-cultural characteristics reminiscent of the era of colonialism and slavery". Indeed, neither President Forbes Burnham of Guyana nor Prime Minister Eric Williams of Trinidad and Tobago, Holder observes, "regarded tourism as a sector he wished to see developed in his country". Ironically, tourism would at times prove a more reliable source of foreign exchange earnings for Barbados and the Bahamas than bauxite for Jamaica and Guyana, or oil and gas for Trinidad and Tobago. Holder asks and answers the question: "Why have Caribbean people had a love/hate relation with tourism although almost everyone would agree it is of critical economic importance to their lives?"

The Caribbean Tourism Research and Development Centre, founded in 1974, and the Caribbean Tourism Organization, after 1989, would transform the way in which the business of Caribbean tourism was conducted. Staffed by university-trained economists, statisticians, physical planners, sociologists and market researchers, the organization was soon able to create a comprehensive database of tourism statistics for the entire region, measuring tourist and cruise arrivals, length of stay, hotel occupancy rates, tourist expenditure and so on, in keeping with the late Peter Drucker's dictum, "What isn't measured doesn't get managed." It also gathered intelligence on the economic impact of tourism. The Caribbean Tourism Research and Development Centre also played an important role in altering public perceptions of the tourism industry through its own publications and by collaborating with both academic and tourism agencies in the fields of education and training, and served as a cradle of senior public servants and managers in the public and private sectors.

Jean Holder is understandably proud of his own role in the establishment of the Caribbean Tourism Research and Development Centre but fully recognizes the important contributions of his fellow workers, many of whom now hold high office in government, diplomacy, academia and the private sector throughout the Caribbean.

Sir Courtney N. Blackman

Preface

During my thirty years as the secretary general of two Caribbean tourism organizations – fifteen years at the Caribbean Tourism Research and Development Centre (CTRC) and a further fifteen at the Caribbean Tourism Organization (CTO) – I wrote many articles and contributed chapters to a number of books on tourism.

After my retirement from the CTO, it was suggested to me by a number of persons whose opinions I respect that I should write a comprehensive book about the Caribbean tourism industry. After five years as chairman of LIAT Airline, I became so consumed with all the challenges facing the Caribbean in the area of air transportation that I was driven to write about them, first and foremost as matters demanding urgent discussion, understanding and, I hoped, solutions. Hence my book *Don't Burn Our Bridges: The Case for Owning Airlines* was given priority and published in April 2010 by the University of the West Indies Press.

I have now concluded that the time spent dealing directly with air transportation has given me a more comprehensive view of the tourism sector as a whole, and I therefore undertook the present project with more confidence than I might otherwise have done. I had to decide, however, on what aspects of the tourism industry I should write after an association with travel and tourism for just under forty years.

The present book is entitled *Caribbean Tourism*. It deals with the history and development of its subject from its earliest beginnings in the nineteenth century to the second decade of the twenty-first century.

My intention was to write a straightforward narrative about the history of Caribbean tourism development and to relate certain of my own experiences. However, as I pondered the struggle that tourism faced in becoming accepted in the Caribbean despite its undoubted contribution to the region's economic development, I was drawn to focus on the history of these territories and how colonialism, slavery and sugar affected almost everything that concerns tourism in the present. It is a perspective which can never be fully understood by the many external tourism practitioners who are our industry partners in our countries, and who must think it is unnecessary and even unpleasant to revive these memories.

Acknowledgements

I wish to state that in my own journey with tourism, which began in 1974, I have had the opportunity to work with a number of tourism colleagues and regional development specialists whose technical and other support I value greatly. I therefore wish to acknowledge the significant contribution which they made to my understanding and knowledge of the tourism industry. There is, of course, a long list, but I make special mention of colleagues from the Caribbean Tourism Association (CTA), Caribbean Tourism Research and Development Centre (CTRC), Caribbean Tourism Organization (CTO) and Caribbean Hotel Association (CHA); James Pepperdine, Audrey Palmer-Hawks, Arley Sobers – all three now deceased – and John Bell, Winfield Griffith, Luther Miller, Michael Youngman, Karen Ford-Warner, Bonita Morgan, Veronica St Louis, Hugh Riley, Sylma Brown, Julia Hendry, Dr Auliana Poon, Vincent Vanderpool-Wallace, Patricia Byer, Harriette Banfield, Johnson Johnrose and Stephen Aymes – some retired, others still in harness at the time of writing.

I wish also to express my appreciation to the now-retired Sir Edwin Carrington, former secretary general of the Caribbean Community (CARICOM) and Byron Blake, former assistant secretary general, for two reasons. First, for their valiant efforts at holding together CARICOM, an association of states which the Almighty and the British Empire had fragmented. Second, for supporting, since 1974, the CTRC, the CTO and Caribbean tourism generally, when it was not fashionable to do so. I also thank the Central Bank of Barbados for its support and must acknowledge the exceptional support of president Dr Warren Smith and the Caribbean Development Bank for sponsoring this publication.

In writing this book I have drawn heavily on the resources of the document centre of the CTO, especially the Caribbean tourism statistical reports, *The North American Demand Study for Caribbean Tourism*; the *European Tourism Demand Study, 1979*; the *European Tourism Demand Study Update, 1983*; and the final report of the OAS/CTRC regional seminar on "Cultural Patrimony and the Tourism Product: Towards a Mutually Beneficial Relationship". I also wish to express my appreciation to the CTO secretary general, Hugh Riley, to the CTO staff, and to the chief commercial officer at LIAT, Leesa Parris-Rudder, and the LIAT staff for the use of tables on tourism and air transportation, to Norma Holder for assistance with editing, and to Janelle Morris and Grace Holder-Nelson for computer and secretarial advice.

I have also made reference to one of my own books *Don't Burn Our Bridges: The Case for Owning Airlines*, published by the University of the West Indies Press in April 2010, to some of my contributions to other books on tourism and air transportation, such as *Practicing Responsible Tourism: International Case Studies in Tourism Planning, Policy, and Development*, edited by Lynn C. Harrison and Winston Husbands; *Tourism: The Driver of Change in the Jamaican Economy*, edited by Kenneth O. Hall and Rheima Holding; *Production Integration in CARICOM: From Theory to Action*, by Kenneth Hall and Denis Benn; and to some other papers, all of which can be found in the CTO library. These papers include "The Challenges of Technological Change in the Travel and Tourism Industry", "Cruise Tourism: The Pros and Cons", "Cruise Tourism in the Caribbean: Towards a Spirit of Cooperation", "Defining the Caribbean's Tourism Position in World Trade Negotiations", "Developing the Sports Tourism Niche Market for the Caribbean", "Human Resource Development: A Key Factor in Building a Sustainable Tourism Industry", "Key Factors of Sustainable Tourism Development", "Meeting the Challenge of Change", "Paradoxes, Sustainable Tourism Development and New Concepts of Sovereignty", "Public/Private Sector Partnership for Excellence in Tourism Development", "Responding to the Present and Future Challenges of Caribbean Tourism", "Tourism Benefits to the Region from Cricket World Cup 2007", "Tourism and Culture", "Tourism Policies and Impacts", "Trade in Services Liberalization Negotiations: Regional Tourism Policy Positions" and "Tourism Summit: Caribbean Tourism Development Program".

Finally, I wish to acknowledge my indebtedness to other source materials, which include *Capitalism and Slavery* by Eric Williams; the "Caribbean Regional Airlines Cooperation Study" executed by Miami Aviation Services and El Perial for CTO; *Caribbean Wars Untold: A Salute to the British West Indies* by Humphrey Metzgen and John Graham; *CARICOM: Our Caribbean Community: An Introduction* by the CARICOM Secretariat; the 1972 Commonwealth Caribbean Regional Secretariat's report; *Confronting Slavery: Breaking Through the Corridors of Silence* by Alvin O. Thompson; *The First West Indies Cricket Tour: Canada and the United States in 1866* and *A History of Barbados: From Amerindian Settlement to Caribbean Single Market* by Hilary McD. Beckles; *A History of West Indies Cricket* by Michael Manley; *Life of Alexander* and *Lives* by Plutarch; *Managing in the Service Economy* by James L. Heskett; *People and Tourism: Issues and Attitudes in the Jamaican Hospitality Industry* by Hopeton S. Dunn and Leith L. Dunn; the 1994 CTO document *Report on the Requirements for Establishing a Regional Regulatory Body and Licensing System to Oversee the Operations of Cruise Ships in the Caribbean Sea* by Ralph Carnegie; *To Hell with Paradise: A History of the Jamaican Tourist Industry* by Frank Taylor; *A Time to Choose: Caribbean Development in the Twenty-first Century*; "Travel and Tourism's Economic Impact 2011: The Caribbean" by the World Travel and Tourism Council and Oxford Economics; The United Nations' *2007/2008 Human Development Report: Fighting Climate Change: Human Solidarity in a Divided World*; *The West Indies* by Philip Sherlock; *Will of the Wind* by the Reverend Andrew Hatch; *The World Bank Annual Report 2005: Year in Review*; and "The Year Was 1951: The CTO Story", by Richard S. Kahn and Johnson John Rose. I consulted in the *Gleaner* newspaper the articles by Rebecca Tortello, "Pieces of the Past: Jamaica's Grand Hotels" (26 November 2001) and "Pieces of the Past: The Great Exhibition of 1891" (28 January 2002). I also used the CTO report on tourism and taxes in the Caribbean, CTO executive briefs by Michael Youngman, and various commentaries by Ronald Sanders, especially his paper "The Commonwealth Caribbean and the New Colonialism: Risks and Resistance in an Age of Globalization". An excerpt from that paper is attached as appendix 6.

Abbreviations

ACP	African, Caribbean, and Pacific Group of States
ALTA	Air Transportation and Caribbean Air Transport Association
APD	air passenger duty
BRIC	Brazil, Russia, India and China
BWIA	British West Indian Airways
CAL	Caribbean Airlines
CARICOM	Caribbean Community
CARIFORUM	Caribbean Forum
CARIFTA	Caribbean Free Trade Association
CARIMOS	Caribbean Plan for Monuments and Sites
CHA	Caribbean Hotel Association
CIDOT	Cayman Islands Department of Tourism
COTED	Council for Trade and Economic Development
CSME	CARICOM Single Market and Economy
CTA	Caribbean Tourism Association
CTO	Caribbean Tourism Organization
CTRC	Caribbean Tourism Research Centre/Caribbean Tourism Research and Development Centre
ECTA	Eastern Caribbean Tourist Association
FCCA	Florida Caribbean Cruise Association
FIFA	International Federation of Association Football
FTAA	Free Trade Area of the Americas
GDP	gross domestic product
IAF	Inter-American Foundation
IATA	International Air Transport Association

ICC	International Cricket Council
ITB	International Tourisme Bourse
LDC	less developed country
LIAT	Leeward Islands Air Transport
MIST	management information system for tourism
NGO	non-governmental organization
OAS	Organization of American States
OECD	Organisation for Economic Co-operation and Development
UNDP	United Nations Development Programme
UNWTO	United Nations World Tourism Organization
WTO	World Trade Organization

Introduction

This book, *Caribbean Tourism,* may be unique in intertwining the history of sugar, the history of slavery, and tourism in the Caribbean. The history of a country or region is often the history of its major economic activities. Caribbean history, from the early seventeenth century to the twenty-first, is perhaps largely the history of sugar and tourism in the region. Many of the Caribbean territories were for centuries chronically dependent on the sugar industry for their socio-economic development. In the last quarter of the nineteenth century the tourism industry had its early beginnings in a number of countries in or close to the Caribbean Basin. In 2013, tourism has become the major industry in most Caribbean countries, and a significant industry in all the others.

The history of Caribbean sugar and of its association with transatlantic slavery has been much researched and published. But little work has been published on the history of tourism. It is therefore one of the objectives of this book to fill a large gap in the knowledge of Caribbean people about an industry of critical importance to themselves.

A country's tourism product reflects its history

It is important to see the relationship between a country's history and the tourism product it offers. The tourism product is often thought of as the hotel, and the amenities and the other hospitality and transport services used by visitors. The product is, however, more than this. It is the cultural experiences offered by the country to the visitor. These experiences derive their authenticity and uniqueness from their being a distillation of the beliefs, values and practices that have been shaped by the country's socio-economic history. For example, one would expect that the entities that comprise a country's cultural and heritage product – domestic buildings, commercial architecture, industrial structures, military works, public buildings, heritage sites, artisans' skills, folklore, folk art and crafts, culinary arts, entertainment, performing and visual arts, religious practices, educational systems, *inter alia* – would reflect what the people did for a living. Life and living would therefore be expected to be somewhat different in a plantation society, built on slavery, than in an industrial society, where all men were born free and equal under the law.

Perhaps a simple example would be illustrative of the point being made here. In a plantation economy, the great houses of the planters could be expected to be counted among the impressive structures of the time. In a tourism economy, certain of the most impressive buildings would be the hotels and the elaborate villas of the rich and famous, and of certain of the other structures in which they spend their time. The nature of the Caribbean's history has sometimes presented challenges to its tourism promoters, about how and what aspects of its heritage they should package and offer as visitor experiences.

The Caribbean's love-hate relationship to tourism

One of the questions which this book raises is why, despite its economic dominance, Caribbean tourism is constantly being asked to justify its existence on socio-cultural and environmental grounds. Why have Caribbean people had a love-hate relationship with tourism although almost everyone would agree it is of critical economic importance to their lives? Three explanations are offered in this book.

One possible explanation may lie in the nature of the activity itself, which will be shown to attract certain negative reactions for reasons which will later be outlined in chapter 1. A second possible explanation may be due to a lack of understanding about how tourism actually serves as a tool of development, a lack which hopefully can be addressed by education and re-education. But the major factor in determining negative attitudes to tourism in the Caribbean is almost certainly this: The sugar plantation culture and slavery created the kind of societies which have made people suspicious of any activity that involves relationships between races that are even remotely reflective of those that existed before emancipation. We cannot therefore avoid discussing what those societies in the New World were like and the legacies inherited by Caribbean people down to the twenty-first century. But given our economic realities, we must also discuss how we have overcome and are still seeking to overcome the challenges posed by our history.

European sixteenth-century decimation of Caribbean indigenous peoples

Even before the advent of African slavery in the Caribbean, the European colonizers visited incredible brutality upon the Native American people who, in 1492, had discovered Christopher Columbus hopelessly lost in their countries. Regrettably, too little attention seems to have been paid by modern Caribbean historians to the barbaric acts performed on the native Tainos or Arawaks, which would in the twenty-first century be labelled as genocide, and which would provoke calls for the perpetrators to be brought before the International Court of Justice.

At the time of the arrival of Columbus in the region, the number of the indigenous population was estimated at 250,000. By 1517, due to the diseases that came with the European arrivals and the oppression by the colonizers, the number had fallen to 14,000. The Spanish then brought in African slave labour to replace the dwindling number of indigenous workers. By 1574 a census taken in the Greater Antilles recorded 1,000 Spaniards and 12,000 African slaves on Hispaniola, the oldest permanent European settlement in the Americas. This island was later divided to become Haiti and the Dominican Republic.

According to Philip Sherlock (*The West Indies*, 1966), the Dominican friar Bartolomé de Las Casas, who was an ardent champion of the native population against the Spanish colonists, persuaded the Spanish Emperor that the only way to save the indigenous Arawaks from extinction was to import African slave labour. Soon every Spanish colony was calling for African slaves, and church and state both conspired to intensify the Atlantic slave trade.

British colonizers arrive in the Caribbean

It would not be long before the British would decide that the Caribbean could not continue to be a closed Spanish Sea. Led by men like John Hawkins and Sir Francis Drake, with the backing of Queen Elizabeth the First, the British and other Europeans therefore decided to establish their own colonies in the region. A number of these colonies began with white indentured labour, but as sugar replaced other crops like cotton and tobacco, the British followed the Spanish in also importing slave labour from Africa to work on their sugar plantations.

It is interesting to ponder what Caribbean societies would have been like in modern times if they had continued to comprise white planters and white indentured servants planting non-sugar agricultural crops. However, apart from any motivation to save the indigenous native population, the falling demand for tobacco and cotton and the rising demand for sugar in Europe in the 1640s were seen by the colonists as sufficient economic grounds for importing black slave labour from Africa.

The fact that the Africans demonstrated an ability to survive the harsh conditions of sugar plantations better than the native Arawaks was simply a bonus. In the British West Indies sugar was the equivalent in value to the gold and silver found by the Spanish in mainland South America. Between 1640 and 1700, some 263,700 Africans were imported into the British West Indies alone – 134,500 for Barbados, 85,100 for Jamaica and 44,100 for the Leewards (Beckles, *A History of Barbados*, 1990).

Sugar and slavery fashioned inhumane and unequal Caribbean societies

Sugar and slavery fashioned inhumane and unequal Caribbean societies. In November 2010, Professor Alvin O. Thompson of the University of the West Indies launched a book entitled *Confronting Slavery: Breaking Through the Corridors of Silence*. In words and pictures it dramatized the horrors of transatlantic slavery and made the point that the time had now come to end the conspiracy of silence which has attended the events of slavery.

Two particular quotations included in that book are relevant to the case being made in this introduction for delineating the connections between slavery, sugar and tourism. One quotation is by Jorge L. Giovannetti:

> If, as Caribbean historians and social scientists, we are committed to facing the problem of racism and ethnic prejudice in the twenty-first century, then we need to engage in truly interdisciplinary research and cooperation, as well as in projects of public education (that is, outside the ivory tower) that would assist in unveiling and unmasking, the racial past of the region with the explicit purpose of crafting a better future for all.

The other quotation is by Doudou Diène, the UNESCO director of the Division for Intercultural Projects. Diène stated:

> The transatlantic slave trade, the most massive displacement of population in history, also constituted a clash of cultures that transformed the vast geo-cultural area of the Americas and the Caribbean into a living theatre in which the fundamental issue of today's world – cultural pluralism – continues to hold the stage. The construction of the ideology of the inequality of races, the cornerstone of racism, is directly linked to the slave trade.

Philip Sherlock put the matter another way in *The West Indies*: "For the greater part of West Indian history, the plantation system reinforced the colour-scale values and the social organization of the slave-colony."

Further impact of Asian indentured labour on Caribbean society

After the emancipation of slaves in British territories in 1834, Asian indentured labour was brought to a number of colonies to work on sugar plantations. The twin factors of colonialism and slavery now created societies structured in a hierarchy of race, colour and wealth, with whites at the top, blacks – who comprised the majority of the population in almost every territory – at the bottom, and Asians distributed across the social continuum as was felt appropriate to their station.

However, it could be noticed, at least by those observers close to the situation, that there were in fact subtle differences, even in more recent times, in the social interaction between the races in each Caribbean country, and it was entirely possible that the kind of society that evolved in each territory was determined by two factors: the extent to which its size and topography permitted the sugar plantation, with its highly structured class and race system during slavery, to dominate the entire life of the country; and whether the sugar plantation system was established before or after the abolition of slavery.

Antigua and Barbados, which were small and flat territories, were almost totally covered by sugar plantations. Jamaica, although becoming a major sugar producer, was large enough, with its flat lands and mountains, to accommodate other activities and, after emancipation, to provide options off the plantation to its peasant farming communities. Sugar plantations were introduced into Trinidad close to the end of the slavery period, and the workforce was fairly evenly divided between free black labour and Asian indentured labour; Trinidad had been captured from Spain in 1798 and had a population at that time of 17,643 persons, of which 10,000 were blacks. There was a shortage of labour in Trinidad which persisted until the middle of the nineteenth century when indentured labour, largely of Asian origin, was imported. The absence of flat land in Dominica, Grenada and St Vincent saved them from being completely dominated by sugar. Instead they were settled by small and middle-sized French farmers who lived on their estates and cultivated cacao, cotton and coffee. This situation no doubt produced different social structures and racial relationships than did the sugar plantations. Finally, the evolved societies were again different in the larger territories such as Cuba and the mainland Latin American countries, where the African did not comprise the largest racial majority, and more mixing between races seems to have taken place.

Post-emancipation Caribbean society

Whatever the subtle nuances of race relations in the different Caribbean territories, generally speaking, colonial and slave conditions during and after a period of hundreds of years created a number of socially dysfunctional and antagonistic societies. The slave trade in British territories was abolished in 1807, and the emancipation of the slaves passed in 1833 as an act of the British Parliament, and became effective in 1834.

The negative legacies of the period of slavery were not restricted to racial and class discrimination. Slavery and colonialism were responsible for the built-in culture of fragmentation which has bedeviled the Caribbean region into the twenty-first century. The Caribbean consists largely of an archipelago: a group of islands separated from each other by water. Despite certain federal administrative arrangements formed by the British in the Windward and Leeward islands (referred to in chapter 3), each Caribbean unit related, generally speaking, to the particular colonial power rather than to each other. This situation was the case especially in matters of trade. The result of this lack of communication was a culture of competition between the territories, rather than one of cooperation.

The mercantilist system of trade, introduced by the Spanish, enforced the doctrine that a colony existed for the benefit of the mother country through which all imports and exports should proceed. All trade with other countries was to be excluded; colonies were to produce raw materials for the mother country, and purchase from her all the manufactured goods, including food. The British and the French were quick to follow, if not to the same extent. To this day, the ability for French Caribbean departments – for example, Martinique and Guadeloupe – to secure international airline services from other countries is tightly controlled by Paris.

The culture of fragmentation survived long after independence status was achieved by the vast majority of the Caribbean colonies, and it is highly probable that it continues into the twenty-first century to affect negatively important attempts at Caribbean integration, including those attempts in tourism.

Diversifying out of sugar into tourism in the mid-nineteenth century

The passing of the 1833 Act freeing Britain's West Indian slaves had at least two important consequences. First, it had a direct impact on the reduction of the availability of African labour, leading, as was described above, to the importation of indentured Asian labour. Second, it created the need to search for a means of diversifying Caribbean economies, many of which were then chronically dependent on sugar. The shock of emancipation on sugar production was followed by another: the abolition in 1845 of the duties that protected West Indian sugar from foreign competition.

As blacks and Asians were fighting during the last quarter of the nineteenth century to reverse social and political inequalities and injustices, another industry, tourism, was introduced into the Caribbean. In the opinion of many academics, especially Caribbean academics, tourism exhibited many of the negative socio-cultural characteristics reminiscent of the era of colonialism and slavery. The search for a means of diversifying economies led to many different initiatives. One of these, for example, was banana production, on the back of which a tourism industry evolved in Jamaica and elsewhere.

This book seeks to tell the story of why, when, how and where tourism, one of the world's oldest industries, came to the Caribbean region, and why its journey has been somewhat turbulent. Its underlying message is that tourism development should always be handled with care. It sets the stage by demonstrating that the tourism activity is in itself a complex and invasive phenomenon, one which does not require a history of colonialism and racism to provoke strong reactions in a society. It also addresses why there is a need for education and re-education about the industry. One of the Caribbean's most experienced tourism ministers, Peter Morgan of Barbados, in speaking of tourism's complex nature, used to say, with tongue-in-cheek, "Better not have it, if you can avoid doing so." But, of course, we in the Caribbean cannot.

The book deals with the economic realities of the region being forced in the nineteenth century to diversify out of sugar – a sector on which the region had been dependent chronically, as the same region is today dependent on tourism. It gives a historical perspective of the settlement, economy and political development of five "touristically" developed countries – Bermuda, the Bahamas, Barbados, Cuba and Jamaica, where colonialism, race and class were critical factors – and argues that the enslavement and decimation of the native population by Europeans, followed by their introduction of African slave labour and later by indentured Asian and African labour, created societies based on hierarchies of race, class and colour. This history, above all else, caused tourism – which, initially, involved situations in which it was almost entirely a case of the black descendants of the slaves and Asian indentured servants serving a white clientele – to be regarded with suspicion and even resentment. These were painful birth pangs which most people in the region, especially tourism practitioners, seem to prefer to remain buried in the distant past, rather than clinically analysed with a view to achieving necessary and desirable catharsis, as is being done here.

This work looks at the history of the regional and subregional organizations through which tourism was organized and developed on a multi-country level, at the efforts of some of those organizations to transform the industry into a developmental economic sector, and at regional education, training and public relations programmes designed to create positive attitudes towards the industry. It provides, for the first time, a record in one place of the roles played in tourism by the Caribbean Commission in 1946, the Caribbean Tourism Association in 1951, the Caribbean Hotel Association, now the Caribbean Hotel and Tourism Association, in 1962, the Caribbean Free Trade Association in 1965, the Eastern Caribbean Tourist Association in the 1960s, the Caribbean Community in 1973, the Caribbean Tourism Research and Development Centre in 1974, the Caribbean Tourism Organization in 1989, as well as the programmatic support given by such organizations as the Organization of American States in 1976, the European Economic Community in 1978, the United Nations Development Programme in 1981 and the Caribbean Development Bank in 1984. In addition, this book

- examines the role of the Florida Caribbean Cruise Association and the socio-economic and environmental impact of cruise tourism in the Caribbean, while addressing the issues involved in its competition with land-based tourism;
- outlines a sustainable strategic plan for Caribbean tourism, covering the first decade of the twenty-first century, and discusses challenges, especially of a financial nature, that faced its implementation;
- deals with the current need for product and market diversification and discusses, in detail, the importance of developing and expanding niche markets, especially those in sports, culture and heritage;
- analyses Caribbean tourism performance in the second decade of the twenty-first century against the background of world economic performance;
- considers the forecasts for global tourism and air transportation, including regional air transportation;
- compares the economic performance of Europe and North America with that of the emerging markets, particularly those of Russia, India, China, Brazil, and Latin America generally; and
- makes recommendations for the survival of Caribbean tourism during the present decade of 2010 to 2020.

Finally, *Caribbean Tourism* makes the point that the tourism industry itself has survived its external challenges for thousands of years. Further, it argues that Caribbean people have been able to overcome the adverse social conditions they inherited and, in modern times, to develop a competitive industry which has permitted them to enjoy a standard of living which remains the envy of several larger developing countries with ostensibly more abundant natural resources. This success, it argues, is connected to this fact: tourism is a response to the need of the human race for adventure and freedom of spirit.

Given both the resource endowment constraints of the Caribbean and the small size of land masses and local markets, Caribbean people and countries need to come to terms with the economic reality of their dependence on tourism and related services. This is the conclusion of this book. It argues that, for the foreseeable future at any rate, tourism and related services will remain the best prospect for the economic development of the Caribbean region.

In spite of the many challenges that face the region in the second decade of the twenty-first century, the author remains cautiously optimistic about the future of Caribbean tourism. He does, however, see a winning strategy as dependent on the region's willingness and ability to embrace the significant technological and policy changes required, and to accept finally that Caribbean collaboration offers the best hope for success.

It is hoped that the general public, as well as those students and scholars who already have access to substantial information about sugar and slavery, will find this new work useful in amplifying their knowledge of the history and development of that other great economic sector – tourism – which has replaced sugar as king in the Caribbean.

1
Coming to Grips with the Complexity and Other Characteristics of Tourism

Perhaps it ought to be explained that tourism is by its very nature a complex and controversial activity that can incite extreme reactions, even in the absence of preconditions like colonialism and slavery. To resident populations anywhere, tourism can seem to be a form of drip-feed immigration or it can mean invading hordes of people with circumstances, ideas and cultures which are different from those of the resident population. Tourism transforms familiar landscapes. It is also an invasive industry which is difficult to isolate in the society. In small societies its presence can be felt everywhere. For years the international development community refused to accept it as an industry: it saw the *activity* rather than the economic impacts *of* the activity.

It is argued later in this chapter that the colonial education system, with its decided class bias, prejudiced people against tourism, and indeed against all the service industries, as professions. This is why a call is made repeatedly in the book for the introduction of tourism education into the school curriculum of tourism-dependent Caribbean countries. The objective is to explain to local residents at an early age the origins and the socio-cultural, economic and environmental impact of an industry on which they have become chronically dependent.

The origin of the word "tourism"

The word "tourism", as opposed to "travel", is of nineteenth-century origin. Its authorship is often ascribed to the Englishman Thomas Cook, who himself arranged tours in the 1840s. He organized railway tours in England, and in 1856 advertised a grand circular tour of Europe. All of these projects gave birth to the concept of travel just for fun, and made places like Blackpool in England and the Catskills in upstate New York famous as places to which working people could take holidays by travelling only a few hours away from their homes.

An *Economist* article entitled "The Pleasure Principal" (23 March 1991) contained some fascinating trivia about travel and tourism. It quoted the American historian Daniel Boorstin as explaining that the English word "travel" was originally the same word as "travail", meaning "work" or "torment", and that "travail", in turn, was derived from the Latin word "tripalium", which was a three-staked instrument of torture. This comes as no surprise to modern travellers, who are subjected to all the international security measures that followed the attacks by terrorists on the United States on 11 September 2001.

Boorstin's article also made reference to claims by the Spanish that the first travel guide was written in 1130 by Aimeri Picaud, a French Monk, for pilgrims making their way to Santiago de Compostela. Boorstin also mentioned an early work on travel called "Narrow Road to the Deep North", written in the 1690s by the Japanese poet Basho, and to a quotation by Dr Samuel Johnson: "The use of travelling is to regulate imagination by reality and instead of thinking how things are, to see them as they are." It is interesting that in efforts to diversify tourist niche markets in the twenty-first century the industry has returned to the concepts espoused by Dr Johnson.

Negative views on tourism

The *Economist* article also said of tourism:

> Massive though it is, the industry is unloved and knows it. In the developing world it is blamed for polluting the beaches, despoiling the countryside and contaminating

the values of native people. In the industrialized world, it is blamed for everything from the haze of diesel fumes above London's Hyde Park Corner, to the death of Venice. Socialists hate it for its supposed unfair practices; Conservatives hate it because it allows the hoi polloi to degrade what was once exclusive.

Richard Tomkins, in an article titled "A Social Evil Called Tourism" (*Financial Times*, 12–13 June 1993), questions the value to Britain of foreign visitors, and details all the evils of tourism as he sees them. Having listed all the measures he thinks the British government could introduce to get rid of tourism he ends with this last proposal: "the trouble is, all this could prove too controversial for Britain's beleaguered government. There is however, an alternative. Last time Britain was faced with the threat of an invasion, during the second world war, its citizens stopped talking to strangers and turned all the signposts round so that they pointed in the wrong direction. Desperate times call for desperate measures. It is time to resume hostilities." So strong was his dislike of the intrusiveness of tourism that he was apparently willing to eliminate an industry that British prime minister David Cameron described in August 2010 as Britain's third largest.

Positive views on tourism

Views in support of tourism are equally strong, however. Dick Onians, former chairman of the Royal Society of Arts in Britain, in his lecture "The Real England?" (*Royal Society for the Encouragement of Arts, Manufactures and Commerce* 146 [1998]: 40–49), says the following about tourism:

> Tourism for leisure encourages an appreciation of the arts, architecture and all manner of man's creations. It encourages an appreciation of one's own and other people's history, their heritage, values, culture, anthropology, cuisines, living and other habits. It exposes one to nature and to the natural environment, including landscapes and climates. It can encourage one to take exercise, thus improving body as well as mind. It takes one to special events of a national, regional and international nature, and in addition to all these splendid benefits, it makes important contributions to economic development and wealth creation in poor and rich countries alike. Lastly, but perhaps more importantly, it is probably the greatest contributor to understanding and friendship among peoples of different cultures and backgrounds.

Lelei Le Laulu, president of Counterpart International, addressing European aviation chiefs in Oslo in November 2007, described tourism as "the world's largest and fastest growing industry, representing the largest voluntary transfer of resources from the rich to the poor in history". He concluded that for those in the development community tourism is the most potent anti-poverty tool ever.

The history of international tourism

Tourism has been around for a long time. From 776 BC, when the Olympic Games, known as the Olympiad, began in ancient Greece, visitors from throughout the Greek world flocked every four years to the Games. This occurrence would now be classified as "sports tourism", a niche market, a concept which is more fully discussed in chapter 11.

In 334 BC, when Alexander the Great entered Ephesus, hundreds of thousands of visitors gathered from far and wide to that city, where they were entertained by acrobats, jugglers, magicians and other performers. This is a good example of what is now called "event tourism".

The pyramids of Egypt and other major attractions of Greece and Rome, which were bringing visitors to those countries in ancient times, continue to do so in the twenty-first century, reminding people over thousands of years of the greatness of those places from antiquity. This is an outstanding example of "heritage tourism".

Criticism about tourism and tourists did not start with modern day journalists. Plutarch, writing in the first century AD, gives us insight into the conflict that, even from those times, existed between visitors and locals. He speaks critically of the Romans, accusing them of globe-trotting over the countries of their empire, and in doing so displaying the attitudes which are normally ascribed to some of today's visitors to the Caribbean from Europe and North America.

Tourism is often seen as an us-and-them issue by local populations; the sight of rich foreign tourists "lording" it over the natives was as annoying in ancient times as it is today. It had as much to do with local envy as with the attitudes displayed by conquering people, people who saw themselves as superior to those whose countries they visited. The manner in which the Caribbean territories were settled and exploited by Europeans in the seventeenth century created societies where race and colour were the determinants of who were "us" and who were "them", and which laid the groundwork for societies where racial discrimination was rampant. This development inevitably had implications for tourism.

Tourism: the world's largest industry in the twenty-first century

Despite the criticisms which the industry has received in several places over many centuries, it has not only survived, but has also become the largest economic activity in the world, and is projected by the United Nations World Tourism Organization (UNWTO) to generate by the year 2020 more than 1.6 billion international tourists, spending more than US$2 trillion. The ability of tourism to survive these kinds of criticisms, shocks and disasters, from ancient to modern times, speaks to its unique appeal to the needs of the human spirit for adventure, discovery, and indeed freedom.

Year after year, more and more people seem driven to engage in this activity of moving within and across national borders in search of new vistas and experiences, sometimes encountering considerable inconveniences, if not personal danger. Between 1950 and 2010, international tourism arrivals grew at an annual rate of 6.2 per cent from 25 million to 940 million, and the income generated by these arrivals reached US$919 billion in 2010. UNWTO reckons that the business volume of tourism equals or even surpasses that of oil exports, food products or automobiles. Even more impressive is this fact: in all those years, the times when international tourism arrivals have decreased, year over year, can be counted on the fingers of one hand (see appendix 1: International and Caribbean Tourist Arrivals: 1970 to 2010).

Clearly the promotional efforts of the public and private sector are important motivators of travel. But given the industry's record for resilience during major economic and natural disasters, and its usual quick recovery thereafter, it is easy to conclude that other motivators are mankind's curiosity: the thirst for knowledge and love of freedom with which travel is associated. One of the first acts of dictators on assuming power has often been to restrict their respective populations from travelling.

Continuing negativity towards tourism

Despite the robust growth in international tourist arrivals over an extended period, doubts continue to be expressed by some about the industry's actual economic value as well as concerns regarding its perceived negative social impacts.

Negative views about tourism as an economic sector may be the result of a misunderstanding of how it works. Certain economists, more accustomed to concepts of visible than invisible trade, seem confused by this fact: tourism does not conform in an obvious way to many ideas they have about exports. The idea of an export that is consumed where it is produced takes time adapting to. They also seem unable to distinguish between the face of tourism and its reality. Tourism presents the face of pleasure and recreation, concealing its reality of hard big business. It sells dreams and experiences for cold cash, while hard-nosed technicians in government and in international agencies seem to prefer to deal with those industries which involve the growing of crops, or the making of goods or the building of bridges, roads and buildings, all of which they can see, touch and feel.

The reality is, however, that tourism, disguised as a simple act of hospitality, conceals a web of intricate business activities, relationships and negotiations often conducted across international borders. It involves the use of high technology and massive amounts of capital investment on a scale often both unknown in and among small agriculturally based developing states.

The foreign tycoons with whom both public and private sector individuals now negotiate – that is, tycoons who work in travel and tourism – tend to be somewhat tougher and probably less sympathetic to their problems than are the diplomats of those developed countries and agencies with whom Caribbean governments normally deal.

This is a world in which the price of one 747 aircraft or a cruise ship could easily dwarf the annual budget of a West Indian microstate. The CEOs of many airlines make no secret of the fact that their business is to put out of business other airlines, especially small carriers owned by developing countries. However, it is a world with which the Caribbean tourism sector has learned to cope.

With respect to the sociological and environmental impacts of tourism, the point must always be made that the industry, while a smokeless one, is still not pollution-free. It can threaten cultural norms, the social values and the built and natural environment. Considerable skill is required to keep the balance between contending forces and especially between the rights of the investors, the tourists themselves, and those who live and have their livelihoods in the Caribbean islands. Chapter 10 explores the issues of cultural diffusion and how cultural products can also be used positively to gain both an economic and social advantage through tourism.

Tourism is an amalgam of several different commercial enterprises that cut across the portfolios of every ministry in a country, and satisfying their respective demands can challenge both the rights of the citizenry and the authority of the governments themselves. Unlike other industries, tourism cannot easily be contained in small areas. It is an invasive activity, especially in small states with tiny land masses. It brings together hundreds of thousands, and in some cases millions of persons of different races, cultures and stages of development. In doing so, tourism combines the confrontations of an invasion with the xenophobia often also associated with immigration of peoples.

It can disturb the status quo. In many colonial and former-colonial societies – where the races were either kept apart or elected to remain separate from each other – tourists from those metropolitan countries largely inhabited by white people created considerable confusion locally. They did this by mixing freely with the black members of society and by even openly flaunting intimate relationships.

Tourism success stories are often found in those countries which have been able to place their special stamp on the products they sell. Tourism is about giving the visitor an experience. Countries, like many in Europe which have been practising tourism before the Caribbean, have sought to distill the national experience and package it for sale. This process starts with being proud of yourself and your culture. This pride seems much easier for those who have been a part of a conquering empire than for the subjects of a colonial or a recently colonial territory. Unfortunately, the colonial heritage seems in large measure to have given Caribbean people a preference for things that are not their own; certainly, in the early stages of Caribbean tourism, some employees appeared to think it desirable even to ape the accents of the people they served. That was probably before the Jamaican Rastas discovered the power of both their own language and of culture generally.

The competitiveness of Caribbean tourism in the future will depend on the ability of the region to sell the essence of what is Caribbean: in tourism terms this and this alone is unique in a globalized world, one where sameness and standardization often seem to be the goal. And this fact is true not only in terms of the on-land experience, but also in respect of the journey to and from the Caribbean.

One of the arguments that can be made in favour of the Caribbean owning some of its own airlines is this: such airlines offer visitors a Caribbean experience from the start of the journey to a foreign marketplace and later extend the memories on the way home. Foreign airlines, however efficient, cannot be expected to provide the traveller with a *Caribbean* travel experience.

The rise of Caribbean tourism

In chapter 2 an attempt will be made to track the origin and growth of tourism in five states in, or associated with, the Caribbean during the second half of the nineteenth century. They are Bermuda, the Bahamas, Barbados, Cuba and Jamaica. These states were selected because they each represent some of the earliest examples of Caribbean tourism, which developed in those countries at a stage when they were governed by colonial norms and when their societies were stratified accordingly.

Special attention is paid to Cuba which, prior to its revolution in 1959, received the largest number of tourists of any Caribbean country. Since tourism spread to many Caribbean countries following the US embargo against Cuba – an embargo which resulted in a serious drop in the number of visitors to that country – many Caribbean countries lived with the fear that, if the US embargo were to end, US visitors would then return in numbers to Cuba, and there would be a concomitant decrease in their own US visitors.

Characteristics of early Caribbean tourism

As the tourism industry expanded in the Caribbean during the first half of the twentieth century it was almost entirely a white, private sector–driven, foreign-owned and -controlled industry. Its capital-intensive nature initially placed it well beyond the financial capabilities of local black entrepreneurs, who did not receive much help for tourism investment from the commercial banks – banks which were themselves foreign owned.

There were isolated instances of local whites becoming hoteliers or major players in the tourism industry before 1950. But, generally speaking, the local white business elite in the Caribbean – that is, those persons who either had the money to invest in tourism or had access to it – tended to remain involved with the management and ownership of plantations, or to evolve into merchant capitalists. Caribbean tourism therefore earned the reputation of being an alien activity, owned by aliens and supported by an alien clientele. Outstanding exceptions evolved in Jamaica. These exceptions will be discussed in the next chapter.

To two important groups of the 1950s, 1960s and even the 1970s these social factors made tourism unacceptable as the main driver of economic development. The first group comprised members of the political directorate that was leading the region out of colonialism. The second group comprised those academics who saw themselves as giving in a post-colonial period the intellectual leadership needed to forge new directions for the socio-economic development of the region. It is not a coincidence that the prime minister of Trinidad and Tobago, Eric Williams – the author of *Capitalism and Slavery* and a person who became a politician after a career in academia – was particularly opposed to the development of tourism as an economic sector in his country.

In the 1950s tourism involved blacks serving whites and sometimes exhibited luxury in the midst of poverty. As such, in the heat of the fight for independence, it was seen by many persons as reinforcing the characteristics of a colonial past. Such persons therefore also failed to see white sands, blue skies and health-giving waters as the rich natural resources they are. Some Caribbean leaders accordingly thought of their countries as being poor in natural resources, countries with few development options. In search of foreign exchange and employment opportunities leaders clung to the industry they knew after three hundred years of slavery and colonialism: export agriculture. But export agriculture was high-cost, in particular sugar production, and it became less and less able to compete with Europe's beet sugar. The Caribbean sugar industry could therefore only be sustained by special quotas and preferential trading arrangements with the United

Kingdom and, ultimately, European importers. Ironically this situation continued to tie the Caribbean countries involved to the coattails of their former colonial masters even after constitutional independence.

The new breed of Caribbean economists that emerged in the 1950s, 1960s and 1970s were unhappy with both the plantation economies and tourism. The economists thought that the Caribbean should diversify out of agriculture into manufacturing, a change they believed was the solution to leading it to developed status. Regrettably, however, the type and scale of that sector was again limited by the resource realities of the region, the size of markets, the costs of production, and the aggression of the competition, especially out of Asia. Once again Caribbean manufacturing industries were dependent for their survival on negotiating special trading and development arrangements, largely with American and Canadian importers.

The record will show that, since independence, the foreign policy of Caribbean states and certainly of the Commonwealth Caribbean countries was largely focused on maintaining and expanding preferential treaties and the negotiation of ever more loans and aid programmes.

Undoubtedly some progress was made with manufacturing, both for exports and for import substitution. But when this new sector, the second Caribbean priority, proved inadequate to carry the load of a region with a great appetite for consumption of foreign goods and a need for more and more foreign exchange, the region grudgingly began to turn towards tourism, and to deal with its undoubted socio-cultural issues as a part of public sector strategy.

Originally, tourism, to the extent that it was considered as a serious development option, was thought of by Caribbean planners as too unreliable and fickle to play the role in a sustained manner. It was regarded therefore as a third priority, a stopgap, until "real development" could take place through the evolution of an industrial sector.

Modernizing Caribbean economies

The modernization of most Caribbean economies we may say began with the recognition of the importance of services among which are tourism and financial services. Neither of these industries required, or had the benefit of, any kind of preferences or quotas. They were forced, from the beginning, to grow and compete with all the best products of their kind available in the international marketplace. In fact, internationally, Caribbean tourism became, in resort tourism, a standard to be aimed for. What is more, financial services became so successful that specific developed countries belonging to the Organisation for Economic Co-operation and Development began to classify them somewhat indiscriminately as tax havens, and resorted to having many of them blacklisted.

By the end of the first decade of the twenty-first century the market-driven liberalization philosophies associated with globalization had begun to close the door on the old-type preferential trading arrangements the Caribbean held with Europe. This shift made the Caribbean even more dependent on tourism and other services for its export earnings, employment and government revenue.

In 2013, tourism remains the undisputed driver of Caribbean economic development, with the potential, if properly planned and marketed, to uplift the total development of the region through linkages with the other sectors of the economy. Its widespread importance was dramatized by the global economic meltdown of 2008, 2009 and 2010, when it was demonstrated that, when the economic contribution of tourism declines in the Caribbean, almost all other economic activity is negatively affected. This confirmation hopefully now sends a particular message to the future: there is a need to refocus on building a sustainable tourism industry, and to place it at the centre of the creation of linkages with old and new industries. The region will, however, have to do this in a new world order, where old paternalistic relationships have been replaced by demands for reciprocity between unequals, and where negotiating skills are as important as having a quality product to offer.

The contribution of colonial education to the denigration of tourism

It can also be argued that one of the factors affecting the acceptance of tourism and other services in the Caribbean was the system of education imported into the region from the metropolitan colonizers. This contribution was particularly true of those Caribbean elite schools, often run by white expatriates. These schools mimicked in tone the English private schools, and were ultra-conservative with respect to their curriculum. They therefore created deep-rooted prejudices about which studies and professions were acceptable.

For many years classical studies were at the apex of educational excellence, and practitioners of law, medicine and theology were ranked the highest of all the professions. The providers of other services were generally regarded as tradesmen, and scored low in the social hierarchy.

Tourism did not, therefore, up to the time of independence, make it on to the curriculum of the leading secondary and first-grade schools in the Caribbean. Even when tourism later became more acceptable as a development sector, many academics did not think that, as a subject of study, it had the intellectual rigour to be taught at the tertiary level. These attitudes helped to reinforce the view that employment in tourism was not for the brightest and best emerging products of the school system.

This history suggests that countries deciding to embrace tourism as a major development sector need to understand its many facets, and to pay a great deal more attention than is now the case to its various social, cultural, environmental and economic impacts, both negative and positive, on their respective societies. Such countries should therefore ensure that tourism education and tourism-related studies, beyond the technical and vocational aspects, are available to their communities as preparation for a better understanding of the industry.

Need for tourism research at tertiary levels

If the conditions stated above are to be met, the tourism research agenda of our tertiary educational institutions needs to be greatly expanded. The process of tourism education should be started in our primary schools and continued throughout the education system.

The Caribbean is a region described by such tourism authorities as the United Nations World Tourism Organization, the World Travel and Tourism Council, the Caribbean Hotel and Tourism Association and the Caribbean Tourism Organization, as four times more dependent on tourism for its socio-economic development than any other region of the world. Yet so little is known about the history of hospitality and tourism in the Caribbean. Even a visit to the Internet in this technological information age reveals that there are large gaps in both the information about the industry and the history of the Caribbean's major tourism institutions and organizations.

This situation may be contrasted with the voluminous research findings and scholarly publications that now flow from the pens of our university scholars about the history and importance of the slave trade and of the sugar industry, and of the social significance of both for the region. It is only recently that any progress is being made in having tourism taught as a subject in Caribbean schools and as part of the curriculum for the Caribbean Examinations Council of the Caribbean Community region. A clear difficulty has been the lack of material from which to teach, a problem which must now be seen by tourism scholars as a priority.

West Indian government attitudes to tourism

Widespread social unrest in the British West Indies during the 1930s resulted in a number of developments. It further polarized black-white relationships, if that were possible; it accelerated the movement towards trade unionism, regionalism and independence; and it made it difficult to endorse fully an industry which was seen as further defining the inferior relationship of blacks to whites.

In the 1950s and 1960s the complex socio-cultural issues left Caribbean politicians ambivalent about the tourism industry. The politicians were therefore reluctant to align themselves with the forces which controlled it, and which were largely seen by both Caribbean academics and the masses as reactionary. It is noticeable that tourism is missing from the regional agendas of West Indian leadership of the 1950s and 1960s. We will return to these matters in chapter 4.

As described above, the phenomenon of tourism, race and class in the Caribbean can be studied more closely if one looks at the historical and social development of the following five countries: Bermuda, the Bahamas, Barbados, Cuba and Jamaica. These countries were the first five where tourism developed to a significant degree. This matter is looked at in detail in chapter 2.

2

History, Race and Tourism in Bermuda, the Bahamas, Barbados, Jamaica and Cuba

What little evidence exists of the early beginnings of tourism in the Caribbean region (loosely defined to include Bermuda and the Bahamas, which, though not in the Caribbean Sea, are members of the Caribbean Tourism Organization), suggests the following. Bermuda, the Bahamas, Barbados, Cuba and Jamaica were five places in the region where the tourism industry first took root in a serious manner. They seemed therefore to be excellent case studies for this book.

The African slaves were brought into the New World to provide labour for the sugar plantations, and while neither Bermuda nor the Bahamas had any history of serious sugar cultivation, African slaves were nonetheless introduced into Bermuda and the Bahamas. This created social conditions not dissimilar to those in Barbados, Cuba and Jamaica, where in all cases sugar became the major economic sector.

Starting with the settlement of the African slaves I will look briefly at the socio-cultural, economic and political structure of those five societies in which attitudes to class and race were formed as a result of the relationship between white settlers and slaves. I argue that attitudes to tourism in the

Caribbean, from its origins in the nineteenth century to the situation in the twenty-first, have been influenced by the historic experiences of colonialism and racial discrimination against non-white people in those states. I then draw conclusions about the situation in all the Caribbean states, with explanations about the reasons for subtle differences in race relations to be found in different particular states.

We need to accept the following realities about Caribbean tourism. A number of surveys, including those carried out in the 1970s by the Caribbean Tourism Research and Development Centre, have showed that, initially, both black and white people in the Caribbean defined a tourist as a white person from overseas taking a holiday in the Caribbean. The first tourist hotels in the Caribbean were built to accommodate white foreigners. Older black Caribbean people have early memories of attempts being made to keep them from "trespassing" on hotel premises. Black people spending holidays in the Caribbean, usually in small guest houses or with friends and family, did not refer to themselves as tourists; the social situation that derived from slavery was that, as a general rule, white people were served by black people across all the services. Given these perceptions about who was and who was not a tourist, the tourism industry – which consisted almost entirely of blacks serving whites – was bound to be seen as a continuation of the social relationships of plantation society. As tourism expanded, industry workers had to be constantly reminded not to confuse service with servitude. Such perceptions no doubt influenced the attitudes of both whites and local blacks to the industry.

As the Caribbean became more and more dependent on tourism for economic development, the tendency was for those persons promoting tourism to live in a world of denial. Such persons pretended that tourism did not come with a negative social price tag, and blamed opponents of tourism for not concentrating on the positive economic impacts of the industry. As promoters they ignored the socio-cultural and even environmental impacts of tourism. The situation, however, in fact called for a far different approach. This approach included recognition of the negative historical legacy of tourism. It also advocated intervention, particularly by governments, in education, training, public relations and planning, to reorient the attitudes both of the local population and of the tourists themselves. To the extent that national governments, regional organizations and other entities have developed such programmes, the nature, image and reality of tourism in the region have all been transformed for the better.

Bermuda

Bermuda is not in the Caribbean Sea but is nonetheless situated only 650 miles east of Cape Hatteras, North Carolina, 750 miles from New York City and 940 miles from Nassau, the Bahamas. Bermuda has maintained strong relations with Caribbean countries from which it has received many immigrants. It became a member of the CTO in 2000, an associate member of the Caribbean Community (CARICOM) on 2 July 2003, and a contributory member of the University of the West Indies in 2009.

In 2005 the population of Bermuda was estimated at 65,365 persons, of which the ethnic makeup was 54.8 per cent African-Caribbean, 34.1 European and 6.4 multiracial. It has a year-round mild semi-tropical climate, with temperatures ranging from sixty-eight to eighty-four degrees Fahrenheit – a climate important for the tourism industry.

Bermuda was first sighted and named by Captain Juan de Bermudez in 1505. It was not claimed for the British until 28 July 1609, however, when the ship *Sea Venture* – part of a flotilla sailing to Virginia under the command of Sir George Somers and Sir Thomas Gates, the governor of Jamestown – was wrecked off the island. This occurrence left the survivors in possession of the territory. Most of the survivors of the *Sea Venture* in fact carried on to Virginia in 1610, and Bermuda was not actually intentionally settled until 1612, with the arrival of the ship the *Plough*. Close relations between Bermuda and Virginia both survived the new settlement and continued.

Bermuda's small size of 21 square miles – 23 miles long by 1.75 miles wide – had a number of implications. One implication was the need to keep the population manageable by constant emigration; another was that the efforts of the Somers Isles Company in the seventeenth century to keep Bermudans in agriculture were of only limited success. Neither the shallow topsoil nor the total dependence on the rain for water fostered agriculture. Bermudans therefore turned largely to maritime trades, and their resistance to the pressures from the Somers Isles Company ultimately led to the dissolution of the company in 1684, making Bermuda a British colony.

Thereafter Bermudans abandoned agriculture for shipbuilding, and replanted farmland with Bermuda Cedar trees. (The exception to this shift was the continued cultivation and export to the United States of such crops as lilies and fresh vegetables.) Then, after establishing control over the Turks and Caicos Islands, the Bermudans began the salt trade on those territories. This trade became the world's largest in salt, and for a century it was the cornerstone of the Bermuda economy. Bermuda became reliant on imports from the American colonies to which it exported sea salt. In addition to the salt trade, Bermudans also turned to whaling, privateering and the merchant trade.

Bermuda's strategic location

Bermuda's strategic geographical location made it an important military base in several wars: the American War of Independence from Britain (1775–83), the War of 1812 (1812–14), the American Civil War (1861–65), the First World War (1914–18) and the Second World War (1939–45). This use by the British caused the Royal Navy to improve Bermudian harbours and dockyards. Later, during the Second World War, US military installations were also located in Bermuda. In fact, the United States constructed an air base on St David's Island, where the international airport is now constructed.

Bermuda, like many of the Caribbean countries, benefited from improvements to the harbours and airports built, for military reasons, by either the British or the Americans. These landmarks would later provide good infrastructure for the cruise and stay-over sectors of the tourism industry. Bermuda itself also benefited economically from the presence of the Royal Navy Dockyard and military garrison, both of which had to be supplied by the local vendors with food and other materials and services.

Race relations in Bermuda

Slaves were first brought to Bermuda in 1616. Some were Native Americans, but most were those brought forcibly from Africa. They were employed as trades people or domestic servants rather than as agricultural labourers. At the time of emancipation of the slaves in British-owned territories in 1834, the number of persons living in Bermuda was given as 9,000, with 5,000 – that is, the majority – listed as black or coloured.

Race relations have come far in Bermuda since the latter part of the twentieth century and the beginning of the twenty-first, but until the 1950s Bermudans were very much racially segregated into blacks and whites. This was the case even with such institutions as schools, cinemas and churches.

After the Second World War women were given the right to vote, and, after several boycotts, certain of the franchise qualifications restricting black voters were removed. Universal suffrage only came to Bermuda through the Bermuda Constitution of 1967. Until then voting was based on property ownership.

It was in the late 1950s that the first two coloured persons were employed by the Bermuda Post Office. They were Shirley Nearon, now Shirley Clarke, wife of Barbadian Cecil Clarke, residing in Barbados; and Phyllis Guishard. In 1963 the Progressive Labour Party was formed to represent the interests of non-white Bermudans in a country governed largely by white landowners. The Bermuda school system was racially desegregated by act in 1965. However, two of the "white schools" opted to become private schools.

In the 1970s there were riots which led to the de facto end of discrimination. Several thousand expatriate workers came from the United Kingdom, Canada, South Africa and the United States, and were employed in such activities as accounting, finance, insurance, hotels, restaurants, construction and landscaping services. But social, cultural and political change was probably accelerated by an influx of West Indian immigration in the twentieth century. Of the total workforce of 38,947 persons in 2005, 11,223 were non-Bermudan.

The Commission for Unity and Racial Equality (CURE), established in 1994, was amended in 1999 to allow the government to collect detailed statistics on black hirings, firings and compensation *inter alia*. Development and opportunity minister Terry Lister was quoted as saying, "Bermuda has one of the highest standards of living in the world, but a professional business base that is effectively lily white."

Tourism beginnings

This was the Bermudian society into which tourism, comprising white visitors, was introduced as early as the last quarter of the nineteenth century. The fourth daughter of Queen Victoria, Princess Louise, the wife of the governor general of Canada, paid an extensive visit to Bermuda in 1883, and is often credited with placing Bermuda on the tourist map. Other persons followed her example in seeking to flee from the long Canadian winter and by the turn of the century many others were seeking the sun in Bermuda. Being situated only 750 miles from New York was a clear advantage and the trip from New York to Hamilton by steamer was an easy one.

On 1 January 1885 Bermuda opened the Fairmont Hamilton Princess Hotel, named in honour of Princess Louise. It was built by Harley Trott of Trott and Cox, a company of steamship agents that provided meat for the British military. It attracted rich white Americans who spent their summers at home and their winters in Bermuda. Among its famous guests were such people as Mark Twain and Ian Fleming.

The Hamilton Princess Hotel became a British Intelligence Centre and home to Allied servicemen during the Second World War. It was purchased in 1959 by American tanker billionaire Daniel Ludwig, who also built a second luxury hotel, the Fairmont Southampton, on the south shore.

By the 1930s there were new incentives to expand the tourism industry in Bermuda. The Smoot-Hawley Tariff Act, passed by the United States in 1930, cut off Bermuda's agricultural exports of lilies and fresh vegetables to the United States, causing the colony to seek to diversify its economy.

There were, however, other factors which favoured the growth of a tourism industry in the 1930s. These were the development of modern transportation and communications systems internationally – a shift which included expanded steamship service bringing wealthy tourists to Bermuda from Britain, America and Canada – and the arrival of air transport to Bermuda.

In 1930, the first airplane to reach Bermuda was a Stinson Detroiter seaplane which flew from New York. In the late 1930s Imperial Airways and Pan American World Airways began operating scheduled flying boat airline services from New York, and from Baltimore to Darrell's Island. In 1948, regular scheduled commercial airline service by land-based planes began to land at Kindley Field Airport, the current Bermuda International Airport. By the 1960s and 1970s Bermuda was a major tourism destination.

Racial discrimination in tourism

It is not surprising that, given the picture of the Bermudian society painted above, the hotels were, until the 1960s, off-limits to black people as guests. It is alleged that in the 1950s the premier of Barbados, Sir Grantley Adams, while in transit from Barbados to Britain through Bermuda, was refused accommodation at the Fairmont Hamilton Princess Hotel based on colour, and had to be rescued by a prominent black Bermudan. This incident regrettably was not an isolated one in the Caribbean prior to the 1960s, and it explains why tourism had difficulty being generally accepted in countries where blacks were in the vast majority and were seeking to effect change through political advancement.

The Bahamas

The Commonwealth of the Bahamas has the distinction of being the place where in 1492 Christopher Columbus first landed in the New World. Believing incorrectly that he was in the Indies, he called the inhabitants he found there "Indians", but the native people in the Bahamas called themselves Lucayans, meaning "Island People". They were the descendants of the Arawaks of Hispaniola where Columbus also landed in 1492. At the time of European contact in that year, the native Lucayan population in the Bahamas Islands was estimated to be about 40,000 persons.

The Arawak population in Hispaniola, estimated as having been 250,000 persons in 1492, had been reduced to 14,000 by 1517, due to disease and harsh treatment by the Spanish overlords who enslaved them. Hispaniola first imported African slaves as early as 1501, and according to a census taken of the Greater Antilles in 1574, there were 1,000 Spaniards and 12,000 African slaves on Hispaniola at that time. The Spanish seemed to have had little interest in the Bahamas except to capture the local Lucayans and transport them to Hispaniola as slave labour. By 1520, there was only a handful of Lucayans left, and the Bahamas remained uninhabited for about 130 years.

The first Bahamian settlement was made by the British in 1648 when Captain William Sayle and a group comprising twenty-five Puritans and Republicans, called the Eleutheran Adventurers, left an over-crowded Bermuda and sailed in search of religious freedom to the island that became known as Eleuthera. (Eleuthera is a mere 225 miles from Miami and Fort Lauderdale, a distance which would later have implications for Bahamian tourism and its markets.) The group was called "The Company of Adventurers for the Plantation of the Islands of Eleutheria [sic]". Its members were farmers. One of the two ships in which they sailed was wrecked on a reef on Eleuthera with the loss of all provisions. Despite additional settlers comprising whites, slaves and free blacks arriving from Bermuda, and provisions from Virginia and New England, the Eleutheran colony nonetheless struggled, and some of the settlers returned to Bermuda.

In 1666 other settlers came from Bermuda to the Bahamas, but this time to New Providence Island. Unlike the settlers in Eleuthera, this group made their living largely from the sea, engaging in such activities as salvaging wrecks, making salt, catching fish, turtles and conch, obtaining ambergris from whales, and cutting the hard woods for lumber, dyewood and medicinal bark. Some farmers, however, followed to New Providence. Neither the Eleutheran nor the New Providence settlements had any standing in English law, and attempts by the Proprietors of Carolina to establish governors in the Bahamas failed miserably.

Between 1666 and 1718, a rather chaotic situation seems to have prevailed in the Bahamas, where wreckers, privateers and pirates preyed at will on shipping (mainly Spanish) without any reference to the existing relationship between Britain and Spain, or between Britain and France. Some of the world's most notorious pirates, both male and female, operated out of the Bahamas.

In 1684 the Spanish burned the settlements on New Providence and Eleuthera, leading to their abandonment, and in 1686 New Providence was settled a second time from Jamaica. Finally, in 1718, Woodes Rogers, who had been appointed governor of the Bahamas by King George the First, sailed for Nassau. By 1725 all the pirates had been expelled, and in 1729 a House of Assembly was established.

After the American Declaration of Independence in 1776, many of the English Loyalists fled from Georgia and the Carolinas to Florida, which was then owned by the English, and to the Bahamas. When under the Treaty of Versailles in 1783 Florida was restored to Spain, several of those Loyalists who had fled to Florida then fled to the Bahamas. By 1788 about 9,300 had fled to the Bahamas and more were to follow. The British issued land grants to the American Loyalists, and the population of the Bahamas thereupon tripled in a short time.

Before the Loyalists arrived there were no more than about 1,000 slaves. Most of the blacks were free, having either been exiled from Bermuda or escaped from there. About 3,000 slaves came with the Loyalists, and a further 1,000 came in 1783 with the second wave of Loyalists from Florida.

Certain of the blacks in the Bahamas were also those who had been set free by the British navy after the abolition of the slave trade in 1807. The Loyalists started cotton plantations on Crooked Island, the Bahamas Lumber Company on Andros Island, and a large salt mine on Great Inagua. The Loyalists also provided stevedores, and brought to the Bahamas agricultural skills. The emancipation of the slaves in 1834 put an end to plantation life.

The Bahamians had made a good living from wrecking, but matters started to shift in 1821, when Florida became a US territory. When, in 1825, the United States decreed that all wrecked goods in the area must be taken to a US port, the Bahamian wrecking business suffered. As the number of lighthouses increased, and steamships replaced sailing vessels, there were also fewer shipwrecks from which to benefit. Sponging and growing of pineapples replaced wrecking, but after 1912, the Bahamas found it difficult to compete with cheap Cuban pineapples, and in about 1938 the sponge industry suffered from a serious disease.

Since they were expert blockade runners the Bahamians benefited from the US Civil War. The Bahamas served the Confederate cause through blockade running, bringing in cotton for the mills of England, and running out arms and munitions. These activities came to an end with the conclusion of the war. The Bahamians also benefited from the passing of the US Prohibition Act in 1919, as their ships acted as rum runners, smuggling liquor into the United States. However, in 1933 the Prohibition Act was repealed, with obvious consequences for the colony.

Because of the strategic and geographical location of the Bahamas, its infrastructure was greatly improved by its being used as bases for the Allied forces during both the First and Second World Wars. During the Second World War specifically the Allied Powers based their flight training and anti-submarine operations for the Caribbean in the Bahamas. The wartime airfield became Nassau's international airport in 1957, and helped to spur the growth of tourism.

Bahamian society

In an online article titled "The Windsors in the Bahamas" (17 June 2009), Carolyn Cash described the Bahamas as being one of the British Empire's most backward colonies during the 1940s, It is alleged that the Duke of Windsor referred to the Bahamas as one of Britain's third-rate colonies.

(Sir Winston Churchill had exiled the duke to the Bahamas after the outbreak of the Second World War because the duke was suspected of pro-Nazi sympathies.) The duke's racial propensities are noteworthy. They may be judged by a report that he said of Étienne Dupuch, editor of the *Nassau Daily Tribune*: "It must be remembered that Dupuch is more than half Negro and due to the peculiar mentality of this race, they seem unable to rise to prominence without losing their equilibrium." At the time the Bahamas had a population of 70,000, of which about 60,000 were black or of mixed race.

After having been briefly king of the British Empire at its most expansive stage, it is not surprising that the former King Edward VIII did not enjoy his term of office as governor of the Bahamas from 1940 to 1945. He earned a place in Bahamian history, however, when, on 8 June 1942, returning from the United States, he helped to calm riots by the black population, which had looted and pillaged Bay Street because of discontent about low wages and their social conditions generally.

This brief summation of the history of the Bahamas suggests a colony where wrecking, privateering and even pirating dominated the business activity for almost two hundred years. Agriculture was pursued, but it never dominated the economy, as had happened in several of the Caribbean colonies. People were able to make a living from various activities at sea. These activities included salt mining and supporting combatants in various wars, specifically wars in the United States and the two world wars. There was also participation in such dubious activities as rum-running during American prohibition. Emigrants from Britain, Bermuda and the relocated Loyalists from the slave plantation states of Carolina and Virginia, often with attendant slaves, created a society structured according to clear concepts of white racial superiority.

Bahamian politics

In the Bahamas, as in the West Indian colonies, it was the white minority which controlled both the political and the economic life of the territory up to the beginning of the 1950s. For decades the white-dominated United Bahamian Party ruled the Bahamas, while a group of white merchants, known as "the Bay Street Boys", dominated the economy. It was in fact the Bay Street Boys who had created the United Bahamian Party. In 1953, the

Progressive Liberal Party, under the leadership of Lynden Pindling, later Sir Lynden Pindling, was formed to represent the disenfranchised black majority.

When Britain gave the Bahamas internal self-government in 1964 it was the leader of the United Bahamian Party, Roland Symonettte, who became the first premier of the Bahamas. However, led by Pindling, the Progressive Liberal Party won the government in 1967, and took the country into independence on 10 July 1973.

Tourism growth in the Bahamas

Two of the best known early hotels in the Bahamas were the Graycliff and the British Colonial. The famous historic Graycliff Hotel situated in Nassau, overlooking Government House, is housed in a 260-year-old mansion which, over many years, has offered high-quality food in its five-star Graycliff restaurant.

A much larger hotel, the British Colonial, was built in the Bahamas in 1920 on the site of an ancient fortress in the middle of Nassau. It is situated to the west of Bay Street, and currently operates as a Hilton Hotel with 291 rooms, including twenty-nine suites. In 2012, with 15,153 rooms, 1.42 million visitors and 4.41 million cruise passengers, the Bahamas ranked sixth in the region.

The American Prohibition Act of 1919 greatly assisted the growth of tourism in the Bahamas as it did also in Cuba. The geographical location of these countries – in close proximity to the United States – provided an easy escape for those persons looking to avoid the deprivations of such legislation. For both good and ill the act also resulted in an overwhelming dependence on the American tourist market. Proximity and good sea and air access to the United States have been of great advantage to Bahamian tourism. But whatever happens to the US economy that is bad is bound to have an associated impact on the Bahamas, and tends to affect it more than it does other tourism-dependent countries in the region, as those countries have more diversified source markets.

Despite the non-progressive social agenda of the white-dominated governments up to the 1960s, they nonetheless have to be credited with an aggressive policy of promoting tourism and financial services in the Bahamas. In 1967, however, the Progressive Liberal Party did indeed come to power with an agenda for change in racial discrimination practices, for power-to-the-people, and for constitutional advancement.

A major step was taken in 1974 when the Pindling government formed the Hotel Corporation of the Bahamas, which took responsibility for seven major hotels – four in Nassau and three in Freeport. It also owned a golf course, a marina and four casinos – in this case two in New Providence and two in Grand Bahama. In 1983 the corporation completed work on a new seven-hundred-room hotel at Cable Beach, a hotel with a convention centre and a casino as well.

The first global energy crisis took place in 1974–75. Many of the foreign private-sector owners of hotels in the Bahamas and Jamaica ceased operations, and the governments were forced to take over the hotels to save jobs in the industry. Over the years there has been much discussion about the stewardship of the Hotel Corporation of the Bahamas, but it cannot be denied that its establishment in 1974 was a major turning point in the ownership patterns of hotels in the Bahamas, hotels which had before been either white, or white and foreign.

The first native non-white Bahamian to become director general of tourism in the Bahamas was Baltrom Bethel. He was a civil servant who, after reaching the rank of permanent secretary in the Ministry of Education, was appointed to the Ministry of Tourism in 1979 as director general, where he then served for fourteen years. He later became chairman of the Hotel Corporation in the 1980s, and returned as deputy chairman and managing director when the Progressive Liberal Party government, led by Prime Minister Perry Christie, returned to office in May 2002.

By the twenty-first century tourism and tourism-related construction and manufacturing were providing some 60 per cent of the gross domestic product (GDP) of the Bahamas. In 1986, the World Bank estimated that the Bahamas accounted for 20 per cent of stopover visitors in the Caribbean region, as well as a large share of the cruise-passenger arrivals. In 2008, it was estimated that tourism employed 50 per cent of the Bahamian workforce.

Issues of race in the Bahamas

The accepted wisdom in the Bahamas and in Caribbean countries, where tourism is the major economic activity, is that it is prudent not to discuss matters of race. The reason for this reaction seems, in part, to be this: white people in the Caribbean would prefer that race not be discussed in case such discussion provokes resentment against them. Black people wish to avoid stirring up old memories of circumstances that are generally agreed either to have changed or to be changing for the better. Both whites and blacks believe that such discussions will scare away the tourists.

This need not be the case, however. A great deal depends on how the discussion is conducted. Moreover, it seems that the issue must be exorcised if tourism is to be accepted by Caribbean people of all races, classes and colours for what it is: the economic activity that puts food on Caribbean tables and roofs over the heads of its people. A similar state of racial discrimination existed with respect to the established Anglican Church in the West Indies, which Anglicans now accept as a part of their colonial past, and have accordingly moved on.

The tradition of silence on racial issues was broken in the Bahamas when, in January 2006, there was the odd event of a white Bahamian, Helen Klonaris, writing a letter called "Whiteness and Being Bahamian" to the *Tribune* newspaper in the Bahamas. In her letter, Klonaris reacted to an alleged comment by a white Bahamian politician who, when asked why white Bahamians find it difficult to celebrate African-rooted culture, responded: "I didn't come that route [that is, of the African slave]. My cultural history isn't based in the navel string of Mother Africa. So how can you ask me to celebrate that heritage?" Her response was as follows: "Are not African slavery and the arrival of white colonialists connected? Are the two histories not integrally and irreversibly intertwined and still to this day rub up against each other, and hurt when rain is coming, when hurricanes start brewing and when it is just another ordinary day in a small place and we don't know how to look each other in the eye and tell the truth?" She expressed the view that when white Bahamians say

> "we should come to grips with our history and move on", they mean, "Black people should accept what happened and move on. I don't want to have to think about how I, as a white person, have developed an identity in an age of racism; I don't want to have to think about how four hundred years of European enslavement of Africans affected who I am today . . . how whiteness developed as a system of standards and values and ways of desiring in the world – a system that thrives still and assimilates

into it anyone standing too close to a television set (or just standing) with ears to hear and hope for sale."

Klonaris's letter forced race in the Bahamas onto the front pages of the country's newspapers and evoked a great deal of comment both for and against the views expressed. The Nassau Institute, which was critical of the letter, described it as "a strident and inflammatory thesis". The institute made the case that slavery had existed among people of all races, that it was the Africans who sold their own people into slavery, and that it was Europeans who put an end to slavery. This last point completely ignored the historical efforts, including several revolts, of the slaves to free themselves, and the economic case made by Williams in *Capitalism and Slavery* of why slave labour was proving an overly expensive form of field labour.

Andrew Allen, in an article called "Racism and Colonialism in the Bahamas", published in the *New Black Magazine*, defended Klonaris's thesis. He supported the expressed views that

> there is in our society a well-defined system of relationships, including educational curricula, the legal system, Judeo-Christian church hierarchies, and the English language itself, whose effect is to suppress, condemn and "ghettoize" other cultures; that the African in the New World is often wrongly thought of as a blank slate who only began accumulating culture upon contact with his new colonial society, although he brought with him a fairly complex system of social rules, beliefs and values, including religious ones.

Allen argued, however, that the New World black must take some of the blame for the situation. It is the black, Allen contended, who internalized the colonial value system and, in doing so, ghettoized himself. The black was psychologically penetrated to the point that he no longer recognized value in anything arising from his own heritage, ancient or modern. In fact, he became an active accomplice in the stigmatization of such things. To the "colonialized" New World black, while Hindu pantheism connotes a neutral Eastern mysticism and Greco-Roman pantheism connotes high classicism, African pantheism instead connotes a savage and unequivocally negative black magic. Allen concluded that none of this needs to be fatal to harmonious national development for the Bahamas "so long as our self-image is constantly 'tweaked' to reflect the interests of the Bahamas as an independent nation of many races".

Chapter 10 of this book deals with cultural tourism. As I argue there, many cultures have contributed for over four hundred years to a new Caribbean civilization which Caribbean people, of whatever ethnic origin, should embrace and proudly claim as their own.

Barbados

A Spanish writer in 1541 described Barbados as having had no indigenous people. Hilary McD. Beckles (*A History of Barbados*, 1990) refutes this claim, and points to evidence of early Amerindian settlements, the existences of which have been verified by more recently discovered evidence. What *is* true is that the English party that first arrived in Barbados – in May 1625 under Captain John Powell – found no inhabitants, nor did the English colonists who arrived in 1627 to settle the colony.

The topography of the land, which was largely flat, and the absence of warlike and hostile natives marked Barbados as ideal for agricultural cultivation. It is a matter of record that the entire island was planted in a remarkably short time. Unlike several of the other Caribbean territories, Barbados was to remain under British rule for the entire period, from settlement in 1627 to independence in 1966. This fact had implications for its socio-cultural and political development.

A parliament was established in 1639 comprising eleven counsellors and twenty-two chosen burgesses, each of the three persons representing one of the respective parishes. According to Beckles, land was allocated mostly to colonists with known financial and social connections in England, so that a small number of prominent men soon owned the vast majority of the arable land, and were well placed to impose their social and political power on the colony. They also had the finances and the connections to do business, and Barbados soon emerged as Britain's most attractive colony in the New World.

From 1627 the Barbadian planters focused initially on the production of tobacco, and when the bottom fell out of the London market, turned to production of cotton and indigo. Their labour force at the time comprised mainly white British indentured servants. It was their expressed intention to continue along this path, and between 1627 and 1645 blacks remained a small minority, not exceeding eight hundred in the 1630s, when sugar cane was first introduced to Barbados.

By the 1650s sugar was king in Barbados. At that time, again according to Beckles, the colony was described as the richest spot in the New World. Colonial officials boasted that the island's value in terms of trade and capital was greater than all the English colonies put together. Between 1640 and 1700, some 263,700 Africans were imported into the British West Indies, 134,500 for Barbados, 85,100 for Jamaica and 44,100 for the Leewards.

It was said in the introduction that sugar and slavery fashioned inhumane and unequal Caribbean societies. In 1655 there were 23,000 whites in Barbados and 20,000 blacks. By 1712 the number of whites had been reduced to 12,528 and the blacks had increased to 41,970. As blacks came to outnumber whites many times over, the planters sought to keep the blacks in subordination by deployment of militia regiments. These regiments were supported by imperial troops and navy, and buttressed by legal machinery designed to control every aspect of their lives. In Barbados, for example, the 1661 Act for the Better Ordering and Governing of Negroes described slaves as "heathenish", "brutish" and "a dangerous kind of people" whose naturally wicked instincts should at all times be suppressed (Beckles, *A History of Barbados*, 1990).

Beckles records the cruel and inhuman punishments slaves incurred in Barbados for certain crimes. These punishments included being branded, whipped, having their noses slit and having a limb removed. For other crimes, such as rebellion, the punishment was death. They could not leave their plantation without a ticket; were not allowed to beat drums, blow horns or use other loud instruments; and, since they were regarded as real estate, they could not own property. They could not give evidence in court against whites until the early nineteenth century, and under the 1688 Slave Code a master could wilfully kill his slave and be liable to a fine of only £15. He could also kill the slave of another master and then, on conviction, be liable to a fine of £25. Not until 1805, two years before the slave trade was actually abolished, did the murder of a slave by a white person become a capital felony in Barbados. A slave could, however, be punished by death for striking or threatening a white person, or for stealing property. It seems that a number of slave codes in other West Indian territories were fashioned on the Barbados model.

In dealing with racism in the Bahamas, as reported earlier, Andrew Allen takes the position that the blacks in the New World must take some blame for internalizing the colonial value system, a process through which they ghettoized themselves, and even became active accomplices in stigmatizing things African. It must be remembered, however, that, at a certain point in time, the majority of the blacks in the Caribbean were born there, and not in Africa. By 1817, only 7 per cent of the blacks in Barbados actually came from Africa, a place which by then was becoming a distant memory. But, more to the point, given the Eurocentric cultural blitz to which they were subjected, underpinned by penalties and punishments for manifestations of African cultural retentions, assimilation of European ways of behaviour was first and foremost a matter of survival.

Barbadian society

The claim that Barbados is a unique society is one made not only by Barbadians but also by other people. This uniqueness is, however, sometimes seen as a positive fact and at other times as a negative one. The Jamaican writer John Hearne – a decided fan of things Barbadian – in an article entitled "What the Barbadian Means to Me" (*New World Magazine*, 1966), writes the following:

> He is English in a way that the rest of us are not . . . More Englishmen, from a wider range of social classes came to Barbados and became Barbadians earlier than in any of the islands . . . It meant that some values, some concept of manners, other than the purely materialistic ones of looting and exploitation, had time to take some sort of root. The simple code of grab and "cent per cent", which was to a large extent the legacy left to Jamaica by an "overseer class", had certain refinements added to it in Barbados that would seem to have been a permanent influence.

Hearne contrasts the state of education in Barbados with that of Jamaica: at the end of the eighteenth century, the former had a well-established foundation for teaching the classics, whereas in the latter, education in reading, writing and arithmetic functioned only at basic levels. He attributes this discrepancy to the number of whites in Barbados, including white women, which were proportionally greater than in any other West Indian colony at the time. He continues:

> This meant more home life and a further gentling influence on domestic and public manners . . . it was a greedy, cruel place, like any other West Indian sugar island, but certain proprieties, a certain sense of style were observed by a larger sector of its

population. The observations may seem to give an undue importance to the whites who were, after all, only a small minority in a community of blacks. But any slave society takes its tone and customary behavior from the masters. And this was particularly true of the West Indian slave societies in which the slaves were reborn, literally naked, into a world that must have been, literally unimaginable, until they saw it and in which their tribal and past family associations were broken or discouraged so as to lessen the danger of revolt. As the captive from the German forests taken to Rome had to become a Roman quickly, if he were not to remain a mere field brute, so the captive from Africa had to become a Barbadian or a Jamaican, if he was not to, perhaps, die of sheer cultural starvation.

The Puerto Rican academic Gordon Lewis, in an article called "The Struggle for Freedom" (*New World Magazine*, 1966), paints a far less sympathetic view of Barbadians and Barbadian society, specifically that of the society in the 1930s and 1940s:

> Each group lived away from the other, feeding the distrust with gross stereotypes that they had of each other. The situation was reinforced by an openly class-prejudiced and class-ordered educational system. For the Barbadian, pride in that system was in reality the pride in a snobbery that graded the school pupil in the educational ladder in terms of his class position, based on the assumptions of the seminal Mitchinson report of 1875: that the purpose of primary education was to create an obedient and honest working class; of middle class education, via the First and Second grade secondary schools (that peculiar Barbadian distinction in itself a reflection of the snob value that attached itself to "white" foundations like Lodge and Harrison College) to aim at an education set within the external terms of the English public school; and of higher education by means of the glittering prize of the Barbados Scholarship, to work up by attendance at Oxford or Cambridge, as the report put it, "the very best raw material" of the island into a "cultivated article".

Lewis concluded that educational culture in this context of values meant, as in England, the ornamental development of the privileged individual, not the general enlightenment of a community. Lewis, speaking more generally of Barbadian society, described it thus:

> an almost pure sugar plantation economy, preserved more completely than in any other West Indian island, produced in its turn a white plantocracy proverbial for its reactionary conceit. Barbados, along with Bermuda and the Bahamas, thus became notorious for the entrenched system of racialist prejudice and at times it seems that almost every coloured West Indian one meets has a half-bitter, half-hilarious story

of what happened to him when he visited "Bimshire"; more than any other West Indian territory, Barbados society recreated the structural configuration of Victorian England, modified, of course, even in "Little England" by the social fruits of slavery, concubinage and colour, but, at the same time, intensified by the fact that the island was a cramped and introspective community. It was a familiar hierarchy; at the top, the white economic oligarchy, along with the professional echelons of law, church, and state; in the middle the various grades, nicely demarcated by income indices of the middle class; at the bottom, the heavily Negro proletariat . . . the stranglehold of the resident whites, not only in estate agriculture but also in commerce, meant that it took years after 1940 for the coloured outsider to break into the trading monopoly of the famous "Big Six" in the Bridgetown trading emporia.

Lewis contrasted Barbados with other West Indian territories, where people of colour, especially Indians, entered the commercial field. In Barbados, he maintained, the world of trade retained throughout an upper-class white image. This exclusion of blacks from commerce was not restricted to their ownership or management of big business. Until 1952 no non-white person had ever been employed even as a teller at the lone Barclays Bank on Broad Street.

Early Barbadian society is shown to be even more complex when another Lewis, white Barbadian Gary Lewis (*White Rebel*, 1999), deals with class stratification among the white people of Barbados. He divides the white community into four segments: at the top, the white planter class comprising thirty elite families who owned 80 per cent of the land and who wielded considerable social, financial and political influence because of that ownership. They were said to be not well-educated, but they nevertheless occupied the majority of the seats in the House of Assembly or the Legislative Council. Just below them was the white middle class. This class comprised principally Bridgetown merchants who controlled commerce and who would later challenge the planter oligarchy for both power and social status. Other members of this second white group were also, variously, the smaller planters, plantation managers, doctors, attorneys, middle-level colonial administrators and the upper tier of the Anglican Church – an institution which played a major part in the running of local government through the vestry system. The third group comprised the lower-income group of whites, who rarely possessed enough property to qualify as voters, and who worked in such jobs as plantation overseers, bookkeepers, Bridgetown clerks, craftsmen, wheelwrights and blacksmiths, both in Bridgetown and on the plantations. At the bottom were the poor whites, who were generally fishermen, estate workers, and even beggars who tended to live in villages along the island's east coast.

The way through the complexity of social stratification in Barbados lay through capturing political power from the small white elite at the top and through broadening the base of education which the planters were determined to keep from the black population. The elite refused education to the slaves, and held that education for emancipated blacks would create among them unrealistic expectations, and make it difficult to accept their social status. It is not surprising, therefore, that the list of national heroes in Barbados, created in 1998 by a black government, includes the four persons who, between them, and beginning with the early nineteenth century, started the process of wrestling political power from the plantation oligarchy until full independence was gained. These were the same four persons who expanded the recipients of education until, in 1961, it became free and available to every Barbadian, from primary to tertiary level. The names of the four men were Samuel Jackman Prescod, Charles Duncan O'Neal, Sir Grantley Herbert Adams and Errol Walton Barrow.

Samuel Jackman Prescod

Samuel Jackman Prescod (1806–71) was born one year before the slave trade was abolished in the British territories. As the illegitimate son of a free-coloured woman, Lydia Smith, and a white planter, William Prescod, he was in 1843 the first non-white person to be elected to the Barbados House of Assembly, as one of the two representatives for Bridgetown.

As a newspaper editor, first of the *New Times* and later of the *Liberal*, he educated the coloureds and blacks about their rights. He succeeded in getting free coloureds to be admitted to vote in 1831 and fought to give some meaning to freedom for the slaves after their emancipation, which took effect in 1834.

As early as 1839 he recommended that adult suffrage be made law, but suffrage was to wait for more than a hundred years, to be realized in 1951 under the political leadership of Sir Grantley Adams. H.A. Vaughan ("The Birth of a Hero", *New World Magazine*, 1966) states that Prescod made *The*

Liberal newspaper the mouthpiece of the labouring and middle classes. Prescod spent a great deal of time agitating for franchise reform.

Charles Duncan O'Neal

The second hero to emerge was a member of a distinguished black Barbadian family, a medical doctor, Charles Duncan O'Neal (1879–1936), who dedicated his working life to helping the poor and agitated against the deep-seated racism of the 1920s and 1930s. This bigotry the planter class perpetrated against blacks in education, religion, at the work place and in housing (*National Heroes of Barbados*, 1998).

In pursuit of his objectives, O'Neal founded the Democratic League in 1924. In that same year the party was able to send its first representative, C.A. "Chrissie" Brathwaite, to the House of Assembly. O'Neal was himself elected to the assembly in 1932. The Democratic League was the forerunner of the Barbados Labour Party, from which the second major party, the Democratic Labour Party, also sprung.

O'Neal agitated unsuccessfully for free education and free dental care for children, for improved housing, for the abolition of the Masters and Servants Act, and for the introduction of universal adult suffrage, as Prescod had done before him.

Grantley Herbert Adams

In 1934, Grantley Herbert Adams (1898–1971), later Sir Grantley, was first elected to the House of Assembly. A brilliant Oxford-educated lawyer, he made many personal sacrifices by championing the cause of the poor and downpressed after the 1937 riots in Barbados, riots which had been provoked by the depressed social conditions. His agenda was to release the masses from the socio-economic bondage of the 1930s under which they had been placed by the planter and merchant classes of the time.

When the Barbados Labour Party was launched on 31 March 1938, he was elected deputy leader while absent in England giving evidence about the island's social conditions. In 1939 he was elected leader, and in 1940 his party won five seats in the House of Assembly.

In 1941, the Barbados Workers Union was formed with Adams as president, a post he retained until 1954. In 1942, he was appointed to the

Executive Committee, and in 1946, he was asked by the governor to submit four names for membership of the Executive Committee, thus conferring a measure of self-government upon Barbados. To him belongs the honour of gaining full adult suffrage for Barbadians in 1951. When full ministerial government was introduced to Barbados in 1954, Adams became Barbados's first premier, and with the introduction of the cabinet system in 1958 Barbados attained full internal self-government. The pinnacle of his success, however, was his becoming the first and then only prime minister of the short-lived West Indies Federation in 1958.

Gordon Lewis expresses some reservations about crediting Adams with the rise of modern Barbados and modern democracy in the country. He describes him as "a liberal constitutionalist, convinced of the primacy of politics and believing that when the political fight is won, economic ills will disappear. Major emphasis was therefore laid upon constitutional advances, in willing cooperation with liberal governors." Lewis criticizes Adams for not introducing certain social legislation.

Lewis, like many other critics before and since, regards as docility and conservatism the Barbadian pursuit of pragmatic strategies based on the art of the possible in a given environment. Adams's painstaking commitment to the steady achievement of constitutional advancement for Barbados witnessed the attainment of desirable major social goals without the social confusion associated with other territories, both outside and inside the Caribbean region. He was a man of his times who, with a measure of success, identified the plantocracy as the enemy and fought their reactionary policies, policies which seemed in the 1930s to have changed little from those of the seventeenth and eighteenth centuries. Adams was for that reason accused by some persons of being a traitor to his own class.

Errol Walton Barrow

Errol Walton Barrow (1920–87) was the son of the Reverend Reginald Grant Barrow and Ruth Barrow (née O'Neal; she was the sister of Dr Charles Duncan O'Neal, discussed above).

Errol Barrow was a Renaissance man: a pilot, a war hero, a sailor and a horseman. He returned to Barbados in 1950 after serving in the Second World War, and then qualified as an economist at the London School of

Economics and as a lawyer at the Inns of Court in London. He was elected to the House of Assembly in 1951 as a member of the Barbados Labour Party but, after disagreements with Grantley Adams, left the party in 1955 to join with the so-called Young Turks in a new party, the Democratic Labour Party. He lost his seat in parliament in 1956, but was returned in 1958. In 1966 he led Barbados into independence, becoming its first prime minister. His party lost power in 1976 but regained it in 1986. Unfortunately, he died a year later.

Barrow described himself as a democratic socialist, explaining that for him this meant commitment to equal opportunity for all. He was the father of most of the life-changing social legislation in modern Barbados. His achievements included the following:

- democratization of the educational process and expansion of free education to every Barbadian child, including secondary and tertiary levels
- creation of the Barbados Community College
- creation of the Samuel Jackman Prescod Polytechnic
- introduction of the national health insurance and social security scheme
- provision of nutritional school meals for Barbados's children
- improvement of health services
- acceleration of industrial development
- support for the establishment of the National Independence Festival of Creative Arts
- expansion of the tourist industry

Barrow was also a committed regionalist and one of three architects of the Caribbean Free Trade Association (CARIFTA). He defined the foreign policy of an independent Barbados as "friends of all and satellites of none", and throughout his life and political career refused to allow the small size of his country to cause it to pursue a policy of mendicancy or of subservience to the large developed former colonial countries.

In comparing Barrow to Adams, Gordon Lewis writes critically that Barrow did not take Barbados in any new ideological direction from Adams. In fact, Lewis argues, the new premier and his colleagues sought less to socialize the economy than to modernize it.

If Lewis expected from Barrow the brand of socialism of a Michael Manley in Jamaica and a Forbes Burnham in Guyana – which would ideologically align Barbados with the countries of Eastern Europe and even Cuba nearer home – again he misunderstood the Barbadian psyche. Barrow's brand of social engineering completed the task of ending the political dominance of whites in Barbados while harnessing their experience and resources for the benefit of the wider population. By strengthening the social and educational infrastructure he vastly expanded the size of the Barbadian middle class that, for the first time, was not based on colour. His educational and social policies set Barbados on the road to becoming the leading developing country at the United Nations.

Politicians can put an end to racial discrimination by policies and legislation, but cannot wave a wand to achieve racial integration, which often seems in Barbados to be desired by neither white nor black people. Locals are quite comfortable with a status quo in which all races meet and interact pleasantly in a work or business situation and then go their separate ways socially. Although there are instances in which white and black Barbadians meet and enjoy social interaction, these are the exception rather than the rule, and Barbadians are sometimes said cynically to have achieved what South Africa during apartheid falsely claimed to be its objective – separate but equal development of the races. A white local person who marries a black person can still be ostracized by the white group. This situation can be perplexing for some white long-stay visitors, persons who have been heard to comment on the absence from certain social functions of local black people with whom they think they have much in common socially and intellectually. They end up seeking out these people themselves. The average white visitors, especially white women, can be rather surprised by the disparaging looks they attract by fraternizing with black men. While this situation may be somewhat generational and is no longer as stark as it was six decades ago, it is time that it is publicly discussed and comes to an end with the next generation of Barbadians.

Reflection on race relations in Barbados, however, brings us back to its effects on tourism. Certainly, until the 1960s and 1970s, when the end to colonialism and the search for independence were uppermost in people's minds, planners, government advisers, and academics, especially historians, social scientists and economists, raised serious questions about whether the negative socio-cultural impacts of tourism, especially those related to race, outweighed its economic benefits in countries emerging from colonialism. The asking of these questions did not help the cause of tourism and militated against its acceptance as a developmental sector.

Major tourism landmarks in Barbados

Hotels

The Royal Naval Hotel, 1780

Given all that has been said above about race and white ownership of business, including tourism businesses, in Barbados prior to the 1950s, the story of Rachael Pringle and her hotel needs to be told. The first hotel, which was opened in Barbados in 1780, was owned by a slave of mixed parentage, Rachael Pringle Polgreen. Her father, William Lauder, a Scotsman, was a teacher at Harrison College, a school founded in Barbados in 1733, and her mother was one of his slaves. Lauder was said to have fled England after he had written and published attacks on the English poet John Milton. Later in Barbados he was discharged from his post as a schoolmaster, having done a pretty poor job of teaching during the eight years, starting with his appointment in 1754, as a Latin master at Harrison College.

Rachael's difficulties are alleged to have begun after she refused to have sexual relations with her father. She was ultimately rescued, first by a certain Thomas Pringle, captain of the ship the *Centaur*, and later by another white man, Mr Polgreen. Under his care she prospered sufficiently to have become the owner of a substantial property which she turned into a hotel.

Prince William Henry, Duke of Clarence, later King William the Fourth of England, while serving as a naval captain with the British navy in the Caribbean, was a guest at Pringle's hotel. He was with certain of his naval companions and, having consumed a great deal of alcohol, the party proceeded to destroy the property. Fortunately the Prince later agreed to meet the cost of the damage presented by Pringle, and she then named the restored property the Royal Naval Hotel in his honour. It was the same Prince William who, at the wedding of Horatio Nelson on the island of Nevis, gave away the bride, Frances Nisbet, to Nelson (Metzgen and Graham, *Caribbean Wars Untold*, 2007).

The Crane Hotel, 1880

The Crane Hotel, located in St Philip, and often referred to as Barbados's first resort, opened in 1880. It was created by transforming a mansion known as Marine Villa, which had been built in about 1790. Today the Crane Hotel, situated at a spectacular site in the South East of Barbados, swept by refreshing breezes, has been developed into a large and luxurious retreat with an excellent reputation among international visitors. The hotel continues, however, to have considerable appeal to local residents.

The Atlantis Hotel, 1880s

The Atlantis Hotel, located in Tent Bay, in the parish of St Joseph, was also one of the earliest hotels in Barbados, and flourished during the 1880s. It became a popular stop when the Barbados railway was opened in 1883. In those days it was owned and operated by a Miss Emmeline McConney. In more modern times it was owned by a black Barbadian, Enid Maxwell, who operated it for over forty years as a favourite retreat of Barbadians. It was best known for its provision of local Barbadian dishes. These meals were enjoyed by many locals, and also visitors who made the Atlantis a stop on their tours of the island. It was closed for a short while in 2007 but was upgraded and reopened on 7 December 2009.

The Marine Hotel, 1887

Another hotel of equal antiquity in Barbados was the Marine Hotel which was built in Hastings by an American proprietor, George S. Pomeroy, and opened in 1887. The original property ceased to operate as a hotel in the 1960s, and was converted to government buildings, housing department offices in the 1970s. It was then demolished and a new property, named the PomMarine Hotel, was constructed on the site. It opened in 1998 as the training hotel of the Barbados Community College.

Barbados's social history is full of stories of the grand social events which took place when the Marine Hotel was at the height of its fame in the 1930s, 1940s and 1950s. Unfortunately, few people of colour participated except in the kitchen or in other places where they were called upon to serve.

Racial discrimination in Barbados's hotels

A white Englishman, former Conservative member of parliament Bowen Wells, attests to the rigid colour prejudice that obtained in Barbados' hotel industry as late as the 1950s. (Wells spent many holidays in Barbados and was a close friend of Peter Morgan, a hotelier who became minister of tourism in a Democratic Labour Party government in 1971.) In the introduction to his book *Bridging the Gap: A Collection of Articles by Peter Morgan*, published by the *Nation* newspaper in 2010, Wells wrote of the 1950s, "Black people were not admitted to any hotel in Barbados that was owned and operated by white people. Peter's was the first white-owned hotel to admit all people on an equal basis." Morgan also stated, in the *Nation* in April 1997, concerning the governor of Barbados, that "John Stow was a friendly man of liberal attitudes. Later he wrote that he was appalled at the level of racial segregation and discrimination he found on arrival in Barbados, far exceeding anything he had experienced in more than 30 years of colonial service." Sir John had come to Barbados in 1959 after serving in the British Colonial Service in Africa – specifically, in Kenya and the Gambia – and in the Caribbean – specifically, in the Windward Islands and Jamaica. He remained in Barbados as governor general after independence.

Air services

The first aircraft to touch down in Barbados was an Avro Avian which landed at the Rockley Golf course in 1913. It was not, however, until the late 1930s that air services to Barbados could be said to have begun. It was then that an airport was constructed at Seawell, a former plantation, and named Seawell Airport. It retained this name until 1976, when it was renamed the Grantley Adams International Airport after Barbados' first premier.

The first plane, belonging to the Royal Netherlands Airlines, landed there in 1939, on what was then a mere grass strip. A terminal building was built in 1949 in time to receive the first commercial service, which was introduced by Air Canada in that year. From that time Air Canada has maintained a service continually between Canada and Barbados. Seawell received its first Pan Am flight in 1957 and its first British Overseas Airways flight in 1959.

Unlike several airports in the Caribbean, Seawell, now Grantley Adams International Airport, was not started as a military base by either the British or the Americans. It was, however, expanded in 1983 as part of an agreement with the United States to facilitate their invasion of Grenada.

Tourism administration in Barbados

A formal structure to promote tourism to Barbados started as early as 1932 with the formation of the Barbados Publicity Committee, which was jointly funded by government and businessmen. In 1956 the Hotel Aids Act was passed with a view to attracting hotels to Barbados, and during the 1950s the first luxury hotels, such as the Colony Club, Miramar Beach and Coral Reef Club, opened along the west coast of the island. Barbados' most famous hotel, Sandy Lane, was not opened until 1961, and the Barbados Hilton in 1966.

The Barbados Hotel Association was formed in 1957 with Peter Morgan, the owner of the St Lawrence Hotel, as its first president. Morgan, the Englishman who had adopted Barbados as his home and who became the minister of tourism, was one of the founders and the first chairman of the Caribbean Tourism Research and Development Centre in 1974. He also served as the executive director of the Caribbean Tourism Association (CTA) from 1976 to 1978.

In 1958, under a Labour Party government, the Barbados Tourist Board was established by an act of Parliament, with businessman James A. Niblock as its first chairman, and Maurice Cave – chairman and CEO of Barbados's oldest and most famous department store, Cave Shepherd and Company – as his deputy. Niblock's association with Barbados' tourism stretched back to his association with the Barbados Publicity Committee, where he had also served as chairman. Cave succeeded him as chairman of the Barbados Tourist Board in 1961 and Morgan succeeded Cave as chairman in 1963.

The first manager of the Barbados Tourist Board, Paul Foster, was appointed in May 1959. He had been formerly employed in public relations and advertising and gave distinguished leadership to the tourist board until he left in 1965 to establish Paul Foster Travel. He was the recipient of three major awards for his service to tourism: the Caribbean Tourism Organization (CTO) Fiftieth Anniversary medal in 2002, the Barbados Hotel and Tourism Association Lifetime Achievement Award in 2006 and the Government of Barbados' Lifetime Achievement Award in 2007.

The appointment in 1965 of Frank Odle, a former permanent secretary in the Barbados public service, to succeed Foster as manager of the Barbados Tourist Board, though not a revolutionary step, was still a significant one, as Odle was the first black Barbadian to hold the post of chief executive officer in the tourism sector. He was to be followed by a long line of similar Barbadian professionals. On his retirement in 1979, Patrick Hinds, a former employee of the Caribbean Tourism Research and Development Centre, became director of tourism. He was succeeded by Patricia Nehaul in 1987. Nehaul's tourism career had begun as early as 1950 when she was employed by the publicity committee, and had lasted as an employee for approximately forty years.

Subsequent chief executive officers, however styled, were Hugh Anthony Arthur, the current Barbados high commissioner to Britain, Earlyn Shuffler, Oliver Jordan, Gene Stuart Layne and David Rice. Other names, which will be remembered for long and distinguished service to the Barbados Tourism Authority, were the former Denise Hope, now Lady Douglas; Hugh Riley, now secretary general of the CTO; Markly Wilson, who subsequently served as deputy secretary general and director of marketing of the CTO and who is now director of international marketing, New York State; and Dr Michael Scantlebury, formerly assistant professor of University of Central Florida's Rosen College of Hospitality Management.

By the time the Labour Party government left office in 1961 significant strides had been made in establishing Barbados as a tourism destination. Certainly the improvements to the airport and the construction of the Deep Water Harbour, which officially opened that year, laid the ground work for growth in both stay-over and cruise tourism. But at that time, Barbados was still very much dependent on sugar as its chief export, employer of labour, and foreign exchange earner, and politicians across the region, many of them with a trade union and labour base, were moving rather cautiously in their approach to the new industry of tourism.

Much was to change with respect to tourism from 1961 to 1976, the fifteen years of the Democratic Labour Party government. These were years in which independence from Britain was gained and the new government committed itself to the modernization of the Barbados economy. This process involved the government seeking to diversify into manufacturing and tourism, and to committing itself to playing a major role in the planning and marketing of tourism. In 1964 Barbados opened its first overseas office, in Toronto, and, starting in 1966, its tourism board also operated out of the Barbados government office in Kensington High Street in London.

In the 1970s commercial banks had no lending policies tailored to the peculiar needs of the tourism industry and black borrowers did not find a welcome mat at their doors. However, government institutions like the Barbados Development Bank were seeking to assist Barbadians to enter the field of entrepreneurship, including the tourism industry.

Across the Caribbean, the membership of national and regional private sector hotel associations consisted largely of foreign owners and managers, and of local whites catering to white guests. Black Caribbean people, whether local or otherwise, were not being encouraged to become hotel guests, and were often viewed with suspicion on entering the premises. When one reflects on those days, it is a pleasure to see even Barbados' luxury hotels thirty years later, in 2009 and 2010, promoting "staycations" – vacation packages for locals – and spreading the gospel that locals are more than welcome as hotel guests. It does not matter that this shift had resulted from decreased foreign business. It is a trend which, once started, is unlikely to be reversed.

In Barbados, by 2013 – because of the aggressive policies of the Barbados Labour Party, under the stewardship of cabinet ministers Billie Miller and Noel Lynch, and of the Democratic Labour Party, under the stewardship of Richard Sealy – tourism continues to be the driver of the economy. It is so recognized by most economic planners, the government and the public at large.

According to the governor of the Central Bank of Barbados, Delisle Worrell, speaking at a Barbados International Business Association's Investment Conference in October 2010, "tourism is by far Barbados' most important source of foreign exchange, contributing about two-thirds of our earnings on the current account of the balance of payments and almost twenty per cent of the country's GDP. Any strategy for renewal of growth of the local economy has to start with the tourism sector" (*Barbados Advocate*, 29 October 2010).

Jamaica

Columbus arrived in Jamaica in 1494 and found the indigenous Arawaks engaged in hunting, fishing and small-scale cultivation of cassava. The

Spanish settlement was then established at Santiago de la Vega, now known as Spanish Town. As had happened elsewhere in the region, the native population did not survive for long. Between 1494 and 1655, however, no large number of either Spanish settlers or African slaves lived in Jamaica, since Spain thought that the best use of the island was as a base to support the conquest of mainland America where gold and silver were to be found in commercial quantities.

With the Treaty of Utrecht in 1713, it was agreed that England would supply slaves to the Spanish colonies in America, and Kingston then became a great centre for the trade. The total population under Spanish ownership was about five thousand persons, composed largely of Spanish farmers and African slaves, all of whom were engaged in farming cassava and maize, raising cattle and horses, and in trading with passing ships as well as with Cuba and the Spanish Main.

In 1655, the face and the fortunes of Jamaica changed when the British admirals William Penn and Robert Venables captured it from the Spanish. The first phase of development took place when the English buccaneers selected Port Royal, which was close to Kingston harbour as an operational base, a decision that led to it becoming one of the richest towns in the New World. From Port Royal the buccaneers led fierce raids on Spanish cities, and as silver and gold flowed into that town, more and more settlers came of their own volition. Other settlers were sent out from Ireland and Scotland by Oliver Cromwell. Some planters, who came from Barbados to settle in Jamaica, brought sugar technology and thereupon began the production of sugar in the colony. In places like Barbados (166 square miles) and St Kitts (68 square miles) most of the land was soon covered by sugar plantations, but the extent to which the plantations could expand was limited by the small size of the islands themselves. Jamaica, however, with a land mass of 4,244 square miles, had comparatively large flat stretches of virgin land available for sugar production, an enterprise which now required large numbers of African slave labour to exploit it.

In 1670 there were 8,000 white persons and 9,504 black slaves in Jamaica. By 1787, there were 25,000 white persons and 210,894 black slaves. By 1750 Jamaica had overtaken Barbados as the largest producer of sugar, and remained so until it was itself overtaken by the larger territory of Haiti (10,714 square miles), which by 1789 had 500,000 African slaves.

Post-emancipation Jamaican society

In small islands like Barbados and Antigua, free blacks, after emancipation, had little land to farm and nowhere to go, and, more often than not, were forced to sell their services to the planters, their former owners. Moreover, they now had to look after themselves in various new ways. During the time of slavery the slaves were the responsibility of the planter, who had to provide social services such as they were. Off the plantation freed slaves were very much on their own.

In the much larger Jamaica, emancipated slaves had the choice of establishing small peasant holdings either in the hills far away from the plantation, or on its borders. Therefore the number of small farmers grew and so did the variety of crops other than sugar. But this was not a situation that found favour with the planter and merchant classes, who had traditionally equated the sugar estate with the prosperity of the country. Lord Grey, the secretary of state for the colonies, in support of the planters suggested a tax on peasant produce to make work on the estates more profitable than peasant farming (Philip Sherlock, *The West Indies*, 1966). Moreover, the planters dominated the House of Assembly and the vestry, and, not surprisingly, were reluctant for the state to take over the responsibility for social services no longer performed by the former slave owners.

The Morant Bay Rebellion

In Jamaica growing poverty, the breakdown of the justice system, the absence of a civil service and a persistent drought all contributed to the misery of the people. This situation climaxed in the Morant Bay Rebellion in 1865, when four hundred small settlers under the leadership of a deacon, Paul Bogle, clashed with the custos and the vestry of a parish. Black and white people were killed, and much damage done to property, both during the event and in the reaction to it. The next year, 1866, Britain made Jamaica a Crown colony, which meant direct rule from Britain. While this was a backward step constitutionally, it permitted the British governor to establish a civil service, to introduce medical and educational services, and to improve the judicial system.

Between 1881 and 1911, the number of Jamaican small farmers is said to have increased from 47,000 to 142,000, and the production of sea-island cotton, cocoa and bananas all increased considerably. However, by the

1930s, due to a number of factors, unemployment had become endemic. Those factors included population growth, emigration restrictions by both the United States and Central America, and the spread of the Panama Disease, which wiped out the banana industry. Other contributors, according to Sherlock, were "the hopeless frustration of people shut out from participating in the government by a limited franchise and confined within narrow social limits by rigid class lines and social attitudes".

The rise of Marcus Garvey, Alexander Bustamante and Norman Manley

These social conditions spawned a range of leaders, including middle-class intellectuals, who were committed both to oppose colonial rule, and to change the doctrine of "black badness" and "white virtue". This doctrine, it should be noted, was, in many cases, believed as strongly by black persons as it was by white.

Marcus Garvey, a black Jamaican born in St Ann's Bay in Jamaica in 1887, founded at this time the Universal Negro Improvement Association, a body which called on black people to promote the spirit of race, pride and love. But it was to be Alexander Bustamante – leader of the Jamaica Labour Party and head of the Bustamante Industrial Trade Union – and Norman Washington Manley – leader of the People's National Party – who, first as colleagues and later as rivals, gave leadership first to constitutional advancement, and then to independence.

The rise of political parties in Jamaica

In 1943 Bustamante founded the Jamaica Labour Party. Under his leadership elections took place – for the first time under universal adult suffrage – in 1944. The party won twenty-two of the thirty-two seats. The new constitution, introduced in 1944, provided for a bicameral legislature in which, for the first time, power rested with an elected House of Assembly and only the Legislative Council contained nominated members.

Across the region it had become clear that only the achievement of political power by Caribbean people, together with constitutional change, would lead both to more diversified economies and to an assault on the race and colour barriers. These barriers were the inevitable corollaries of sugar plantation societies, and had persisted well into the twentieth century.

The West Indian sugar crisis, 1838 to 1900

Knowledge of the roller-coaster economic fortunes of the West Indian colonies between 1834, the date of emancipation, and the 1930s, when depressed social conditions resulted in the eruption of riots across the region, is critical to the understanding of the beginnings of both the Caribbean tourism industry and how it was viewed by locals.

In *The History of Barbados* (1991), Hilary Beckles discusses the crisis in the West Indian sugar industry between 1838 and the end of that century. This crisis followed the emancipation of the slaves and the abolition, in 1838, of the apprenticeship system. The apprenticeship system was supposed to work in this way: slaves older than six years were entitled to be registered as apprenticed labourers and to acquire thereby all rights and privileges of freedom in return for food, clothing and lodging, but without wages. They were also to work for their former owners three-fourths of the day. The barely disguised purpose of this unjust scheme was to provide the sugar planters with a cheap source of labour on their plantations after emancipation. Fortunately it did not last beyond 1838. Beckles describes the sugar crisis in the following manner:

> The deep end of the sugar crisis was reached in 1884 and continued until the turn of the century. For the first time since emancipation, planters sincerely expressed their inability to cope with market trends, and confidence in the industry declined rapidly. The root cause was the sudden drop in European sugar prices – the result of rapidly increasing subsidized domestic sugar beet production. Between 1884 and 1897 planters reported the disappearance of their small profit margins. Production levels fell marginally and even then most major producers were operating at cost levels above what was required to make a profit. The volume of exports did not show any appreciable decline, though with collapsing prices, returns fell off sharply. In 1886, for example, the value of exports was about 40 per cent below the 1884 level. The crisis within the industry was reflected in the collapse of sugar estate values; estates sold in 1884 at between £65 and £70 per acre while in 1887 sales were recorded as £25 to £30 per acre. The worst years were the mid-1890s . . . The Agricultural Aids Act of 1887, which was passed to allow government to provide short-term financing for sugar planters, had some positive effects, but the economic crisis was seen to be leading to social unrest among the laboring poor.

After emancipation the resort to indentured labour from Asia and even from Africa – labour which went also to Guyana and Trinidad – did not entirely solve the labour problems of the plantations. It instead allowed Jamaica some breathing space in transitioning from slave labour. The time had come, however, to pursue other solutions.

Diversification out of sugar

The reality was that the sugar crisis represented a larger problem for governments than could be solved by importing indentured labour. There was a clear need to diversify the economy away from the almost total dependence on sugar. In this respect Jamaica led the way with the banana trade and through it to tourism. Frank Taylor, in his book *To Hell with Paradise* (2003), makes the connection between the sugar crisis and diversification into tourism, and locates the tourism industry in Jamaica in the 1870s at the back end of the banana trade with the United States.

Bananas were introduced to Jamaica by the Spaniards, by means of the Canary Islands into Port Antonio in Portland. The trade flourished beyond all expectations. In 1871, an American sea captain, Lorenzo Dow Baker, took bananas on board in Port Antonio, and traded them in Boston at such a profit that he was encouraged to buy land in Jamaica and organize a shipping line to transport the fruit. He was to become a major partner in the United Fruit Company, the body that dominated the banana trade in Jamaica and Central America for more than a century. Baker is credited with single-handedly starting the production of bananas for export in Jamaica at a time when the island was experiencing a decline in sugar production and increased competition from beet sugar.

Early Jamaican tourism: A by-product of the banana trade

Baker, having become both a large landowner in Jamaica and a shipowner, soon conceived the idea that the same ships which transported bananas could transport tourists. For a successful tourism industry to develop, however, Jamaica, and other Caribbean countries, had to find a solution to their health problems.

For a large part of the nineteenth century the Caribbean had health problems due to malaria and yellow fever, and had accordingly earned the reputation of "the white man's grave". In the West Indies both civilians and the British military had died in significant numbers during the first part of the nineteenth century. It was reckoned that between 1817 and 1836 the average death rate among the British troops stationed, for example in Jamaica, was as high as 121.3 per thousand.

According to Taylor, from as early as 1851 the Jamaican authorities were interested in attracting men and money into Jamaica from the United States for the expressed purpose of aiding the post-emancipation reconstruction of the economy of the island. As such it was important to give entrepreneurs assurances about the health conditions of the country. Emphasis was therefore placed on promotions for business opportunities in Jamaica's "genial" climate. Such advertisement, however, required a comprehensive rebranding job for "the white man's grave".

In the twenty-first century, when emphasis is being placed on ecotourism and inland tourism, it is fascinating that a place like Jamaica, now known and celebrated for its beaches, was first promoted as offering healthy mountain retreats because the beaches were notoriously unhealthy places. Visitors were therefore invited to spend time instead in the highlands of Jamaica where they would find "dry mountain retreats pleasing in panorama and invigorating in atmosphere, ideal for the hypochondriac and dyspeptic". Visitors were assured that "the clear, rare atmosphere of Jamaica's higher elevations, will do more for the individual than Egypt, Mentone, Nice or the Riviera for the Europeans, and California, Nassau, Bermuda or Florida for the American".

The availability of the banana boats and the need to promote Jamaica as a pleasant and healthy place to do business was a happy coincidence which fostered the development of tourism. The United Fruit Company operated some sixty steamers, ferried visitors to and fro between Jamaica and the United States, and built modern facilities for their guests in Jamaica.

It was not long before the Jamaican banana trade was paralleled on the other side of the Atlantic by the Imperial Line of Elder, Dempster and Company, which also traded in bananas. The company operated from the United Kingdom, and advertised vacations to Englishmen, who then came to Jamaica on the banana boats. From as early as 1908, the UK banana-trading interests of the company were advertising regular fortnightly sailings between Bristol and the island. The company was also promoting Jamaica as the "New Riviera".

Historic hotels in Jamaica

According to the Jamaica *Gleaner*'s special feature "Pieces of the Past: The Grand Hotels of Jamaica", published in November 2001, the Jamaica Hotels Law was passed, in 1890, to jump-start the hotel industry. This was to meet the needs of the over 300,000 people expected to attend Jamaica's Great Exhibition of 1891. By the end of the nineteenth century and beginning of the twentieth, Kingston was teeming with thousands of visitors who arrived by steamship, and consequently the Myrtle Bank, Constant Spring and Queen's Hotel proved major hotels.

The Myrtle Bank, built in the mid-1800s, was acquired by government and modernized specially to accommodate guests for the Great Exhibition. It was destroyed in the earthquake of 1907, but rebuilt in 1918, with some 205 rooms, then sold to the United Fruit Company.

The Constant Spring Hotel, with one hundred rooms, was also built for the Great Exhibition, and was situated some six miles outside of Kingston at the end of an electric tramcar line. The hotel was taken over by government by the mid-1890s. It was situated on 165 acres, and became known for its golf course. It boasted quite luxurious accommodations and amenities, but in 1941 had to be sold because it was not making a profit. It was bought by the Franciscan Sisters and used as a convent and a school. In 1941 it became the Immaculate Conception School, which was attended mostly by the daughters of wealthy Jamaican, Cuban, Haitian and Canadian Catholic families.

Another Kingston hotel, built about the same time as the Constant Spring, was the Queen's Hotel. It was erected to house the working classes at the time of the Great Exhibition, but was afterwards used largely by country folk coming to Kingston and looking for reasonably priced accommodation.

However, not all the early Jamaican hotels were situated in Kingston. The Moneague Hotel, built around 1890 in St Ann, is now the Moneague Teachers' Training College. However, in the early 1900s it was a charming hotel establishment known for its food, tennis, croquet and shooting. It used to be reached by visitors travelling by train to Ewarton and onwards by hotel carriage. It seems to have suffered, as many hotels before and since, because of changes in modes of transportation and in the transportation infrastructure. There was also the Rio Cobre Hotel in Spanish Town, and the Mandeville Hotel, set 2,000 feet above sea level in the Manchester Hills, which began life in 1875 as the Waverly Hotel.

One of the most famous of the great hotels of Jamaica was the Titchfield Hotel, first built in 1895 by Baker as a small property in Port Antonio, Portland, then Jamaica's second most important town. However, by 1905 the hotel had four hundred rooms and was well-known for its amenities and facilities. The Titchfield Hotel was closely linked to the development of the banana trade, and consequently suffered with the decline of that industry in the 1930s. It was finally destroyed by fire in the late 1960s.

The Great Exhibition of 1891

More needs to be said about the Great Exhibition of 1891 ("Pieces of the Past", *Gleaner*, 28 January 2002). It was organized to display the main agricultural products of Jamaica at the time, such as sugar, rum, coffee and cocoa. The exhibition displayed cigars, cigarettes and tobacco as well. The event must, however, also be seen as having played an important role in placing Jamaica on the map as a tourism destination.

The exhibition was the idea of Jamaican A.C. Sinclair who persuaded Governor Blake to raise the funds needed to mount the exhibition. It was a massive undertaking. The exhibition building which covered forty thousand square feet was expected to cost £15,000, which, at the time, was a large sum of money. The funds were raised by public contributions from the business sector matched by a contribution from the treasury.

The Prince of Wales, later King George V of Britain, was the exhibition's patron. Eight thousand persons are estimated to have attended the opening day. Five hotels, including the Queen's, the Myrtle Bank and the Constant Spring, were either modernized or built to accommodate guests attending the exhibition, and roads, bridges and railways were either constructed or improved to secure transport from the countryside. The exhibition, which closed on 2 May 1891 after four months, had received 302,831 visitors.

Beginning of modern tourism in Jamaica

The period from 1944 to 1962 may be said to mark the beginning of modern tourism in Jamaica. It was a period of impressive economic and political development in the country, as it witnessed economic expansion beyond sugar to include bananas and other agricultural sectors. The period also included the substantial mining of bauxite and alumina, and the development of manufacturing, and tourism, which latter spawned a vibrant construction industry.

The tourism industry leader during this period was Abe Issa, who had convinced his father, Elias Issa, to buy the Myrtle Bank Hotel in Kingston in 1943. The venture was successful, and in 1948 Abe Issa built the Tower Isle Hotel on the north coast of the island. The hotel hosted such movie stars as Eva Gabor, Debbie Reynolds and Errol Flynn, as well as the boxer Joe Louis and the playwright Noel Coward. This success helped to further publicize Jamaica as an international tourism destination.

The Tower Isle was the first hotel in Jamaica to operate all-year-round. As chairman of the Jamaica Tourist Board from 1955 to 1963, Abe Issa presided over major growth of visitors to Jamaica, an expansion which reached 227,000 persons per year. In 1978 his nephew John Issa, founder of the Superclubs chain of hotels, pioneered the concept of the Jamaican all-inclusive hotel, turning Tower Isle into the Couples Tower Isle Hotel. This implementation was followed by that of the Couples Sans Souci, the Couples Swept Away and the Couples Negril. Abe died in 1984 and was succeeded by his son, Elias Issa.

The Superclubs all-inclusive concept was later to find a major competitor in the Sandals Resorts, founded in 1981 by Gordon "Butch" Stewart. By 2013 Stewart's multi-billion-dollar hotel empire has grown to twenty hotel resorts, inside and outside of Jamaica. They include the Sandals all-inclusive, couples-only resorts; the Beaches resorts for families; and four boutique hotels. In November 1994 Stewart's company, the Air Jamaica Acquisition Group, also became the majority shareholder in Air Jamaica, a Jamaican airline which had been launched in April 1969. In 2004, however, the Government of Jamaica regained the ownership of the airline, ending a ten-year period of privatization.

Jamaican ownership of hotels

There are two significant aspects of the Issa and Stewart enterprises that dominate the local Jamaican hotel scene. The first aspect is that they are both home-grown Jamaican efforts, in contrast to the foreign ownership of the large and luxurious hotels of a former era. Foreign ownership of large, luxurious hotels continues to be the norm in several other Caribbean countries. The second aspect is that the Stewart and Issa hotels are all-inclusive products, the social and economic implications of which are discussed below.

The CTO, in a 1994 study of all-inclusive hotels, defines them as "resorts or vacations where all or most hotel guest services are included in one pre-paid package price. This includes airport transfers, accommodation, all meals, drinks and snacks, alcoholic beverages, entertainment, sports facilities, water sports, government taxes and gratuities." Such an arrangement contrasts with that of the European plan, in which the rate charged covers accommodation only, and meals are paid for only as they are consumed. There are several other variations on these two plans, depending on whether breakfast, lunch and dinner are included in the price paid by the customer.

The available statistics from the Jamaica Tourist Board for 2000 to 2004 indicate that the all-inclusive hotels comprise 73.7 per cent of the room stock as compared to 28.2 per cent in the European plan hotels. The all-inclusive hotels also out-perform the non-all-inclusives in terms of occupancy – specifically by approximately 69 to 70 per cent for the all-inclusive ones, as compared to 35 to 39 per cent on the part of the European plan hotels (*Tourism: The Driver of Change in the Jamaican Economy*, 2006). A study in 1997 by the Organization of American States (OAS) suggests that the all-inclusive hotels in Jamaica contributed almost 50 per cent of total earnings.

Government's role in Jamaican tourism development

Jamaica's massive private sector effort has always been strongly supported by the Ministry of Tourism, which came on board in this regard as early as 1922. It was in that year that the government created the Jamaica Tourist Trade Development Board, the forerunner of the Jamaica Tourist Board.

The Jamaica Tourist Board was reorganized in 1963 and received immediately its first full-time director of tourism, John Pringle, CBE. Pringle has been described as dynamic, creative and innovative, and is credited with transforming Jamaica's tourism sector from a marginal enterprise to both an industry and the island's economic mainstay. He served until 1967. Under his stewardship the tourism earnings of Jamaica tripled. Pringle also introduced many innovations, all of which were said to have revolutionized Jamaica's marketing programmes, and several new aspects of the product.

He was followed by a long line of high-profile directors which included Stewart Sharpe, Eric Anthony Abrahams, Adrian Robinson, Desmond Henry, John Gentles, Carrole Guntley-Brady, Robert Stephens, Fay Pickersgill, Paul Penny Cook, Basil Smith and John Lynch.

The racial dimension

The expansion of the tourism industry at the beginning of the twentieth century took place through the banana boats. Many of the clientele using the boats out of the United States were from the racially segregated southern states, and brought with them the social and racial attitudes which had been absorbed in their society. It is not difficult to imagine what happened when these attitudes were grafted on to the attitudes that had already existed at that time in a colonial plantation society. It goes without saying that the early hotels we have been describing in Jamaica, as in other Caribbean islands, were places of privilege, frequented at that time largely by patrons who were wealthy, famous and white. These hotels were off limits to blacks as guests.

Frank Taylor records that the early banana-boat tourists had found the attitudes of black Jamaican workers somewhat different from the more docile blacks they had left at home in the southern states. Early travelogues spoke of Jamaican staff as being "ignorant and impudent". They were described as behaving "as if it were gall and wormwood to their haughty souls to have to wait upon the white person" and "in a way, unmistakably denoting that they were revenging themselves for the indignity of having to accept such service".

The racial practices in Caribbean tourism were affected by a number of factors, some of which affected Jamaica differently from the eastern Caribbean. In the smaller islands of the eastern Caribbean it was possible to perform any task and return home to sleep in one's own bed. On these islands it was understood and accepted that hotels were, from the beginning, built to accommodate foreign tourists who, initially, were almost by definition white. This situation continued to be the case until a black American tourist market was developed in the 1970s. Even so, the record shows that, initially, American blacks had some difficulty being accepted and treated by black staff with the same courtesy and respect as the white guests. Prior to that period, black Caribbean families travelling on business or on holiday within the eastern Caribbean stayed largely with friends or family or at small guest houses, and often did not refer to themselves as tourists.

In Jamaica, a country of much larger size, two distinct types of hotels developed. The first type was those built to accommodate tourists in places like Montego Bay, Negril and Ocho Rios. The second type comprised those built in Kingston to accommodate both locals, who needed to stay overnight in the capital, and business people doing business away from home, whether that business was located in some distant part of Jamaica or overseas.

By their respective locations, marketing and type of operation, the tourist hotels, especially the all-inclusive ones, created the suggestion that they were not catering to local Jamaicans as guests. This practice changed significantly when, in the 1970s, Jamaica shifted to socialism under the Michael Manley government, a change that resulted in a loss of foreign-tourist business. The response of the Jamaica Tourist Board was to develop a strong marketing campaign inviting Jamaicans to take their holidays in the hotels on the north coast of the country.

History repeats itself: a similar situation occurred in 2009 and 2010 in the eastern Caribbean, where difficult global economic circumstances led even luxury hotels to develop "staycation" programmes, where they marketed their product aggressively to the local population. Once a shift like this takes place, however, it is difficult to return to the status quo ante, and both hoteliers and local populations become accustomed to the notion that the only relevant criteria for the use of the hotel is that the client can afford to pay for the services rendered.

In their important book *People and Tourism: Issues and Attitudes in the Jamaican Hospitality Industry* (2002), based on research carried out in 1999, Hopeton Dunn and Leith Dunn explored the relationships between the Jamaican people and the tourism industry. In the introduction, Jamaican hotelier James Samuels, speaking about tourism development in around the 1950s, states:

> Jamaicans who worked in tourism mainly occupied line staff positions. The Jamaican middle class had very little to do with the tourism industry, mainly equating the various jobs with that of the house slaves. There was little meaningful interaction between the visitors and the Jamaican people at large. The process reinforced the syndrome of "them" and "us". The fact is, that this was a business that was not integrated within the Jamaican economy and enjoyed negative perceptions among

sections of the population. Arguably, this may well mirror the rest of the Caribbean during this period.

Samuels goes on to elaborate the role that the Jamaican government played in the 1970s, through the Urban Development Corporation (UDC), in developing both a superstructure and an infrastructure of a tourism industry. In Jamaica it was the UDC which spearheaded the construction of foreign-owned-and-managed hotels such as the Holiday Inn, Wyndham Rosehall, Trelawny Beach, the Hilton Kingston Hotel, the Courtleigh Hotel, the Le Meridian Jamaica Pegasus, as well as the Ocean and Forum hotels, now closed.

It is suggested that this effort to integrate Jamaicans into the industry failed, initially, because steps had not been taken to train Jamaicans and bring them on board. However, this situation changed when a new state agency was created: the National Hotels and Properties. One objective of the agency was to infuse Jamaican professionals into the sector. The government, which was a major equity owner in the hotel industry, enforced a policy of having Jamaicans understudy management in the foreign hotel chains. This policy paid off when there was a flight of foreign hotel owners and investors during the mid-1970s and the government was left to take over the hotels both to save jobs and to keep the industry going.

There were three factors responsible for transforming Jamaican tourism during the 1970s. First, as was mentioned earlier, the government had developed a policy of encouraging local Jamaicans to spend holidays in the country itself. In 1976 there were 9,000 Jamaican hotel visits by Jamaicans, and by the end of 1977, the number of visits to both large and small hotels had jumped to 129,000. Second, because of state planning, Jamaicans had now been trained in tourism and were working as professionals in the industry. Third, all these shifts coincided with the birth of major local hotel entrepreneurship as demonstrated by the Issa family and Stewart with the Superclubs and Sandals chains. These developments have resulted in a tourism industry in Jamaica that is now over 80 per cent locally owned, as other locals have since joined the Issas and Stewarts as investors in the industry.

Major hotel initiatives by Jamaican investors who were of local white and Middle Eastern origin was an important development, one which distinguished Jamaica from other English-speaking Caribbean countries. In most of those territories, the white entrepreneurial business class diversified out of sugar plantations into commercial services other than tourism, a sector which continued to be dominated by foreign owners and managers. In Barbados, for example, the first major hotel investment by the white local private sector business enterprise was the acquisition of the Almond Beach hotels by Barbados Shipping and Trading in 1991. It is interesting that when, in 2011 and 2012, the chain, now largely owned by Trinidadian interests, was losing money, both the Barbadian and Trinidadian investors decided to bail out of the hotel industry and put the hotels up for sale.

The ownership situation in much of the CARICOM region began to change as a result of government intervention into the investment process. After the first energy crisis of 1974 and 1975, foreign investors became wary of investing in hotel real estate, and preferred instead to manage hotels built by governments on land owned by governments. This development also facilitated the emergence of a local black managerial class in the hotel industry.

The growth in Jamaican ownership and guests did not, however, immediately eliminate some of the social and racial problems that were experienced in the hotel industry. As had happened when the black American visitors started to arrive as hotel guests across the Caribbean, adjustments had to be made in the attitudes of staff and guests of Jamaican hotels. When Jamaicans began to show up at their own hotels as guests, both staff and locals generally who had been acclimatized to think that hotel guests were foreign, if not white and foreign, had to be socialized differently.

The perception in the Caribbean by ordinary people of who is and who is not a tourist has certainly undergone changes due to many developments, not least the training and education tourism programmes sponsored by governments, regional organizations like the CTO and the Caribbean Hotel Association (CHA), and by the enlightened members of the national private sector itself. In one of the surveys carried out in Jamaica by the Dunns, 54 per cent of Jamaicans expressed the view that tourists are ordinary people just like them, 46 per cent saw tourists as visitors from overseas, 27.3 per cent all races, 19.2 per cent white foreigners, and 7.2 per cent guests in a resort hotel. However, most people did not see Jamaicans on holiday in resort areas as tourists.

While Jamaicans seem to be in no doubt about the importance of tourism to their national economy, even if facing a number of challenges, especially with respect to crime, the debate continues about whom the industry benefits and how the proceeds are shared.

The Dunns' research produced some interesting answers. Some 86.4 per cent of Jamaicans thought tourism as being very important, 10.5 per cent as reasonably important and only 3.1 per cent as unimportant. But when asked about tourism's benefits to their own community, 38 per cent perceived it as not providing any benefits at that level, 36 per cent as being moderately beneficial and only 26 per cent beneficial. Responses also differed by age group, with the older, over-fifty-five-year-olds seeing it as most beneficial, the females as moderately beneficial and the twenty-to-forty-four-year-olds as least beneficial. The overall general perception was that the "big man" benefits most and the "small man" least. Perceptions of who are the "big men" include owners of large all-inclusive hotels, overseas travel companies, airline and cruise ship operators, and owners of in-bond shops. The "small men" were seen as including small business people, such as taxi operators, craft vendors, higglers, local farmers, operators of local villas and guests houses, as well as low-level workers in the industry.

An interesting finding of the surveys is that Jamaicans do not rank tourism as the priority sector to improve the economy and create more jobs. The rankings in terms of what were the priority sectors are as follows: agriculture, 48 per cent; tourism, 38 per cent; manufacturing, 30 per cent; information technology, 23 per cent; bauxite, 19 per cent; and other, 44 per cent. These discoveries would not have been the findings for the Bahamas, Bermuda, Barbados or of any survey carried out in or close to the beginning of the twenty-first century. The Jamaican findings probably reflect the existence of a relatively more extensive and sustainable local agricultural sector, continuing concern about the nature of tourism, the challenges tourism faces, and the perception that tourism continues to benefit the "big man" more than the "small man".

Cuba

Christopher Columbus landed on Cuba on 12 October 1492 and claimed it for Spain. In 1511, the first Spanish settlement was founded by Diego Velazquez de Cuellar at Baracoa, and other towns then followed. The future capital, San Cristobal de la Habana, was founded in 1515. At the time of settlement there were about 100,000 indigenous people, called Tainos or Arawaks, living in Cuba. However, within a century the entire population of indigenous people had been wiped out, either by disease or by repressive measures of subjugation by the colonizers. From 1511 until 1898 Cuba remained a colony of Spain. Under the social and economic domination of a Spanish landowning elite Cuba developed an economy based on exporting sugar, coffee and tobacco to Europe and later also to North America. As with other Caribbean colonies, African slaves were brought to Cuba to work on the plantations, with the first group arriving in 1790.

Cuba is the largest island in the Caribbean with an area of 42,427 square miles and a population estimated in 2008 at 11,236,444 persons. Unlike the four English-speaking islands discussed above, the whites comprised the vast majority of the population, some 65.05 per cent prior to the Castro revolution in 1959. (They were largely of Spanish origin.) The rest of the population was divided proportionally into 10.08 per cent African and 23.84 per cent Mulattos and Mestizos. These ethnic proportions may be compared with those of 1817, which were 219,021 whites, 115,691 free blacks and 224,268 black slaves. The balance in population shifted due to periods of intensive emigration of whites to Cuba from Spain and other European countries, both before and after Cuban independence. It has, however, been suggested by some sources, to be discussed later, that, due to mass emigration to the United States of whites after 1959, the number of whites and non-whites remaining in Cuba has become almost equal.

Independence movement

The 1820s was an active period for independence in Latin America, but for a long time the Cubans seemed content to remain under the rule of Spain. There were a number of abortive attempts at independence. One attempt was in 1868, and led by Carlos Manuel de Céspedes. Another one took place in 1895; during this uprising José Martí, who had formed the Cuban Revolutionary Party in New York in 1892, was killed in the battle of Dos Rios. The Spanish army, which greatly outnumbered the rebels, had put down the insurrection with a considerable amount of brutality.

However, the break with Spain in fact came after the detonation of the US battleship *Main* in the Havana Harbour on 25 January 1898, with the loss of 252 crew members. Spain was suspected to be the perpetrator of the *Main* incident, and this perception led to war between Spain and the United States. Under the Treaty of Paris in 1898, Cuba, Puerto Rico, the Philippines and Guam were ceded to the United States for the sum of US$20 million, and on 20 May 1902 the United States, under the presidency of Theodore Roosevelt, granted Cuba its independence.

American dominance in Cuba

Under the new Cuban independent constitution, the United States retained the right to intervene in Cuban affairs and to supervise its finances and foreign relations. Furthermore, under the Platt Amendment, the United States leased the Guantanamo naval base from Cuba. This right to intervention in Cuban affairs by the US government was exercised on a number of occasions: in 1906, for example, during a period of unrest, the United States intervened and established a governor named Edward Magoon, who remained in power until 1908, when self-government was restored under José Miguel Gómez. It is difficult to understand present-day relations between the United States and Cuba, and Cuba's reaction to US dominance, unless one is familiar with the history in which the United States took for granted proprietary rights in the country.

Constitutional government existed in Cuba until 1930, when Gerardo Machado y Morales seized power. During the next four years Cuba was to have several different presidents all installed by coups: Carlos Manuel de Céspedes y Quesada succeeded Machado; Céspedes was then replaced by Ramón Grau; and in 1934 Grau was replaced by Carlos Mendieta, through the instrumentality of Fulgencio Batista and the Cuban army. In 1940, Batista, about whom much more is said below in respect of tourism in Cuba, was elected president.

Tourism in pre-revolutionary Cuba

If the dates of hotel openings are valid means on which to depend, tourism began in Cuba in about the 1830s. There are historic hotels such as the Hotel Florida, built in 1836, the Hotel Telegrafo, which opened in 1888 and Hotel Sofitel Sevilla, which started in 1902. The Hotel Santa Isabel in Old Havana was first opened in 1867, offering splendid and sumptuous comfort. It was the favourite of ship chandlers, merchants, artists, scientists, and famous travellers that frequented Cuba at that time. It closed, but reopened a century later with all its former elegance. Hotel Inglaterra recently celebrated 130 years of operation and there are others which have now been restored to their former glory, making Old Havana a living history of Cuba's tourism industry.

The Hotel Ambos Mundos in Old Havana was built in the 1920s, and in the 1930s became famous as the favourite place of the author, Ernest Hemingway who is supposed to have written a chapter of his book *For Whom the Bell Tolls* in room 511. Some of his possessions are still kept in the room, which has become one of the tourist attractions of Old Havana.

The Hotel Nacional de Cuba, Cuba's most famous hotel, was opened on 30 December 1930. It is an imposing building which commands an impressive site on Taganana Hill. During the pre-revolution era it counted among its famous guests, such artists, actors and writers as Johnny Weissmuller, Buster Keaton, José Mujica, Jorge Negrete, Agustin Lara, Tyrone Power, Romulo Gallegos, Errol Flynn, Marlon Brando and Ernest Hemingway. Winston Churchill and the Duke and Duchess of Windsor also stayed there.

In the period from 1920 to 1933 Cuba could not have wished for a greater tourism incentive than the passing of the eighteenth amendment to the United States Constitution, which banned the sale, manufacture and transportation of alcohol nationally in the United States. Cuba, as it was situated just ninety miles off the Florida coast, became the Mecca for casino gambling, prostitution, horse racing, drug running and alcohol consumption, and was now known as the Latin Las Vegas. Among the famous persons who were now to be found at Cuba's hotels therefore were not only royalty, the movie stars and politicians, but also gangsters such as Santos Trafficante, Meyer Lansky, Lucky Luciano and Frank Costello, all of whom were reputed to be close associates of Batista. It is alleged that a full-scale meeting of the American underworld leaders took place in December 1946 at the Hotel Nacional. Lansky was able to obtain approval to operate a casino in the hotel, and it opened in 1955, with a show featuring Eartha Kitt. Lucky Luciano, who was paroled from prison after the Second World War on condition that he return to Sicily, nonetheless found his way to Cuba, where he not only ran a number of casinos, but also continued his operations as part of the American Mafia until he was finally deported.

In 1955 Batista announced that Cuba would grant a gaming licence to anyone who invested US$1 million in a hotel or US$200,000 in a new night club, and that the government would provide matching public funds for construction, a ten-year exemption from taxes, and impose no duties on imports of equipment and furnishings for new hotels. From each casino the government was to receive US$250,000 for the licence, and a percentage of the profits. The background checks that were required to operate casinos in the United States were waived, leaving the door open for corruption and money laundering.

The influence of dictator Fulgencio Batista on Cuban tourism

As president of Cuba, Fulgencio Batista y Zaldiver influenced the kind of tourism for which Cuba became infamous in the pre-revolutionary period. He exercised power in Cuba from 1933 to 1944 and again from 1952 to 1959, ostensibly with the support of various US governments. Batista seems to have been the most corrupt of the Cuban political leaders. He was a man of mixed European, African, Chinese and Amerindian ancestry who, from humble origins, came to prominence through a career in the Cuban army. He first became a sergeant and then launched his political career when he led a successful coup. That coup became known as the "Revolt of the Sergeants", and took place on 4 September 1933 against the government of Gerardo Machado.

Assuming the position of army chief of staff, Batista was the power behind a series of puppet presidents until he himself was elected president in October 1940, holding office until 1944. He gained favour with the Allied governments during the Second World War by declaring Cuba's strong support for the war effort against the Germans, Japanese and Italians.

In 1944, at the end of his first term, Batista went to live in the United States, spending time between Florida and New York, but continued to participate in Cuban affairs from his American bases. Those locations probably reflected the haunts of certain well-known gangsters in the United States. In 1948 he was elected *in absentia* to the Cuban Senate, and in 1952, once more back in Cuba, he ran for president. On 10 March 1952, however, three months before the elections which he seemed likely to lose, he staged a coup, with army backing, and assumed power in Cuba for a second time.

There seems to be substantial independent testimony, by authoritative US sources, to the state of corruption and neglect of the welfare of the Cuban population during Batista's second term as president of Cuba.

Arthur Schlesinger Jr, when then asked by the US government to comment on Batista's Cuba, stated: "The corruption of the government, the brutality of the police, the regime's indifference to the needs of the people for education, medical care, housing, for social justice and economic justice is an open invitation to revolution" (Schlesinger, *The Dynamics of World Power*, 1973). David Detzer, an American journalist, commented as follows after visiting Cuba in the 1950s: "Brothels flourished. A major industry grew up around them; government officials received bribes, policemen collected protection money. Prostitutes could be seen standing in doorways, strolling the streets, or leaning from windows. One report estimated that 11,500 of them worked in the trade in Havana. Beyond the outskirts of the capital, beyond the slot machines, was one of the poorest, and most beautiful countries in the Western world" (Detzer, *The Brink: Cuban Missile Crisis, 1962*, 1979).

But perhaps the most damning words came from John F. Kennedy himself, both as a candidate for the presidency and after he became president. At a Democratic dinner in Ohio (6 October 1960), he said: "In 1959 United States companies owned about 40 per cent of the Cuban sugar lands – almost all the cattle ranches – 90 per cent of the mines and mineral concessions – 80 per cent of the utilities – practically all the oil industry and supplied two-thirds of Cuban imports." Kennedy also argued, in October 1960 during his campaign:

> Fulgenio Batista murdered twenty thousand Cubans in seven years ... and he turned democratic Cuba into a complete police state – destroying every individual liberty. Yet our aid to his regime, and the ineptness of our policies, enabled Batista to invoke the name of the United States in support of his reign of terror. Administration spokesmen publicly praised Batista – hailed him as a staunch ally and a good friend – at a time when Batista was murdering thousands, destroying the last vestiges of freedom and stealing millions of dollars from the Cuban people, and we failed to press for free elections.

In an interview with Jean Daniel that same month Kennedy also remarked:

> I believe that there is no country in the world, including any and all the countries under colonial domination, where economic colonization, humiliation and exploitation were worse than in Cuba, in part, owing to my country's policies during the Batista regime. I approved the proclamation which Fidel Castro made in the Sierra

Maestra, when he justifiably called for justice and especially yearned to rid Cuba of corruption. I will even go further: to some extent it is as though Batista was the incarnation of a number of sins on the part of the United States. Now we shall have to pay for those sins. In the matter of the Batista regime, I am in agreement with the first Cuban revolutionaries. That is perfectly clear.

The years 1952 to 1959 in Cuba were years of frequent rebellions against the regime and the brutal police and of army responses against the citizens. Until 1958 Batista could count on US support in terms of arms, tanks and planes, but finally, US president Dwight Eisenhower decided that enough was enough, and informed Batista that he could no longer count on US support.

Fidel Castro – who, on 26 July 1953, was the leader of the first albeit unsuccessful assault on the Batista regime when the Moncada Barracks in Santiago were attacked – was arrested and imprisoned. Many of the other leaders were executed, but Castro was only imprisoned. By 1955 Batista was so confident of his power in Cuba that he released from prison Castro and other survivors of the Moncada Barracks attack. Castro and other associates sought refuge in Mexico from where they planned the Cuban Revolution. On 2 December 1956 the small group of Cuban rebels on the yacht Granma landed in Cuba and established themselves in the Sierra Maestro region. In late 1958 the rebels launched a full-scale attack on the Batista regime. After the rebels captured Santa Clara the dictator fled into exile in Portugal.

The first president of the new government in 1959 was Dr Manuel Urrutia Lleo, but after some disagreements in the party, he was replaced in the same year by Osvaldo Dorticos, who served as president until 1976. Castro was made prime minister in February 1959.

The racial dimension in Cuba

It will be seen that the concerns about the tourism industry in the Bahamas, Bermuda, Barbados and Jamaica differed radically from those in Cuba. In those four former colonies, where there was a black majority, the major socio-cultural issue was, that after years of European colonialism, slavery, and racial discrimination, tourism was seen as simply continuing the same negative practices that the plantation economy had brought.

The Cuban initial situation appears to have been somewhat different than that of the other four countries. Prior to the revolution there was a decided white majority in Cuba, and the social issue for Cubans was this: tourism was seen as part of a package in which corrupt dictators, for personal gain, handed over the country in its entirety to American businessmen and the US Mafia. In Batista's Cuba, blacks were a deprived, but relatively small proportion of the population. Blacks had hoped, however, that after Castro's revolution, their circumstances would be greatly improved.

Black Cuban professor Carlos Moore Wedderburn is the author of the book *Pichón: Race and Revolution in Castro's Cuba: A Memoir*. He claims in the book that he himself was repeatedly harassed by Cuban government authorities, and finally exiled from the country, because of his fight for equality for blacks in Cuba. Wedderburn has argued that in post-revolutionary Cuba, following the fall of Batista, non-white people continued to be bitter because of both continuing racial discrimination and exclusion from participation in the exercise of power in the country. He also states that their expectation of improved circumstances in return for supporting the revolution were not then met. Wedderburn argues as well that, as more and more whites left for Miami, the balance in the number of whites and non-whites in Cuba became more even, with the added complexity that non-whites were stratified according to their various shades and racial characteristics to an even greater degree than had happened in the small Caribbean islands which had been dominated by the sugar plantations. These charges of racial discrimination against blacks in Cuba are denied by government sources.

Impact of the American embargo on Cuban tourism in post-revolutionary Cuba

Prior to 1959, Cuba was the largest tourism destination in the Caribbean, with more than 350,000 annual visitors from the United States, Europe and Latin America. All this changed as a result of the developments that immediately followed the revolution. The state took over ownership of private newspapers and radio and television stations; during its first year the Castro government also nationalized private property, tightened controls on the private sector, and closed down the gambling industry that had been controlled by the Mafia. Given the extent to which both American business and the criminal element owned property and businesses of every kind in Cuba, Americans were set to be the chief victims of the widespread state expropriation, without compensation.

In October 1960, the American government hit back with a partially imposed commercial, economic and financial embargo against Cuba, which the United States then strengthened to a near-total embargo, in February 1962. There was therefore a complete breakdown in relations between the two countries. The situation was further exacerbated by the fact that, by 1961, Cuba had become a client state of the Soviet Union, exhibiting Soviet tanks and other weapons in its 1961 New Year's Day parade. Cuba was also reputed to have the second-largest army in Latin America. All of this was happening at the time of the Cold War.

In April 1961 there was an unsuccessful invasion of Cuba at the Bay of Pigs by a force of Cuban exiles trained and supported by the United States. The next year the peace of the entire world was threatened by the Cuban Missile Crisis when, under Kennedy, the United States demanded the withdrawal of Soviet missiles from Cuba, and succeeded in this regard. By this time, inevitably, American tourist flows to Cuba had come to a standstill.

Indigenous tourism in Cuba

It is often held that after its revolution Cuba did not pursue tourism development until after the collapse in 1991 of the Soviet Union and the consequent loss of Soviet financial support. It is argued, however (Ward, *Packaged Vacations*, 2008), that there were two distinct periods in Cuban tourism development. The first period took place from 1959 to 1981. During this time Castro, having nationalized foreign-owned tourism properties immediately after the revolution, began the development of a domestic tourism infrastructure, with the focus on showcasing the achievements and talents of the revolution, the beauty and hospitality of Cuba, and retaining valuable foreign exchange in the country. The second period started in earnest in 1973 and was consolidated in 1981. This period was seen as muting the nationalist and revolutionary content of Cuban tourism, and looked to foreign-tourist spending for earning revenue.

Unintended consequences of the American embargo

The US restrictions imposed by the embargo were intended to cause the death of organized and legitimate American tourism to Cuba, which was a major source of its employment and foreign exchange earnings. But there were two developments, probably neither fully foreseen by the United States.

First, the impact of the American embargo was blunted by the expansion of European investment, and especially Spanish investment, in Caribbean tourism, beginning in the 1980s. Spanish companies like Sol Media and Guitart, which were in any case expanding in several Spanish Caribbean countries, took the opportunity to fill the vacuum in Cuba left by the United States. Spanish tourists were later joined by Canadians, who paid little attention to the US embargo, preferring instead to take advantage of the competitive hotel rates in Cuba.

Second, the embargo had made Cuba heavily dependent on the Soviet Union and Eastern Europe for almost all aspects of its economic life. During the Cold War the Soviet Union was reported to have generated US$5 billion annually in financial aid to Cuba.

Impact of Soviet collapse on Cuban tourism

A serious twin blow was therefore dealt to the Cuba economy by the collapse of the Soviet Union in 1991 and the drop in world prices for agricultural products. Castro now found himself more dependent than ever on tourism, and set out to establish fresh goals for the sector. He turned aggressively to foreign direct investment, creating joint venture partnerships between Cuban agencies and foreign investors, largely from Europe, but also from Canada and Latin America. Five Cuban agencies – Cubanacan, Gran Caribe, Gaviota, Horizontes and Marinas Puertosol – were established to manage the hotel industry, and the geographic areas of focus for development were Havana, Varadero and Cayo largo.

By the mid-1990s Cuba had 180 hotels with, between them, more than 23,000 rooms and another 10,000 in the planning stage. In 1994, tourism in Cuba surpassed the sugar industry for the first time as the strongest economic sector in the country, and, according to the Cuban government, now attracted more than 700,000 visitors. Moreover, the goals set for achievement by the year 2000 were aggressive. These included:

- attracting 2.5 million tourists per year – 3.5 million if the embargo were lifted
- generating US$3.12 billion in hard-currency earnings
- doubling hotel rooms to 50,000
- investing US$2.4 billion in development projects
- operating cruise ships from three ports
- adding fourteen hotels in Old Havana
- expanding airport facilities
- developing four golf courses
- replacing aging fleet of the country
- developing the island's water-sport infrastructure

A new incident, on 24 February 1996, and the US response to it, seemed to threaten the achievement of the tourism goals of Cuba. It was on that date that Cuban MIG fighters shot down two civilian planes. Each plane carried Cuban-Americans who were working for a Miami-based group of Cuban exiles called Brothers to the Rescue. The US government claimed that the incident had taken place in international airspace and not in Cuban airspace, as Cuba argued. On 12 March 1996 the US Congress responded to Cuba's position by further strengthening the embargo against Cuba. Specifically, Congress passed the Helms-Burton Act, which restricted US citizens from doing business with or in Cuba, and which mandated restrictions on giving public or private assistance to any successor government in Havana until certain claims against the Cuban government were met.

More than fifty years after the US embargo against Cuba was introduced it is clear that it has not only failed to achieve its objectives of isolating Cuba, especially with respect to the tourism industry, but is now also disapproved of by almost every country. Moreover, American business – which during the Batista era, owned the vast majority of Cuban businesses – has seen other countries in both North and South America fill the vacuum they left behind.

During 2008 and 2009, two of the most difficult years for international tourism performance, Cuban tourism continued on its growth path. In 2008, according to statistics provided by the Caribbean Tourism Organization, Cuba's arrival numbers were 2,348,340 visitors (an improvement of

9 per cent), and in 2009, 2,429,809 (a further improvement of 3.5 per cent). On 20 October 2010 the *Caribbean News Digital* carried a report of significance. According to the report the Cuban Ministry of Tourism had announced that, by 18 October 2010, the country had welcomed two million tourists, and was on the way to a 3 per cent growth over the 2009 figure. Cuba had reached the two-million figure for the seventh straight year.

Additional figures are also striking. According to an article written for the Associated Press, and carried by *Caribbean News* on 22 November 2010, tourism revenue through September 2010 was US$1.3 billion, up 3.5 per cent over the previous period. In 2010 Canada sent the most tourists to Cuba, with 733,000 visitors in the first nine months of 2010, followed, in order of number, by Britain, Italy, Spain, Germany, France, Mexico, Argentina and Russia.

By the end of 2011, 2.7 million tourists visited Cuba, an increase of 8.2 per cent over 2010, according to the Cuban minister of tourism, Manuel Marrero. The number was expected to grow even further in 2012, with some 2.9 million foreign visitors expected. The Dutch carrier KLM returned to Cuba at the end of September 2011 after an absence of sixty-eight years. The largest market is now Canada, which was expected to produce 1 million tourists in 2011. The second-largest market is the United Kingdom, but Italy, Spain, Germany France, Argentina, Mexico and Russia are also well-represented. Seventy-two thousand Russians came in 2011, a 140 per cent increase over 2010.

When Castro assumed power in Cuba he was quick to criticize the tourism industry, which he saw as largely reflective of all that was wrong with the Batista regime. It is ironic that, in the twenty-first century, Castro, like many others before him, has had to recognize that tourism has been and continues to be the main driver of his country's economy.

The return of tourism to Cuba has, however, not been without its share of negative socio-cultural impacts. In fact, prostitution still exists in revolutionary Cuba, and seems to be practised by a cadre of unlikely prospects. Unlike during the Batista era, however, it is blamed on the economic scarcities created for the general population by the US embargo.

Failure of the American embargo to halt the growth of Cuban tourism

The US embargo, in place since 1960, has hurt the Cuban people, but it has failed to destabilize the Castro government or halt the growth of Cuban tourism. It is highly probable that, had the US government permitted its citizens and residents to travel freely as tourists and businessmen to Cuba, bringing American cultural influences and freely spending US dollars, it might have brought about more radical socio-political changes in Cuba than did all the alleged CIA plots against Castro's life, had any of them been successful. Moreover, despite the entire existing US legislative and other barriers, a significant number of American tourists continue to make their way to Cuba by diverse and devious routes. While no American president has yet found the political courage to abolish the embargo, if for no other reason than that it has failed to achieve its objectives, it can only be a matter of time before that abolition nevertheless happens.

In February 2008, Castro announced his retirement from the Cuban presidency, after holding office for forty-nine years. He had survived all the US presidents since Dwight. D. Eisenhower, who left office in 1961. It is an interesting bit of trivia that in 1959, when CTA representatives attended the annual World Travel Congress, hosted that year in Havana by the American Society of Travel Agents, Cuba was then a member of the CTA, and Castro, who had just come to power, was then made a lifetime member of the society.

3
Regional Integration in the Caribbean and the Birth and History of Regional Tourism Institutions

Some background on the historical efforts to integrate the British West Indian territories in the Caribbean, both economically and politically, is necessary for a better understanding of regional Caribbean tourism efforts and of the creation of the regional Caribbean tourism organizations. For persons without an intimate knowledge of the history of this region, it needs to be explained that the term "West Indian" is often interchanged with "Caribbean" when referring to the above mentioned subregion, which is sometimes also referred to as the "Commonwealth Caribbean". CARICOM comprises fifteen states. Thirteen of these states are members of the Commonwealth. Haiti, the fourteenth state, was French before becoming independent on 1 January 1804; and Surinam, the fifteenth, was a Dutch possession before its independence, on 25 November 1975.

Regional integration in the Caribbean is a delicate flower that must be watered and nurtured with considerable care if it is to be sustained. Efforts by Caribbean people to integrate Caribbean countries, politically or economically, have faced great difficulty. This difficulty persists despite the acceptance by most persons that, in a fiercely competitive global environment, the interests of small entities would be better served by their working together than by doing so apart. As late as 2013, however, the debate continues about whether the Caribbean community will survive, and whether it will achieve the goals of greater socio-economic integration in a single market economy that it set for itself at various times throughout the twentieth century. An ominous sign is that, in 2012, those doubts were being expressed from within the leadership itself.

The Federation of the West Indies was established in 1958, but collapsed after only four years. One of several reasons advanced by some commentators in explanation of its fragility, was that it had been imposed by Britain, an external power, on the territories concerned. The facts would suggest, however, that both Britain and the West Indies were involved in the creation of the federation. What is more, external pressure does not explain adequately the tendency to fragmentation that has attended regional integration efforts since the independence of all but a few of the territories concerned. Perhaps Caribbean people – a people who live in a geographically fragmented area and who have endured more than three hundred years of divisive forms of colonial government – need to dig deeper into their psyches and history to explain the propensity to secede from regional entities. Professor Gordon Lewis of Puerto Rico once declared that the Caribbean's philosophy is this: "If at first you don't secede, try, try and try again."

The West India Committee

Challenges have always plagued Caribbean integration efforts. In this context it is tempting to compare how another agency, one created externally to represent external interests in the West Indies, has been able to adapt itself to changing circumstances over a period of more than two hundred years, thereby surpassing all records for survival. The reference is to the West India Committee which, as late as 2011, has been performing an advocacy role in Europe for Caribbean tourism interests.

The West India Committee was formed in the eighteenth century by a permanent association of London merchants engaged in the West Indian trade, and by absentee owners of West Indian estates who lived in London and its environs. The interests of both planters and merchants appear to have first joined on a permanent basis in 1775. The committee acted as a pressure group for West Indian interests, principally in support of the sugar and rum trades (West India Committee, Official Archives, 1899 to 1998). The role of the committee then evolved as circumstances demanded. After first advocating for the sugar and rum trades, the members then argued on behalf of the enslavers, and opposed emancipation and the abolition of slavery. Then, the committee fought in support of compensation for the planters and merchants whose slaves had now been freed. After that, the members advocated for the importation of indentured Asian labour to replace the freed slaves. Later, the committee acted in support of the harvesting of cane sugar over beet sugar. Afterwards, the members operated as trade agents for the individual colonies. Finally, after the independence of several of the Caribbean countries, members worked on behalf of the West Indies as a whole, as representatives of the region in trade relations with the European Union, the United States and the other countries in the Americas.

As the role of the West India Committee changed to suit changing circumstances, a number of significant autonomous bodies were created within the agency, two of which were the Caribbean Council for Europe and the Caribbean Trade Advisory Group. More recently, the committee argued the case for European support of Caribbean tourism, and opposed the unfair imposition by the British government of the UK air passenger duty (APD) on visitors to the region. Here, clearly, is a lesson to the Caribbean in adaption and survival, if nothing else.

British administrative federal arrangements

The first federation in the West Indies did not in fact occur in 1958. From as early as the nineteenth century, the formation of various subregional units had actually been introduced by the British government in some of their West Indian territories. The Windward Islands of Grenada, St Lucia and St Vincent were associated in a federation from 1833 to 1958. From 1871 to 1956 there also existed the Federation of the Leeward Islands, which comprised Antigua and Barbuda, Dominica, Montserrat, and St Kitts–Nevis–Anguilla. Dominica was later transferred to the first regional unit. These arrangements were, however, nothing more than attempts by Britain to facilitate the administration of her West Indian possessions, and did not derive from any desire or act by the local inhabitants for federation or independence.

The road to integration of the Commonwealth Caribbean states

The road to Caribbean integration, as both a goal of Caribbean people and as a precursor to independence, can be dated from the early 1930s. It has been long and hard. It was driven by a need to transform the socio-economic conditions of the vast majority of people whose quality of life, from the 1640s, was determined by the fortunes of the sugar industry. From the first quarter of the seventeenth century sugar had been "king" in the Caribbean, meaning that it was the driver of their economies at that time. As went the rise and fall of sugar, so went the fortunes of those persons, whether slave or free, who lived in the region.

The destruction of beet sugar in Europe during the First World War had helped the recovery of the West Indian cane sugar industry from its low point at the beginning of the century. However, by the 1930s, the region was again experiencing yet another cyclical downward spiral in its economic fortunes related to sugar exports, and the planters were exploiting the workers to the greatest possible limit. Unemployment was high and wages low, and history records that the state of misery among the working class – the class which comprised the majority of the population in the British West Indies – had reached its breaking point. The situation then erupted into the various riots which, collectively, now represent a watershed in West Indian socio-political history.

In 1936, Grenadian-born Uriah Butler had organized a strike of the oilfield workers in Trinidad. The strike led to riots and the loss of human life, and to the imprisonment of Butler. In 1937 Clement Payne, born of Barbadian parents in Trinidad, had entered Barbados and fanned the flames of rebellion of the poor against the oppressive conditions that the white oligarchy had imposed. His subsequent arrest and deportation led to rioting among the normally conservative Barbadian population. A commission was then established by Sir Mark Young, the governor of Barbados, with Sir George Dean to examine the reason for the riots. That examination painted a grim picture of an island of economically disenfranchised people, people for whom the social landscape had progressed little since the emancipation of the slaves one hundred years earlier. The committee reported that there was among the population of residents deprivation, hunger and general despair, with a deep-seated resentment towards those persons who were, or were perceived to be, responsible for the prevailing inequities. Around this time disturbances were also occurring in British Guiana, St Vincent, Trinidad, Jamaica and St Kitts. In May 1938, Alexander Bustamante – later Sir Alexander and the first prime minister of Jamaica – instigated a strike in Kingston. That strike led to rioting and to his own imprisonment.

The 1930s were periods of great social and political turmoil, a situation which continued, to some extent, for another two decades. The period was marked by the emergence of the West Indian labour unions, and by the creation of political parties which, more often than not, grew out of these unions. Several of the political leaders, especially those who emerged after the Second World War, were caught up in the fervour of resistance to colonialism worldwide, and in the struggles to achieve independence that were then taking place in Asia and Africa. A number of these leaders had lived and studied together at universities in Britain, the "Mother Country". They were deeply involved in student politics, and it was almost inevitable that their thoughts would turn to national politics and to political and economic cooperation between their countries of birth on their return home. The social ills which had exploded across the Caribbean subregion in the 1930s had created common interests among its labour and political leadership, resulting in the call for some form of political collaboration among the territories.

First calls for the creation of a federal West Indian state

As early as 1932 there had been calls from a few West Indian political leaders for a federation of the West Indian states as a basis for independence. The small size and slender resources of many of those territories which comprised the British West Indies suggested to them that independence could only be realistically pursued through an economic and political union or a federation. At that time, few leaders believed that any of the territories could each proceed to independence alone. Among some of the earliest of those persons calling for federation were T.A. Marryshow of Grenada and A.A. Cypriani of Trinidad and Tobago. These calls became more strident and widespread as social unrest broke out in the region in the 1930s, incited by the deplorable living conditions of the West Indian masses.

In 1938 the West Indian Labour Congress, later the Caribbean Labour Congress, met with the Moyne Commission. The commission had been established to look into the cause of the unrest and pose solutions. One of their recommendations of the Congress was the formation of a federation of the West Indies.

The Second World War was a defining period in the history of the world. The concepts of freedom introduced through the war were not only global, but also national, and colonial people who had joined with the Allied Powers to free the world from the tyrants in Germany, Italy and Japan consequently felt that they had earned the right to be free themselves.

As Asian and African states looked to their own independence, Caribbean territories, comprising mainly an archipelago of tiny islands – later likened by President Charles de Gaulle of France to "specks of dust" – contemplated the prospect of independence, but feared that, even as a federal unit, their collective resources might be too slender to take complete charge of their own affairs. Norman Manley, chief minister of Jamaica, while addressing the Canadian Mount Allison Summer Institute at the University College of the West Indies in 1957, observed:

> If one looks at the map of these small dots which represent the ten islands that are to federate, by comparison with the vastness of the Canadian wildernesses, and if one considers the expanse of water that separates us, and if one considers the size of the population struggling for a living, it is so small a part of the world, that one is bound to come to the conclusion, and of course it is a conclusion that has been come to on several occasions, that the people who thought of this federation were indeed crazy. It is the most improbable venture that one could imagine.

West Indian leaders had met in 1947 at a conference called the Closer Association of the West Indian Colonies, and agreed there, in principle, that there should be a federation of the West Indies. The British government supported the concept, and negotiations began in Britain in 1953, resulting in agreement to establish the West Indies federation in 1958.

Collapse of the federation and the "Little Eight"

Despite its short life, the federal government was able to establish a number of regional institutions, each seen as critical, and to take over responsibility for other institutions that predated the federation. These bodies included the West Indies Shipping Service, which was established in 1962 to operate two ships, *The Federal Maple* and *The Federal Palm*. The ships had been presented by the Government of Canada, and visited each island of the federation twice monthly. As well, the federal government also started negotiations to acquire from British Overseas Airways its subsidiary, the British West Indian Airways (BWIA). The government also took over the meteorological service. (The body was first established in 1951 as the British Caribbean Meteorological Service and became the Caribbean Meteorological Service in 1963.) Finally, the federation also assumed responsibility for the University College of the West Indies, which opened in 1948, and which became the University of the West Indies in 1962.

After both Jamaica and Trinidad and Tobago left the federation in 1962, the remaining eight territories of Antigua and Barbuda, Barbados, Dominica, Grenada, Montserrat, St Kitts–Nevis–Anguilla, St Lucia, and St Vincent and the Grenadines – which came to be known as the Little Eight – tried to form a federation among themselves. One of the reasons motivating them to stay together in an association was that the existing regional institutions and services mentioned above needed to be kept going. The "Little Eight" worked under the umbrella of the Eastern Caribbean Commission with headquarters in Barbados, under the chairmanship of Sir John Stow. As noted in the previous chapter, he was the governor of Barbados. He was later the first governor general of the country. Barbados's decision to go into independence on its own in 1966 signaled the beginning of the collapse of the "Little Eight" group.

Creation of CARIFTA and CARICOM

The logic of regional cooperation did not disappear with the collapse of the federation, and enlightened Caribbean leaders continued to work towards some form of pragmatic cooperation between the territories. In 1965, a year before the breakup of the "Little Eight", agreement had been reached at Dickenson Bay, Antigua, between the prime ministers of Antigua and Barbuda, Barbados, and Guyana – Vere Bird, Errol Barrow and Forbes Burnham, respectively – to form the Caribbean Free Trade Association (CARIFTA), and on 15 December 1965 the agreement was signed to give effect to CARIFTA. Trinidad and Tobago, which only signed later, was nonetheless regarded as one of the founding members. Trinidad and Tobago signed before 1 May 1968.

After the collapse of the federation in 1962, Commonwealth Caribbean heads of government had continued at their various meetings to establish other important regional institutions. These included the Caribbean Development Bank in 1969, the Caribbean Broadcasting Union and the Council of Legal Education in 1970, and the Caribbean Examinations Council in 1972.

In November 1972, at a meeting of heads of government held at Chaguaramas, Trinidad, it was agreed that CARIFTA should become the Caribbean Community (CARICOM). This event took place the following year with the signing of the Treaty of Chaguaramas. Both CARIFTA and CARICOM, its successor, continued to carry on the functional regional services. With respect to the economic agenda, however, the focus of the two bodies was on visible trade matters such as agricultural exports, of which sugar was the largest and most important, and manufactured goods.

It is important to note that neither tourism, nor any other service industries, were then seen as an important part of the agenda of CARICOM and were therefore never discussed at the meetings of its heads of government in the early days of CARICOM. Indeed, two of the movers-and-shakers among the Commonwealth Caribbean political leaders of the 1950s and 1960s, Prime Minister Forbes Burnham of Guyana and Prime Minister Dr Eric Williams of Trinidad and Tobago, did not regard tourism as a sector to be developed in their respective countries. Williams was on record as saying that he did not wish to see Trinidad and Tobago become, like Barbados, a nation of "bus boys" – that is, low level employees in the tourism industry. The attitude of these leaders to tourism no doubt reflected their own political philosophies, but it also spoke to the social issues surrounding Caribbean tourism and the way it was perceived at the time when the two men were in office.

Nothing said above is meant to suggest that the secretariats of CARIFTA and of CARICOM had no interest in the tourism sector. On the contrary, they closely followed both tourism developments and the tourism issues which began to surface in a significant way in other forums at the end of the 1960s. But the mandate of the secretariats was about visible trade matters and, while the leadership accepted that tourism could make a contribution, its ability to drive the development of the region was neither recognized nor accepted in the 1960s and 1970s.

The 1972 CARIFTA report *From CARIFTA to Caribbean Community* set out the secretariat's views on the weaknesses of the tourism industry as it then existed and made recommendations about how problems with the industry should be corrected, certain problems of which continue to have relevance in 2013. These problems will be addressed in detail in chapter 5.

Tourism agencies: The first pan-Caribbean organizations

It is somewhat paradoxical that tourism, which has become the driver of the economies of almost every Caribbean state, and especially of the former British West Indian territories, was not initially seen as the priority sector by the federation, CARIFTA or CARICOM. It has in fact continued to struggle into the twenty-first century to be included as an item on the agenda of the CARICOM heads of government.

The Caribbean tourism agencies are unique in at least two important ways:

1. The first tourism body, the Caribbean Tourism Association (CTA), was created by foreign governments. The second, the Caribbean Hotel Association (CHA), was an offshoot of the first. The third, the Caribbean Tourism Research and Development Centre (CTRC), was the product of the joint efforts of non-governmental organizations (NGOs) and governments.

2. Despite the fragmented nature of the Caribbean archipelago, all three bodies were able, from the start, to attract a pan-Caribbean membership from among the English, Spanish, French and Dutch-speaking countries of the Caribbean region.

The details will be expanded on later in this chapter.

The CTA, which was established in 1951, was the brainchild of the Caribbean Commission, an agency established by Britain, France, the Netherlands and the United States in 1946. The events leading to the birth of the Caribbean Commission are detailed below.

The birth of the Caribbean Commission in 1946

It was suggested earlier, in discussing the West Indies federation and the regional agencies that followed its demise, that the experiences of the Second World War changed fundamentally the way colonial persons thought about themselves. The war increased their knowledge of world affairs and of the interconnectivity of people and events. Thereafter Asians, Africans and Caribbean people shared common ideas about their future. Foreign universities often provided an incubator in which future Caribbean leaders met as students and started to know each other personally.

But the Second World War was also a defining moment for the Allied colonial powers. They too realized that there was no possibility of returning to the status quo ante in their colonies and, even before the war ended in 1945, began to discuss the future of these territories and of the Allied strategic bases scattered all over the world. The war no doubt dramatized the importance, especially to Britain and the United States, of the Caribbean sea lanes, through which critical supplies had to pass. The war also certainly made clear the significance of the strategic military bases located in a region sometimes referred to, in military circles, as "the soft underbelly" of the United States.

Franklin D. Roosevelt and Winston Churchill on 14 August 1941 established an eight-point declaration known as the Atlantic Charter, which set up the principles on which they wanted the post-war world to be run. Arising out of this meeting, Roosevelt appointed Charles W. Taussig, a businessman with interests in the American Caribbean territories, to head a commission to make a survey of the British West Indian colonies. Out of this exercise came the idea of the Anglo-American Caribbean Commission, which was set up on 9 March 1942 through an exchange of notes between the Americans and the British. It was intended, among other responsibilities, to encourage social and economic cooperation between the United States, including its possessions and bases in the Caribbean, and the United Kingdom, including its colonies in the same area. The commissioners were to concern themselves with labour, agriculture, housing, health, education, social welfare, finance and related subjects in those Caribbean territories under the British and American flags.

The Anglo-American Caribbean Commission first met in 1944 in Brooklyn, New York. In October 1946, one year after the end of the Second World War, the commission was expanded to include the Netherlands and France, both of which had been wartime allies of Britain and the United States, and renamed the Caribbean Commission. One of its first meetings was held in the school hall of Harrison College, Barbados. A plaque on the wall just outside the front entrance of the hall bears testimony to this fact.

The Caribbean Commission recognized that tourism was an economic sector that could be common to all the Caribbean territories and which had considerable development potential. Many of the military airports and harbours built by the Europeans and the Americans would later become part of a major infrastructure for tourism development in the Caribbean. A subcommittee of the Caribbean Commission, called the Caribbean Interim Tourism Committee, was established, and recommended the creation of the CTA, a public and private sector organization which, as noted above, eventually came into being in 1951. One of the members of the interim committee was a distinguished Caribbean journalist, E.L.C. Cozier, the father of Tony Cozier, a prominent West Indies cricket commentator.

An even more famous name associated with the Caribbean Commission, first as a consultant, and then as an employee, was Eric Williams. After teaching at Howard University in the United States he was appointed to the staff of the Anglo-Caribbean Commission in 1944, and in 1948 returned to Trinidad as the deputy chairman of the commission's research council. In 1955, Williams and the commission had a disagreement and his contract was not renewed. On 15 January 1956 he launched his own political party, the People's National Movement, in Trinidad. By September 1956 he had become the chief minister of Trinidad and Tobago, and in 1962 became its prime minister as he took his country into independence.

Birth of the Caribbean Tourist Association in 1951

In 1949, the Caribbean Interim Tourism Committee met in Haiti and concluded the arrangements for establishing the CTA. The Interim Committee described the purpose of the new organization as follows: "To focus the thinking of tourists on the Caribbean, rather than on particular territories of the region, and to seek to promote cooperative efforts in regard to attracting investment, encouraging airlines and the like."

In 1951 the office of the CTA was registered in Curaçao, in the Dutch Antilles. It began its operations in St John's, Antigua, in that same year. The CTA membership comprised all the Caribbean colonies of Britain at that time, except Guyana. The membership also comprised the Caribbean colonies of France, Holland, Spain and the United States, in addition to the independent countries of Cuba, Costa Rica, the Dominican Republic, Haiti, Panama and Venezuela. It was therefore the first pan-Caribbean organization, the membership of which covered English-, French-, Spanish-, Dutch- and indeed Papiamento-speaking territories. Panama and Costa Rica later left the organization, although Costa Rica rejoined for a brief period in the 1990s.

Its membership also included private sector entities such as hotels, airlines, cruise lines, travel agencies, travel media, glossy magazines and various other-allied agencies. This affiliation with the private sector was of critical importance, as it involved the specific persons and companies who had a vested interest in the success and expansion of Caribbean tourism. It will be seen that companies such as those airlines and cruise lines which from the very beginning were members of the CTA would continue to play important roles in Caribbean tourism development at a later stage, when the leadership of the organization itself became Caribbean.

It was decided that the official language of the CTA would be English as it was the language of international tourism. All the members of the board of directors members of the CTA, other than the English-speaking ones, were at least bilingual, and sometimes spoke more than two languages. The inclusion of both public and private sector members on the board of directors of the CTA was certainly a futuristic idea, one which reflected the real nature of the tourism industry. However, to keep the balance of influence in favour of governments, if matters came to a vote, each government was given two votes to each private sector vote.

Location of the CTA

In 1955, the CTA's offices were moved from St John's, Antigua, to New York because the private sector membership of the organization, which was largely from New York, had argued that the CTA was a marketing organization, and should therefore be based in what was then the main marketplace of the region. This move to the United States, with an accompanying change in focus to the US market almost to the exclusion of all other markets, was to have consequences which will be dealt with later in this book.

CTA budget and staff

The CTA's first budget was set at US$200,000, and its mandate was to promote the region as the world's leading warm weather destination. The CTA began operations with a staff of twelve persons, and engaged in advising and coordinating activities for its members. It organized forums, seminars and programmes for interaction between visitors and nationals, and successfully demonstrated, for the first time, that there was something called a *Caribbean* tourism product and a *Caribbean* tourism destination, in addition to those products and destinations of individual Caribbean countries.

CTA directorate

When the CTA was established in 1951, the first chief executive officer was an Englishman on secondment from the British Tourism Authority, and until 1978 his successors were all white, male and foreign. As a joint public and private sector body, its directorate comprised a mixture of Caribbean government appointees and of members appointed by the largely foreign private sector tourism and travel organizations, including businesses. However, the private sector directors, representing, as they did, large enterprises in the marketplace doing business with the Caribbean, were the movers and shakers of the organization, and more often than not, saw the CTA as representing *their* interests in the Caribbean.

Birth of the Caribbean Hotel Association in 1962

The CHA, which in more recent times has been renamed the Caribbean Hotel and Tourism Association, began its life as one of the technical committees of the CTA – the hotel committee, which was formed in 1959. This committee comprised individual hotels that wanted to discuss ideas on how to work together with the government tourist offices to promote tourist destinations. In 1962, the CTA Hotel Committee took a decision to become a separate entity as the CHA, and established its headquarters in San Juan, Puerto Rico. There it remained until 2009 when the headquarters were moved to Miami.

The CHA was established as a federation of Caribbean national hotel associations. The directors of the CTA did agree, however, to a request from the CHA to become a member of the CTA and be represented on its board. It was equally important that the CTA – and the CTRC, which came into being in 1974 – be represented on the board of directors of the CHA. This presence ensured a high level of cooperation in regional tourism between the public and private sectors, and helped to foster the development of tourism throughout the countries of the Caribbean Basin.

CHA directorate

In 1962, the year of formation of the CHA, its directorate was drawn from the pool of hotel owners and managers, largely white and male, who lived in the member states. This racial and gender imbalance continued for several decades until the transformation of the industry saw the emergence of a number of eminent black male and female Caribbean managers and even owners.

Tourism and Caribbean development

The arrival of the jet engine in the post–Second World War period had fuelled an escalation in world travel, and provided just the opportunity needed by some Caribbean countries to diversify out of export agriculture and a nascent manufacturing sector. Other Caribbean countries, which did not have even these resources and had few options for development, began to find a use for the white sands and blue waters which had formerly been seen simply as undeveloped infertile coastal areas.

As described in chapter 1, in mid-nineteenth-century Europe modern tourism had already been developed by people such as Thomas Cook, and was helping to soften and civilize certain aspects of the industrial revolution. The rest of the world would now, in the 1950s, discover the good and bad aspects of tourism development.

Between 1950 and 1980, international tourism arrivals grew from 25.3 million persons to 165.8 million in 1970 and to 278.2 million in 1980. Tourism receipts went from US$2.1 billion in 1950 to 17.9 billion in 1970 and 106.5 billion in 1980. In the Caribbean specifically, tourism arrivals in 1970 were 4.2 million persons and in 1980, 6.7 million (see also appendix 1, "International and Caribbean Tourist Arrivals: 1970 to 2010"). It therefore became impossible to ignore tourism as a development sector.

In a few decades the number of people traversing the globe had moved from a trickle to a flood, and some of that flood had come in the direction of the Caribbean. It became necessary, therefore, as never before, for the Caribbean to plan and cater for the increased movement of people of different cultures, languages and races. In the 1950s and 1960s, Caribbean national tourism boards, where they existed, were largely marketing agencies, and were not geared or staffed to deal with the broad developmental issues. Similarly, the CTA was a regional tourism marketing organization based in New York, and the United States was the region's chief market.

Prior to 1970, the CHA, situated in Puerto Rico, represented the interests of its hotel constituency and had little to do with the local politicians, who were only then beginning to see the possibilities of tourism as part of national economic development. In the 1950s and 1960s, the two groups of marketers and hoteliers, from the CTA and the CHA respectively, may be said to have been pursuing their legitimate business of running their hotels. This pursuit included the marketing, advertising and other public-relations activities by which their hotel rooms and airline seats were filled. The two groups did not see themselves as having any mandate to deal with the socio-economic development issues of the Caribbean. This attitude was even more that of the cruise industry, for some members of which interest in the region was thought to end at the port of entry.

By 1970, however, the impact of tourism could no longer be ignored. The Caribbean was receiving 4.2 million stay-over arrivals, and countries in the eastern Caribbean and the Dutch Caribbean were becoming players in an industry formerly dominated by only five countries – Bahamas, Barbados, Bermuda, Cuba and Jamaica. In 1970 the countries of the Organisation of Eastern Caribbean States alone received some 177,198 tourists or 3.9 per cent of all Caribbean stay-over arrivals.

Government involvement in the tourism sector

In chapter 2 it was shown that, at the national level, government involvement in the tourism sector, especially in Jamaica, had made an important difference in the direction of the industry. Institutions had been established to plan the sector, and training had been instituted to produce human resources to crack the glass ceiling placed there by white foreign ownership and management, beyond which local Caribbean people could not go.

As tourism spread across the Caribbean, especially after the Cuban revolution in 1959 and the subsequent US embargo against Cuba, there was a growing awareness, especially by certain NGOs, of various negative tourism impacts and of the need for them to be addressed by national planning processes.

The focus of the tourism private sector in the 1950s and 1960s had been on growing the numbers. The emphasis was placed on the demand side: how, by marketing and promoting the destination, could more and more visitors be brought to the region. A number of individuals and organizations mentioned below were, however, concerned about such factors as unplanned physical growth of tourism, the carrying capacity of the countries involved, alienation of scarce land resources, competition with agriculture, the lack of linkages with the rest of the economy, the lack of strategic planning based on research and statistics, and the near-absence of Caribbean ownership and control of the tourism industry.

In 1972 the CARIFTA Secretariat did an analysis of the tourism sector and was somewhat unhappy with what it found. Sugar had left a bitter taste in its mouth, and tourism, which clearly had certain economic possibilities, seemed to bring with it some of the social and racial baggage of the colonial and sugar era. These findings are discussed in detail in chapter 5.

The call for change in the direction of Caribbean tourism

The call for a change in the direction of tourism came from an unlikely coalition of individuals representing both NGOs and governments. The persons included Peter Morgan, minister of tourism in Barbados; Carlos Diago, deputy director of the Puerto Rico Tourism Development Company; Sir Philip Sherlock, vice chancellor of the University of the West Indies; the Reverend Andrew Hatch, an Anglican priest and member of Christian Action for Development in the Caribbean; Byron Blake and Edwin Carrington of the CARIFTA Secretariat; and Herbert Hiller, an unconventional American who happened at the time to be the executive director of the CTA, and who was on loan from Caribbean Norwegian Cruise Lines.

Hiller at a personal level had rejected many of the trappings of modern American lifestyle and had strong views about personal diet, the environment, and the damage he felt mass tourism was doing to small developing states everywhere. He was an advocate of banishing mass tourism from the region and replacing it with a small-scale product which would be far more indigenous than that which then existed. It is possible that some of Hiller's thinking found its way into the 1972 CARIFTA document recommending changes in the tourism industry.

In the early 1970s, a series of consultations about tourism change, largely dominated by the persons mentioned earlier, was held in the region. Perhaps the best known was that held in 1971 in Haiti and organized by the Caribbean Council of Churches. The second consultation, also held in 1971, took place at the Windsor Hotel in Barbados, and ended with a call for the establishment of an institution not only to examine the benefits of tourism, but also to study its social and environmental costs. It gave a mandate to Morgan and Sherlock to travel the wider Caribbean both to speak to governments about the need for such an institution and to gather support for its establishment. Among the persons with whom Morgan met and who strongly supported the idea was P.J. Patterson, then the minister responsible for tourism in Jamaica and later the prime minister.

In January 1972, the CTA held a meeting in San Juan specifically to review the progress with respect to the Haiti and Barbados consultations, and to take decisions about how the proposed institution was to be funded and established.

Creation of the Caribbean Tourism Centre

Arising out of the CTA meeting in San Juan, its executive director, Herbert Hiller, was given a mandate to prepare a proposal. The proposal would set out terms of reference and identify possible funding agencies willing to provide seed money for the establishment of an institution for change in the tourism industry. That body was to be called the Caribbean Tourism Centre (CTC).

Approaches for funding were made to several agencies, and eventually in 1973, the Inter-American Foundation (IAF), an institution of the United States Congress, agreed to donate for that purpose, a grant of US$291,000 over a three-year period. The IAF had agreed to do so on the understanding that governments would each contribute a small counterpart amount of cash, as well as support the institution in kind, with practical administrative requirements.

Had the IAF not come to the table, the proposal might have languished and died, since no other source of funding had been found. This was a most unusual decision for the IAF. It did not normally fund projects other than those which focused on supporting social or agricultural programmes for the poor, largely in rural areas of Central and South America. Tourism was outside of its usual areas of concern. An explanation of this shift on the part of the IAF may be found in the Reverend Andrew Hatch's book *Will of the Wind*, in which the backing of the proposal by the church organization Christian Action for Development in the Caribbean is credited for winning the support of the IAF. The IAF would also have been positively influenced by the somewhat revolutionary nature of the proposal Hiller submitted: it strongly criticized Caribbean tourism as it then existed, and emphasized small-scale development, community programmes such as campsite projects, and local Caribbean ownership. In agreeing to fund the project, the IAF made it clear that this was to be its one and only financial contribution.

Once the funds had been identified for the CTC, the protagonists commenced a search for a chief executive officer in 1973. Hiller offered to serve as the first executive director and to establish the centre, but the national ministers of tourism in the CTA, after a great deal of thought, agreed that, given the centre's mandate for change, it was important to appoint an executive director who was a native of the Caribbean.

Their first choice was a well-known economist at the University of the West Indies, Bisnodat Persuad, the father of Professor Avinath Persuad, currently executive chairman of the Paradise Beach, Four Seasons project in Barbados, and himself an economist of international repute. When Persuad later proved unavailable because he had accepted a position at the Commonwealth Secretariat in London, the job was offered to Barbadian diplomat Jean Holder, who had served with the West Indies federal government – "the Little Eight" – and the Barbados Ministry of External Affairs. He took up the responsibilities of executive director of the CTC on 1 September 1974, on secondment from the Ministry of External Affairs of Barbados.

The establishment of the CTC presented many challenges. Holder had not been a party to any of the discussions that had taken place before agreement to establish the centre, nor had he any prior experience of the tourism industry. There was also no blueprint for the centre except the project funding document Hiller submitted to the IAF. Beginning with a staff of himself and his secretary, Pat Byer, the first executive director had the responsibility of identifying a building for the headquarters, establishing the organization with the available funding, seeking additional funding from other sources to keep it going, determining exactly what the three-year programme for which funding was available should comprise, and recruiting suitable staff to implement the project.

The initial CTC agreement was signed in October 1974 by only eleven countries, but the membership would grow to over thirty. It was decided that the centre would be based in Barbados and would have a board of governors comprising ministers of tourism, and the three founding institutional members, the CTA, the CHA and the Christian Action for Development in the Caribbean.

Peter Morgan, the minister of tourism of Barbados, was elected the first chairman of the board of governors. A traditional Barbadian house, called Mer Vue, in Marine Gardens, Christ Church, was selected as the headquarters of the centre. At the first meeting of the board in October 1974, the executive director was charged with putting together a work plan. This project posed a number of challenges since it was difficult to produce agreement among those members who had supported the creation of the centre as to what exactly its programme should be.

One change was readily accepted at that meeting: a proposal by Morgan that the name should be changed from the Caribbean Tourism Centre to the Caribbean Tourism Research Centre (CTRC). That name was itself changed, after the programme was agreed upon, to the Caribbean Tourism Research and Development Centre, although the acronym CTRC was never consequently altered.

The CTRC programme

Initially, various CTRC directors and other interested parties held different views on the subject of what the CTRC programme should be. Hiller felt a certain degree of ownership and was understandably insistent that all his detailed proposals for small-scale indigenous tourism, and related ideas that had been mentioned earlier and put to the donors, should comprise the core of the centre's programme. (Hiller, who had prepared the project document of the centre, had by this time been replaced as executive director of the CTA in New York by an American hotelier, James Pepperdine.) The CHA, which, as described above, was run and controlled by owners and managers of hotels, the most influential of which were large and foreign-owned, was certainly not in agreement with Hiller's position.

The CHA had supported the call for the creation of the CTC, but saw its purpose mainly as providing the research data needed for planning the hotel industry. It therefore distanced itself from the talk by Hiller of indigenous ownership, small-scale hotels, and the negative socio-cultural and environmental impacts of mass tourism, talk which was making them uneasy. Many of the private sector directors and allied members of the CTA saw the role of the centre as that of strengthening and informing tourism marketing from their base in the United States. These directors did not really understand why there was this strident call in the Caribbean for change in what seemed to them to be already a growing and successful tourism industry. However, the chief proponents of the creation of the centre as a tourism change agent, proponents who included Sherlock, were equally insistent on a programme which, in their opinion, would make Caribbean tourism more developmental in specific terms. They wanted to see a changing of the guard with respect to the leadership of Caribbean tourism and to have issues of socio-cultural, environmental and economic impact moved to the centre of the agenda.

Governments' ambivalent attitudes to the CTRC

In the 1970s governments were often somewhat ambivalent about their respective positions on what the focus of the CTRC's programme should be. Although the CTRC, unlike the CTA and the CHA, was largely overseen by a board of governors comprising tourism ministers, many governments at the time were at an early stage of launching and growing their tourism industries and were therefore somewhat concerned about the centre developing a programme which made the assumption that tourism had both positive and negative impacts.

In 1975, the centre, in cooperation with the London-based Commonwealth Secretariat, held a seminar in the Bahamas on the social and economic impacts of tourism, based on a paper prepared by Byron Blake and Edwin Carrington of CARICOM. An article in a newspaper on the following day accused the CTRC of having come to the Bahamas to destroy its tourism industry.

Creation of the CTRC action programme

Some eyebrows were raised when, after an economist first identified as the executive director of the CTRC was unable to take up the post, a diplomat was then chosen. It soon became clear, however, that a director with extensive diplomatic experience was needed to map and resolve the controversies that the conflicting views about the centre's ideal programme had created. There was a need to find common ground among the various tourism protagonists whose support would be necessary for the centre to be established. There was also a need to make alliances with regional and international donor agencies whose financial support would be needed for continuing and sustaining the work of the centre beyond the life of the IAF grant.

The management retained the consultancy services of Peat, Marwick, Mitchell and Company, then headed by Ian Bertrand of Trinidad and

Tobago, to work with it on creating a work programme which would at least in part satisfy all participating parties. The end result was a programme comprising tourism planning, research and statistics, education and training, and technical assistance to the membership.

The next step was to begin to put in place a technical team of people qualified in marketing, economics, finance, physical planning, information management, statistics, environmental studies, sociology and education who could deliver the programme as devised. This was ambitious, given the small size of the CTRC in-house budget, and steps had to be taken to secure additional resources from international donor agencies. This latter step therefore took some time to achieve.

The first employees of the CTRC

The in-house team initially put together by the CTRC was as follows: executive director, later termed secretary general, Jean Holder (Barbados); executive secretary, Patricia Byer (Barbados); director of research, Timothy Prime (Trinidad and Tobago); administrative officer, Margaret Sardinha (Trinidad and Tobago); economist, Ione Marshall (Barbados); director of finance, Patrick Hinds (Barbados); sociologist, Dr Rustum Sethna (Canada); and economist, Len Prudent (St Lucia). As the staff expanded the team was joined by Vera Anne Bereton (St Vincent and the Grenadines), Larkland Richards (St Kitts–Nevis), Jane Belfon (Grenada), Maria Laville (Dominica), Cynthia Wilson (Barbados), Luther Miller (Barbados), Auliana Poon (Trinidad and Tobago), Harriette Banfield (Barbados), Colleen Wint (Jamaica), Hugh Cresser (Jamaica), Richard Sherman (Grenada), Rudyard Robinson (Jamaica), Llewyn Rock (Barbados), Sherman Williams (Trinidad and Tobago) and Patrick Alexander (Guyana). These persons were all university graduates, trained either in tourism studies or in various branches of the social studies and finance, certain of them with first class honours, with doctorates, or with both distinctions. The significance of their respective educations will be addressed in the next chapter.

Technical assistance employees

Beginning in 1976, the centre was provided with highly qualified and experienced international tourism experts under various strategic alliances negotiated with such donor institutions as the OAS, the Caribbean Development Bank, the European Economic Community (EEC), the Inter-American Development Bank, and the United Nations Development Programme (UNDP).

The CTRC and the OAS

The CTRC's first strategic alliance with the OAS was signed in 1976 when Ambassador Alejandro Orfila of Argentina was the OAS secretary general. The agreement has been renewed continuously since then, and in April 2006, Vincent Vanderpool-Wallace, who succeeded Holder in 2005 as the second secretary general of the CTO, was able to continue this alliance by signing yet another agreement between the CTO and the OAS.

The original 1976 agreement was a tripartite arrangement between the Government of Barbados, the CTRC and the OAS, and the relationship first came about when the CTRC was able to negotiate with the OAS that it be seen as part of what was called the CICATUR system, established as part of an inter-American system for the delivery of tourism training and research.

In 1970 the OAS had taken a policy decision to establish three such centres – one in Argentina, one in Central America and the third in the Caribbean. It was serendipitous that, as a Barbadian diplomat, Holder had taken part in Bogota in the discussions on the creation of the CICATUR system. In 1976, with the support of the Government of Barbados, the centre was designated under the agreement as the third CICATUR Centre in the Americas.

Under the strategic alliance with the OAS, the secondment of high-level OAS tourism staff greatly strengthened the technical capacity of the centre. In the area of marketing, the centre was joined at first by Jean Saurel, marketing adviser (Haiti); Eberhardt Von Hauenschill, marketing specialist (Germany); Edward Smith, physical planner (United States); Bernard Spinrad, economist (Uruguay); and Jasmine Tarr, environmentalist (United States). After two years, Eric Anthony Abrahams (Jamaica) replaced Jean Saurel as marketing adviser.

The CTRC and the European Economic Community

Under the first Lomé agreement, the CTRC was identified by CARICOM as the executing agency for regional tourism development programmes. The first aid programme from which the CTRC benefited was agreed to in 1978, and Steigenberger Consulting GmbH of West Germany was contracted to carry out a European Tourism Demand Study for the region. This was the beginning of many years of close collaboration between the centre and the Steigenberger team of German tourism marketing and research experts, a team led by Dr Bernd Bienek, and which included Gernott Ott and Werner Geirsh.

The CTRC and the United Nations Development Programme

In 1981, an Englishman, Esmond Devas, came to the centre under a UNDP programme, and through it brought the CTRC into the computer age. He laid down the template for the regional tourism statistics. His work was then built on by Laurie Berman, a former head of the British statistical services, who joined the staff of the centre as part of the UNDP technical assistance component.

The CTRC and the Caribbean Development Bank

In 1984 Arley Sobers joined the statistical department under a programme supported by the Caribbean Development Bank, but was taken onto the permanent staff of the CTRC after the aid programme ended. He was to remain at the CTRC and then the CTO – formed by a merger of the CTA and the CTRC – for some twenty-four years as head of research and statistics, until his untimely death in 2008.

4
The Changing Face of Caribbean Tourism

The CTRC was created to be an agent for change in Caribbean tourism, and the record shows that in many ways it succeeded in so doing. From its beginnings in September 1974, the CTRC exhibited clear differences from the existing tourism agencies. It was a *Caribbean* tourism agency, based in the Caribbean, led by a Caribbean person and with a senior staff comprising highly qualified Caribbean university-trained personnel. Prior to the founding of the centre it was unusual for tourism agencies to be staffed with economists, statisticians, physical planners, sociologists and market researchers. Such Caribbean graduates did not normally look for jobs in the tourism sector and the tourism industry did not provide opportunities requiring their skills. Of even greater importance were the CTRC's alliances with the international development agencies for which it began to perform the role of executing agency for regional aid programmes. This shift sent a signal, both locally and internationally, that the CTRC was an important development agency, and that tourism was beginning to be treated as a serious development sector.

CTRC: Cradle of Caribbean tourism experts

In another sense, the CTRC changed the face of Caribbean tourism by being the cradle from which, in the 1970s and 1980s, came a significant number of future Caribbean directors of tourism and other key personnel. In fact, the vast majority of the technical staff mentioned in the past chapter as being the first employees of the CTRC were in fact later recruited for the top jobs in national tourism agencies, or in regional or hemispheric ones. Eight of them became directors of tourism in Barbados and the Eastern Caribbean, one the director general of the Organisation of Eastern Caribbean States, one the minister of tourism of Jamaica, three international tourism consultants, and the rest senior officials at the Caribbean Development Bank, the OAS, the Caribbean Centre for Development Administration or the Caribbean Knowledge and Learning Network.

It was a matter of considerable pride for the secretary general of the CTRC to attend its board meetings in the 1980s and 1990s, and to see that many of the country delegations of member states were now being led by former employees of the centre, several of whom had held their first job there.

New tourism programmes

Tourism database

Of all the changes the CTRC fostered through its programmes, perhaps the most important was the creation of a tourism database for the entire region. Caribbean governments usually had good statistical departments, staffed by experts at varying levels, producing information relating to trade, agriculture, industry, health, education and finance, among many other sectors. However, until 1974 when the centre was established, no comparable body of tourism statistics existed in the region.

The CTRC recognized from the start that if tourism were ever to become a serious development sector – and to be recognized as such by the political directorate, bureaucrats, consultants, researchers and investors, among others – then a range of basic tourism data needed to be available to them for their various planning purposes. Furthermore, giving reality to the concept of a regional tourism product which could be marketed and promoted to the external world required the existence of a regional tourism database comprising national statistics which were in every way comparable. This required a serious statistical initiative to be executed simultaneously at both the national and regional levels across the entire Caribbean region.

The CTRC and later the CTO programme set out to cover annual tourist and cruise arrivals for the region set against the background of international arrivals. It collected market information for the American, Canadian, European, Caribbean, South American and even Japanese markets. It dealt with tourist profiles such as place of stay, purpose of visit, average length of stay and arrivals, further classified by age group and sex. It covered tourist accommodation capacity and room occupancy rates. It included tourist expenditure and the budgets of national tourist organizations. It collected information both in respect of employment in accommodation establishments and concerning total employment dependent on tourism. It gathered market intelligence in the major markets and data about the economic impact of tourism.

It is often taken for granted that one can quote tourism figures for the region, compare one Caribbean country's performance with another and compare the Caribbean's performance both with that of the other regions and with the rest of the world. It is also taken for granted that these numbers are easily available in a comprehensive publication and are surprisingly up to date, given the many sources from which they must be collected, compiled and analysed monthly and then annually. Creation of and access to important, at times vital, data came into being in the Caribbean because of the CTRC programme that started in 1974.

The task was monumental. It consisted of setting up the regional system while providing technical assistance at the national level to achieve systems compatible with the central system. Clearly it did not happen all at once. It owed much to the early technical assistance received from the UNDP. But the person who has made a lasting and distinguished contribution to the organization in this area was a Barbadian, Arley Sobers, whose statistical skills were legendary both at the CTRC and in the wider region.

The CTRC and its successor, the CTO, were, for several decades, the first source from which Caribbean comparable tourism statistics were drawn. The two organizations served as the tourism Bible, to which governments, donor agencies, consultants, investors, marketers, academics and students, among other groups, have gone for vital tourism information. Despite various resource constraints, efforts have been made at the CTO to bring its information technology capacity into the twenty-first century.

While considerable progress has been made, some thirty-nine years later, in 2013, much remains to be done about the manner in which tourism statistics are collected and analysed, not only in the Caribbean, but also worldwide, if the real economic contribution of the sector to the economy is to be adequately captured. This factor is of no small importance when political and economic decisions have to be made about the industry. Hopefully the efforts now being made to put in place a system of Tourism Satellite Accounts by the United Nations World Tourism Organization, the World Travel and Tourism Council, the CTO and a number of tourism destinations will come to fruition and change the basis on which tourism economic impacts are measured.

Tourism research

Little tourism research existed in the region prior to 1974, and the CTRC was now expected to do a great deal of work in this area. However, the CTRC soon realized that research is both expensive and time-consuming, and from the start the centre was forced to establish certain priorities. The research done by the CTRC was therefore, in response to the priorities now set, largely in the areas of investment, market intelligence, market research, visitor expenditure, employment, economic impact, accommodation capacity, air transport issues and information technology. Many of the issues that had driven the creation of the centre, such as socio-cultural impacts, carrying capacity, environmental impact, land usage, physical planning, and similar principal concerns, were not adequately addressed, largely for budgetary reasons.

However, the CTRC, as a regional organization, was able to tackle some sensitive tourism issues. These issues include crime, which national agencies tended to shy away from, either for political reasons or because of other sensitivities they felt had to be observed.

It remains true, however, that even in 2013, some of the most critical research work in travel and tourism remains to be done, and is best done in institutions which have the time, resources, and freedom from pressures of any sort to follow a programme dictated by the best interests of the society.

Much more can be done, for example, by students in master's programmes. Certainly, universities are major candidates for such a role, and the good news is that in more recent times several of them, including the University of the West Indies, are currently responding to the challenge.

Tourism training and education

The CTRC may also be said to have made an important contribution to the development of human resources within Caribbean tourism: it broadened the concept of what needs to be taught to meet the needs of an industry which covers many more skills and disciplines than first meets the eye.

In the Caribbean, tourism education traditionally meant hospitality and vocational training for those persons intending to work in the hotel and restaurant sector, and Caribbean governments seeking to expand the opportunities for employment began to establish hotel schools in the 1960s to provide basic skills training. Initially, locals were being prepared only for the level of jobs available to them in the hospitality industry, there being a glass ceiling in management areas, which few could hope to rise through. This situation happily has changed, and there are a number of sophisticated hospitality schools throughout the region that maintain, and teach, from a broad tourism curriculum. This curriculum functions at all levels.

In the 1970s, those persons who worked in tourism outside the accommodation and restaurant subsectors were largely expected to learn on the job. As tourism grew in importance, however, it was increasingly understood that it in fact meant more than hotels and restaurants, unlike what had been previously supposed. Persons who were expected to work for tourism ministries, for tourist authorities, however named, and for travel and transport businesses, were to be performing jobs for which they needed specialist training. This growing need served to explode the lie that those persons who could not meet the high academic standards of other disciplines would easily find a place in the tourism industry, whether male or female, especially if of attractive physical appearance and sartorial excellence. This misconception proved a self-fulfilling prophecy, since the best and the brightest of our scholars did not seek employment in the industry, nor was it an area into which parents ambitious for the best for their children pushed them to go. Consequently, at least in the Commonwealth

Caribbean, tourism was, initially, not being taught in schools at any level, and later only as an optional part of the social studies syllabus of the Caribbean Examinations Council. More importantly, the educational system did not then provide students with that all-important certificate at the end of the course. All of this led to the inadequate knowledge of tourism, a gap which then plagued the industry for many years.

The CTRC played an important role in changing these perceptions by the educational papers it published. The organization did so through the curricula it helped to design, and through its work in the field of education and training, which it did in collaboration with both academic and tourism agencies. Later, when the CTRC and the CTA were merged to become the CTO in 1989, the new organization created the Caribbean Tourism Human Resource Council, which raised tourism education and training to a new level.

One of the early CTRC publications was a careers guide to tourism, setting out all the various jobs that needed to be done in a well-run industry and the career opportunities available. These ran into hundreds of types of jobs in an industry which is an amalgam of various kinds of enterprises, requiring staff, both at high levels of specialization and at lower levels, across a wide range of service industries. The Caribbean came to learn that a high percentage of the workforce of many of the developed countries they were seeking to emulate were employed in tourism or in jobs that would not otherwise exist if there were not a tourism industry.

Teacher workshops

One of the centre's early programmes was the organization of tourism workshops for teachers across the Caribbean region. These programmes taught teachers about the positive and negative socio-cultural, environmental and economic impacts of tourism, and about the opportunities for employment in the industry for Caribbean people. Equally importantly, they provided material through which the instructors taught aspects of the social studies curriculum.

Frequently, teachers who had initially been negatively disposed towards both the tourism industry and to the teaching of tourism in schools began, after a workshop, to be fascinated by the industry to the point of enquiring about employment opportunities for themselves in the field.

Scholarship programmes

The region has come a long way in tourism education and training since the 1970s. The CTO and the CHA scholarship programmes have contributed to this. Every year the CTO spends as much as US$70,000 providing scholarships, more often than not, at postgraduate levels, to enable Caribbean students to study at institutions of higher learning, both within and outside of the region. The CTO scholarships are given to persons who have to demonstrate excellence both in their studies and in other fields of endeavour. Some of these have earned master's and doctoral qualifications, and have found employment both in foreign and Caribbean universities. The University of the West Indies, of which many of the teaching staff were initially dismissive of tourism studies, is in 2013 a major centre at which tourism can be studied at both undergraduate and postgraduate levels.

CTRC technical assistance

The CTRC in-house budget did not allow much room for major technical assistance to its member states. However, as a regional coordinating and executing agency for regional and international aid programmes, it brought to the table mixed local and foreign teams of highly qualified experts to advise a number of Caribbean countries, countries which were then in their tourism infancy. The presence of tourism experts from the Caribbean delivering technical assistance services in the CTRC member states was also a significant advance on what obtained before.

New leadership at the CHA and the CTA

In dealing in chapter 2 with the country case studies, a number of significant changes were seen with respect to tourism leadership at the national level in the 1970s.

What is also arguable is that the creation of a Caribbean tourism organization such as the CTRC – dealing, as it did, with research and development matters, and from 1974 closely linked to the CTA and the CHA through exchange board membership – affected their programmes positively, causing them to pay greater attention to similar issues. The appointment at these organizations of new CEOs, who served with their presidents on the CTRC's board of directors, reinforced this trend.

In 1973, the president of the CHA, James Pepperdine, described above in chapter 2, appointed John Bell, an Englishman, as the executive director. Bell, later termed director general and the CEO, was to hold this post for some twenty-eight years, and succeeded in transforming the CHA into an effective federation of Caribbean hotels, one which offered meaningful programmes for Caribbean hoteliers. The shift also moved the CHA beyond the "old boys club" image which it was alleged to possess before his appointment. The composition of the board of the CHA, however, continued for many years to reflect the reality of national Caribbean hotel ownership and management – largely white and expatriate. It is important, therefore, to record that the following black Caribbean nationals succeeded in being elected to the CHA presidency: Osmond Kelsick, Martin Donawa, Berthia Parle, Sir Royston Hopkins, Ralph Taylor and Peter Odle.

In 1974, Pepperdine was himself appointed executive director of the CTA, replacing Herbert Hiller. Pepperdine had been recruited by an Englishman, Michael Youngman, who at the time was the international director of marketing for American Airlines and the secretary treasurer of the CTA. James, better known as Jim, had been a US Marine, and on discharge, had become a hotel owner in the US Virgin Islands. He was a congenial person, absolutely fearless and outspoken in his views, loyal in his friendships and creative in the field of marketing. Although he remained with the CTA for a period of only two years, he left an indelible mark on the association and continued to contribute to Caribbean tourism as a partner in the Orlando marketing firm of Robinson, Pepperdine and Yesawich, and as a board director of CHA.

Like Hiller, Pepperdine was committed to Caribbean people and Caribbean development. It was Pepperdine who created the first Caribbean-wide promotional film, *The Caribbean: A World of Its Own*. The movie gave visual evidence, from a tourism perspective, that there was something which could be regarded as a single Caribbean tourism destination.

CTA chapters

James Pepperdine, Michael Youngman, Lloyd Cole (a New York travel agent) and Jim Furey (of the New York marketing company Furey and

Associates) created the first CTA chapter in 1975. The chapter comprised largely US travel agents organized to promote the Caribbean in the United States. These chapters were to become a powerful promotional and educational arm of the CTA, and were to spread across the United States, Canada, Europe, and to reach even Australia, until they were some forty-four by the 1990s. In 1975, Pepperdine mounted the first CTA tourism trade shows in the United States and launched the first Caribbean tourism cooperative advertising programme.

CTRC launch of the first Caribbean tourism conference

In 1974, the three regional tourism organizations were based internationally in three places. The first was in New York, and was responsible for marketing; the second, in San Juan, and was responsible for serving the hotel industry; and the third in Barbados, where it dealt with research and development programmes. It was the major global energy crisis of 1974 and 1975 that brought them together, for the first time, to discuss how best to work together.

In the midst of the Israeli–Arab conflict, after Syria and Egypt had launched a surprise attack on Israel on 6 October 1973, the Organization of Petroleum Exporting Countries decided on 16 October to raise the price of oil by 70 per cent to US$5.11 per barrel, and also stated its intension to raise it by 4 per cent over time until their published objectives were met. By 1974 it had risen to nearly US$12 per barrel and an oil embargo was in place. One of the first casualties of the crisis was the global tourism industry, and the CTRC, as the organization responsible for tourism research and development, was called upon by its government members to convene a pan-Caribbean, public and private sector conference, at the highest possible level, to discuss, as the title of the conference phrased it, "The Present and Future of Caribbean Tourism Industry in the Wake of the First Energy Crisis of 1973–5".

Organizing the conference was a major challenge for the CTRC, an organization that was only a few months old. The CTRC invited the CHA and the CTA to collaborate with it in this endeavour, and the three CEOs met in Caracas in January 1975 with the Venezuelan head of Corpoturismo, Frank

Bricenio, then president of the CTA, to discuss the logistics and programme of the conference. The Government of Venezuela, which was a member of both the CTA and the CTRC, offered to host the conference. The president of Venezuela, Carlos Andres Perez, agreed to chair the proceedings. Invitations were extended to Caribbean governments, including prime ministers, some of whom attended. The delegates, however, comprised largely ministers of tourism, and delegates from the tourism, banking and financial private sector.

The conference produced many learned papers several of which were published in 1979 by the secretary general of the CTRC in a book called *Tourism Policies and Impacts*. The conference met some of its goals of examining the state of Caribbean tourism and reinforcing the commitment of all parties to Caribbean tourism. However, promises of financial and other support for the sector from oil-rich Venezuela were not fulfilled.

An important outcome of the Caracas meeting, however, was that the CEOs of the three regional public and private sector organizations – Bell, Pepperdine and Holder – established close personal relationships, which resulted thereafter in the three regional tourism organizations working closely together. The personal relationships lasted for almost thirty years, broken only by the death of Pepperdine in 2005, and resulted in many joint initiatives in Caribbean tourism. The first of these initiatives was an unsuccessful attempt, in 1976, to create one regional public and private sector tourism organization in the Caribbean region by merging the CTA, the CHA and the CTRC, to be called the Caribbean Tourism Organization.

First attempt to create a Caribbean tourism organization in 1976

The three executive directors, as they were then called, secured approval from their boards to form themselves into a working group for the purpose of creating a Caribbean tourism organization. They then proceeded to elect to the group Yvonne Maginley, later Dame Yvonne Maginley, the executive director of the Eastern Caribbean Tourist Association (ECTA), a subregional tourism organization of the countries in the Organisation of Eastern Caribbean States.

After they had met several times over a period of six weeks, consensus was reached among members of the working group on the terms of reference and organizational structure of the proposed CTO. A draft CTO constitution was prepared. The vision in 1976 was to create a single, powerful Caribbean tourism body, of both the public and private sectors. It was to involve all the Caribbean countries, all the hotel associations in the Caribbean Basin, and the existing Caribbean and non-Caribbean private sector membership of the CTA. It would have been a formidable force in global tourism. Regrettably, in 1976, it was a vision the time of which had not yet come.

The breakdown of the CTO talks in the Virgin Islands

A joint meeting of the respective boards of directors of the four organizations was held in April 1976 at Frenchman's Reef Hotel, in St Thomas in the US Virgin Islands. The meeting took place to discuss and, it was hoped, approve the merger. The CARICOM Secretariat was represented at the meeting by Byron Blake.

At the level of the four boards of directors there were a number of matters to be settled about which no agreement was reached. These matters included determination of which country should function as the headquarters of the new CTO, of the means and extent of staff relocation, and person to be the CEO. That person, it was understood, had to be one of the three existing CEOs – one an American, the second an Englishman, and the third a Caribbean man.

It seemed like a recurrence of the issues which had surfaced when the ten West Indian states had sought to form the West Indies federation. One proposal was that the CTO headquarters should be based in Barbados, and that the then secretary general of the CTRC, who was the only Caribbean candidate, should be the one appointed CEO. The CTA and the ECTA were in agreement, but the proposal did not receive the approval of the CHA.

The meeting ended in disarray, concluding that the Caribbean tourism organizations would not merge in 1976 to become the CTO, but would instead continue to work closely together, hold their meetings at the same time and place where practical, and hold one common annual convention. This convention was the Caribbean Tourism Conference (CTC). The agreement that the three organizations would hold one annual CTC lasted until 1983, when the CHA decided to separate from the body. The CTA and the CTRC continued to hold an annual conference together and kept the CTC logo.

After the failed attempt in 1976 to form one Caribbean tourism organization out of the existing agencies, the CTA, the CHA, the CTRC and the ECTA, remained separate organizations, and the region then had to wait until 1989 for a CTO to be formed out of a merger of the CTA and the CTRC.

The CTA's first Caribbean CEO in 1978

In 1976, Pepperdine resigned as executive director of the CTA. He was succeeded by an Englishman, Peter Morgan. As described above, Morgan had established the St Lawrence Hotel and later became the minister of tourism in a Democratic Labour Party government. In 1976 when that government was defeated by the Barbados Labour Party, he was appointed to succeed Pepperdine as the CEO of the CTA in New York.

Morgan, as the minister of tourism and a member of the CTA board of directors, had been one of the strongest voices in regional tourism matters during the 1970s. He had played a leading role in the creation of the Caribbean Tourism Research and Development Centre in 1974, of which he became the first chairman of the board. As a professional hotelier, he was one of the most knowledgeable and capable ministers of tourism to have served in Barbados or the Caribbean. He found the transition from minister to official a difficult one, however, and he left the New York post after only two years.

With the departure of Morgan in 1978 from the post of executive director of the CTA came the end of a tradition begun in 1951, of that post being held either by an Englishman or a white American. When Audrey Palmer, a black Caribbean woman, then the public relations director of the CTA, applied for the post, questions were raised by certain members of both the CTA and the CHA about whether or not she would be able to perform the job in a satisfactory manner.

Palmer was a Grenadian who had been minister of tourism in the Eric Gairy government. After resigning from that office she had gone to New York to represent Grenada in its New York tourism office. Pepperdine, who had recruited her as the CTA public relations director in 1974, strongly supported her for the post of executive director, and the Caribbean governments approved her appointment.

With Palmer's appointment in 1978, "Caribbeanization" and gender equality at the CTA may be said to have begun. Other Caribbean nationals, many of them female, were recruited to the staff, and they confounded the doubters about their ability to run the office effectively. An area in which it was thought Palmer might be weakest, that of relating to the US private sector, in fact proved her strongest. Women held many of the managerial positions in the world of glossy magazines, travel press, travel agencies, advertising, public relations and credit card companies. In North America in the 1970s, many of these agencies comprised the CTA-allied private sector membership. Palmer was able to create strong alliances in the marketplace which greatly strengthened the resources of the organization. Some of the outstanding allied members of the CTA were Ellen Asmadeo and Barry Brown of Travel and Leisure, Jacqueline Johnson of Condé Nast Bridal Group, Doria M Camaraza of American Express Travel Related Services, Madigan Pratt of Madigan, Pratt and Associates, Deborah Turner-Russell of Publicitas Globe Media, and Jonathan Splitz of Foote, Cone and Belding. All the contributions of these persons to Caribbean travel and to support of the CTO deserve to be recorded.

Under Palmer's leadership at the CTA, an even closer working relationship developed between the New York–based CTA and the Barbados-based CTRC, which, ten years later, made compelling the logic of forming one Caribbean tourism organization, the CTO, out of the two existing organizations. While not initiating the formation of the pan-Caribbean tourism organizations, the CARIFTA Secretariat had been involved in the discussions about the need for a new brand of Caribbean tourism, and in its 1972 report it set out its views of what national and regional strategies were needed to make tourism more developmental.

5
CARIFTA: Views and Strategies Relating to Caribbean Tourism

In the 1960s and 1970s, when the pan-Caribbean tourism organizations – representing the English, French, Spanish, Dutch and US Caribbean – were dealing with issues of unifying the tourism sector of the entire Caribbean Basin, the ten English-speaking Commonwealth countries that had formed the unsuccessful Federation of the West Indies (1958–62) had already commenced efforts to salvage the integration movement in their subregion. This new process began with the formation of the Caribbean Free Trade Association (CARIFTA) that came into being with the signing of the Dickenson Bay Agreement in December 1965 in Antigua (Randle, "Our Caribbean Community", 2005).

As described in chapter 3, the founding members were Antigua and Barbuda, Barbados, Guyana, and Trinidad and Tobago, which signed before 1 May 1968. Dominica, Grenada, St Kitts–Nevis–Anguilla, St Lucia, and St Vincent and the Grenadines signed on 1 July 1968. Jamaica and Montserrat signed on 1 August 1968 and British Honduras, now Belize, in 1971. CARIFTA may be said to have taken over from the federal government its responsibilities for the regional development of its member states. What were those responsibilities?

CARIFTA objectives

CARIFTA's objectives were as follows:

- increase trade by buying and selling more goods among the member states
- diversify trade by expanding the variety of goods and services available for trade
- liberalize trade by removing tariffs and quotas on goods produced and traded within the area
- ensure fair competition by setting up rules for all members to follow to protect the smaller enterprises

In addition to providing for free trade, the Dickenson Bay Agreement sought also to

- ensure that the benefits of free trade were equitably distributed
- promote industrial development in the less developed countries (LDCs) of CARIFTA
- promote the development of the coconut industry (through the Oils and Fats Agreement, which was then significant to many of the LDCs)
- rationalize agricultural production, but also, in the interim, facilitate the marketing of selected agricultural products of particular interest to the LDCs through the Agricultural Marketing Protocol
- provide a longer period to phase out customs duties on certain products which were more important for the revenue of the LDCs

It is important to note that the focus of CARIFTA, a subregional governmental organization, was in fact on trade in goods, both agricultural and manufactured. Whereas one of the stated purposes, mentioned above, of CARIFTA was "expanding goods and services", nowhere was the word "tourism" actually mentioned. No importance was given to tourism development in the CARIFTA agreement.

It has already been shown in chapters 3 and 4 that the initiatives taken to create the CTA, finally established in 1951, were at the pan-regional level and took their beginning from the Caribbean Commission, an agency of the then European and American colonial powers. While the creation of CTRC resulted from a joint government/NGO initiative, it was not the result of a formal CARIFTA or CARICOM policy decision. In fact, Commonwealth Caribbean governments remained ambivalent about the tourism industry for a long time and their concerns were spelt out in some detail in the CARIFTA Secretariat's 1972 report, entitled *From CARIFTA to Caribbean Community*, which is analysed below.

The 1972 CARIFTA Secretariat report

The CARIFTA report was about the Commonwealth Caribbean's cycle of socio-economic dependence and the national and regional strategies needed to break it. The report begins by restating the colonial legacy of the Commonwealth Caribbean:

> The institutional and structural features of the post-war West Indian economy represented in many ways new forms of the same old dependence that has characterized the economies ever since they were brought into the international economy as sugar producing plantation colonies in the days of European mercantilism in the 17th and 18th centuries. In those early days the present patterns of taste for imported goods were formed through the export of sugar and the import of practically everything else. From those early days also derive the predominance of the outside investor; the absence of technological innovations; the absence of a numerous nationally oriented entrepreneurial class; and the absence of locally controlled mechanisms and financial institutions for mobilizing national savings for productive investment domestically. Last, but not least, from those early days also derive metropolitan preferences for sugar – the predecessor of today's special arrangements and tariff preferences for West Indian agricultural exports in the markets of the UK, and Canada and the USA particularly the UK market in the case of sugar, bananas and citrus. It is difficult to dispense with these arrangements since the region is high cost and uncompetitive in these products. Consequently, when the UK joins the EEC, the West Indies will have to negotiate a relationship with the enlarged Community in order to safeguard the market for these traditional export crops.

It can be seen from what follows that in 1972 CARIFTA perceived tourism, as it then existed, as reinforcing many of the colonial dependencies created by sugar and other agricultural export crops.

CARIFTA/CARICOM assessment of the tourism industry

The 1972 CARIFTA report provided the following analysis of the tourism sector:

- Excessive foreign ownership and high import content had led to external leakages: over 40 per cent in Jamaica, and Trinidad and Tobago; 40 per cent in Barbados; and higher than Barbados in some of the smaller islands. This resulted largely from payment abroad of profits, high interest and imports of food, furniture, fittings, draperies and many of their inputs. This situation was blamed on the failure of governments to integrate the tourist sector with other productive sectors of the economy, such as agriculture and light manufactures – a reflection of the underdeveloped character of the entire regional economy and particularly of the decay of agriculture.
- Foreign control of the tourism sector led to only limited use of indigenous resources, ideas and culture. It was held that the following problems were both interrelated, and inherent in foreign ownership: the predominance of large luxury hotels, the high leakages, the limited integration into the regional economy, and structural inhibitions to indigenization.
- It was believed that "smaller hotels, different and cheaper in structural design, priced and organized to service regional as well as foreign visitors for the whole rather than a part of the year, utilizing more local capital as well as more local inputs, would be a much more economically desirable pattern of development for the regional tourist industry".
- There was high concentration and extreme dependence on the North American market.
- Business was seasonal, resulting in large unused resources in the off-season (May to November) and high prices in the high season (December to April).
- Travel costs were high, constituting high revenue primarily for foreign carriers, due to discriminatory rates of airfares set by external agencies.
- Hotel rates were high and uncompetitive, arising from the preponderance of the luxury-type tourism facilities.
- The undemanding nature of tourist employment, and the high level of wages it paid, had together led to a labour shortage in those

economic sectors incapable of offering comparable work conditions. An example of such a sector was domestic agriculture. An example of the soft aspect of the tourism industry was the granting of tax incentives.
- A serious social crisis that faced the tourism industry exacerbated its economic problems. This crisis was the juxtaposition of foreign luxury and local poverty, a situation in which a luxurious form of tourism inflames the white-black, master-servant syndrome. Piqued by a history of slavery, elements of the predominantly black population guard their new nationalism and their black pride, and warn against the dangers of a renewed era of black servitude.
- If the trend of the indiscriminate sale of land on a freehold basis were to continue, the West Indian would soon be crowded out of his own islands. A proper policy on foreign land ownership, as well as comprehensive national land use planning, was required to meet this situation, which the report judged to be serious.

As long as thirty years ago important conclusions were drawn by the secretariat about tourism. They were as follows.

- There was the necessity, on grounds of national self-interest, for a regional strategy in the development of tourism.
- One of the key areas for a regional strategy was in marketing, both extra as well as intra-regional. There was the need to tap into the markets in western Europe, in Latin America and within the Caribbean itself.
- There was the need for a joint campaign to encourage people from the region to spend their vacations within, rather than outside of, the Caribbean. Both trade unions and the Caribbean Congress of Labour were exhorted to negotiate with employers for vacations to be spent by employees in the less-developed countries of the region.
- The Caribbean islands needed to be promoted abroad as a region and less as single units, more as people, places and activities rather than as sea, sand and surf only. The "diversity amidst unity" of the region needed to be emphasized.
- Regional action was required to address the high airfares between the Caribbean and the North Atlantic, and among the Caribbean islands themselves.

- With respect to regional transport policy it was noted that (1) the operations of a single international regional air carrier – owned and controlled by the government, or the people of the region, or both – could be doing much to stimulate the development of tourism in the region as a whole; and (2) the operations of passenger cruise ships intra-regionally could do much to increase tourist travel by both West Indian and non-West Indians within the region.
- There was a call for the simplification of travel requirements for those persons moving between member states, and a call for a meeting of immigration authorities to work out the necessary guidelines.
- The question was posed "whether the countries should go all out to maximize the number of foreign tourists visiting their shores, or whether they should concentrate on promoting the maximum linkages between the tourist sector with other sectors, particularly those producing food, furniture and fittings, building materials and handicrafts". The conclusion reached was that, although the two options were not in fact mutually exclusive, economic prudence as well as social and cultural considerations would seem to require placing greater emphasis on the second approach rather than the first.

To counter the inherited weaknesses of the colonial legacy, the CARIFTA Secretariat in 1972 identified two macro strategies at the national and regional level and several things to be done within each one. They apply to the economy generally and are not specifically related to tourism.

National strategies

The four national economic strategies identified by CARIFTA were as follows:

1. *Localization*
    - The governments and peoples of the region must assume control over key economic sectors, which included minerals, tourism and sugar.
    - There must be control of the freehold alienation of land to foreigners.
    - There must be a clearly defined policy concerning foreign investment, with certain sections of the economy reserved for national or regional ownership and control.

- There must be rejection of foreign domination of the key sectors of the economy, but not of foreign investment as such.
- Ownership of the economy must be distributed between the public sector, the private sector and the people, the latter participating through small business and small industry; workers banks; small and medium farms; cooperatives; and shares in nationally controlled public companies or in state enterprises.
- There must be the reorientation of the mass and advertising media in the service of localization and in the participation of the people in the economy.
- Techniques must be developed for mobilization of personal savings to meet the needs for a tremendous increase in national savings.
- There is a need for wage and salary restraint in the public sector and greater efficiency of operations to guarantee larger surpluses.

2. *Priority sectors*. Agriculture, particularly domestic agriculture, must come first, followed by industry with tourism last. There must be a vast expansion of the farm schools and introduction of land reform aimed at converting mini-farms into medium-sized farms.

3. *Linkages and local inputs*
   - The pattern of industrial and tourist development must be changed to provide more local inputs.
   - There must be greater emphasis on exports of manufactures, not only to regional markets but also to the outside world. The reason given for this was that "the extent to which a country can export manufactures to the outside world is an important index of its stage of development and this is particularly so in the case of small countries such as those in the Caribbean".

4. *Employment creation*
   - More popular participation in the economy would create more employment. This shift would take place through, for example, small businesses, small hotels and guest houses, and cooperatives.
   - More linkages and fewer leakages would create more jobs.

- Giving priority to agriculture would stem the drift from rural to urban areas.
- There needed to be a reorientation of all levels of the educational system to change values towards agriculture and manual work and to place much greater value on vocational and technical subjects.
- There needed also to be a range of change agents such as double shift work; more agricultural education; more on-the-job training, and so on.

Regional strategies

Three regional strategies were proposed as follows:

1. Widening of markets was to be achieved by

    - creating an integrated regional market by means of free trade and a common external tariff and common protective policy in place of a more restricted national market for both industrial and agricultural production
    - widening the regional grouping by bringing in neighbouring Caribbean countries, that is, non–Commonwealth Caribbean territories. Through the CTA and the CHA this situation already existed in tourism, as the two organizations were pan-regional in scope
    - striving at large increases in exports of manufactures to third countries outside of the region

2. Creating more linkages between the national economies of the region by

    - pooling national natural resources so that "regional production complexes" or "regional integrated industries" drawing their inputs from the entire region and selling their outputs in the entire regional market can be created
    - promoting complementarity between the countries – and a certain amount of specialization *among* them – in respect of agricultural and industrial development

3. Creating joint action and common policies by

- harmonization of approaches and policies with respect to fiscal incentives to industry, financial, legislation and company law
- planning of regional integrated industries
- rationalization of agriculture in the region
- achieving a closer degree of monetary and financial cooperation
- creating a common policy on foreign investment
- cooperation in extra-regional shipping and air transportation
- joint bargaining over air rights
- joint bargaining over foreign aid and technical assistance
- formulating a common approach to the United Nations Law of the Sea, including the Regime of the Ocean Bed
- joint promotion of tourism and exports of both agricultural and manufactured products
- joint negotiations with external trading blocs like the EEC
- the establishment of trading links with socialist countries

Analysis of certain CARIFTA strategies

It needs, first of all, to be stated, that many of the criticisms currently being made about tourism and about strategies being presented for its transformation were first put forward some forty years ago by the CARIFTA Secretariat. Certain of the strategies were implemented and others fell by the wayside. A highly relevant question, therefore, which must be answered is this: why so many of them were never implemented? Some answers are as follows:

- CARIFTA in 1972, followed by CARICOM in 1973, did not see tourism as the lead sector of the region, given the many shortcomings it detailed in the report. In fact, as noted above, tourism was ranked by CARIFTA as third after agriculture and manufacturing.
- While CARIFTA made many relevant recommendations for improving the industry, tourism was not a part of its agenda. It strongly supported, however, the work of the CTRC, established in 1974, and of the CTO, which was formed by the merger of CTRC and CTA in 1989.
- Certain of the recommendations, in respect to tourism as well as other sectors, while desirable, were not easily implemented because of political and economic considerations.

- Some of the tourism recommendations were taken forward by the CTRC, and others at a later period by the CTO. But neither of these agencies operated at the level of heads of government, which is critical for decision-making in the Commonwealth Caribbean.
- Other recommendations are still not implemented at 2013.

These views are further expanded below.

Localization

Of all the above recommendations, perhaps the most far reaching was that the Commonwealth Caribbean countries should employ a "localization strategy" – that is, "assume control over key economic sectors, for example, minerals, tourism and sugar".

This was a goal which was always going to be difficult for former colonies to achieve. Former colonial powers may relinquish control over constitutional matters, but they are less willing to lose control of those businesses and resources in their former territories which have benefited them, in some cases for centuries. The CARIFTA recommendation, made in 1972, about the former colonies assuming control over major industries attracted even more suspicion from the West when this was linked with the establishment of trading partnerships with the socialist countries.

Caribbean experience of assuming control

Caribbean politicians who tried, during the era of the Cold War, to assume control over key economic sectors, or to begin trading relationships with the Eastern Bloc, or both, ran into serious difficulty. This fact can be seen from the following examples:

- In 1953, Prime Minister Cheddi Jagan was removed from office in British Guyana with the help of Britain and the United Sates, as his Marxist leanings had become more evident.
- In 1960, as described in chapter 2, the US government imposed a trade embargo on Cuba after that country changed its political ideology following the 1959 revolution and the confiscation of US property. The embargo remains in force fifty-three years later in 2013.

- When in the 1970s, Guyana and Jamaica, under the socialist leaders Michael Manley and Forbes Burnham respectively, moved left-of-centre ideologically, and sought more control over their bauxite industries, they were warned off by those developed countries to which they exported raw materials and which produced the finished product.
- Attempts by these same two countries during this same period to have closer relations with the Eastern European Bloc and with Cuba were frowned upon and even actively discouraged by the United States, which had refreshed the Monroe Doctrine for their benefit. Jamaican tourism, which was heavily dependent on the US market, suffered seriously in the 1970s because of the reaction of the US government to Manley's socialist policies.
- When, in the 1980s, the Maurice Bishop government in Grenada openly espoused the communist cause and allied itself closely with Cuba, US forces, supported by the more conservative leaders in the Caribbean, invaded Grenada.

The limitations of small size and meager resources have always imposed on Caribbean states the need to be evolutionary, rather than revolutionary, in matters of ownership and control, and led them instead to adopt the pragmatic approaches in politics needed for their survival. The wiggle room which the Commonwealth Caribbean did in fact have for changes in ownership and control was as follows: Caribbean people were trained to do jobs done by foreigners, and to develop forms of Caribbean ownership alongside that of foreign ownership and control, with the hope of gradually taking greater local control. "Assuming control" could therefore never mean, for the Commonwealth Caribbean countries, "expropriation" of property owned by the citizens of any of the Western powers. Certainly Cuba, which is considerably larger than any of the other Caribbean islands, has paid a high price for its confiscation of US properties over fifty years ago.

Taking control of tourism

It was said earlier in this book that tourism was seen in the Caribbean, at one time, as an alien activity, owned by aliens and catering to aliens. Given the region's history of colonialism and slavery, it would be expected that one of the goals of independence would be to gain control over key economic sectors, including tourism. The importance of this goal was increased by the fact that, despite the recommendation of the 1972 CARIFTA report – that the economic sectors of the subregion should be ranked as agriculture first, manufacturing second and tourism third – the entire region gradually became progressively more dependent on tourism as several global economic factors marginalized the value and importance of the other two sectors. Much of this book is about how difficult it is for Caribbean people to assume control of the tourism industry because of both its history and its structure. There was a need, nevertheless, to expand the areas under Caribbean control and to maximize its benefits for Caribbean people.

Economic and social realities of Caribbean tourism

The tourism industry comprises land-based activities and the related infrastructure and superstructure; sea-based activities and related assets; air transportation activities and assets; and market-based operations dealing with marketing, sales and distribution.

The industry is capital-intensive at every level and depends heavily on direct foreign investment for several aspects of its land, sea, air and market-based activities. At the time of tourism expansion in the 1960s and 1970s, some of this capital might have been available from local sources if large Caribbean businesses had been interested in the tourism industry. They, however, preferred less high-risk commercial activity. Local large-scale hotel investment was a late development, beginning first in Jamaica. On the plus side, the Caribbean was attractive to foreign investment for tourism purposes. But with foreign investment came foreign management and expertise, and a number of social issues related to these realities.

Since tourism development is largely about real estate, a necessary consequence of foreign investment and ownership was large-scale alienation of scarce Caribbean land resources. As the Caribbean moved from sugar to tourism, the debate continued about a small and often white elite section of the population owning over 90 per cent of the land. This debate took on other dimensions such as the utilization of land formerly dedicated to export agriculture and the growing of food for local consumption, now in fact being used for tourism superstructure and infrastructure, especially golf courses and shopping malls.

Perhaps most disturbing of all, the increased demand of land for tourism was seen as inflationary, with land prices escalating out of the reach of the local inhabitants. The concept of "owning a piece of the rock" therefore took on a special significance for the general population beyond ownership. It was seen as a badge of freedom and independence.

The 1972 CARIFTA report suggested that the problem of alienation of land resources might be solved by making land available to foreign investors on a leasehold, rather than freehold, basis. This solution is, however, more apparent than real, since for leases to be attractive to foreign investors they would have to be of a duration long enough to make little difference relative to being freehold.

Small hotels and local ownership

Herbert Hiller, one of the major proponents of the creation of CTRC, was a firm believer in the theory that mass tourism associated with large hotels should be replaced in the Caribbean by small-scale, locally owned and locally managed properties. This was an attempt to solve the problem of foreign ownership and extensive leakage associated with it. However, that sort of small-scale operation could never have generated the kind of resources the region needed for its development or to compete internationally as Caribbean tourism had to. Tourism is now the world's largest industry and one in which there is fierce competition for business at a global level. No allowances are made for small or developing countries. This situation suggests that, to be competitive, a mix of local and foreign ownership and of large and small hotel plant is highly desirable, not only with respect to product, but also to marketing reach and power. Over the years it has been demonstrated that brand name hotels like the Ritz-Carlton and the Four Seasons cater to people who are recession-proof and who make a destination more attractive than it might otherwise have been. The development in the 1980s and 1990s of the major and highly competitive hotel chains of Sandals and Superclubs by Jamaicans Gordon "Butch" Stewart and John Issa was a major breakthrough and ended the lie that, for a hotel to be large and successful, it had to be foreign owned and managed.

While Hiller's idea of replacing mass tourism with small-scale tourism was not feasible, the development of a small hotel sector as a means of entry into ownership and management, was a sound idea. It therefore took root when it was supported by government policies of human resource development and provision of access to development financing, which the commercial banks were not providing in the 1970s and 1980s.

From time to time, governments were also forced to become owners and managers of large hotel plants, either to replace foreign ownership, which had left the region for its own reasons, or to jump start projects that might not otherwise have started. This kind of intervention, which is much criticized by the private sector, can work as long as government puts in place professional management which understands the business of commerce and allows it to operate along business lines.

Regional cooperation in travel and tourism

CARIFTA must be credited with a great deal of foresight in recommending, as long ago as 1972, a regional approach to several aspects of Caribbean tourism. This approach received a mixed reception, however.

Collaboration in foreign direct investment

Little collaboration ever took place between Caribbean states with respect to foreign investment in tourism, as was recommended. In fact, attracting foreign investment remains one of the greatest areas of competition between the member states.

Cruise tourism

Forty years after CARIFTA suggested that the operations of passenger cruise ships owned and operated by Caribbean people could do much to increase tourist travel by both West Indians and non-West Indians within the region, the Caribbean, which is the world's preferred area for cruising, owns not a single cruise ship. Moreover, as will be shown later in this book, Caribbean governments have been unable during that same period to devise and agree on any regional strategies thought likely to increase their control of the cruise industry and to maximize the benefits of cruise tourism to the region.

Diversification of tourist markets

CARIFTA's identification of over-dependence of the region on the US market was insightful and the CTA and the CTRC, as well as individual countries, did a great deal in the 1980s to diversify the region's tourist market in Europe and beyond. The regional efforts are dealt with at some length in chapter 6.

The Caribbean as a market

CARIFTA in calling in 1972 for the development of the Caribbean market was well ahead of its time. In fact, it took a long time for people, whether as entrepreneurs or as vacationers, to take the Caribbean region seriously as a tourism market.

The reasons for neglect of this market were twofold; first, historically, tourists were thought of in the Caribbean as white people from Europe and North America and second, the majority of Caribbean people taking holidays thought of going to those European countries with which they had colonial connections or to the United States (largely Miami and New York) where they had family connections and opportunities to shop for goods not available at home or obtainable at bargain prices abroad. Their stay was largely with family and friends.

It followed that for a long time neither the public nor private sector in the region had any incentive to establish, within the Caribbean, the apparatus for tourism promotion and packaging that, as a necessary part of doing business, had been established in European and North American markets. Further, initially, people who travelled within the region for any purpose, even the comparative few that took holidays there, did not think of themselves as tourists.

In the 1970s it was the Caribbean Tourism Research and Development Centre that pushed the CARIFTA idea of the need to set up tour operations and other systems in the Caribbean for developing and promoting an intra-Caribbean tourism market. The Caribbean hotel industry did not initially warm to the idea of putting in place the kind of rates and packages for Caribbean visitors which they had put in place for visitors from outside the region. There was no real incentive to do so, since only a few Caribbean people were staying in hotels, and those persons who travelled within the region for private or government business were happily paying rates which were double those being paid by packaged foreign visitors on holiday. Eventually CARICOM rates were negotiated at some hotels. Intra-regional tourism on any scale has therefore been of comparatively recent vintage.

By 2013, however, intra-regional tourism comprised the core of visitors to a number of small states in the eastern Caribbean and is a significant market even for certain of the other states which are comparatively more developed in tourism.

The Latin American market

The Commonwealth Caribbean has traditionally ignored the Latin American tourism market for many reasons related to the colonial history of the region. Historically, the lack of any significant relationships, whether political, cultural or economic, with neighbours in Latin America, was determined by the policies of colonial powers. The powers had fought each other for hundreds of years to gain possession of the resources of the Caribbean and South America, and accordingly had Balkanized the region in their own interests, especially in relation to trade. It is to be noted, however, that the same metropolitan countries were able to bring together all their territories in the Caribbean Basin – English, French, Dutch, Spanish and American – under the one umbrella of CTA when they wished so to do.

Later, despite shared membership in organizations such as the OAS, the gap between Latin America and the Commonwealth Caribbean was not closed significantly. Basic transport connections between countries derive from ethnic, trade and cultural relationships, and these were not in place. Differences in language are also serious barriers to communication between peoples.

With respect to tourism specifically, CARICOM countries, generally speaking, did not know enough about Latin America to see it as a productive tourist market, and starting to put in place the structures needed to promote and market tourism business seemed a job that was both difficult and expensive, given the lack of air connections.

The exception to some extent has been Venezuela, which has had long standing diplomatic, business and some social relationships with Barbados and with Trinidad and Tobago, from which at one point it is separated by a distance of only seven miles. The extent of this relationship between the Commonwealth Caribbean and Venezuela decreased with the advent in the country of a deteriorating economy and of currency depreciation. As a result of this economic shift, the number of air links between Venezuela and the CARICOM states fell in the 1990s. This change resulted in a significant decrease in the number of people travelling between the Commonwealth Caribbean and Venezuela.

In recent times Venezuela has strengthened its relationships at the political level with other CARICOM countries, such as Antigua and Barbuda, Dominica, and St Vincent and the Grenadines, which are members of the Bolivarian Alliance for the Americas and with other countries with which it has signed a Petrocaribe agreement. This development may have been driven by recent international events which have motivated Venezuela to seek greater support from those independent countries within the region that both have a voice and a vote at the United Nations. It remains to be seen whether these new relationships will lead to more tourist arrivals from Venezuela.

Product diversification out of sand, sea and surf

The positioning of Caribbean countries in the marketplace as sea, sun and sand destinations is sometimes greeted with ridicule by some observers who do not understand the history of tourism and the context in which it developed in this region. The Caribbean countries were the colonial possessions of European countries, and one of the benefits for Europeans of ownership was the consequent ability to travel to the islands of perpetual summer in escape of the rigours of winter in their temperate climates, to enjoy sea bathing in warm temperatures and to experience the beauty of the Caribbean environment. In their own countries going to the seaside in summer was a large part of the holiday for those who could not afford to go abroad, but those who went to places like the Caribbean knew what they were missing. When CTRC carried out motivational surveys in the 1980s, it found that the Caribbean climate remained at the core of demand for the region. At any period when there is extremely cold weather in northern climes, the Caribbean can still expect a spike in arrivals, provided that international transport continues to function. It is important that those planning Caribbean tourism remain conscious of this fact. However, the call by CARIFTA for the diversification of the Caribbean tourism product was insightful for a number of reasons. These reasons became clearer as time progressed.

First, the complete focus on the sea, sun and sand in promotion of the Caribbean had resulted in several Caribbean countries with no beaches of exceptional beauty not being regarded, either by themselves or other countries, as tourist destinations. This self-perception was the case despite the exciting flora and fauna, and interesting cultural products that these countries had. It might also explain why neither Trinidad nor Guyana initially supported tourism development.

Second, the product needed to be expanded to suit shifting demand in the marketplace due to changes in the demographics and psychographics of customers. There was a need to cater to a traveller who wanted to do more than lie on the beach in the sun. Indeed, this shift was also driven by the circulation of information that overexposure to the sun can be a source of skin cancer, if the proper precautions are not taken.

Third, as Caribbean people gained more control over their industry, they saw themselves and their countries as more than a beach. (That phrase became a Jamaica tagline.) Caribbean people saw and projected themselves as real people engaged in their normal daily lives in the same kind of activities which occupy the attention of visitors in their own country of origin. Caribbean people also projected their countries as exciting places with exotic cultures and fascinating histories.

In the past forty years, the ferocity of the global competition for tourism business has brought almost every country to the table, some with vast financial resources, able and willing to promote their tourism product as the best, whatever it is. The difference between traditional markets and destinations has therefore been blurred.

In that context sand, sea and sun is not enough to win and keep the attention of a travelling public whose circumstances and interests have changed. More emphasis is now being placed everywhere on things to see and do, on events and attractions, festivals, sports tourism, cultural and historic monuments, museums, shopping, on people interaction and, where credible, on ecotourism, which was strongly promoted by the Caribbean Tourism Research and Development Centre after its establishment. Shopping, events and festivals have a particular appeal to Caribbean visitors for whom fine beaches are not the main attraction as each country contends that its own beaches are unparalleled.

In the twenty-first century, diversifying and enriching the product offer is more a matter of survival than of choice. Catering creatively to the various tastes is the secret of attracting new business. If something can be packaged, priced and promoted attractively, it can be sold.

One regional airline

In 1969, when the Government of Trinidad and Tobago owned BWIA and a controlling interest in the Leeward Islands Air Transport (LIAT) Airline, Kamaludin Mohamed, the minister of West Indian Affairs in that government, stated: "the integration process has, for many years, been hampered by the lack of fast, cheap and reliable inter-island transport . . . this void is to a large extent being filled by British West Indian Airways and its subsidiary LIAT". He therefore called for BWIA to be designated the regional carrier with participation by the other regional governments. It was in that same month in April 1969 that Air Jamaica was launched. It was therefore possible for the CARIFTA report to say:

> there has been no progress whatever in developing a regional approach to air transportation. In this area, fragmentation, divisiveness and disintegration continue apace. Three member states now have their own individual international airlines and the number of intra-regional carriers is multiplying daily. A UK-based company has acquired a controlling interest in LIAT because the previous company with a majority control, could not afford to infuse the new capital necessary for the improvement of the services offered by LIAT.

This company was Court Line which went bankrupt in 1974, leaving LIAT to be rescued by the CARICOM countries.

It is clear that in 1972, and for many years thereafter, CARICOM governments did not understand the relationship of regional air transportation to regional integration, did not understand the importance of developing the intra-Caribbean tourism market, and were unaware of why the costs of intra-regional travel are high. As a result, regional carriers experienced a chequered existence for the next forty years, as will be discussed later in this book, and which was discussed at length in the book *Don't Burn Our Bridges: The Case for Owing Airlines* by this same author. Sufficient to say for the moment that, as late as 2013, a satisfactory solution to regional air transport problems was still being sought.

Other CARIFTA issues

Other tourism issues raised by CARIFTA, such as the facilitation of intra-regional travel, the creation of linkages, and joint marketing, are discussed in detail in chapter 10, as part of an exploration of strategic planning.

Factors militating against tourism progress

It was mentioned earlier that CARICOM had no tourism mandate and therefore no tourism division. An option would have been to seek to make the CTRC an organ of CARICOM, which would have provided it with access to the decision-making process of the heads of government, the level at which the important decisions are made. One of the difficulties posed, however, was that the CTRC had a wider Caribbean membership than did CARICOM.

One inescapable factor was the fact that in the early 1970s, the leadership of the secretariat and certain of the most eminent political leaders of CARICOM did not really believe in tourism development, and operated in an environment in which the contemporary intellectuals, especially historians, sociologists and economists, both in academia and in certain international donor agencies, were equally sceptical.

Scepticism among thinkers

In the 1970s a number of eminent thinkers in the region continued to hope that one day their dream – that there would be a Caribbean economic miracle based on the successful development of agriculture and manufacturing, with "real" visible exports like those in the countries of the four Asian Tigers – would indeed materialize.

Forty years later, when it is difficult to deny that many, if not most of the countries of the region, have achieved high and sustained levels of economic development through tourism, the scepticism continues. Some of the region's most eminent commentators, who at times do seem won over to the idea of tourism being the driver of Caribbean economies, at other times are seen to backslide into the old thinking. This slip takes place when tourism suffers a decline, as has indeed happened in such circumstances as the events of 9/11, the SARS epidemic or the global financial crisis that began in 2008. No one, however, would think that agricultural crops like wheat or rice are fickle because they failed after a series of monstrous natural disasters, or that oil is fickle because frequent civil and political unrest in the Middle East causes fluctuations in its price.

Sectoral priorities set by CARIFTA in 1972

Several other important regional and international development agencies shared CARICOM's views on tourism as expressed in 1972.

Caribbean Regional Negotiating Machinery

It is regrettable that, when the Caribbean Regional Negotiating Machinery was created as late as 1997, its focus was entirely on merchandizing trade objectives and did not include services which, even then, were more important for the Caribbean. A shared focus with services came with the negotiations for the Doha Round and probably only as a result of the abandonment of the European Union's special support for Caribbean sugar and bananas.

Views of the Caribbean Development Bank on tourism

In 1974, eminent thinker and economist William Demas, the secretary general first of CARIFTA and then CARICOM, became president of the Caribbean Development Bank, a post he then occupied until 1988. When he moved from CARICOM to the bank, he took his views on tourism to the bank with him.

Demas once expressed his view that tourism was a stopgap until the region could implement its manufacturing industry. This view contradicted the fact that, at that time, there were a number of small countries in the Caribbean which relied largely on tourism and financial services, had little else by way of economic diversification, but were palpably those with some of the region's highest standards of living and per capita incomes. They remain so some forty years later in 2013.

Sir Neville Nicholls, who succeeded Demas, and who served as president of the bank from 1988 to 2001, made it clear in his first official speech, in St Kitts, that the region, with few exceptions, had become largely dependent on tourism development and needed to recognize this reality going forward. The policies of the bank underwent radical changes thereafter and the institution became a firm supporter of tourism projects.

Views of the World Bank view on tourism

In the 1970s and 1980s, after a brief period of support for tourism projects, the World Bank changed its position as to its development possibilities, ultimately closing its own tourism division. The Caribbean region therefore then had an uphill battle receiving support for tourism programmes from that quarter. This was especially noticeable in the annual meetings of the Caribbean Group for Economic Development held at the World Bank in Washington, at which Caribbean countries presented their development projects for funding to donor agencies.

The Caribbean Tourism Research and Development Centre was represented at these meetings and submitted several tourism projects for consideration, arguing that tourism was the one industry in which its member states were resource rich and had the potential to compete internationally without special protection. Further, it argued that tourism should be used to strengthen linkages with the other sectors.

The World Bank's view at the time was that tourism was not only a fickle and unsustainable sector, but also a private sector concern, which accordingly should be left to the private sector and not be a recipient of aid. It was the view that was also prevalent in US government circles, and one which influenced those development agencies, the leadership of which tended to be American. This American government view has long been fought by its own US travel industry and it came as no surprise when the American federal tourism institution, the US Travel and Tourism Administration, was itself closed for a period.

Little attention was paid in US official circles at the time to the fact that Caribbean tourism annually bought about US$5 billion in goods and services from the United States. Furthermore, US politicians from the tourism-dependent US states of Florida and Hawaii saw the Caribbean as a tourism competitor and were opposed to any suggestion of their federal government supporting its product with aid flows.

Later the World Bank and other international agencies would totally reverse their views on the role of tourism both in developed countries and in the Caribbean. Chapter 15 will outline a radical shift in the policies of the US government under President Barack Obama, and the UK government under Prime Minister David Cameron, with respect to the role of tourism as an export industry in their economic policies.

Views of European Economic Community on tourism

The attitude of European aid agencies at the Caribbean Group for Economic Development was in sharp contrast to those of the World Bank- and American-dominated agencies generally. This difference may in part have been because EEC countries such as Britain, France, Spain and Italy then had a better understanding of tourism as a development sector, and may indeed be said to have invented the modern tourism industry.

Further, the EEC better understood that a prosperous tourism industry in the Caribbean served the mutual interests of both the Caribbean and Europe. European citizens were travelling to the Caribbean largely in European planes to consume a Caribbean product sold and promoted by European tour operators, European travel agents and European advertising companies, and to consume goods often made in Europe and exported to the Caribbean. This situation created jobs at home for Europeans. The Caribbean sold Europeans a packaged tourism experience, and in doing so earned foreign exchange, created jobs and created government revenue to finance Caribbean social services. Everyone benefited from the exchange.

In 1979 the European Community made the first of several tourism grants to the Caribbean Tourism Research and Development Centre, under the umbrella of their Regional Assistance Programme. This support continued over the next three decades and was critical in expanding the reach of the Caribbean into the European market. Chapter 6 deals with the steps taken by two regional tourism organizations, the CTA and the CTRC, to expand Caribbean tourism activity, with the support of the European Community, into Europe.

6
Caribbean Tourism Expands to Europe

The ability to develop an overseas tourism market is a function of many factors. There must, of course, be some form of transportation connecting the market with the destination. For transportation services to be sustainable, however, there must also be a critical mass of business that derives from one or a combination of the following situations and conditions: a major ethnic presence wishing to move between the countries concerned; an established pattern of that trade which creates business traffic; a demand in the market for the tourism products on offer; and established structures that promote and sell those products.

Until the 1970s there was some high-end traffic of the rich and famous between Europe and the Caribbean. Other traffic between the continent and the Caribbean comprised, for the most part, colonial students studying in Europe, civil servants taking "long-leave" in their various "Mother countries" and immigrants travelling one way, seeking work and a new life in Europe.

With respect to the Commonwealth Caribbean, serious immigration to Britain began in the late 1950s and became a flood in the 1960s. These immigrants would later become a productive source of vacation traffic. But in the 1950s, 1960s and 1970s trade between CARICOM countries and Britain consisted largely of agricultural exports, mainly sugar, and of manufactured goods to the Caribbean.

As late as the 1950s, when most travel across the North Atlantic was by ship, it could take as long as seventeen days to make the journey one way. The rapid development of air transportation and the jet engine after the Second World War cut the time and distance to Europe drastically and brought European tourist markets within reach of a much-expanded group of travellers. There was now a case for giving serious consideration to Europe as a tourism market for the Caribbean.

Need to diversify Caribbean tourist markets

The CTA and the CTRC took seriously the 1972 CARIFTA recommendations to seek to diversify the tourism markets of the region. The CTA – which, as noted, was based in New York and had been actively promoting the North American market since the 1950s – therefore joined with the CTRC at the end of the 1970s to research the European market potential and to determine which structures and systems were needed for the promotion and sale of tourism products there. Their ability to do this was due to the enlightened policy of the European Community which, in 1975, had signed the first Lomé agreement with the African, Caribbean, and Pacific Group of States (ACP) countries, covering both aid and trade, and including tourism services. The Europeans understood the symbiotic relationship between Caribbean tourism and their own economies, and were willing to offer financial aid to assist the tourism industry.

Major market studies

Prior to 1978, the Caribbean marketing and promotional operations did not have the benefit of any scientific analysis of the market potential. The North American markets had been developed by US and Canadian travel and tourism businesses, jointly with support from national tourism entities. These entities combined representation in major cities like New York and Toronto with aggressive periodic promotional tours. Only a few Caribbean countries had any tourism representation in London or in other European cities in the 1950s and 1960s.

The CTRC's first work programme in 1974 had identified market research as an important part of its agenda, but found it impossible to do a great deal within its limited annual budget. It therefore turned for financial support to two aid agencies, the Inter-American Development Bank and the European Economic Community (EEC), for assistance in carrying out the first major tourism market demand studies ever undertaken by the Caribbean states in North America and western Europe.

Between August 1980 and March 1981, a major North American demand study, financed by the Inter-American Development Bank, was carried out by Travel and Tourism Consultants International, in collaboration with the CTRC. The findings confirmed much of what was already known about those markets from the region's long experience of working in them. What was in fact looked forward to, with great anticipation, was this finding: the discovery of the potential for the Caribbean of the European markets. About this potential relatively less was then known.

In 1978, with funds negotiated with the EEC under the Caribbean Regional Programme of the Lomé agreement, the CTRC contracted two German firms – Steigenberger Consulting GMBH and Lufthansa Consulting – to execute the study in collaboration with a joint CTA/CTRC team. This team comprised Audrey Palmer-Hawks of the CTA and Jean Holder, Luther Miller and Maria Laville of the CTRC.

The first European market demand study

The first study, which began in February 1979, demonstrated that there was a high potential for expanding the number of arrivals to the Caribbean from Europe. Based on this finding, and based on this study and a follow-up study in 1983, significant EU financial and technical assistance became available to Caribbean countries for tourism development in Europe under various national and regional programmes.

The findings from the first European tourism demand study in 1979 were as follows:

1. **Number of arrivals:** The number of European visitors to the Caribbean had grown from 104,000 in 1970, to 640,000 in 1978, representing

some 9.5 per cent of the region's arrivals. These visitors went to only a few Caribbean destinations, among the most visited being the Bahamas, Jamaica, Barbados, and Martinique and Guadeloupe, which as departments of France received almost all those French tourists taking holidays in the Caribbean. Eighty per cent of these visitors went to one destination and 15 per cent to two or more islands.

2. **Visitor profiles:** Typical European visitors were found in 1979 to be couples without children, between thirty and sixty years of age and from higher-income groups, with a small trend developing of younger and middle-class visitors travelling in the summer.

3. **Motivation for travel:** Those travellers surveyed gave the excellent climatic conditions all year round and the attractive beaches as the chief motivations for visiting the Caribbean. The travellers also mentioned entertainment, excursions and land sports, such as tennis and golf, as important.

4. **Knowledge of the region:** In 1979 few Europeans were able to identify the exact geographical location and demarcation of the Caribbean countries, and were therefore not particularly able to differentiate between the varying touristic offers within the region.

5. **Product strengths and weaknesses identified by the consultants:** The consultants made it clear from the beginning, that the views expressed about product strengths and weaknesses in the European surveys were those of the Europeans and could differ from any views expressed by North Americans. The European assessment of the Caribbean product strengths in 1979 were

- excellent climatic conditions
- great beaches
- wonderful topography
- high quality of accommodation
- good sports facilities (largely marine and tennis)

The weaknesses were

- a lack of tourism-related cultural attractions

- poor intra-Caribbean air connections
- a lack of excursion programmes
- bad attitudes of immigration and customs officials
- poor quality of shopping
- high price levels
- poor service quality
- lack of knowledge of foreign languages

6. **Competition to the Caribbean:** The tour operators surveyed identified the region's main competition for the European markets as the Seychelles, Kenya and Mauritius, followed by Thailand, the Canary Islands, Sri Lanka and Mexico, some of which were seen, unlike the Caribbean, as offering other equally valid attractions, such as cultural assets, history, safaris, and so on.

7. **Role of the European tour operator:** The European holiday business to the Caribbean was defined as tour-operator driven, with about 80 per cent of all trips from Europe implemented through tour operators. The other 20 per cent comprised business and ethnic travel, not seen by the travel trade (for their purposes) as part of tourism.

8. **Forecast for 1985 and 1990:** The forecast for European travel to the Caribbean, set by the study for 1985 and 1990, was optimistic, about 1.34 million and 1.85 million persons, respectively, but these numbers were not achieved by the times suggested. It is to be noted, however, that by 2001, European arrivals had reached in excess of 4.8 million or 24.3 per cent of the total arrivals to the region. Over the years Europe was to gain ascendancy as the most significant market for many Caribbean destinations, and in fact the biggest for Barbados. This transformation of the European prospects was achieved, to a large extent, by the implementation of the broad strategies recommended by the 1979 and 1983 studies, even if a great deal of that implementation was in fact done at *both* the regional and the national levels.

The recommendations of the first study included specifics on multi-destination, horizontal presentation, price, market development, product improvement, and image strategies. It dealt with the need for increased accommodation facilities and for many of the small properties to be properly marketed. Marketing had by then been largely restricted in many of the smaller destinations to the production and distribution of a few brochures and folders. In the 1970s, even the CTA, the CHA and the ECTA, on which many small destinations depended for exposure, were not well known by tour operators in Europe because they were only really active in North America.

9. **European product preferences:** It became clear with the first study that the demands made of the Caribbean product by European guests differed, to some extent, from those made by North Americans. This covered areas like the environment, airport facilitation, organization of taxi services, tour guide services, familiarity with European currencies and willingness to accept them, hotel staffs' ability to speak some of the languages of Europe, wider offering of fresh fruit, vegetables, sea food, local foods, more varied sports facilities, culture-related entertainment, and a wider range of shopping, including good quality handicraft articles of national origin.

10. **Pricing in Europe:** It was held to be critical for Caribbean hoteliers to understand how pricing is done in Europe as opposed to the United States. The package prices as published by the European tour operators are decisive for the European tourist for assessment and judgment of the Caribbean. Contrary to American tour operators, Europeans deal on the basis of net prices, whereby they aim either at a uniform annual price (to be able to determine their own seasonal differences) or at five to six different seasonal prices (to cover shoulder periods).

11. **Publicity and promotion:** The study gave specific recommendations of how the region was to promote itself, stressing:

    - advertising in periodicals and magazines jointly with tour operators and airlines
    - creation of films to present realistically the holiday destination, especially to first-time visitors
    - making of audio-visual shows which were easy to transport, flexible in terms of adding information, and not costly to produce
    - direct mailing to specific target groups

- creation of prospectuses which fulfil the function of providing information and creating meaningful images
- the creation of a uniform, complete and permanently up-to-date manual, offering information on all aspects of all the Caribbean destinations
- regular visits to European tour operators and retail travel agents by representatives of Caribbean tourist boards and Caribbean hoteliers
- familiarization trips for travel agents to the region
- participation in the most important European trade fairs including but not limited to those in Berlin, Milan and Paris.

12. **Organization and budget:** The study recommended the establishment in Europe of a Caribbean tourism presence to deliver the marketing activities. This agency would work with the tourist boards, the European tour operators, the airlines flying from Europe to the Caribbean, the hotels, and other tourist facilities in the region.

    On the assumption that in 1979 a minimum annual budget of US$300,000 was then required for a country marketing in Europe, it suggested that some thirteen of the countries in the Caribbean region could afford such a sum and the others should operate through a regional entity. It set a budget guideline for national tourism offices of some US$6 to US$8 per European room night to cover promotional expenditures, and payroll and overhead costs.

13. **Establishment of marketing offices in Europe:** A specific proposal was that there should be

    - a CTA office established in Frankfurt, followed by offices in London and Paris
    - representation within the CTA offices of those destinations which were heavily dependent on tourism but unable to afford an office of their own
    - multi-destination marketing services within the CTA

    All the tourism agencies in Frankfurt were to be brought together in what was to be called a "Caribbean House". The building was to be in a good business location, and gain additional publicity through the existence of a building of this name.

The 1979 study also called for the immediate implementation of the following recommendations:

- improving and standardizing tourism statistics
- introducing regular visitor surveys
- hospitality training
- training in foreign languages
- providing the general population with information on the importance of tourism
- providing technical assistance to the national tourism organizations
- creating a model project for the linking of the tourism and agricultural sectors
- creating a similar project for the promotion of local handicrafts
- creating a Caribbean hotel classification concept
- preparing a Caribbean manual
- establishing a CTA office in Frankfurt
- preparatory studies on special interest markets and reservation systems for Caribbean hotels and airlines
- elaborating a uniform graphic design concept
- producing an audio-visual show entitled *The European Tourism Market for the Caribbean*

On completion of the study, the region had not only a blueprint for marketing in Europe, but also a guide to improvement of the tourism product generally in the region from which promotion of other markets would benefit.

Caribbean and Europe air transportation

Air transport connections between Europe and the Caribbean, and within the Caribbean, were seen as significant factors affecting the overall development of the region. In 1978, thirteen Caribbean destinations were served directly from Europe, most frequently from London, Paris and Amsterdam, while some twenty-five local carriers operated between twenty-six Caribbean countries, usually within a limited area. The study recommended, on the supposition that an efficient feeder service could be established, that instead of opening more direct routes to Europe from smaller islands, six

Caribbean gateway hubs should be established at (1) Nassau, (2) Kingston or Port-au-Prince or both, (3) San Juan, (4) Guadeloupe or Antigua or both, (5) Barbados or Port of Spain or both, and (6) Caracas and Curaçao or both.

The six-gateway strategy was based on a number of other implementations, however:

- services to at least two of the gateways from each of the important European countries
- direct flight connections between all six gateway hubs to neighbouring islands
- distribution of passenger volume over four peaks per day:
  1. local traffic in the morning
  2. intercontinental North American traffic at noon
  3. intercontinental European traffic in the afternoon
  4. local traffic in the evening
- standardized booking systems and mutual acceptance by all local carriers of each other's travel documents and those of intercontinental airlines
- pooling agreements between local carriers regarding maintenance, engineering services, handling and accounting
- improvement of service standards with regard to punctuality, safety, flexibility, in-flight service, and passenger and baggage handling
- replacement in the medium term of old aircraft by modern better performance planes with seating capacity for one hundred persons
- separation of passenger flows by three different passenger halls serving domestic traffic, international traffic and transits
- streamlining of immigration and customs control procedures
- provision of a guidance system for passengers in the form of multilingual signs indicating the most important airport sections
- installation of night landing facilities at all Caribbean airports

Creation of the first Caribbean tourism village

Through the instrumentality of the German consultants Steigenberger GNB, Audrey Palmer-Hawks and Jean Holder – the CEOs of the CTA and the CTRC, respectively, accompanied by two staff members of their organizations, Sylma Browne and Luther Miller – attended in 1978, for the first time, the International Tourisme Bourse (ITB). This was the largest tourism fair in the world. It was an eye opener to witness this event, as almost every country in the world was exhibiting tourism products. It was possible to see at first hand the enormous competition which any country faces in this industry. There was no consolidated Caribbean presence there, simply a number of isolated countries, mostly small islands, lost in the crowd, and separated from each other at the fair by significant distances. This isolation made it difficult for consumers and the trade press to find them, or for them to find each other.

It was at this event in 1978 that the CTA and the CTRC made the simple suggestion that it would be far better if all the Caribbean countries could be brought together in one exhibition hall. This building would be suitably organized and decorated to present a single Caribbean image and presence to the rest of the world. This creation would need to be professionally done, however, and required a consistent source of funds with which to do it.

After the end of the 1978 ITB, Palmer-Hawks and Holder travelled directly to Brussels to meet with officials at the offices of the European Commission to discuss financial support for the creation of a "Caribbean village" at the Berlin Fair. This would create an identifiable Caribbean presence where all Caribbean countries could be easily found by anyone wishing to do business with the Caribbean, where the countries could be in constant contact with each other, and the CTA could provide common services.

In hindsight, it all seems such an obvious act, and yet it had never been done before. The European Commission not only agreed to fund the village, but also saw it as a prototype for the creation of other such villages representing the African and Pacific countries as well – countries which, like the Caribbean, were recipients of funding under the regional programmes for those countries covered by the ACP Lomé agreement.

The first Caribbean Village at the ITB provided, in a physical sense, a striking spectacle. Its stands had thatched roofs, and there was abundant Caribbean flora, a bubbling waterfall and streams of running water. The ITB authorities deemed it the best exhibit at the fair in 1979.

From the first year, the Caribbean immediately made its presence known through the introduction of lively Caribbean music into the hitherto sombre atmosphere of the German winter. This drew large numbers to the Caribbean Village, so much so that the Fair organizers were forced to request the Caribbean to reduce the amount of noise of the music and other activity that took place in the village. An annual Caribbean party was introduced at the Fair and attracted attendance from many of the countries exhibiting. When, due to considerations of space, the Caribbean annual party was moved out of the village and into the hotels in Berlin, the numbers of those exhibitors and Germans resident in Berlin attending annually grew to several hundred per year. Caribbean performers of the quality of David Rudder of Trinidad and Tobago were now being invited to perform, and ultimately steps had to be taken to limit the size of the event.

Caribbean tourism villages spread to the Italian Tourism Fair and later to the French Fair Top Resa which were serviced from the CTA office when it was opened in Frankfurt in 1984.

With the year 2013 the Caribbean had been represented at ITB in Berlin, each year since 1979. In 2004, when the secretary general of the CTO retired he was honoured by the fair authorities for having participated in twenty-six consecutive annual shows in Berlin.

Presentation of the 1979 European study

Work on the 1979 European Demand Study was completed in January 1980. Its findings and recommendations were presented to Caribbean governments at the fourth tourism conference held in Santo Domingo in June 1980. The discussion that followed, however, confirmed that real progress in Europe required that a Caribbean marketing presence be established in Europe. A further study was proposed to identify the extent to which Caribbean countries had tried from 1978 to 1983 to implement the recommendations of the first study, and to seek to justify the aid funds needed to establish CTA offices in Europe.

European study update, 1983

In 1983 the CTRC again obtained funds from the European Commission for the purposes stated above. The 1983 study found that steps had been taken to address product areas in many ways. There had been, to start with, many improvements in the Caribbean infrastructure, including water and power supplies, and sewage and waste disposal. Postal, telex and telephone services were satisfactory in almost all countries. There were also good road networks in most nations although in the smaller countries there were problems of road maintenance. The airport and airfield facilities were satisfactory. The beaches were being improved through the introduction of pollution controls, and studies on beach erosion were now being done. The cultural environment was also being improved, and steps were being taken to improve as well the cultural assets: as an example, there was now a regional plan for their restoration and maintenance, specifically the Caribbean Plan for Monuments and Sites.

The quality and quantity of accommodation still varied from country to country and relatively little new accommodation had been built between 1978 and 1983, except in Antigua, Aruba, Barbados, the Dominican Republic and the Bahamas. Room rates were regarded as high, although seldom were rack rates achieved. Criticisms continued about the high cost and lack of variety of food and beverage and insufficient use of local food, a criticism which separates the European visitor from the American. Land and sea sports were being seen as available and well-organized, and both sporting and entertainment facilities were stated to have been greatly improved. The variety and quality of available products, particularly handicrafts, continued to be perceived as limited and their prices high, leading tourists to restrict their purchases to necessities.

Air transportation revisited

Air transportation issues were again addressed in the 1983 study. It needed to be understood that air transportation links often follow the flag, meaning that certain historical links help to create "traditional markets".

The 1983 study found that a number of air transportation issues still remained between Europe and the Caribbean depending on whether or not historical links in fact existed. The links varied heavily between the region and those countries in Europe with which they had been linked historically, ethnically, economically and politically, and those with which they had not. There were therefore strong air links between countries like Britain, France, the Netherlands and Spain and those particular countries with which each one had a long colonial relationship. It is important to understand that these links were unlikely to cross the historic divide: French airlines, for example, did not fly to British territories. And there were virtually no direct air transportation links between the Caribbean and countries such as Germany, Switzerland, Austria, and Italy.

Historic linkages also form the reason why there are still today excellent intra-Caribbean transportation links between the English-speaking Commonwealth Caribbean countries, which were colonies of Britain, but almost no connections between those and the various Spanish- and Dutch-speaking countries of the same region, which were connected historically and in terms of family and trade with the *other* countries in Europe that had each formed their respective colonial empires. For similar reasons there remain few direct air transportation connections between the Commonwealth Caribbean countries and Central and Latin America.

In 1979, some 73 per cent of European passenger traffic to the Caribbean came from the "traditional markets". By 1983 this percentage had grown to 88 per cent.

Another factor affecting the growth of European business to the Caribbean, as compared to competing countries situated in Asia, concerned airfares to the Caribbean: they were much higher if calculated on a passenger-kilometre basis. One reason for the difference was this: whereas the competing Asian long-haul destinations were well served by non-scheduled charter services, the Caribbean was not. The European tour operators' changeover to wide-body equipment had resulted in the industry not having the resources to assume the risk of contracting for an entire flight or series of flights; this was the case even with the larger tour operators. It became necessary, therefore, to form a seat-buying consortium, thereby dividing the capacity of the aircraft between a number of tour operators. The success of these operations depended on each tour operator being able to sell its respective seat allocation. One such consortium – formed to market the Caribbean in West Germany by Neckermann, Touristik Union International and Terramar – had collapsed with the bankruptcy of Terramar.

A second issue concerned connecting flights. Many of the intra-Caribbean connecting services were scheduled to connect to flights arriving from North America. Their times of departure often did not accommodate passengers arriving from Europe.

Strengths and weaknesses revisited

The updated 1983 study gave the strengths of the Caribbean tourism industry as follows:

- year-round pleasant climate
- high-quality and attractiveness of the beaches in a tropical setting
- variety and standard of accommodation
- availability of a wide range of water sports activities

The weaknesses as described were:

- high prices
- inconvenient flight connections
- less-interesting supplementary attractions

The European consumer revisited

The European consumer to the Caribbean has traditionally been upscale, highly educated (more often than not to university level), from the liberal professions, self-employed or top-level salaried professionals, travelling, more often than not, with a partner.

Since 1979, there was a discernible change in the socio-economic characteristics of the European visitors to the region. By 1983, the shift from the higher-end social groups of thirty to sixty years of age was more pronounced than had been recorded earlier, to more middle-class younger tourists. Nevertheless, the predominant tourist group remained couples without children.

Establishing a Caribbean marketing presence in Europe

Many factors suggested that not only had the time come to intensify the Caribbean's marketing efforts in Europe, but also that a Caribbean marketing presence based in Europe had become urgent and essential. An important consideration was that the nature of the European tourism market was heterogeneous and the structure of the travel trade in the principal generating countries of the United Kingdom, West Germany, France, Switzerland and Italy, diverse.

The consultants recommended that a CTA office should be established with its headquarters in Frankfurt. This proposal was questioned by several people who felt that it should have been in London and wondered whether the proposal derived from the fact that the consultants were German. The consultants' arguments in favour of their recommendation were as follows:

- The traditional markets like the United Kingdom and France already had established ties and good air transport services to the Caribbean.
- There were, at the time, few visitors to the Caribbean from the non-traditional markets of Germany, Switzerland and Italy, although they travelled in numbers to the Caribbean's competition countries. These markets were therefore seen as having a great deal of growth potential.
- Germany is well located for servicing the needs of the German, Swiss, Italian markets, and convenient for the Benelux countries and Austria.
- The British and French markets could be served through representation on a smaller scale.

It was proposed that a pool of marketing specialists should be established in the Caribbean at the offices of the CTRC, with the objective of acting as the interface between the Frankfurt office and the member states of the CTA.

It was further proposed that a CTA European office would initiate a tourism marketing programme within the principal European source markets, concentrating on promotion to the trade, cooperative advertising, public relations and all aspects of product development, including air transportation. A full range of collateral materials for the regional tourism product was to be developed in the five principal languages – English, French, German, Italian and Spanish – for distribution to the European travel trade. The experts based at CTRC would concentrate in close collaboration with the CTA on such matters as product improvement, market research, specific research topics and general market development.

The European Commission now agreed to finance the implementation of the recommendations made with respect both to Europe and the Caribbean. Having these arrangements put in place for both the CTA and the

CTRC could be seen, it was argued, as the first step taken in bringing the two organizations together as one organization: the CTO.

Steigenberger Consulting GMBH, which had also executed the second European demand study, was contracted by the CTRC, with European funding, to establish the marketing project. The Steigenberger research team had been led by Bernd Bienek and included at one time or another, Gernott Ott and Werner Gersh, all of whom were later to serve as members of the product development team of experts based at the CTRC. This was to be the first in a series of national and regional tourism programmes funded by the European Commission in many of the African, Caribbean and Pacific states and the names of these same consultants appear and reappear as the implementers in the last two decades of the twentieth century and the first decade of the twenty-first.

Funding for the Frankfurt and Paris sub-offices was provided by the EEC for three years, 1984 to 1987, on the understanding that it would be sustained by Caribbean governments at the end of that period. The Caribbean governments were responsible for the maintenance of the London office, which was headed by an Englishman, David Barber, who before the end of the Steigenberger project was transferred to Frankfurt and replaced in London by Carolle Guntley, a former Jamaican director of tourism, assisted by Veronica St Louis of Grenada.

Through the operations of the Frankfurt office, many important contacts had been established for the first time with the non-traditional European tour operators, travel agents, airlines and other travel partners. Through them, the initial steps were taken to form a network of CTA chapters, beginning in Germany, Paris and London. Once formed, however, these chapters differed in structure somewhat from the traditional CTA chapters in North America – which were in fact quite separate organizations from the CTA and the membership of which largely comprised retail travel agents.

The membership of the European chapters comprised, not travel agents, but national tourist boards, tour operators, airlines, cruise lines and other suppliers who had products of their own to sell, and whose programmes constituted more direct involvement in putting business together than simply serving as "middle men". They saw themselves as equal marketing partners with the CTA. This was reflected in the integrated structure of the European chapters with that of the CTA offices. As a result of this situation it was constantly necessary to ensure – if a cliché may be used – that the tail was not wagging the dog.

Closure of mainland Europe offices in 1987

The year 1987 was rather traumatic for the CTA; the European funding, and with it the Steigenberger project, ended; and Palmer-Hawks, director general of the CTA, died at the untimely age of forty-four. For a short while a Dominican, Sylma Browne, acted as officer-in-charge until she was succeeded by a Barbadian, Markly Wilson, who served as director general until 1989. The London office survived these events, but the offices in Frankfurt and Paris did not. Caribbean governments were unable to continue to finance the German and French CTA programmes without the aid funds.

The European travel trade on the continent perceived itself as having lost momentum following the end of the programme, but the gap was filled, to some extent, by those national tourism offices, which existed in Europe working with the CTA London office and the CTA chapters to continue the regional presence and programmes.

Between 1987 and 1989, the CTA London office struggled on within the scarce financial resources of its membership, until two significant events occurred, in 1989 and 1991 respectively. In 1989 the CTA and the CTRC merged to become the CTO and in 1991 the CTO negotiated new funding from the EEC to support and strengthen the efforts of the new organization.

In November 1991, the CTO appointed Michael Youngman as its director of marketing international. Michael had served the CTA in many capacities while working in New York as the international marketing director for American Airlines. When that company moved its headquarters from New York to Dallas, Michael remained in New York where the CTO benefited not only from his marketing expertise, but also from the many contacts he had made while with American Airlines.

Through a comprehensive development programme the relationship between the EEC, the CTA and the CTRC had broken new ground in tourism aid. This programme was later to be duplicated in the African and Pacific countries of the ACP group.

7
The Creation of the Caribbean Tourism Organization

In 1976 the creation of a single Caribbean organization by merging the Caribbean Tourism Association (CTA), the Caribbean Hotel Association (CHA), the Caribbean Tourism Research Centre (CTRC) and the Eastern Caribbean Tourist Association (ECTA) had failed, largely because the private sector members of the CHA and the public sector members of the other three organizations had failed to reach agreement on a number of issues. This history was detailed in chapter 4.

In 1988, the idea of the Caribbean Tourism Organization (CTO) resurfaced among the directors of the CTA and the CTRC, this time excluding the participation of the CHA. In the period following the joint activities of the CTA and the CTRC in Europe (1979–87) it seemed that a good case could be made for merging the marketing activities of the CTA with the research and development activities of the CTRC. These activities complemented and supported each other because, from a macro strategic planning perspective, the merger would allow an integrated approach to managing an industry which had traditionally focused on marketing, to the neglect of adequate planning and research.

But there were other practical considerations. With the appointment of a Caribbean CEO and, from 1978, more Caribbean staff at the CTA office in

New York, the working relationship between the CTA and the CTRC had become closer. In developing the European market, the two agencies had worked almost as one body, with the CTRC giving leadership in both the statistics and research area, and in the negotiations for funding. Another positive consideration was the prospect of cost savings for governments. The CTA had a mixed board of private and public sector members, but the public sector members were invariably the same persons, now largely Caribbean, who were serving on the CTRC board of governors. A merger reduced the number of meetings needed, with attendant savings in costs for regional and international travel.

Perhaps more compellingly, the changing face of Caribbean economies, and the growth in the importance of tourism as a development sector, demanded more direction and control of its major tourism agency by those Caribbean policymakers based in the region. Over the years, the CTA had become an important and influential organization, with the government membership of thirty-four Caribbean countries and the private sector membership of many of the major travel and tourism persons and groups that operated in and to the Caribbean region. These persons and groups included, but were not limited to, the CHA, airlines, cruise lines, travel agencies, travel media, publishers of glossy and business magazines, and public relations and advertising companies. The 1972 CARIFTA report had spoken in terms of the need for Caribbean states to take control of their major economic sectors, including tourism. What better way to start than work to ensure that the leadership of the major regional tourism organization should be Caribbean and the policy-making process be located in the region?

Public and private sector divide on the new Caribbean Tourism Association

Understandably, this view was not shared by all of the CTA's US private sector members, who had dominated the US-based CTA since 1951. There was therefore some opposition from that quarter to a merger of the CTA and the CTRC. Further, it was believed that, even if the merger took place, the focus of the organization should be largely marketing, and its direction, location and headquarters be in the US marketplace.

It would be naïve also not to understand that, even as late as the 1980s, the factors of race and colour were never far beneath the surface in any discussion about who should be in charge of a major Caribbean tourism project or organization. The CTO would be the Caribbean's biggest tourism agency in existence, and traditional logic did not suggest that any black Caribbean person had the experience and know-how to lead it.

With respect to location, there were persons who genuinely saw the United States as the Caribbean's natural marketplace and saw many reasons why Caribbean tourism should be run from there and directed largely by the US private sector, which had a vested interest in tourism's success. Further, those persons did not anticipate the expansion to, and the growth in Europe, which for a number of countries was to become the largest market.

The differences between the parties ran deeper than that, however. Those in the marketplace were envisaging an enhanced marketing organization with a research agency attached to it to serve selected tourism objectives. The Caribbean leadership was looking for a tourism development agency that sought to make tourism the servant of development in the region and part of larger national strategic planning exercises. It was an organization of this latter kind into which international and regional development agencies could plug, and which they could support with aid funds. It is entirely possible that this divide still operates, to some extent, between the public and the private sectors in Caribbean tourism.

The negative discussions that broke out on every hand in 1988 revived shades of the 1976 discussions about merging the CTA, the CHA and the CTRC. Fortunately over the years there had also been important social and political development at the national level in the member states. Chapter 2 dealt with the social and political changes that took place in the Bahamas, resulting in the appointment of Baltrom Bethel as director general of tourism in that country in 1979. In 1988, Bethel was elected chairman of the CTA. Bethel was the ideal person to promote a merger between the CTA and the CTRC. The CTRC management therefore reopened the discussion with him.

A joint meeting of the CTA and the CTRC boards was held in the Cayman Islands in 1988 to discuss the matter. The then-CEOs of the two organizations were Markly Wilson of the CTA, based in New York, and Jean Holder of the CTRC, based in Barbados. It was decided at the meeting to establish a working group to create the proposal for a merger, including draft terms of reference and a draft constitution for the CTO.

When the working group reported, however, recommending the merger and presenting the draft terms of reference and constitution, serious opposition was ranged against the proposal to create the CTO by merging CTA and CTRC, against basing the new organization in Barbados, and against appointing Holder the first secretary general of the CTO.

Creation of the Caribbean Tourism Organization in 1989

In 1988, unlike in 1976, the Caribbean governments, led by Bahamian Baltron Bethel, president of CTA, and Jamaican Dr Marco Brown, minister of state for tourism in Jamaica and chairman of the board of directors of the CTRC, were committed to the merger and had no intention of having the process frustrated. A second joint meeting of the CTA and CTRC boards was held in January 1989, at Almond Beach Village in Barbados, and the decision was taken to merge the two organizations, thus creating the CTO. The organization was officially launched in a ceremony at the Frank Collymore Hall at the Central Bank of Barbados, where Bethel was confirmed as its first chairman of the board and Holder as its first secretary general.

Birth of the Association of Caribbean States

The CTO was later to play a key role in the creation of another pan-Caribbean organization. When, in 1994, a decision was taken by heads of government across the Caribbean Basin to create the Association of Caribbean States, the CTO, of which almost every Caribbean country was a member, was given the principal part in bringing the parties together. To assist in this process, Michael Manley, the former prime minister of Jamaica, was contracted by the CTO as a consultant, with financing from the OAS. Manley was the political figure known to have had a personal relationship with the heads of government of the wider Caribbean, including Cuba and Mexico. It is now a matter of record that his efforts were very successful. The CTO was thereafter declared a founding member of the association.

Cuba applies for membership in the Caribbean Tourism Organization

The Government of Cuba had been in the 1950s one of the early members of the CTA, but had given up its membership in 1960 after the Cuban revolution. In the 1980s the US embargo was in force against trade with Cuba, and the country found itself in a state of isolation, especially in the Americas, where the US influence was dominant.

By 1989 a great deal had happened, including the ending of Russian aid to Cuba, and Cuba was once again back on the tourism trail in an effort to earn the scarce and valuable foreign exchange the country so badly needed. US foreign policy was, however, ranged against any relief for Cuba from any source, and opposed to Cuba being given membership in any of the regional or hemispheric organizations, including the CTO.

The Cuban ambassador to Barbados, however, came to the Almond Beach Village hotel during the January 1989 meeting, and sought every opportunity he could find to speak to persons relevant to Cuba's goal of CTO membership, especially those ministers of tourism who were attending the meeting.

His remarks in seeking membership were memorable. He said, "This is the Caribbean Tourism Organization. My country, Cuba, which is very dependent on tourism is in the middle of the Caribbean Sea. To which part of the world would you like us to move our country? We have a right to be members of the Caribbean Tourism Organization."

His logic seemed irrefutable and resonated well with Barbados which, under the leadership of Prime Minister Errol Walton Barrow, had long been committed to a foreign policy of "being friends of all and satellites of none". In 1972 in the OAS forum, the diplomatic representatives of Barbados, Guyana, Jamaica, and Trinidad and Tobago had strongly defended their right to open diplomatic relations with Cuba, a position which was equally strongly opposed by the US government.

However, in 1989 the CTO ministers decided to place Cuba's application for membership of the CTO on their agenda for discussion and decision at a later date. It was not approved until 1991, at a meeting of the board of directors in Curaçao.

The decision to admit Cuba was important. It was a decision which might not have been made in 1991 had the organization been headquartered in the United States, with a US CEO. It underscored the fact that the creation of the Caribbean Tourism Organization had had significance beyond giving birth to an enlarged public and private sector organization. It was to be a place in which Caribbean sovereignty could be exercised in the region's most important economic sector, in a manner impossible if the countries were acting in isolation or if decision-making were in the hands of non-Caribbean people.

Defining relationships between public and private sectors

It is important to understand that the CTO, formed by a merger of the CTA and the CTRC in 1989, was a different kind of organization from the old CTA, based in New York and with a large private sector membership, whose interests – whether they were marketers, hoteliers, cruise lines, airlines or travel agencies, to name only five classes of private sector members – were confined to creating and developing business to the region.

The CTO, with its headquarters in the Caribbean, under Caribbean leadership and closely linked to a number of development agencies, had an expanded portfolio. This portfolio included social, cultural, environmental and economic impact issues which sometimes brought it into collision with its own private sector members.

In the 1990s the relationship between the CTO and the CHA noticeably deteriorated for reasons which will be addressed later. The fact of this decline does however suggest the need for some comment on the state of public and private sector tourism relationships generally.

The ideal arrangement, especially in tourism, is that the public and private sector should work closely together in the public interest. It is an idea that constantly returns to the table, however often it is tried and fails. Efforts range from attempts at close collaboration to actual mergers, as was tried between the CTRC, the CTA, the ECTA and the CHA in 1976. The reality is that people often underestimate the difficulties involved and the real reasons why success is so difficult to achieve.

Disagreements which arose from time to time between the largely public sector organization, the CTO, and the private sector association, the CHA, were seldom, if ever, due to personal antagonism between the leadership of the two organizations. In fact, the leaders came over many years to know each other well, to become personal friends and to give and receive mutual respect. The reality is this: private sector and public sector agencies have different constituencies and often different objectives which their respective CEOs are expected to pursue aggressively. Although there is an obligation, where they operate in the same space, to collaborate wherever possible, it is in the national interest that both sides, especially at the level of leadership, remember the real differences between their mandates.

The business of a private sector organization is to protect the interests of its membership and, where relevant to this function, make profits for the shareholders. The business of a public sector organization is to expand and protect the public good, which may or may not involve serving some particular interest of a private sector group. In fact, there are instances where the objectives of the public and private sector are in direct conflict. Moreover, where the membership of the private sector is largely expatriate, differences can be expected to arise, both from different interpretation of what is the public good, and sometimes from misplaced attitudes of disrespect for persons and things local. There are few areas of socio-economic development where these challenges arise as frequently and obviously as in tourism, where public and private sectors often differ on what is growth and what is sustainable development.

However, the search for solutions must always continue and the CTO over many years has sought to discover a modus vivendi with its two major private sector members, the CHA and the Florida Caribbean Cruise Association (FCCA) – which, incidentally, have themselves been serious competitors relative to each other, and at odds for a long time.

CTO's initiative for public and private sector cooperation, 2004

In June 2004, after a particularly difficult period in the public and private sector tourism relationships, the chairman of the CTO, Obie Wilchcombe, minister of tourism of the Bahamas, assisted by deputy chair commissioner Pamela Richards of the US Virgin Islands and CTO secretary general Jean Holder, convened a meeting of the CTO, the CHA and the FCCA in Nassau. The purpose of the meeting was to discuss a more strategic alliance between the three organizations and to lay the groundwork for future cooperation. These efforts continued even after the retirement of Holder at the end of 2004.

At the twenty-eighth Caribbean Tourism Conference, in October 2005, a memorandum of agreement was signed by four officials. Those persons were Richards, the commissioner of tourism for the US Virgin Islands and now the new chairman of the CTO; Dr. Charles Turnbull, the governor of the Virgin Islands; Berthia Parle, the president of the CHA; and Vincent Vanderpool-Wallace, who, as recorded in chapter 3, had just become the secretary general of the CTO. The memorandum set out fourteen areas of cooperation between the CTO and the CHA to reduce any duplication of effort between the two bodies.

The articles of the memorandum were as follows:

1. The tourism industry in the Caribbean functions best when both the private and public sectors work towards a common set of goals.
2. The CHA, being an Association of Associations, and recognizing that many of its constituent associations also represent non-hotel tourism interests, will be seen to be the principal regional representative of the private sector of Caribbean tourism and CTO will be seen to be the principal public sector representative and we wish our collaboration to be a model that our members can follow in their national jurisdictions.
3. We recognize that by reason of the differences in constituencies that we represent, there are, and will always be, some fundamental areas of natural conflict in style and focus between the public and private sectors. But we will acknowledge and respect those differences as long as they are not inimical to our long-term goals.
4. We will establish joint commercial projects as far as legally and constitutionally possible, and we will share the proceeds of those projects on a 50/50 basis, unless we agree to do otherwise and the alternative arrangements are agreed in writing.
5. We will establish a joint Annual Caribbean Tourism Summit (ACTS) to bring the highest focus on the needs of Caribbean Tourism to the attention of the leaders of the Caribbean and the leaders of our industry in both the public and private sectors.
6. We will cross promote attendance at all of our individual conferences by ensuring that some specific content of each conference has a clear appeal to the membership of the other organization.
7. We will develop and trademark a single Caribbean logo; we will have a common consumer web site that will be promoted jointly by both organizations and we will seek to have all of our members promote the site along with their corporate or national sites. Any new logo developed under this agreement, and any new

website "URL", or "URL's" will be equally owned by both organizations. The logo can be used by one of the two organizations only with the prior written approval of its counterpart hereunder. This restriction will survive the termination or expiration of this agreement. Also, upon termination or expiration of this agreement, both organizations will agree to remove the website from the Internet unless under mutually agreeable terms and conditions one of the parties to this agreement receives the right to maintain the site upon the expiration or cancellation of this agreement.

8. We will explore the possibility of having a single site for both our memberships and if that is not feasible we will look at the possibility of enabling members from each site access to the content of both members' sites.

9. In most of our commercial ventures, we intend, whenever necessary, to engage partners with the appropriate expertise in the relevant area to manage and execute the venture as an independent business with a contractual arrangement to compensate CTO/CHA for our direction/endorsement and for lending our Caribbean name to the venture. We will ensure that CTO/CHA have minimum or no liability arising out of the particular activity. All of these commercial ventures will be overseen by a joint Executive Committee comprising four members from each organization that must include the Chairman and President of CTO and CHA, respectively, and the Secretary General and Director General of each organization, respectively. Each Executive Committee will appoint two additional members from their respective Executive Committee for a period not to exceed two years.

10. In the area of external advocacy, especially in the United States and in the European Union, it will be necessary to deliver, jointly and separately, lobbying activities in a coordinated manner in order to enhance the development of Caribbean tourism. To this end, there will be regular exchange on matters of mutual interest and where appropriate, there shall be coordinated actions. The objective shall be to make the best use of resources, relationships and information flows.

11. For the purposes of developing annual business and operating plans, the Executive Committees of each organization will be treated as a common Executive Committee to enable full and complete input before our plans are presented to our respective Boards for ratification. We each understand fully, that each Board has the right to accept or reject any and all recommendations.

12. In order to establish the long-term recognition of our intent both symbolically and actually, CTO and CHA will engage a linchpin employee whose compensation and expenses will be covered by CTO/CHA on a 50/50 basis.

13. The ultimate intent of this collaboration is to provide the peoples of the Caribbean with ever increasing economic and social benefits from tourism and

to provide our membership with ever expanding services while keeping their membership contributions to a minimum.
14. This Memorandum of Understanding will remain in full force and effect unless modified in a manner agreed and approved in writing by both parties or terminated by either party with six months written notice and agreed disposition of any assets accumulated under this agreement.

Life has its ironies. It was not planned, but the memorandum between the CHA and the CTO was signed during the Caribbean Tourism Conference taking place at the same hotel, the Marriott Frenchmen's Reef in the US Virgin Islands, at which the talks of a merger between the CTA, the CHA, the CTRC and the ECTA into a CTO, had broken down twenty-nine years before, in 1976.

Creation of the Caribbean Tourism Development Company, 2007

By 2007, a joint CTO–CHA marketing agency called the Caribbean Tourism Development Company was formed. In 2008, Vanderpool-Wallace resigned as secretary general of the CTO to return to his native Bahamas as its minister of tourism. The development of the joint agency remained a work-in-progress, to be carried forward by the new secretary general of the CTO, Hugh Riley. He was appointed in 2009. During the period of 2009 to 2011, however, the promise of the Caribbean Tourism Development Company as envisaged was not fulfilled and, in fact, relationships between the CTO and the CHA, by this time renamed the Caribbean Hotel and Tourism Association, once more seemed to be strained.

However, in 2011 the CTO secretary general announced that the Caribbean Tourism Development Company would be resuscitated and would be fulfilling its mandate to be the marketing entity for the Caribbean. This function had been the intention when the Caribbean Tourism Development Company was formed in 2007. It was proposed in 2011 to:

- proceed with a plan to redevelop Caribbean Travel.com and hire a CEO for the Caribbean Tourism Development Company during the first half of 2012

- transition the assets of the CTO New York office to the Caribbean Tourism Development Company and bring an end to the CTO in New York, in its present form
- consider whether there should be any ongoing presence of the CTO in New York

The decision to close the CTO office in New York, if carried through, would end one of the region's most remarkable organizations. Its origins date back to 1951 and its framers brought together the tourism private and public sectors of every country in the Caribbean Sea, whatever its language or political ideology, in the cause of regional tourism and the development of the region's people. It will be far easier to bring an end to this institution than to replace it with something that will serve the larger interests of the people of this region and endure. We wait to see how these matters develop and strongly advocate that the Caribbean does not once again return to an era when it was not clearly understood that tourism marketing without serious investment in product development, human resource development and research is an exercise in futility.

In chapter 8, the spotlight will be shone on the FCCA, which in 2013 had already been a member of the CTA and its successor the CTO, for forty-three years. No history of Caribbean tourism would be complete without a comprehensive record of the history of the FCCA, its role and function in Caribbean tourism and an evaluation of the socio-economic and environmental impacts of cruise tourism on the Caribbean region.

8
The Role, Contribution and Impact of Cruise Tourism in the Caribbean

The World Trade Organization (WTO) 2003 study *Worldwide Cruise Ship Activity* explains the difference between the traditional transatlantic voyages and the modern cruise tourism activity, both in concept and business type. In the case of the former, the ship is conceived as transportation; with respect to the latter, which dates from about the early 1970s, the ship is conceived as accommodation.

Comparisons between the land-based and cruise product

The modern cruise ship, according to the referenced study, is a floating hotel or resort, with a central atrium, accommodation on various floors, ship's crew holding titles like "hotel manager", and resort services including, for example, swimming pools, interactive television, stores, library, golf courses, art galleries, business centres, cinemas and spas. Caribbean hotels, not surprisingly, were somewhat annoyed when a cruise line company ran an advertising campaign based on the theme that the last resort for a vacation should be a hotel.

There are therefore many similarities between the hotel and the cruise product, the significant difference from a land-based resort being the *mobility* of the floating hotel, a difference which is often used to great advantage by the cruise lines.

The fact that the cruise industry has moveable assets gives it a great advantage: ships can be based in any friendly port, which makes it possible for them to escape many of the taxes, duties, levies and other onerous expenses that land-based industries have to pay, by reason of their situation. Further, if any particular government comes to be regarded as "uncooperative", the cruise itineraries can be changed to exclude its destination.

From time to time, the question is raised whether cruise lines really need the destinations and could operate cruises to nowhere – passengers could be taken on a trip by sea without landing in any territory.

Studies have proven this premise to be false. Cruise itineraries and geographical location are important motivators for the passenger. Whereas it is true in theory that a ship, with all of its on-board activities and attractions, could be marketed as though it were a destination in its own right, this in practice can only be done on a limited basis. Over a period of time, cruise line companies have been made more and more aware by their clientele that destinations in the geographical areas in which they sail greatly influence the demand for a cruise holiday. In particular, they recognize that the major strength of the Caribbean is its year-round warm and salubrious climate, and its attractive natural environment, enhanced as a destination by its proximity and accessibility to the greatest source of cruise business – the United States. This perception was confirmed by a study carried out by the Cruise Lines International Association in 2008, which showed that the Caribbean remained in that year the preferred destination of cruise visitors (Holder, *Don't Burn Our Bridges*, 2010).

These advantages give Caribbean governments a bargaining chip – a chip which they have never fully exploited by negotiating with the cruise industry as a united regional force. The modern cruise industry has been built around the strength of the Caribbean product, as will be seen from what follows.

History of global cruise expansion

From the 1970s and 1980s, cruise tourism operated in the Caribbean largely with a North American clientele. In the 1990s the clientele spread to the United Kingdom and the rest of Europe and then to the Asia Pacific region. However, in 2000 when cruise demand reached almost ten million trips, North America still accounted for almost two-thirds of world demand.

The Florida Caribbean Cruise Association

The Florida Caribbean Cruise Association (FCCA) is a trade organization comprising fifteen member cruise lines. These lines operate more than one hundred ships in the region, bringing passengers who annually spend between 9 and 10 per cent of the US$21 billion of the foreign exchange earnings of Caribbean tourism. Cruise tourism is therefore of significant economic importance to the Caribbean. Much of the interaction between Caribbean countries and the cruise industry is through the FCCA, which is a member of the CTO.

The FCCA was created in 1972 and its mandate is to

- provide a forum for discussion on legislation, tourism development, ports, safety, security and other cruise industry issues
- foster an understanding of the cruise industry and its operating practices
- build cooperative relationships with its partner destinations and develop productive bilateral partnerships with every sector
- work with governments, ports, and all private and public sector representatives to maximize cruise passenger, cruise line and cruise line employee spending
- enhance the destination experience and the amount of cruise passengers returning as stay-over visitors.

The FCCA became a member of the CTA soon after it was created, but individual cruise lines had been among the earliest members of the CTA when it was created in 1951 and subsequently relocated its headquarters from Antigua to New York in 1955.

From 1951, the cruise industry shared a joint interest with the CTA, the New York–based regional marketing agency, in bringing visitors to the Caribbean, and was, in a sense, complementary to it, rather than competing with it. There was therefore little reason for conflict between them.

Relationship between the CTRC, the CHA and the FCCA after 1974

When in 1974 the Caribbean Tourism Centre, later to become the Caribbean Tourism Research and Development Centre was established, it was with a mandate not only relating to tourism research, planning, education and training, but also to seek to maximize tourism's contribution to GDP, foreign exchange, revenue and employment, and to minimize negative socio-cultural and environmental impacts. From the time of its founding, the organization began to ask the following questions about the cruise sector:

- What is the environmental impact of cruise tourism?
- Should cruise tourism, which makes large profits operating in Caribbean waters and utilizing Caribbean on-land resources, make an even greater economic contribution to Caribbean economies than it already does?
- Could the region exercise more and better control over the cruise lines with their movable assets, and if so, how could this be done?
- Why does the Caribbean, the world's best known cruise destination, itself not own a single cruise ship?

Land-based tourism organizations also argued that one of the ways in which the cruise industry's economic contribution to the region could be enhanced would be by increasing the per capita taxes on cruise line passengers, a fee which was then about US$1 or US$2. This argument met with serious opposition from the cruise lines, which, based as they were outside the region, would in fact often threaten to withdraw services from any country that decided to raise these specific taxes.

Caribbean relationships with the cruise industry became even more complicated when the CTA – the New York–based regional marketing agency – merged in 1989 with CTRC, the research and development agency based in Barbados to become the CTO.

The relationship of the CHA with the cruise lines was, from the beginning, somewhat adversarial because hoteliers saw the cruise lines' product as a major competitor with theirs, while not operating, in its opinion, on a level playing field. Cruise lines were perceived as operating "floating hotels", but were able to avoid paying many of the taxes and duties which land-based hotels and other tourism entities paid.

Outlook for cruise tourism in 2003

The year 2003 has been taken as an important base year for examining the cruise industry. It was in that year that Caribbean governments considered a proposal to fund their regional strategic plan by imposing a controversial per passenger tax on cruise passengers.

While the European market accounted for about two million trips and the rest of the world for a small share in 2003, the Cruise Lines International Association estimated potential demand in North America alone at some 43.5 million people over the next five years.

There were over US$14 billion worth of new ships on the order books in 2003. This fact indicated that the cruise lines had a great deal of confidence in the future of cruising and as the memory of 9/11 receded, could be expected, in a more tranquil world, to restart their aggressive programme of cruise expansion worldwide. In 2003, cruise lines were expecting high annual growth rates going forward and, prior to the global economic meltdown of 2008, were able to achieve them, even in difficult economic and geopolitical circumstances.

Capacity

From 1985 to 2000, North American cruise capacity had grown by 7.4 per cent per annum and continued to grow by 7.1 per cent per annum, to 234,200 berths, through 2005. While the new ships built during 1996–2000 averaged 1,505 berths, those built during 2000–5 averaged 1,914 berths. Most of these newer, larger ships were assigned to the Caribbean. As a result, the region received more passengers on fewer ships. Between 1997 and 2001, for example, while cruise passenger visits to the region *increased* by 23 per cent, the number of ships visiting these destinations *declined* by 0.6 per cent.

Repositioning of ships after 9/11

Prior to the terrorist events of 9/11 the cruise lines had embarked on an aggressive European expansion programme but had been forced by the reality and perception of insecurity in the Mediterranean after 9/11 to reposition a large number of their ships to the Caribbean and US ports. This shift allowed passengers, now more conscious about security than before, to drive, rather than fly, to the ports where they commenced their vacations. This, in turn, led to more itineraries and greater visitation to the more northerly Caribbean destinations, and fewer itineraries in the southern Caribbean.

Executive vice president Dean Brown of Princess Cruises announced in 2004 that their company would increase its capacity in the Caribbean by 75 per cent. The plan was to base its 109,000-ton Grand Princess in Galveston, Texas, and offer a seven-day western Caribbean cruise to Belize, Costa Maya, Grand Cayman and Cozumel. It was also proposed to start some itineraries for cruises out of Fort Lauderdale.

In 2004, Holland America Line based ten ships in the Caribbean, hosting 191 cruises in the region. Departures were all out of Baltimore, Philadelphia, and Norfolk, Virginia, however – all new ports for Holland America Line. The increasing use of US ports as base ports, however, was an important development, one which had important implications for Caribbean itineraries, as it determined which countries would be included and which excluded.

Cruising as competition to land-based tourism

It is clear from the data reproduced above that the Caribbean has been for many years the major area of operation of the cruise ship industry. This prompted the question, and increasingly so after the 1970s, to what extent is the industry in competition with land-based tourism, even to the point of doing it harm. The simple answer is, that as floating hotels, cruise ships were very much in competition with land-based hotels, and this fact was as a result of the cruise industry having adopted an aggressive marketing strategy which changed the image of what cruising was about and who were the cruisers.

In the early days of cruise tourism there was a stereotype of the cruise passenger as "old and rich", and the picture painted was that of old people sitting in the library and reading books, with blankets covering their knees, but these stereotypes are no longer valid.

Cruise line companies, especially Carnival, have worked hard at their marketing strategies to target anyone likely to choose a vacation of any kind and who have radically changed the demographics and psycho-graphics of those who cruise.

According to the WTO 2003 study, many cruise passengers are taking a cruise for the first time, and come from all segments of the population, especially in the more mature markets of the United States and Canada. The average age of cruisers was given as forty-six and, in the case of American cruisers, the average household income some US$50,000. They perceive a cruise holiday as good value, which results from the ability of the cruise lines to manage many aspects of the trip in a controlled environment, not least of all, their costs and security. (See appendix 2 for key cruise tourism statistics on passenger numbers, capacity, market-share, head taxes, port charges, provisioning and expenditure.)

Discounting in the winter seen as unfair competition

By 2003 and 2004, the changing strategies of cruise lines, and their expansion in the Caribbean, removed all doubt about modern cruise tourism being in direct competition with several land-based vacation products. It was targeting all segments of the travelling public, and providing attractive incentives to the travel trade to promote its products as a preferred experience. As far as the land-based hotels were concerned, the competition issue was exacerbated by this fact: many of the cruise ships' plans for expansion were scheduled to take place during the winter and spring. It follows that competition from the cruise lines becomes more fierce in the winter when, unable to operate in several temperate destinations, they not only return the majority of their ships to the Caribbean, but also offer heavily discounted prices at the very time period when land-based vacations are at their most expensive and therefore most uncompetitive. (This time period is the Caribbean high season, which runs from November to April.) Land-based tourism has thus always seen this as unfair competition.

In response to this situation, the cruise lines raised a number of counter-arguments to the criticisms offered, such as the following:

- the mere fact of competition cannot be held against them since all the various land-based vacation products compete against each other
- after 9/11 and indeed, after every other major political crisis, every type of tourism product resorts to heavy discounting, regardless of season, to survive
- a major and an important difference with a land-based product is that ships offer the visitor a virtual "fam trip" – that is, familiarization trip – around several destinations, and expose him or her to samples of various products in one trip, making it possible for the passenger to become familiar with an area and develop an interest in returning there for a stay-over land-based holiday
- land-based tourism practitioners often fail to take advantage of the opportunities offered them to convert cruisers into stay-over visitors
- unlike with land-based tourism, governments make no input into their marketing costs and their successes are due to their better management and marketing practices

The larger question which hoteliers have always called on governments to address is whether cruise tourism has built-in unfair advantages in competing with land-based tourism which result in negative consequences for national economies.

Growth comparisons

Cruise tourism in the Caribbean has grown faster than land-based tourism, increasing its relative importance. Between 1990 and 2002, cruise passenger visits grew by 5.9 per cent per annum, compared with 3.0 per cent for tourist arrivals.

After several years of gradual decline, from 58.4 per cent in 1987 to 45.8 per cent in 1999, the Caribbean's share of the total cruise capacity marketed out of North America grew to 48.5 per cent in 2002. In 2002, Caribbean destinations received 15.5 million cruise passenger visits, 4 per cent more than in 2001.

Economic impact comparisons

Cruise passengers spent an estimated US$1.6 billion in 2001, or 9 per cent of the US $19.4 billion spent by all visitors to the region. Cruise passenger expenditure varies widely between destinations, based mainly on the amounts spent on shopping. Although average spending per passenger visit was US$109 in 2001, this ranged from US$18 in Grenada to US$269 in the US Virgin Islands.

According to a study executed in 2001 for FCCA by PricewaterhouseCoopers:

- the ships' crews spent US$376 million in Caribbean ports in 2000
- cruise tourism generated an estimated 60,000 jobs in the region in 2000, of which 34,000 were direct and 26,000 indirect
- a typical cruise ship with 2,000 passengers and 900 crew members generated an estimated US$259,000 in total expenditure during a port visit

CTO forecast in 2003

Given the projected growth in capacity and the fact that the cruise industry had demonstrated its ability to fill its ships, the CTO forecast in 2003 that the Caribbean would retain its share of the cruise market, and that cruise visitation would grow to around 6 to 7 per cent per annum through to 2005. It was also of the view that, although the cruise industry had sought to diversify the range of destinations it serves, the Caribbean would continue to receive the major share of the cruise business marketed out of the United States. As was stated earlier, few competing destinations can offer the full set of advantages for cruising which the Caribbean has, such as close proximity to the US market, an amenable year-round climate, relatively short distances between ports of call, and a large number of ports permitting numerous itinerary variations.

In 2003, the CTO believed that the recovery in the cruise industry after 9/11 would be fast because past performance had shown that, after setbacks due to external factors – hurricanes and political instability being examples – the cruise sector has consistently been the first to rebound. This pattern is demonstrated by the figures given in table 8.1.

The region's highest ever share of the cruise market – 60 per cent – was reached in 1991, when the First Gulf War led to a substantial re-positioning of capacity to the Caribbean from other cruising regions. The turmoil in the travel market resulting from the Second Gulf War, economic uncertainty and SARS, contributed towards significant re-positioning of ships which benefited the Caribbean.

Table 8.1 shows that the six major cruise lines serving the region increased their Caribbean allocation by 13.4 per cent in 2003, while the capacity allocated to other markets increased by 2.5 per cent. Only one line, Celebrity, reduced its Caribbean allocation.

Private sector taxes and subsidies

Cruise tourism is not burdened by many of the costs which land-based tourism has to meet in creating its product. Those advantages are as follows: Many of the ships are built with considerable subsidies. Their recruitment practices, of largely non-unionized low-paid staff, lead to considerably lower personnel costs than would be possible on land. They are able to purchase many of their supplies from a wide variety of sources, free of tax and

Table 8.1 Major Cruise Lines: Capacity Deployment, 2003

Market		Carnival	Royal Caribbean	Norwegian	Princess	Celebrity	Holland America	Total
Caribbean	Capacity	2,094,584	1,713,612	379,392	343,200	346,554	274,084	5,151,426
	Share	82.4	81.8	44.5	43.1	52.4	45.6	68.2
	% change	18.2	14.5	25.4	7.0	−22.3	34.4	13.4
Other Markets	Capacity	448,840	380,766	474,020	452,438	314,278	326,648	2,396,990
	Share	17.6	19.2	55.5	56.9	47.6	54.4	31.8
	% change	−1.8	−8.9	10.4	−6.8	27.0	8.7	2.5
World	Capacity	2,543,424	2,094,378	853,412	795,638	660,822	600,732	7,548,406
	Share	100.0	100.0	100.0	100.0	100.0	100.0	100.0
	% change	14.1	9.4	16.6	−1.3	−4.7	19.1	9.7

Note: *Princess* and *Holland America* are part of Carnival; *Celebrity* is a subsidiary of Royal Caribbean.

at competitive prices. Finally, their movable assets give them a decided advantage when they negotiate with governments about anything, but especially about taxes and levies.

Both cruise lines and land-based tourism enterprises are subject to specific taxes. However, land-based enterprises find that, in addition to specific taxes on their industry, customers or both, their cost inputs are affected by all the taxes which are normally payable by anyone living and operating a business in a society. These taxes differ from jurisdiction to jurisdiction, but in some cases can be severe. There is therefore a continuous call from this quarter for a heavier tax burden to be placed on cruise tourism, one which would have the twofold advantage of leveling the playing field between competitors while generating income to be applied to tourism development.

Certain of the issues above have been cited by land-based tourism as unfair competition between them and the cruise lines, and from time to time – during, for example, the negotiations dealing with liberalization of trade in services under the General Agreement on Trade in Services and the Free Trade Area of the Americas – there has been talk of raising them. (See appendix 3 for examples of taxes in five different Caribbean States.)

Public sector concerns

In 2003 concerns were also being raised about certain aspects of cruise tourism which affected the public sector. While admitting that governments benefit from cruise tourism's visitor expenditure – the annual benefit, as noted above, is US$1.6 billion – and the employment it generates, there was a concern about the need for growing investment in port facilities to accommodate bigger and bigger ships, ships which carry more and more resort and shopping operations that compete with land-based facilities. According to the 2003 WTO study, "on board spending is an ever more important part of the cruise line revenue, with figures often reaching 35 per cent of total".

Increasing size was also held to have implications for negative environmental impact on the coral reefs, now being said to be suffering phenomenal losses. A *Travel Weekly* report of 26 July 2002 mentions a particular cruise line having been found guilty in 2002 of "discharging oil-contaminated waste and falsifying oil record books". Caribbean coral reefs were said, in a BBC News online environmental report in 2002, to have declined by 80 per cent in three decades, and while all the blame cannot be laid at the door of the cruise lines for this, some ships have, from time to time, been cited for poor environmental practices.

A pattern of bigger but fewer ships also meant more bunching of ships on some days and little business on others. There were also some cost issues. The International Maritime Organization projected in 2003 that increased security at ports would require a major expenditure. There was evidence of this fact. Local enterprises serving the cruise industry began to experience the need for increased insurance costs to meet the security standards now being demanded by the cruise lines.

Pros and cons of cruise tourism summarized

The annual expenditure of some US$1.6 billion by cruise passengers and crew members in the CTO member states makes an important contribution to local economies. Although it is based offshore, the cruise tourism industry has a strong on-land constituency which benefits directly from its existence. This constituency comprises largely taxi drivers, department stores, duty-free shops, local tour operators, handicraft shops and attractions.

However, Caribbean governments and suppliers face the reality that the cruise lines constitute a powerful oligopoly operating within their territories, but largely outside of their regulatory jurisdiction. Despite the many cruise brands operating under different names in the marketplace, and covering all the segments of the market, the four largest companies – Carnival, Royal Caribbean, P&O and Star Cruises – accounted for 72 per cent of the world supply of berths in 2003. Carnival by itself had, in 2001, a capitalization of over US$15 billion, a fleet of forty-six ships with more than 60,000 berths and annual revenues of US$3.78 billion. It has since merged with P&O.

The power of the cruise lines has often made it possible for them to avoid attempts by individual Caribbean countries to impose on them any regulations or fiscal regime that they think unreasonable or injurious to their bottom line. They have the option to move or to threaten to move their ships to other countries in the region or to other regions – a move which would have an immediate negative economic impact on the countries that would lose this business, and especially on those businesses that were identified above as the cruise line on-shore constituency.

The obvious Caribbean response should be to leverage their real assets of climate and geographical location, which make them the preferred destination of cruise passengers, together with a consolidated and unified Caribbean negotiating stance. The fact is that Caribbean countries have never found a way to manage such a response successfully. On the contrary, there have been occasions when a mere promise by the cruise lines to an individual country of a better deal, even if gained at the expense of another Caribbean country, has been enough to ensure a break in the governments' ranks.

The proposal of Caribbean governments in 2003 to impose a US$20 per capita cruise levy – it was to create a Tourism Development Fund for the purpose of implementing a sustainable tourism development plan – therefore became a real test case of the region's ability to achieve its objective by negotiating as a block. As will be seen, the region failed the test. However, it is important to step back a year from 2003 and examine in detail the specifics of the ambitious strategic plan which was created in 2002, at the direction of CARICOM heads of government, to point a direction for Caribbean tourism covering the first decade of the twenty-first century.

9

Creating a Sustainable Tourism Strategic Plan for the Caribbean

The previous eight chapters have traced the history of Caribbean tourism, first at the national level in those five countries which were seen as the region's earliest exponents of the industry, and then from the perspective of regional and subregional organizations involved, either directly or indirectly, with the development of land-based and cruise tourism in the Caribbean. The time span covered stretches back to the nineteenth century when governments, concerned about the negative economic impact of the emancipation of slaves on the sugar industry, looked for means of achieving economic diversification from sugar. This quest led, in some cases, to the banana trade and tourism industries, which developed by utilizing ships that transported bananas to carry passengers also.

The 1960s witnessed the expansion of tourism across the entire Caribbean after the Cuban revolution in 1959 and Cuba's initial retreat from international tourism. For a further two decades this growth was driven largely by the external private sector and bore few signs of physical planning or concern about the socio-economic, cultural and environmental impacts normally attendant on the industry. The result was that the expansion attracted a great deal of negative comment from several quarters, and initially failed to win the support of the newly independent governments and of the local planners and academics who expressed a preference for other types of economic development.

When, at the beginning of the 1970s, the CARIFTA Secretariat, led by the noted economist Secretary General William Demas, was considering how Caribbean economies could be transformed from their colonial state of dependency, one of the sectors examined was tourism. Close analysis of the industry found it wanting in many aspects, and recommendations for its improvement were published in the 1972 CARIFTA report.

However, since neither the CARIFTA Secretariat, nor the CARICOM Secretariat, which replaced it in 1973, had a tourism division, it was left to the national and regional tourism entities to consider the recommendations and see if they could be incorporated in their own respective agendas.

The public sector agencies, the CTA and the CTRC, which became the CTO through a merger in 1989, while not constitutionally a part of CARICOM, worked in the closest possible association with it and assumed responsibility for implementing many of the tourism recommendations contained in the CARIFTA report. However, the agencies operated at ministerial level and, not being part of CARICOM, had no direct access to the CARICOM heads of government, whose involvement and blessing were often critical to having major policy decisions implemented. Regrettably, tourism never appeared on the agenda of heads of government except in response to major crises which they thought had the potential to destroy the Caribbean tourism industry. Three such crises did occur between 1974 and 2001.

Global threats to Caribbean tourism

The first event which threatened to destroy the tourism industry was the energy crisis of 1974 and 1975. This event led in January 1975 to the public and private sector conference in Caracas, Venezuela, the theme of which was "The Present and Future of Caribbean Tourism". The conference was held under the chairmanship of Venezuelan president H.E. Carlos Andres Perez, to which heads of government were invited and some attended.

The next event was the second energy crisis and the First Gulf War from 1990 to 1991 after which heads of CARICOM governments met in Jamaica in 1992, under the chairmanship of Jamaican prime minister

Michael Manley, and agreed to the first major regional tourism marketing campaign. This initiative was strongly supported by Gordon "Butch" Stuart of the Sandals Resorts chain and by Robert Crandall, chairman and CEO of American Airlines, who each pledged US$1 million in support of the campaign.

The third event was the horrific terrorist attacks of 11 September 2001 on the United States, which were seen as creating the greatest crisis for international tourism ever. The CARICOM heads of government responded quickly to the crisis, and the CARICOM Secretariat convened a meeting of the boards of directors of both the CHA and the CTO in Nassau in December 2001 to examine what measures needed to be taken in support of the Caribbean tourism sector. Certain leading private sector hoteliers operating in the region also attended. The meeting was chaired by the Rt Hon. Hubert Ingraham, the prime minister of the Bahamas.

The Nassau conference took two important decisions as follows:

1. to raise US$16 million to mount what would be the second regional Caribbean marketing campaign, as an immediate and short-term solution to problems created by 9/11
2. to create, for the first time, a comprehensive regional tourism strategic plan which would include proposals for an annual regional marketing programme across many markets and a sustainable funding mechanism to meet the costs of implementing the recommendations

The short-term marketing programme was eventually launched jointly by the CTO and the CHA in 2003, after some inter-organizational controversies, the details of which are better left untold. The CTO was, however, given the responsibility for developing the strategic plan with the assistance of European consultant Victor Curtin. The plan was seen as embracing four steps:

1. defining the Caribbean area to be covered by the plan
2. reviewing Caribbean tourism performance, especially during the decade of 1990 to September 2001, preceding the events of 9/11
3. indicating priority recovery actions, in addition to the 2003 regional short-term marketing programme
4. defining long-term development measures and resource requirements post-9/11 up to, and including, the year 2010

The Nassau meeting may therefore be said to have set a tourism agenda for what was left of the first decade of the twenty-first century, 2002 to 2010, to be implemented by the region as a whole.

Geographical scope of the Caribbean tourism strategic plan, 2002

Although the decision on the plan was made at a CARICOM level, it was agreed that it should be developed covering the countries of the wider Caribbean, reflecting the CTO membership. This membership in 2003 covered some thirty-one island states scattered in the Caribbean Sea, and mainland territories that border that sea. Those islands were Anguilla, Antigua and Barbuda, Aruba, the Bahamas, Barbados, Belize, Bermuda, Bonaire, the British Virgin Islands, the Cayman Islands, Cuba, Curaçao, Dominica, the Dominican Republic, Grenada, Guadeloupe, Haiti, Jamaica, Martinique, Montserrat, Puerto Rico, St Barts, St Eustatius, St Kitts and Nevis, St Lucia, St Maarten, St Martin, St Vincent and the Grenadines, Trinidad and Tobago, the Turks and Caicos Islands, and the US Virgin Islands. The mainland territories were Belize, Guyana, Suriname and Venezuela.

The size of the CTO member states ranges from small islands like Anguilla (35 square miles with a population of 10,300 persons), and Montserrat (39 square miles with a dwindling population of 5,164) to the large island of Cuba (44,218 square miles and a population of 11,050,729) to the mainland territory of Venezuela (352,143 square miles and a population of 22,576,000) with varying implications for resources and economies of scale.

In looking at the strengths and weaknesses of Caribbean tourism, the CTO first examined the role played by the region's geographical location, history, ecology and weather. Obvious strengths were seen as follows:

- **Geographical location:** From the perspective of land-based tourism, the Caribbean territories are situated at the crossroads of the Atlantic and Pacific Oceans, with easy access to Europe and close to the major tourist markets of North America.
- **History and language:** Because of their colonial history, the official languages of the Caribbean territories are English, French, Spanish and Dutch, the languages of the major tourism markets. However,

given the rapid expansion of India and China as tourism markets, the Chinese and Indian languages will in the future challenge this assertion. It is interesting therefore that a number of Caribbean countries in the region, because of their history of receiving Asian indentured labour in the mid-nineteenth century, have had significant immigration from India and China.

- **Culture:** The peoples of Europe, Africa and Asia were brought together in the Caribbean with the native peoples of the Americas, creating a unique mixture of cultures that may be said to offer the world in microcosm.
- **Ecology and beaches:** With respect to its natural environment, the Caribbean Sea is home to about 29 per cent of the world's coral reefs, covering about twenty thousand square miles, most of which are located off the Caribbean islands and the Central American coast. As a result, the region has some of the world's most beautiful beaches.
- **Climate:** The tropical location of the sea helps the water of the Caribbean Sea to maintain a warm temperature, ranging, most of the time, from a low of seventy degrees Fahrenheit to a high of the mid-eighties, depending on the season. Such climate is excellent for sea bathing.
- **Territorial situation:** From the perspective of cruise tourism, the Caribbean region is the world's optimum cruise destination. Its territories are situated about one night's sail by cruise ship from each other, which has important implications for the scheduling of cruise ship itineraries. This advantage is further enhanced by a year round warm and salubrious climate which allows for operations twelve months of the year. In 1991, the Caribbean's share of cruise tourism was as high as 60 per cent of all bed days marketed out of North America, although it later fell for reasons which will become clear later in the book.

The following may be considered as weaknesses, however:

- An annual hurricane season, one that lasts officially from June to November (although the number of storms that occur each year differs), and which can be destructive both of built structures and the environment.

- The territories, especially given their small size, are now seen as potentially liable to the negative effects of global warming. Certainly, there have been several earthquakes during the first decade of the twenty-first century, which is an unusual occurrence.
- The area comprises largely an archipelago of beautiful island territories but their separation by water tends to make intra-regional transportation expensive and certainly more of a challenge than if the region were one connected land mass.

Unity out of diversity

One of the challenges posed in designing a common strategy for the region is the difference in size, population, resources, and in the level and stage of tourism development among so large a number of countries. This challenge also creates a compelling argument for regional collaboration between the CTO member states. The plan therefore sought to bring unity out of the region's diversity and to provoke the entire region to see itself as a single destination and brand, and to act accordingly.

Sustainable tourism development

Since the plan was being conceptualized at a time when the world was consumed by talk of what in fact comprises sustainable development, it was believed that any new tourism plan should accordingly seek to embrace sustainable tourism development principles.

In 1996, the secretary general of the CTO, Jean Holder, offered his definition of sustainable tourism development in a chapter he wrote in the book *Practicing Responsible Tourism: International Case Studies in Tourism Planning, Policy, and Development* (1996). Holder's chapter, "Maintaining Competitiveness in a New World Order", stated that sustainable tourism development has traditionally been addressed from an environmental perspective. Examples of this approach include carrying capacity, solid and liquid waste disposal, coastal pollution, erosion, water quality, deforestation, air pollution, and the protection of natural assets. More recently, the environmental perspective had been coupled with socio-cultural concerns. Holder advanced the view, however, that to be sustainable, Caribbean tourism, in addition to addressing the above, must also be profitable, competitive, safe, and acceptable to Caribbean communities, with Caribbean people sharing in its ownership, management and control. He made the following points:

- Global strategic alliances created under the New World Order – that is, as a consequence of globalized markets – have endorsed the philosophies of "survival of the fittest" and "marginalization" of the weak. The processes of deregulation, liberalization, free trade, privatization, and consolidation cannot, however, be taken in a vacuum as inherently good. They have obvious advantages, but they are often reactions to past problems caused by bureaucratic over-regulation, state control, and protectionism through tariff and non-tariff barriers to trade.
- There are some cases, however, where regulation is required, some protection is desirable, and some limits to privatization and other processes must be set. This system of protection must take place either to protect the weak, or because what may be regarded as gains from a particular process could also produce other consequences which have greater negative than positive effects overall. For example, complete deregulation of air transportation in 1978 resulted in a fivefold expansion of passengers travelling in the United States, but created an unstable financial condition for legacy carriers from which they have never recovered.
- Caribbean tourism-dependent states must develop alliances among themselves to provide the critical mass required to compete in a world of giants that have developed ground rules in their own interest.
- Short-term solutions which cede total control of the key industries in developing countries to foreign companies will ultimately lead to problems worse than those solved.
- Sustainability is threatened by potential negative environmental impact, escalating competition, an unprofitable hotel sector, loss of control over air access, significant levels of crime in some destinations, and the failure of local populations to benefit from the increased jobs and wealth likely to flow from better development of linkages between tourism and other economic sectors.

- By aggregating resources to tackle problems that are regional in scope, functional cooperation, both among the states and at the public and private sector levels, seems to be the key to future economic survival because it can lead to the creation of a competitive force.

The expansion of the definition of sustainable tourism development to include profitability, competitiveness, safety, acceptability to local communities, access by land and sea and significant ownership and control by Caribbean people was new, important and controversial. Indeed, the air access factor was seen by Holder as so overwhelmingly important that it was made the subject of the book *Don't Burn Our Bridges: The Case for Owning Airlines* (2010). The book develops a theme mentioned in *Practicing Responsible Tourism: International Case Studies in Tourism Planning, Policy, and Development* (1996), which states:

> Air transportation is an important instrument of trade, tourism, employment, defense and economic development. It is the very breath of life in the Caribbean region. Its role in making possible intra-Caribbean travel for social and business purposes is also critical and its absence would reduce the population of several small states to being virtual prisoners on their island. No set of countries, economically and geographically placed as are Caribbean countries, can depend solely on foreign carriers that understandably must take decisions about services, routes and schedules according to the best interests of their owners. These decisions will not, and cannot, always coincide with the best interests of the Caribbean states. Moreover, the Caribbean has seen major carriers that served the region disappear almost without a trace.

In the global economic meltdown of 2008 and 2009 these words came close to being prophetic.

Review of tourism performance, 1990 to September 2001

In the aftermath of the horrors of 9/11, almost every failure in the Caribbean tourist industry was being blamed on that event. Therefore, in developing the strategic plan in 2002, it was thought necessary to examine the performance of Caribbean tourism in the period prior to 9/11, and to determine what were long standing structural weaknesses and which impacts were, and which were not, a direct result of the 9/11 events.

Statistics given below will demonstrate that a certain decline in Caribbean tourism had begun prior to the terrorist attacks of 9/11, and that while world tourism suffered immediately after 9/11, the Caribbean region actually benefited, at least in the short term, from some of the fall out. This is often a feature of Caribbean tourism. In support of the view that Caribbean tourism was weakening before 9/11, the numbers speak for themselves:

- **Stay-over tourist arrivals:** Stay-over tourist arrivals to the CTO member states had increased by 59 per cent from 12.8 million in 1990, to 20.3 million in 2000, at an annual rate of 4.7 per cent per annum, which was somewhat in excess of the 4.3 per cent growth rate for world tourist arrivals over the same period.

    A decline of about 2.7 per cent took place in 2001, for which 9/11 was only partly responsible. An important contributing factor prior to 9/11 was the weakening of the US economy, an economy which is a major tourism source market for the Caribbean.

- **Cruise passenger arrivals:** The share of the region in cruise tourism marketed out of North America declined from a high of 60 per cent in 1991 to 48 per cent in 2000. Cruise line capacity was expanding exponentially, however. Between 1990 and 2000, the number of berths marketed out of North America had grown from 83,500 to 155,500, or an average of 6.4 per cent per annum, and according to the Cruise Lines International Association, contracts had already been signed for a further 94,000 berths by 2005, with a further 14,000 planned but not yet contracted.

- **Visitor expenditure:** In 2000, gross expenditure from stay-over tourists, cruise passengers and other same-day visitors, reached an estimated US $19.8 billion. In 2001 it was US$19.5 billion and in 2002, US$18.9 billion.

- **Market share:** The review also demonstrated some interesting features about market shares within the Caribbean itself; the Hispanic Caribbean, comprising Cuba, the Dominican Republic, the Mexican Caribbean (Cancun and Cozumel) and Puerto Rico was outperforming other language groups and between 1995 and 2000 had increased its share of stay-over tourists to the region from 47 per cent to 52 per cent. Somewhat concerning, was that all other regions had suffered declines in their share of market.

- **Market performance:** There was a general decline in the region's share of the US travel market, which had fallen from 57 per cent in 1990 to 50 per cent in 2000.

  In 2000, Canadian visitors, once a major source of business to a number of Caribbean countries, now represented only 6.1 per cent of total arrivals. Canada, where the value of the Canadian dollar had fallen substantially, was now a price-sensitive market, supplying business largely to Latin American and Cuban destinations. In 2001, Canada was replaced as the third largest market, by the intra-Caribbean market, which then represented 7 per cent of total stay-over business to the Caribbean.

  The intra-Caribbean market grew both before and after 9/11, which is explained later in this chapter.

  From the mid-1980s, Europe had been the region's fastest growing market and by 2000 represented some 26 per cent of total arrivals to the region as compared with 17 per cent in 1990. There was, however, a noticeable decline in the rate of growth in 2000, when European arrivals grew by only 2.5 per cent as major tour operators, particularly in Germany, gave notice of their intention to cease operating to several small Caribbean countries.

- **Tourist accommodation:** Between 1990 and 2000, the Caribbean tourist accommodation stock increased from 152,000 rooms to 252,000, but not surprisingly, nearly half – some 48 per cent – were now concentrated in Cuba, the Dominican Republic and the Mexican Caribbean. Aruba, the Bahamas, the French Caribbean, Jamaica, Puerto Rico and specific niches in Barbados, such as the Villa market, also showed significant growth. However, in the Eastern Caribbean during this period, there was little new investment in the accommodation sector.

The business outlook for the Caribbean in July 2001

Public and private sector tourism industry officials, meeting in Barbados in retreat in July 2001 – three months before 9/11 – issued the following statement: "The industry is facing a serious crisis, experiencing a slow summer, increasing layoffs, temporary closures of hotels, falling market shares, reduced airlift from Europe, an uncertain US economy and a growing recession mentality that needs short-term solutions as well as a longer range plan of action."

In 2001, therefore, apart from 9/11, the Caribbean had real reason to be concerned about its performance. The US economy was beginning to recover, but the threat of recession had not quite gone away, and what was needed in that market was sustained growth. Europe, with the exception of the United Kingdom, was experiencing economic difficulties, unfavourable exchange rates and tough competition.

The pre 9/11 situation may therefore be characterized as follows:

- **Land-based tourism:** The decade of the 1990s had witnessed growth in competition to the Caribbean's land-based tourism, both from old competitors like Hawaii and Mexico, and from new competitors like Dubai, Mauritius, and from many states in the United States which had formerly been considered more as markets for the Caribbean than as competing destinations.
- **Cruise tourism:** Prior to 9/11, the cruise industry had begun to diversify out of the Caribbean, with new itineraries to Europe. As was seen in the previous chapter, the issue with cruise tourism was somewhat complicated by the fact that the Caribbean sought to extract from the sector the maximum economic benefit, largely by taxation. This approach was to take place while ensuring that the expansion was not to the detriment of land-based tourism, which was responsible for 90 per cent of the visitor expenditure in the region. Caribbean governments therefore trod carefully around any policy likely to result in the reduction or termination of cruise traffic, which clearly benefits major constituencies like the duty-free businesses, the usually vocal vendor communities, and those ground tour operators who supply both tours and other attractions widely used by cruise passengers.
- **Nature of tourism investment in the Caribbean:** A number of characteristics could be identified with respect to investment, especially foreign direct investment, in the Caribbean hotel industry:

    1. It was skewed in favour of the Hispanic Caribbean.
    2. Both in the Hispanic Caribbean, and in other Caribbean places, such as the Bahamas and Jamaica, investments were being made largely in places where large hotels were located.

3. It tended to be missing in the smaller destinations, places which relied on smaller hotels. Many of these hotels were in the Eastern Caribbean and continually in financial trouble.

- **Air access:** In 2000, a number of European carriers and tour operator companies decided to discontinue service to a large part of the region. The Caribbean countries consequently saw, probably for the first time, the danger of almost all of the carriers connecting them to the European market being owned by foreign companies. Decreased airlift from such markets as Germany had served to reduce the Caribbean's business in mainland Europe. Major tour operators from continental Europe had all but ceased to operate to the Caribbean, except for operations with Cuba, the Dominican Republic and Jamaica. This situation made the Eastern Caribbean particularly a victim of these circumstances.

  The Eastern Caribbean and Jamaica were fortunate in having the Caribbean carriers, with Air Jamaica and BWIA still operating on both sides of the Atlantic. It became clear that the decisions of airlines to come or go were made in board rooms in which Caribbean decision-makers do not operate.

  The intra-Caribbean routes had an adequate quantity of local services, but from 1999 the intra-regional carriers were involved in suicidal fare wars, and competition in which many more seats were on offer than were passengers. They were all surviving by receiving subsidies from their various shareholders, whether of the public or private sectors, to make up the difference between the cost of operation and the revenues. For all these reasons, the quality of service suffered. Ultimately, they began to go bankrupt, one after the other, until there were few carriers left. Initially, from a passenger perspective, there were plenty of seats and the fares were at an all-time low, which would have assisted growth in the market, assuming other strategies had been put in place.

- **Functional cooperation in air transportation:** In 1993, the CTO contracted consultants to execute an air transportation study. It recommended as a solution to some of the region's air transportation problems a plan for functional cooperation between all the Caribbean-owned carriers, both long haul and intra-regional. The plan was, however, never implemented, and eventually in 2007, two of the surviving intra-regional Caribbean carriers, Caribbean Star and LIAT, started merger negotiations. These negotiations ended with the latter carrier taking over the assets of Caribbean Star, which then ceased operations.

- **Airport safety and security:** Up to 2001, none of the airports in the CARICOM subregion had Category One status, which meant they did not satisfy the International Civil Aviation Organization safety oversight standards. Those Caribbean-owned airlines operating out of these airports could therefore not extend any services they already operated in the United States or make new interlining and codeshare arrangements with US carriers.

Impact of 9/11

Since Caribbean tourism was already deteriorating prior to 9/11, its condition was intensified by that event accordingly, and the impact was worse on those countries which depended heavily on the US market, in some case for between 60 and 80 per cent of business. All flights from foreign carriers into the United States were suspended for an entire week following 9/11. Estimates of the average decrease of global visitor flows during that period were approximately 30 per cent in the US market and 11 per cent to 12 per cent in Europe.

Decreases in the Caribbean intensified the number of employee layoffs and the closures of properties and enterprises that were already happening prior to 9/11. Caribbean governments post-9/11 were faced at one and the same time with reduced revenues and with multifarious claims from almost every subsector in tourism for increased budgetary support. These funds were alleged to be needed to reverse the effects of the crisis. A reduction in government fees, levies and taxes was also requested.

The CTO was asked by governments to put a figure on the costs to the region of this disaster. It found it comparatively easy to obtain information from airlines and cruise lines. It was almost impossible to acquire useful information from the hotel, amenities and attractions subsector. This problem sent a message that adequate systems were lacking to track, on an ongoing basis, information on hotel occupancy levels, pricing and financial performance – information necessary not only to deal with crises when they occur, but also for forecasting, forward planning and reacting swiftly, on an everyday basis, to changes in our market environment.

Impact of 9/11 on airlines

The acute fear-of-flying factor after the 9/11 attacks was most pronounced in the United States, but it was also present to a lesser extent in European countries, especially those countries seen as major allies of the United States in the war on terror. This fear immediately reduced airline traffic to about two-thirds of what was normal for that time of the year.

This put great financial pressure on airlines, especially US carriers serving the region, to the point of endangering their long-term viability. American Airlines, for example, which was then responsible for about 70 per cent of US travel to the Caribbean, had reported losses of US$525 million before 9/11. After 9/11, AMR, the parent company of American Airlines, reported a further net loss of US$414 million in the third quarter, despite a bailout from the US government of half a billion dollars.

United Airlines reported a third-quarter loss of US$1.16 billion, the worst in its seventy-five year history, and the CEO notified staff that the airline could perish if the hemorrhaging of cash did not stop soon. Canada 3000, Canada's second largest passenger airline, ceased operations, effective 9 November 2001, citing the impact of 9/11 and problems finalizing a deal with its unions. It had promised it would restructure and proposed to cut 1,500 staff and make a 30 per cent reduction in capacity.

Sabena and Swissair had already gone out of business. Caribbean carriers, without benefit of the government bailout which US carriers had received, were experiencing severe cash flow problems. Like European and Latin American carriers, they felt that the US bailout had placed the US carriers at a serious competitive advantage.

All carriers were affected by both the increased cost of security and the escalating cost of insurance, which in the case of BWIA, for example, went from about US$40,000 annually to about US$3.2 million. In addition, some Caribbean governments had to provide guarantees for the insurance coverage against terrorist attacks on their national carriers. In the case of Air Jamaica, the Jamaican government was called on to guarantee a sum of US$750 million and to hope that it was never called upon to deliver on such a promise. Not for the first time, those Caribbean governments that owned airlines were concerned that they alone were bearing a burden for regional carriers that provided a vital service to many other Caribbean countries.

Needless to say, the need for increased security at airports and seaports led to increased costs to the governments of the region. It also meant the slowing down of the facilitation of passenger traffic and the shipment of cargo.

Impact of 9/11 on cruise lines

Micky Arison, the chairman and CEO of Carnival Cruise Lines and the then-chairman of the FCCA, was reported in *Cruise Industry News* as saying that five or six weak cruise lines might not survive in the market as it was after 9/11.

Carnival's other brands, such as Holland America Line, Windstar Cruises, Cunard Line, Seabourne Cruise Line and Costa, were all scrambling to change itineraries away from ports considered to have high terrorist risks and away from regions where Americans may not want to travel for the rest of 2001 and in 2002. In fact, all cruise lines fled the Eastern Mediterranean and repositioned ships largely to the northern and western Caribbean region, including the Mexican Caribbean, and to those US ports to which Americans could drive.

Cruise lines were offering large discounts and paying travel agents commissions as high as 20 per cent to serve as incentives to sell cruises.

Impact of 9/11 on tour operators and wholesalers

Tour operators and wholesalers – who package business and supply the vast majority of customers to the region and who operate on tight margins – began to feel the squeeze from reduced traffic. A great deal of their money is made from money management, holding money and paying accommodation establishments for their allocations in arrears. There was a fear that some operators might go out of business, owing hotels significant sums of money. Tour operators and wholesalers therefore bargained for heavily discounted rates, which the hotels were willing to accept rather than lose business in a falling market. From the perspective of the hoteliers, it was hoped that this situation would not continue throughout the 2002 winter season. For while it did help to maintain the level of employment, it also led to a difficult financial situation as the year progressed.

Benefits of 9/11 to Caribbean tourism

The picture painted above about the state of Caribbean tourism both prior to and immediately after 9/11 is not a pretty one. But it must be admitted that the horrific events of 9/11, after the initial hit from which all countries and persons suffered, may actually have benefited Caribbean tourism in a number of ways. It certainly gave the industry some respite from which to recover some of the ground it had been losing to competition, competition that prior to 9/11 was beginning to outclass the industry in terms of both product and marketing power. Because of 9/11 the Caribbean tourism industry began to regain advantages:

- Those major competing destinations with high-end quality products in the Middle East, Asia and the Indian Ocean were now less attractive to travellers, as the places were perceived areas of insecurity, with some being places were travel was not an option.
- Certain US destinations had become less attractive for domestic travel, and the United States itself had experienced some considerable decrease in traffic from European visitors, some of whom were already being persuaded to go instead to the Caribbean.
- Because of the decrease in passengers, airlines had more spare capacity and were looking for a place to use it, if they could fill it.
- The fear of flying, which had become acute in the United States, favoured destinations like the Caribbean, which was close to the United States but nevertheless perceived as safe.
- Advertising rates had never before been so competitive.
- In the years that followed 9/11, the world was afflicted in quick succession by such acts of God as the SARS epidemic, mad cow disease and tsunamis. This situation gave the Caribbean a breathing space in which to address new competitive strategies, although everyone knew it was only a matter of time before the competition, especially from new destinations in the Middle East, would return.

It was therefore important in 2002 for the region to address the issues – and to seek to implement, as soon as possible, the mandate for a regional strategic plan issued by the CARICOM heads of government in December 2001.

New approaches required in Caribbean tourism

The region had found itself in 2000 at the bottom of a bust cycle. But more importantly, it perceived that the industry was changing from a meet-and-greet mode to one with an emphasis on scientific analysis, research and information technology. Several persons voiced opinions on whether the Caribbean was prepared to compete in such an environment. The call now was for a radical re-engineering of the Caribbean tourism industry.

The point of the proposed strategic plan was to bring a far more strategic approach to all its programmatic activities, setting clearly defined goals, whenever possible, in quantitative rather than qualitative terms, and institutionalizing processes to monitor success and failure.

One of the realities the region had been forced to face was this: when the crisis of 9/11 struck, the region had been caught gathering, on an ad hoc basis, for the purpose of providing answers to the same crisis, information which should have been easily available from existing systems. More will be said later about this failure when we speak about information management.

Following the performance review it was decided that the regional strategic plan should address ten critical issues to regain lost ground. It established a tourism action programme and related goals for the region which in 2013 remained a work in progress. The critical issues on which it was suggested that a sustainable Caribbean tourism industry must be built are as follows:

1. product quality as widely defined
2. investment climate and strategies
3. affordable and efficient air access to and from markets and on intra-Caribbean routes
4. airport safety and security
5. maximizing the economic benefits of cruise tourism
6. designing and implementing modern up-to-date information management systems
7. effective marketing in old and emerging markets
8. relevant human resource development
9. institutional strengthening
10. funding

Analysis of review findings

What follows below is a review of the state of Caribbean tourism as it was in 2000 in respect to the ten key areas cited above.

Issue 1: Product quality as widely defined

Accommodations: The Caribbean has always offered a varied accommodation product, varying not only from country to country, but also from one subregion to another. The fact that the construction of hotels in the Spanish Caribbean outdistanced that in the rest of the region and that the competitive nature of their pricing accelerated growth in visitors was seen as resulting from a completely different cost structure, available in some countries but not others. Costs tend to be lower in the Hispanic Caribbean. However, if the Caribbean is taken *as a whole* for 2000 a number of aspects remained the case for all accommodation:

- Seventy-five per cent of the total accommodation stock comprised small locally owned hotels with one hundred rooms and under. Most of the hotels in the Eastern Caribbean fitted this description, but there were important differences among them. Some small properties were successful boutique hotels, with great repeat business. These small luxury properties, known for their personal touch and service, commanded rates in considerable excess of resort or business hotels in many parts of the world; others were undercapitalized with a high ratio of debt to equity, and often unwilling to take partners on board. This had resulted in their being unable to refurbish, expand, manage or market themselves to the extent desirable. They had therefore few amenities, inadequate service and were seen as somewhat overpriced.
- The most successful hotels were large upscale foreign-owned hotels or locally owned all-inclusive hotel chains. Regrettably many of the smaller countries lacked the famous hotel brands which have the resources and the marketing reach to sell both their properties and their destinations.
- Given the high costs of inputs into the industry – including costs of land, labour, imported goods, high costs of protected local goods, direct

and indirect taxes and levies – hotels of all types and sizes in the majority of Caribbean countries perceived that their high start-up costs and operating costs put them in a non-competitive position versus the external hotel competition. Such hotels believed themselves further disadvantaged by the competition offered by cruise companies, which, as has been described above, were able to avoid many of the costs for which hotels are liable.

- Most of the room stock was being sold through tour operators or wholesalers who largely determine the price obtained by the majority of properties. Many of the hotels had little bargaining power, especially as the concept of joint approaches was weak. Some hoteliers were fortunate to negotiate deals in which they and the tour operator were partners, and therefore a consistent level of business was guaranteed. Discussions about establishing Caribbean tour operating companies had always come to naught due to fear of reprisals from existing foreign operators.
- The quantity, type and terms of financing available to the sector in the region, from the commercial and even some development financial institutions, were largely unsuited to the needs of the hotel sector.
- The most frequent complaints from visitors about the amenities in or out of hotels had to do with quality of service and high prices.
- Although Caribbean restaurants had gained a reputation for excellent food, Caribbean cuisine was not being exploited as much as it could be.
- It was perceived that increased competitiveness would depend on the region's ability to diversify its product to respond to a variety of niche markets, and to reach them by innovative means.

Tourist attractions: Tourist attractions worldwide – apart from natural phenomena, man-made wonders of the world and heritage and cultural relics – comprise a host of activities, such as sports, festivals and entertainment of all kinds. These are activities with which it is difficult, but not impossible, for small countries to compete.

Mature destinations, especially those in the United Kingdom and mainland Europe, are rich in history and proud of their own culture, and have always understood the economic value of tourist attractions. Castles, palaces, museums, *inter alia*, have always earned their keep and more.

The United States, a relatively late comer in tourism when compared to Europe, has caught up, using all the ingenuity and creativity which wealth can buy. What does not exist naturally or historically in the United States can be built.

The Caribbean's reputation as a tourism destination has been built on its sun-sea-and-sand product and with good reason. Fifty-seven per cent of those polled by the CTO in the 1990s gave sand-sun-and-sea as their major reason for choosing a Caribbean holiday, and it is doubtful that the percentage has changed much since then. Its tourism reputation had been founded on the understanding that it offered, more often and better than any other place, the opportunity to do nothing but lie in the sun on the world's most beautiful beaches, take the occasional dip in the sea, retreat to the shade for a drink and a nap in the afternoon, dine well in the evening, the most strenuous physical activity for some being partying until the early hours of the morning. Traditional Caribbean tourism was certainly not closely associated with cerebral or spiritual activity. Far too little emphasis had traditionally been put on the development and exploitation of tourist attractions except as extensions of the sea-sun-and-sand product. The CTO had for many years discussed with its member states what comprises a tourist attraction and what is required to turn an interesting natural phenomenon into a marketable product. Moreover, the region had also tended to underestimate the value of its own considerable historical, cultural and natural resources, especially to a European clientele.

Changing demographics and psychographics of visitors have, however, forced the region to offer far more activities with which to occupy the time of visitors, to entertain and to educate them. This change has the additional benefit of enticing visitors to travel more widely at the destination and to spend more money across various communities in each country.

The challenge was to identify both the funds and the creative resources needed to fashion attractions that would draw clientele on a sustainable and profitable basis.

Infrastructure: Despite its resource constraints, the Caribbean has an infrastructure that surpasses that of many of the developing countries of the world. This achievement can be placed squarely at the feet of tourism, which has been a great motivator of infrastructural development in the region, a factor which has benefited both local residents and visitors.

However, the review process still drew attention to some of the infrastructural areas to which Caribbean countries needed to pay more attention:

- the poor state of roads in rural areas
- the high cost of water and energy
- the high cost of communications, strictures on use of telephones for long-distance calls, and outrageously high cost of telephone calls in hotels (these complaints were made, of course, before the more recent widespread ownership and use of the cell phone in the region)
- the growing problems of disposal of waste by both locals and visitors
- inadequacy of pavements for pedestrians and of arrangements generally to accommodate persons who are physically challenged in any way
- failure to beautify public places which could be done at reasonable costs and with the help of the private sector and the communities
- airport and seaport structures in some countries that fall below the expectations of the users in respect of convenience, comfort, cleanliness and facilitation. Entry points were frequently inadequately manned at peak times of arrival and immigration, and customs officials were thought not always to be as courteous and enabling as they might be.
- E/D (emigration and disembarkation) cards with a core of common information, remained an elusive objective and too often were not available at times and places expected
- the arrangements for shopping and financial facilities at air and sea ports, especially targeting both departing and arriving passengers, needed to be greatly improved

The environment as a key component of product: Tourism is environmentally dependent and environmental mistakes can show up in the bottom line. It was felt, therefore, that in addition to any new ideas about sustainability, the tourism strategic plan should be fully aware of, and take into consideration, the concepts of sustainable tourism development that were concretized as a result of the Rio Summit Conference in 1990. Some of the ideas flowing from Rio were as follows:

- Global concepts about environmental and health matters have led to a body of international standards and regulations, which, if breached,

not only attract penalties, but can also lead to loss of business. Participating in such programmes as Quality Tourism for the Caribbean, Green Globe and Blue Flag, are now seen as necessary, rather than desirable.
- The changing nature of tourism into a more activity-led mode – what may be called an "off-the-beach mode" – required countries to be more aware of the health and safety hazards that can await a visitor in the formerly un-trodden interior of a country.
- Due to the reappearance of certain communicable diseases long thought obsolete and to the lethal health hazard of HIV/AIDS, health issues now hold a central place in planning sustainable tourism development.
- Issues of traveller safety, security and health were among the key drivers of tourism business, and worrying signs of increased crime and harassment in the region needed to be addressed frontally and immediately.
- Increasing the scope and depth of community tourism was likely to make tourism safer and more acceptable. There is some logic in the argument that a community which benefits significantly from various tourism economic and social linkages would also be motivated to be guardians of the quality and integrity of the industry.

As a result of all the above, it was thought that any action programme going forward should include

- creating public awareness of both the positive and negative impacts of tourism, in particular, sensitizing the public about the real dangers of unhealthy practices, including unprotected and indiscriminate sexual behaviour
- creating policy, legal and regulatory frameworks and standards that ensure balanced development and prevent the irreversible damage that is often derived from lack of planning
- avoiding undue pressure on sites and attractions due to lack of regulation and management
- avoiding unplanned land development, poor conservation, and use of scarce resources
- minimizing diffusion and bastardization of cultural forms

- legislating building standards that respond to the various hazards of the local environment
- proper management of the waste created by both visitors and the local populations

Issue 2: Investment climate and strategies

It was thought that the drafters of the plan should be fully cognizant that the required improvements in superstructure, infrastructure and marketing activities involved high capital costs. Serious thought would therefore have to be given to how, for the Caribbean environment, the attracting of both local and foreign investment could be significantly improved.

In looking at investment, the CTO revisited a 1997 investment study which had been carried out for it by the Commonwealth Secretariat. This study had come up with some interesting findings and preconditions for investment, among which were the following:

- In 1997 the region was thought to require about US$3 billion to US$4 billion annually to meet the need for growth of new accommodation and attractions, and refurbishment of existing facilities. Translated into 2013 figures a far greater sum would be required.
- Gaining access to this kind and level of investment even then was being frustrated by high operating costs and taxation, both of which reduced hotel profitability and returns on investment.
- An industry that is either a growing industry or competitive industry, both of which provide opportunities for investment, was a precondition for investment.
- A favourable investment climate with macroeconomic stability, positive policies towards the tourism sector and attractive investment incentives was necessary.
- The need for adequate infrastructure was self-evident.
- Effective promotion and investment facilitation were necessary.
- There had to be less state bureaucracy in dealing with investors.
- Clear and transparent policies on incentives available to investors were needed.
- Access to local sources of capital, such as insurance and pension funds – then largely off limits to tourism entrepreneurs – should be facilitated.

- Commercial and development banks must be changed to a development mode of lending.
- Special funding mechanisms suited to the special needs of the tourism sector needed to be created.
- Specialized investment promotion institutions needed to be created by the public and private sector dedicated to the business of procuring investment.
- Government needed to frame policies which clearly recognized the special role of tourism in Caribbean economies.
- An adequate return on investment was most important. The study felt that investors needed to secure at least a 15 per cent return on investment, which was available in other regions, but not in a number of the Caribbean countries.

Overall, it was believed that the region's governments, financial institutions, and hotels needed to devise ways of improving profitability, new avenues of access to finance, especially for the small hotel sector, and ways to mobilize regional capital. This later was important, as it would reduce the dependence on foreign capital investment.

Issue 3: Affordable and efficient air access to and from markets and on intra-Caribbean routes

The events of 9/11 underscored the critical importance of air transportation to the Caribbean archipelago. The events dramatized the reality that the Caribbean was dependent on foreign carriers for its communication with the external world, and for the pursuit of its major development activity: tourism. Immediately after the crisis some of these carriers sought financial and other assistance from Caribbean governments. The crisis also demonstrated, as never before, the need to have at least some carriers owned and controlled by the region, carriers which could be deployed as necessary in a crisis.

The review recognized the need to continue strengthening relationships with foreign carriers, but saw as a priority the creation of a strong and viable Caribbean air transportation system to supplement the services being provided by the external carriers. Caribbean carriers were called on to work more closely with each other and to return to the blueprint for cooperation detailed in the CTO Functional Cooperation study.

Issue 4: Airport safety and security

It was acknowledged that everything possible must be done for airports and airlines in the Caribbean region to gain or, in some cases, regain Category One status, and for the region's civil aviation authorities to be strengthened.

Issue 5: Maximizing the economic benefits of cruise tourism

Prior to 9/11, there had been calls in some quarters for the governments to take a stronger stand with respect to the industry, and to reach agreement on the imposition of higher taxes on cruise lines. There was a minority and even more extreme point of view that cruise lines should only be permitted to operate in the Caribbean on the basis of a franchise, one to be sold to them by governments at great cost, and that they should be made to bid for the privilege.

However, immediately after 9/11, a much softer approach was thought to be desirable. The new thinking was that governments should work more closely with the cruise lines with the goals of arresting declining market shares; mitigating the trend towards larger ships, a trend which was putting pressure on existing port facilities; implementing new programmes to convert cruise visitors to stay-over visitors; and increasing the regional sourcing of supplies, services and employment. It was believed that the cruise lines, along with other members of the private sector, might be persuaded to contribute voluntarily, along with governments, to a tourism development fund, the details of which follow.

Issue 6: Designing and implementing modern up-to-date information management systems

Of the ten critical areas that needed to be addressed in the strategic plan it is possible that information technology and research could be said to have been the weakest area in national and regional tourism planning. Going forward, therefore, there was the need to focus on exploring the various uses of the Internet and generally to improve the research and statistical tools accessible through electronic information systems.

The Internet: The Internet was seen as the new major force in tourism. It is described as "the global network of networks of interlinked computers, operating on a standard protocol, which allows data to be transferred between them". The Internet originated in 1965, but it was only in the early 1990s that it became the buzzword in communication and information services. The communications services included e-mail, e-mail-based discussion lists and net news. Those information services such as Telnet, Gopher and anonymous file transfer protocol (FTP) allow users to access data that have been made available by other users. According to Zhenhua Liu, in a paper presented at the fourth international conference on Tourism in Southeast Asia and Indo China (26–26 June 2000):

> Since 1993, the Internet has been transformed completely, by its newest component, the World Wide Web (www). The web not only integrates other file transfer protocols like Gopher and FTP, but also allows the user to access hosts through Telnet, read newsgroups and use e-mail. Through an Internet browser, a user can link to any web sites and may explore the Internet resource in an unprecedented way for both leisure and commercial purposes. Moreover, the Web's capacity to blend text, pictures, sounds and video clips into multimedia documents, played the key role in popularizing the Internet beyond its traditionally academic boundaries and in it becoming an effective communication means in business and everyday life.

The Internet plays a critical role in tourism distribution and is a powerful force in tourism marketing. Its use and related technologies have created endangered species across a wide spectrum of operations, as it connects suppliers and product directly and serves to cut out more and more middle men. Those enterprises which cannot adapt are therefore likely to go out of business.

As early as 2000, the CTO decided that if it was going to fulfil its mandate of "reinventing" Caribbean tourism, it would have to give the research and information functions a much higher role in tourism structures and strategies across a number of areas than had formerly been the case. It began therefore by creating the tools of the trade and identifying the areas in which they were to be used.

CTO created its first website, www.doitcaribbean.com, in 2000, with the help of Peter Warren, president of DOT Media of the United Kingdom. The company launched a redesigned site in January 2001.

The company also created a management information system for tourism (MIST) which was structured to serve both as a national and regional integrated management information system. It comprised three main components:

- performance: a database of such features as arrival and departure statistics, and annual economic indicators
- product inventory: a database of tourism facilities such as accommodation, cruise, carriers, attractions and destination information
- marketing: a database of source information and marketing intelligence

The system was designed to meet certain objectives, such as serving as a repository of tourism information, and as a planning, research and development tool. While initially MIST users would collect and input information relevant to themselves, it was designed ultimately as a means of sharing information of a non-competitive and non-confidential nature among all MIST users. In the aftermath of 9/11, it had become clear that it was not only important to have collected information, but also have the means to retrieve it and massage it electronically in many ways and with dispatch.

MIST was conceived to

- improve the ability of the Caribbean destinations to manage and develop a sustainable tourism industry
- enhance their ability to respond to the changing market environment in which they operate
- strengthen their information infrastructure and enhance their management capability

Tourism statistics: From as early as 1974, the Caribbean Tourism Research and Development Centre had realized that the lack of sophistication in tourism statistics reinforced the early conception that tourism was not a serious development sector and therefore had not been treated as such. A priority for the future was to focus on a great deal of data-gathering across the areas of economic impact, socio-cultural-environmental and health data, crime, market intelligence and what may be described as general research in areas that relate to the tourism sector. These general research data include those matters about which there is a great deal of controversy that is frequently not informed by actual information. Examples include casino gambling, land ownership, alienation of land and land use, and the pros, cons and profitability of all-inclusive hotels, as opposed to other types of hotels and establishments.

Economic impact data: The need for economic impact data must be singled out. One of the traditional weaknesses of the tourism industry is that often when it needs to make a case to policymakers for the importance of its contribution to the socio-economic development of the country, it is hard-pressed to come up with reliable scientific quantitative data produced by experts in the field of economics. Instead the focus of statistics in tourism has largely been on collection and analysis of numbers of people crossing borders.

Governments and marketers, however, need to know much more. They need to know, for example, how much visitors spend, what they spend it on, and, equally important, what they *would* spend it on if the goods were available. Governments and marketers need to be able to track more scientifically and accurately the type and number of jobs created by tourism, especially indirectly. They need to know more accurately than is currently the case what revenue and net foreign exchange earnings tourism produces for governments. This information is, after all, the private sector's best argument for government support. Planners also need to know more accurately what is the financial performance of private enterprises, information which cannot be revealed only when the industry is in trouble and needs government support.

There has also been inadequate attention paid to visitor demographics – who the travellers are – and their psychographics – that is, their preferences, life styles and motivations. Often when such information is collected there is some doubt about the extent of its use in the marketing and planning process. Good marketing has to be a function of good marketing intelligence, and it is not obvious that consumer and trade behaviour and other related trends in tourism are being tracked on a scientific and structured basis.

If the analysis above is accurate, it is clear that, in the absence of the data listed above, those governments which have to allocate scarce resources could not be aware of what was the real return on their tourism investment.

And finally, there is the need for a far more precise definition of the sector than currently obtains before one can collect better data. This lack of proper definition of the tourism sector was to cause serious problems for all those persons and governments seeking to deal with tourism issues in the World Trade Organization negotiations on trade in services.

Issue 7: Effective marketing in old and emerging markets

US market: Until 2002, when the strategic plan was being considered, nothing of any significance had been done in regional marketing since 1992, when Caribbean heads of government and the private sector – that is, the private sector that operated both to and in the region – had joined together and put forth the funds to mount a serious regional marketing and advertising campaign in the US market.

This was an important market for all the Caribbean countries, but for the Bahamas, Puerto Rico, Jamaica and the Cayman Islands, the percentage of US arrivals was over 60 per cent and therefore a lifeline. On that occasion the well-known US musical group the Beach Boys had been contracted to produce a version of their famous song "Kokomo", already a hit in the market, for use in promoting the region. The campaign was generally agreed to have been a major success.

By April 2001, leisure sales in the US market had taken a sharp decline for the following reasons:

- The Caribbean had the lowest share of voice in the US marketplace in several years. Sufficient advertising was not being done by individual countries, and no television advertising at all by any of the regional organizations. Further, the promotion and public relations programmes were inadequate for the needs of the market.
- Competing destinations, both domestic and international, were being promoted heavily in both television and print.
- Posted airfares for the summer months on scheduled carriers from the United States and Canada were, in comparison to those to other competing destinations, high.
- Heavy discounting by the cruise lines due to increased capacity was intensifying that competition being experienced by land-based tourism.

Canadian market: In 2001, the situation in the Canadian market was far worse than it was in the US market. Canada had fallen to fourth place as a supplier of business to the Caribbean. The diagnosis was much of the same:

- There was a lack of market presence, especially outside of Ontario and Quebec. The CTO was represented only by a small firm, one which had several other clients.
- The region was unable, through lack of resources, to develop better co-op programmes and partnerships with the Canadian travel trade.
- The television and print advertising by national entities was inadequate and nonexistent at the regional level.
- The same situation was true for promotion and public relations programmes.
- Canada 3000 had gone out of business, although, on the positive side, Air Canada had announced an increase in its scheduled flights.

European market: Prior to 2000, the European market had grown for a decade by double-digit percentages. Growth in 2000 slowed to less than 1 per cent. Poor performance was due to the following:

- Most of the economies in major source markets in Europe were weak, Germany being a prime example.
- There was non-competitive package pricing in the European originating markets due to the strong dollar against the euro and sterling.
- Vertical integration and consolidation of the major and small tour operators across the United Kingdom and Europe were causing diversions of wholly owned charter services, either to destinations outside of the Caribbean or to specific destinations within the region, largely the Hispanic Caribbean.
- There was a reduction of airlift from Europe, including scheduled services, which negatively affected traffic to the region. One of the major factors cited for this reduction was the high price of fuel.
- The competition to the Caribbean in the European market was better organized and better financed, and succeeded in diluting an already limited Caribbean presence in these markets.
- Very little television advertising was taking place in the markets of Europe by individual countries and none by regional public and private sector entities.

The intra-Caribbean market: The growth in this market presents an interesting phenomenon. It had traditionally been motivated by festivals, sports, the visiting of friends and relatives, meetings and conferences, and shopping rather than pure leisure traffic. The major beneficiary countries had been Cuba, Puerto Rico, Trinidad and Tobago, Venezuela, St Maarten, and a number of the other Eastern Caribbean counties.

The year 2001 can perhaps be claimed as the year in which the intra-Caribbean market truly started to become a leisure market. The potential for growth in leisure business had always been there, but for many years it was hampered by a number of the following factors:

- The failure by both private and public sectors to create an awareness of travel and holidays within the region. The sector had not provided the same kind of human resources, promotional activities and sales tools applied to other external markets.
- The shortage of unique regional products that would be attractive to regional travellers.
- An inadequate distribution system to develop and provide packaged tour programmes.
- The difficulties regional carriers faced in moving people at affordable costs around and across the region.
- The fact that Caribbean hoteliers gave low priority to Caribbean leisure business and, generally speaking, were not at that time willing to provide incentives to travel agents to sell rooms to Caribbean tourists.
- Strict visa requirements imposed for citizens to travel between CARICOM and certain non-CARICOM countries.
- The absence of government incentives to motivate Caribbean people to take holidays either at home or in other Caribbean countries.

The South American market: In 2000, the South American market, which comprised largely Venezuela, Colombia, Brazil, Chile and Argentina, accounted for some 4 per cent of Caribbean business. Countries active in the market were largely Cuba, the Mexican Caribbean, the Netherlands Antilles, Aruba and French St Martin. Some of the countries mentioned above benefited from proximity to the mainland of South America and to certain cultural affinities such as language. The diagnosis about performance of this market was:

- weak economies in the source markets
- facilitation challenges such as visas and language differences
- difficulties for many potential South American travellers to obtain direct flights to and from the Caribbean or by means of South American gateways – it was much easier to travel by way of Miami
- weak links between South American and Caribbean travel partners
- minimal Caribbean presence in the countries concerned, either on a permanent or visiting basis

Japan and the Eastern markets: In 2000, Japan was the only tourism market in Asia that had been seriously pursued by the Caribbean and was at that time responsible for about 40,000 arrivals, highly concentrated in a few countries, such as Aruba, Jamaica, the Bahamas, the Cayman Islands and the US Virgin Islands, all of which had undertaken the work to establish a meaningful presence in Japan.

Japan was conscious at that time that it sold a great deal of goods to the region with which it had a large trade imbalance. About 1990, therefore, it had begun to encourage outbound Japanese tourism to a number of countries, including the Caribbean. In 1992, the secretary general of the CTO led a Caribbean mission to Japan to meet with the Japanese tourism officials and to explore opportunities for increasing the business. A great deal of optimism was generated by this visit. However, Japanese business to the region nevertheless began to decrease starting in about 1995. This drop was due to

- a weakened Japanese economy
- the costs of representation and promotion in Japan, which needed to be in Japanese
- scarce Caribbean resources and therefore a need to prioritize market focus
- a propensity of Japanese tourists to move on after experiencing a specific destination

Issue 8: Relevant human resource development

There can be little disagreement with the proposition that human resources are a major factor in competitiveness. Traditionally, however, much of the focus in tourism with respect to human resources, has been on achieving skills and service quality with respect to those persons employed in the core subsectors – such as accommodation, amenities and attractions – and in such other frontline-related activities as immigration and customs, airline and cruise line service personnel, and ground transport services. The importance of service quality in these areas remains high, especially since the Caribbean has been unfavourably compared to some other regions of the world, particularly Asia, with respect to quality of service.

But tourism in the twenty-first century requires a far more scientific approach to human resource development than was formerly the case. First, proper manpower planning requires, for example, that there are adequate data about the size of the workforce, their conditions of service, and the attitudes of the workers to the industry. Second, the changing face of tourism, driven as it is by information technology and research, requires a range of new and sophisticated skills. This set of requirements has training and recruitment implications for public and private sectors, and for academia.

New human resource strategies therefore need to focus on

- creating a culture of training throughout the industry
- improving access to quality training for both the public and private sector, especially at the level of the small entrepreneur
- creating the human capacity and resources needed to address systematically the real issues of the industry in marketing, transportation, social, environmental, economic and cultural impact
- implementing continuous and professional public awareness programmes to educate the public and to change behaviours in respect of tourism
- introducing or developing tourism education at all levels in the schools and the tertiary system of education
- developing more financial mechanisms for training and education for the sector
- creating career paths and a better understanding of the real opportunities at every level available to Caribbean people in tourism
- taking all possible steps to make tourism in the Caribbean more *Caribbean* in terms of the ownership, management and product

Issues 9 and 10: Institutional strengthening and funding

The concluding statement, after reviewing all the issues in 2002, was that the national and regional tourism authorities were often not structured, staffed and financed to preside over and to manage an industry which earned billions of dollars, and on which, for its socio-economic development, the region would need to rely to a great extent for the foreseeable future. At the time both the governments and the private sector were said to be making too small an investment while expecting a large return.

There was a clarion call therefore for the *institutions* to be reinvented along with the reinvention of Caribbean tourism itself. There was also a call for some mechanism or mechanisms to provide national and regional organizations with adequate financing on a continuing basis.

The vision for the plan

The vision established for the strategic plan was that, by 2012, a developed Caribbean Tourism Industry would be fully understood and embraced by the peoples of the region, an industry which, through cooperative action among governments and the private sector, would make a significant and sustainable contribution to development in both mature and emerging destinations.

The objectives set to be achieved by the strategic plan by 2012 were to:

- achieve growth while intensifying economic impact and distributing the benefits more equitably, both within countries and across the region, with particular reference to poverty alleviation and gender issues
- pay more attention to the marketing and other special needs of emerging tourism destinations and of small and indigenous operators of tourism enterprises
- build a tourism product that is sustainable, competitive and profitable
- modernize Caribbean tourism institutions, structures and systems to compete in a dynamic global environment

- create mechanisms for cooperation, nationally and regionally, between the public and private sectors, and between Caribbean countries
- provide adequate and sustainable funding to finance Caribbean tourism development in all its aspects – this envisioned the establishment of a sustainable tourism development fund and a Caribbean tourism investment fund or bank

Recommendations and assumptions for success

The realization of the vision was seen as dependent on the following action being taken across a number of the following areas:

1. **Sustainable development**
   - making the Caribbean tourism product a model of best environmental practice through adoption of environmental certification and rating programmes and through the provision of improved infrastructure
   - integrating "best practice" tourism industry environmental policies into national environmental policies, with the primary aim of maintaining one of the region's most vital and marketable underpinning assets
   - placing tourism squarely within a national policy framework of social and economic development, one that encourages and strengthens linkages with other sectors, and speaks to the issues of poverty alleviation, sustainability, and conservation of the national patrimony, by reorienting policies, attitudes, and perceptions related to tourism
   - enhancing the reputation of the Caribbean as a safe, secure and healthy tourist destination

2. **Product**
   - creating new and improved industry accommodation, attractions and infrastructure which could cater to a more sophisticated, higher spending, and discerning customer in a growing market
   - investing in new facilities and refurbishment of existing facilities (backed up by marketing) to spread the benefits of tourism growth

throughout the region – including emerging tourism destinations – and reduce the current imbalances in the level of tourism development across the region
- adopting optimum standards in product quality and service as benchmarks for excellence in the industry
- implementing a small hotel-branding scheme, backed up with access to finance for improvements
- designing product that increasingly caters to visitors in special market niches, persons who will be spending more per diem than the standard holidaymaker
- adopting measures to conserve, develop and promote the region's cultural heritage as an integral part of the tourism product

3. **Profitability and investment**
   - adoption by the region of a strong pro-business environment which generates increased tax revenues, provides more jobs and higher wage rates by growing the business
   - improving business profitability through reduction in operating costs and more efficient plant utilization
   - developing a targeted investment programme for new and enhanced products to make the industry attractive for investment
   - making finance more accessible and more available, especially to small hotels

4. **Aviation policy**
   - implementing appropriate national and regional aviation policies, committing additional resources to improve aviation safety and airport security to meet revised international standards and increasing cooperation, including functional cooperation, between regional carriers
   - providing marketing support to specific carriers on specific routes to open new gateways and support existing markets

5. **Cruise tourism**
   - establishing and maintaining strong relationships with the cruise industry at the national level to ensure mutually beneficial initiatives and outcomes, including visitor conversion programmes and

increased regional sourcing of supplies, services and cruise ship employees

6. **Information management**
   - utilizing, at all levels, appropriate information technology that provides timely and accurate information for decision making and business delivery
   - developing regional and national websites as fully as possible to take advantage of the opportunities afforded by Internet and niche marketing
   - improving the timeliness and coverage of existing tourism information systems dealing with such concerns as visitor arrivals, hotel performance and economic impacts of tourism
   - agreeing at the level of the CTO, the CHA, the University of the West Indies and other tertiary institutions in the region, together with relevant national entities, to implement an ongoing tourism research programme

7. **Marketing**
   - launching a sustained marketing programme, to include regional television advertising and other appropriate mechanisms, in key markets and focused on the Caribbean brand image
   - increasing efforts to grow holidays in both absolute and market-share terms, through increased investment and promotion, and through sustained national and regional marketing
   - putting in place special subregional marketing programmes that will benefit emerging Caribbean tourist destinations
   - recognizing the importance of direct marketing, particularly in targeting special interest and niche groups
   - taking steps to put in place Caribbean-owned and -operated distribution channels, initially in North America and later in United Kingdom and Europe, through appropriate private sector collaboration
   - fully exploiting the possibilities and opportunities for growth in the intra-Caribbean market
   - seeking to achieve a better distribution of tourist arrivals throughout the year – thus achieving a reduced disparity between high and low seasons – through giving greater support to new markets which

would include new niche markets, the performance of which, in terms of seasonality, is complementary to the existing main markets

8. **Human resource development**
    - strengthening the Caribbean Tourism Human Resource Council to foster an enhanced training culture, involving both government and industry through the implementation of a new tourism learning system
    - substantially improving the professionalism, at all levels in the industry, through the implementation of industry education, and through training programmes and the development of new programmes focused on identified needs
    - improving the tourism industry performance by a better trained and more professional workforce
    - accepting quality control as a key factor in the provision of a quality end product
    - using tourism awareness programmes to improve public perceptions of tourism, including perceptions of careers in tourism

9. **Organization and funding**
    - creating effective partnerships between the industry and government through formal arrangements and mutual commitments for the benefit of both national exchequers and the tourism industry
    - providing the CHA and the CTO with the human and financial resources necessary to fulfil their respective mandates
    - creating a sustainable tourism development fund to provide an adequate and sustained source of funding for regional and subregional tourism development programmes

10. **Source and structure of the proposed fund**
    It was proposed in the strategic plan that the fund be created and managed in the following manner:
    - A mandatory per capita ticket tax would be levied on incoming visitors by air and sea.
    - The proceeds would be paid directly into a regional escrow account.
    - The fund would be managed by an independent authority and board of trustees.

- The board of trustees managing the fund would comprise about seven to nine members, appointed by contributing governments but drawn from both private and public sectors.
- The trustees would be advised by a committee of private and public sector tourism representatives, supported by its own secretariat, which would have the responsibility for preparing annual marketing and other proposals for funding.
- A detailed work programme would be prepared on an annual basis.

The funds would be used to (a) mount ongoing regional marketing and public relations programmes in agreed priority markets; (b) support programmes intricately related to the marketing efforts. Examples would include market research and intelligence, and website development; (c) fund programmes, including both the CTO and the CHA programmes, adjudged by the authority to be contributing to the development of excellence in the tourism product.

It was believed that, given the number of tourists arriving annually to all the CTO member countries, the contribution of a relatively small sum on the part of the tourists could raise about US$50 million per year for the region, increasing annually by some 5 per cent thereafter. One of the short-term recommendations concerned the period 2003 to 2005. For that period, given the state of the market, 80 per cent of the fund should be spent on marketing, including market research.

It was hoped that agreement on the fund could be reached by the public and private sectors early so that the proposals could be considered by the CARICOM ministers of finance in September 2002.

11. Growth scenarios

The assumptions made were that, should the above recommendations be largely implemented, the following outcomes could be expected by the year 2012:
- Total stay-over visitor arrivals would increase 64 per cent to thirty-three million, representing annual growth of 4.6 per cent per annum from 2000 and 5.7 per cent from 2003.
- Above-average growth rates were projected for the US, Canadian, UK and intra-Caribbean markets.
- The CARICOM share of total stay-over arrivals would increase from 26 per cent in 2000 to 29 per cent in 2012.

- Total visitor expenditure would increase by 77 per cent, compared to the 2000 figures, to US$35 billion at 2002 prices, representing an annual growth rate of 5.3 per cent per annum.
- Approximately 100,000 new or refurbished rooms would be added to the stock of tourist accommodation.
- Total tourism-related employment – direct, indirect and induced – will have increased by an estimated 300,000 or more persons.

The importance of the Caribbean Regional Strategic Plan

In 1951, when the CTA was first established, the concept of a region comprising many countries, cultures, histories and languages, being seen and treated as a single tourism destination, was a creative one, considerably in advance of its time. The ability to create and promote a single Caribbean brand was even more challenging.

A second milestone was reached and passed in 1974 when the marketing activity was underpinned by a research and development programme at CTRC, one that transformed Caribbean tourism from a strictly marketing mode to a process of socio-economic development.

The vision was complete when regional marketing, and research and development, were fused by the merger of the CTA and the CTRC into one organization, the CTO in 1989. Those observers who repeatedly seek to separate the two organizations do not fully understand the symbiosis between these two arms of tourism. Marketing that is not driven by research, statistics and development operates somewhat like a man who is strong and powerful but also blind. Unless such disparate bodies are under common management and direction they will drift apart according to the priorities and ambitions of the respective separate leaderships.

The 2002 Caribbean Tourism Strategic Plan was *sui generis*. Never in the history of tourism development has any region, comprising several sovereign and individual states, conceived of the possibility of establishing goals, strategies and a vision that, between them, encompassed all the member states, and established a blueprint for development which is equally capable of guiding the direction of both the individual states and the region as a whole.

The strategic plan had come about in response to the difficulties created for Caribbean tourism largely, but not entirely, by the events of 9/11. It was intended to be implemented over an eight-year period – 2002 to 2010. Eleven years have now passed in 2013. It will be important before the end of this book to estimate what progress has been made in the context of many variables. In such matters, the best case scenario is often not achieved because all the assumptions made on which that level of success is anticpated do not materialize. As was feared, the competition – especially from Asia and the Middle East, which diminished immediately after 9/11 – returned as strongly as before, if not more so, as oil revenues enriched some countries beyond even their wildest dreams.

In July 2008 the price per barrel of oil, which had been about US$30 in 2003, reached US$147 before it retreated, and climbed again in 2010 to the mid-eighties – a figure which, in 2003, would have been regarded as much too high. By 2011, oil prices had once again risen to over US$100 per barrel.

The growth scenario for Caribbean tourism contemplated in 2002 could not have foreseen the global economic meltdown of 2008 and 2009, which left all regions guessing about the point at which some normalcy in economic matters would return to the world. The global recession was followed in 2010 by cautious optimism for slow recovery, but in 2011 the Greek economic collapse and the growing Italian financial crisis threatened the very existence of the euro, with serious implications for the United States and other economies.

Funding constraints

The breadth and depth of the recommendations made in the strategic plan for re-engineering Caribbean tourism demonstrated that Caribbean people are seldom at a loss for ideas. The challenges often come at the implementation stage of a project. Between 2002 and 2013, the region continued to be frustrated by its inability to identify a sustainable source of funds needed to finance the plan and to effect the transformation targeted. The failure of the region to find the money to implement the plan is a sad story which is told at greater length in chapter 10.

10
Failed Attempts to Create the Regional Tourism Fund

The desirability of Caribbean countries operating as a single united force in global tourism has been promoted for several decades. But this is easier spoken of than done. The stumbling block has been their inability to create a pool of regional funds, separate and apart from national resources, one which is both sustainable and adequate to serve the needs of the region. As a result, regional tourism programmes, at the desired level, cannot be properly planned in advance. The programmes are also in danger of being reduced to relative insignificance or a wish list, aspects of which can be implemented only as funds are identified gradually and in small amounts from a variety of unsustainable quarters.

The need for sustainable funding

While many persons have advocated both the need for strong regional action and the advantages of promoting the entire Caribbean as a single destination, raising the money for so doing has been as unattainable a goal as the Holy Grail. In fact, devising an equitable and acceptable system of funding regional programmes has been a fertile ground for disagreements between countries. Even more frequently, it has been the cause of disputes between public and private sector agencies.

From the earliest conception of joint regional marketing programmes, it has seemed reasonable that they should be financed jointly by contributions from both government and the private sector. The contributions from government were originally perceived as coming from annual budgets and the consolidated fund – that is, from various forms of taxation – and the contributions from private sector establishments either from their revenues or from specific levies on their customers. While seldom agreeing on the specifics, the CTO and the CHA always bought into the ideal of a contributory fund idea of some type. However, the Florida Caribbean Cruise Association never did.

From the beginning, the cruise lines, although members of the CTA and later the CTO, refused to be part of the discussion. They maintained that the funding of regional tourism programmes other than their own was not their responsibility, since they did not see themselves as the beneficiaries of such programmes and since they fully met the costs themselves for their own activities. The land-based tourism operators contested this view and argued strongly the case for governments levying more taxes on the cruise sector.

Failed attempts to increase cruise passenger taxes

In the 1980s and 1990s Caribbean governments had tried repeatedly to levy what they regarded as an adequate per capita cruise passenger tax. They failed miserably because of lack of agreement among the governments – both at the wider level of the CTRC and the CTO and at the CARICOM level – on the quantum of such a tax and how it should be collected. Understandably, the cruise lines were actively engaged in one-on-one discussions with governments to ensure that such agreements were not reached. The closest the parties came to an agreement was at a CARICOM heads of government meeting in the Bahamas in 1993, at which a US$10 per capita tax was discussed. Ultimately, however, the then prime minister of Barbados did not agree to it, and the consensus needed for a decision to be taken by the heads of CARICOM governments on matters of this kind was not achieved.

Proposal to establish a cruise regulatory authority

In 1994, the governments' focus changed from the simple idea of increasing per capita cruise passenger levies to establishing a regulatory authority to impose some kind of control over the cruise industry. The view had been canvassed by certain individuals that the region should cease trifling with such matters as per capita taxes and should instead create a regional agency which would have the authority to license cruise ships at an appropriate fee to operate in the Caribbean Sea. Such a system would reduce their ability to exploit to the full, the advantage the ships received from being moveable assets. Consideration was given, therefore, to whether or not a regulatory authority for the licensing and control of cruise shipping in the Caribbean Sea could be lawfully created and operated as proposed. In June 1994, the CTO sought a legal opinion from Ralph Carnegie, the head of the Faculty of Law of the University of the West Indies. The opinion given in his report ("The Report on the Requirements for Establishing a Regional Regulatory Body and Licensing System to Oversee the Operations of Cruise Ships in the Caribbean Sea") was as follows:

> The Montego Bay Convention extensively protects shipping which is merely in transit through a coastal state's maritime zones from regulation by a coastal state which would impede the movement of such shipping. A licensing system for such in-transit shipping could generally speaking not be established by such a coastal state without contravening international law. The principally relevant exceptions to the exemption of in-transit shipping from coastal state regulation, would relate to environmental protection and routing measures, and could not extend to charging such shipping for the privilege of access for the purposes of transit. It follows that a regulatory scheme based on the rationale of charging for access to the Caribbean Sea would to that extent not be acceptable under international law.
>
> A coastal state would under the Montego Bay Convention have extensive regulatory authority over ships visiting or landing passengers in its ports once such a ship enters its contiguous zone en route to such a port. States parties to the FAL Convention of 1965 relating to Facilitation of International Marine Traffic, have agreed to restraints on the controls to be applied to visiting cruise shipping, however.
>
> Although a regulatory system cannot consistently with international law, be based on charging for access to the Caribbean Sea, there is scope for a regulatory authority to coordinate the regulation that coastal states are entitled to exercise, including the coordination of taxation on a graded basis, and in the process to provide a service to cruise shipping which will ultimately be revenue enhancing.

Carnegie's report included a draft international agreement for the regulation of cruise shipping in the Caribbean. The report outlined how the regulatory authority should be constructed and provided a draft budget and financial projections for its operations. (See appendix 4 for a copy of the draft agreement proposed for consideration.)

In 1994, the CTO member states decided not to pursue the establishment of the regulatory cruise authority option. The proposal consequently lapsed, and while discussions about per capita levies took place on occasion, no major action was taken on the matter. The situation had eased due to raising of the level of the per capita levies. This shift took place through various bilateral agreements between individual countries and cruise lines. It was a more palatable solution to the cruise lines – which, as a matter of policy, tended to resist regional approaches, realizing the danger to themselves of the countries of the region acting as a block. In fact, the cruise lines insisted that their business was with individual states, and consequently saw no reason to negotiate with a regional entity such as the CTO. Interestingly, the same companies saw no problem being members of the CTO, the regional tourism agency, where all aspects of tourism were discussed.

9/11 attack leads to a more conciliatory policy on cruise tourism

After the terrorist attack on the United States on 11 September 2001, with its negative impact on both land-based and cruise tourism, the drafters of the document that followed – "The Caribbean Tourism Strategic Plan" (December 2001) – were in general agreement that, in the prevailing circumstances, confrontation with the cruise lines should, as far as possible, be avoided, and other means explored for increasing the positive impacts of cruise tourism in the region.

The cruise section of the Regional Strategic Tourism Development Plan therefore spoke in terms of focusing on visitor conversion programmes, increasing the number of regional sources from which supplies could be purchased by cruise lines, and the hiring of more Caribbean employees by the cruise lines. Further, it expressed the hope that both public and private sector members of the tourism industry, including the cruise lines, would be willing to contribute voluntarily to the creation of the regional fund proposed to meet its declared objectives.

However, this did not happen. The CTO ministers and commissioners of tourism, having been provided with a strategic plan in 2002 to deal with the negative impacts of 9/11, had been unable by 2003 to identify the funds to implement it. No volunteers appeared on the horizon to contribute to the cause. They therefore established a sustainable funding committee under the chairmanship of Dwyer Astaphan, the minister of tourism of St Kitts, to examine what money was needed and how it could be raised.

Report of the Astaphan funding committee

The funding committee reported to the CTO ministerial caucus in New York in June 2003. The report recommended that the proposed sustainable tourism development fund should be financed by imposing a levy of US$20 on each ticket sold by the cruise lines for a cruise to a CTO member state. The proposal was submitted to and agreed upon by the tourism ministers and commissioners, subject to approval by national ministries of finance or their respective equivalent bodies at the national level. This move was a bold one, considering the fate of the proposal for the US$10 levy per cruise passenger ten years earlier at the 1993 meeting of heads of CARICOM in Nassau.

The declared purpose of the fund in 2003 was somewhat broader than in 1993, when the focus had been entirely on marketing. This time the declared objective was as follows: "to provide resources for the enhancement of regional marketing programmes, human resource development, cultural, environmental and other product development programmes of the region, as articulated in the Regional Strategic Tourism Development Plan."

The cruise lines were outraged by the proposed tax, not only because they thought the level was punitive, but also because the hotels, airlines and other tourism establishments were excluded from that particular tax. It may also be coincidental, but the fact that Astaphan was transferred to another ministry did raise questions in the public domain about whether pressure had in fact been exerted by the cruise lines to have this done.

The recommendations on the US$20 levy were thoroughly discussed in the region at many levels, first by individual CTO member countries, then by COFAP, the CARICOM agency comprising ministers of finance and planning, the committee on finance and planning, and then by the CARICOM heads of government at their meeting in July 2003 in Montego Bay.

At every level, arguments for and against the levy were advanced, without any final resolution on the matter. Finally, the proposal was sent back to the CTO secretariat for the further elucidation of a number of issues. At their meeting in July 2003, the CARICOM heads had expressed the need to be further advised by the CTO on the legality of the levy. The CTO therefore once again sought legal expert advice on the matter from Ralph Carnegie, who, as noted above, had carried out the study in 1994 on the requirements for establishing a regulatory authority. He attended the CTO ministerial caucus at its meeting held at Frenchman's Reef Resort, St Thomas, US Virgin Islands, on 15 October 2003, and gave a legal opinion.

The central points made by Ralph Carnegie were as follows:

- The terms of reference called for the proposed regional cruise passenger ticket levy to be tested in two particular areas of international law, those two being the international trade law obligations of members of the World Trade Organization, and international maritime law.
- The issue of the legality of the proposed cruise ship passenger levy could depend on the detailed manner of its structure.
- The imposition of the tax would depend on the law of any state which is enforcing it. Common action therefore meant that the levy would have to meet the restrictions applicable to the action of any party to the implementation scheme.
- Consideration would need to be given to the sources of possible constraints which were not considered in the opinion, such as the bilateral agreements and the CARICOM Single Market and Economy regime.
- An accounting study needed to be conducted to support the reasonableness of the quantum of the proposed levy.

The conclusion was that the levy was legal and implementable, provided that the conditions outlined in the opinion were met.

The case to heads of government in justification of US$20 tax

The CARICOM heads of government were not, however, prepared to agree to the tax without a great deal more information. Accordingly, the heads asked the CTO secretariat to present more arguments in support of the imposition of the tax.

The CTO provided the following clarifications to a number of questions:

What were the specific proposals of the ministers and commissioners of tourism with respect to the levy?
The ministers and commissioners had proposed that

- a minimum charge of US$20 be imposed on every cruise ticket sold by cruise lines for travel into the CTO member territories
- the funds generated by this charge should be collected by the cruise lines and paid into a regional fund
- any necessary appropriate legislative or other steps would be taken by individual territories to allow for implementation with effect from 1 October 2003
- the ministers and commissioners of tourism would appoint trustees of the fund who would in turn appoint a committee of private and public sector members to design programmes to be submitted to the trustees for approval and funding
- a professional fund manager would be appointed to manage the funds

Why a US$20 levy?
In 2003 it was estimated that the region needed about US$50 million to US$60 million per year to meet the various needs of Caribbean tourism identified in the plan. The US$20 added to the cost of each of the three million cruise line tickets (a conservative estimate) expected to be sold annually in the region for cruising to the CTO member states would, accordingly, generate US$60 million a year. This money would be spent on major regional marketing campaigns in the Caribbean's chief source markets; support for human resource development and other product development programmes; economic impact analyses; information technology development; enhancement of air transportation services; responses to specific and demonstrated tourism needs of member states, responsibilities to be clearly defined under the fund terms; and other research areas, such as statistics.

Why place the levy only on cruise line tickets and therefore on cruise passengers alone?

It was proposed that the levy be imposed at that time only on tickets sold for cruising. The reasons for this restriction were as follows:

- Land-based tourism already contributes 90 per cent of the visitor expenditure and the revenue Caribbean governments collect from tourism. Care needed to be taken, therefore, not to tax it further to the level of diminishing returns and so reduce its contribution.
- In all the discussions held by both public and private sector tourism agencies in the region, preference was expressed for the fund to be created by the imposition of a levy on the consumer. The Caribbean hotels and airlines serving the region and their clientele argued strongly that they were already heavily taxed and since 9/11 both were struggling to survive. The only consumer left who it was thought could be taxed further without significant fall out was the cruiser.
- There are specific travel and tourism fiscal impositions – such as departure taxes, head taxes and port duties – to which both hotels and cruise lines are subject. In addition to those impositions, the land-based units and their customers – unlike the cruise industry, which operates offshore – are also subject to an extensive list of taxes, direct or indirect, which the entire resident population and businesses operating in the territory must pay. Many of the inputs into the land-based product are taxed at some level. These taxes produce accordingly an expensive and uncompetitive land-based product, leading ultimately to reduced revenues for governments.
- While it was generally accepted that much of the credit for the significant growth and profits of the cruise lines must be accorded to them for their entrepreneurship and good management, it was also felt that they were free from several of the taxes land-based tourism bears at every stage of operation. This discrepancy gave the cruise lines certain advantages which, under many of the rules now operative or being established in the regimes for trade liberalization, might well be considered unfair competition.
- Generally speaking, cruise lines were seen as not contributing enough to any of the regional tourism programmes from which, despite claims to the contrary, they were thought to be benefiting. These programmes included the national and regional public and private

sector marketing efforts of other stakeholders in Caribbean tourism, and the regional statistical, research and training programmes.
- Cruise tourism, as with other tourism, was held to be responsible for some of the negative environmental impact on the region, and it was felt that it should bear more of the costs of rectifying this impact than currently was the case.
- Governments' costs for the development of infrastructure to support the cruise industry were increasing as bigger ships were built and security considerations addressed.
- An additional US$20 added to each cruise line ticket at 2003 prices was thought unlikely to act as a deterrent to passengers to buy a cruise. The 2003 World Trade Organization study quoted the president of one of the major cruise lines as saying: "Holidays in a hotel cost 50% more than on a cruise. Cruise lines could increase their profits by up to 50% and still be on a par. They could even lower prices by 20%, given that the hotel sector suffered so much during the nineties that it can no longer reduce its prices and still make a profit."

Who would have access to the fund's resources?
It was proposed that all the CTO member states that signed the agreement legitimizing the cruise levy would benefit from the programmes financed by the fund.

When and where would the cruise levy be collected?
It was proposed that the cruise lines would collect the US$20 levy at the point-of-sale of any ticket sold to a passenger whose cruise takes him or her to any the CTO member state and pay the funds into a regional escrow account. The number of tickets sold should be verifiable from ships' manifests, tickets which would need to be submitted by the cruise lines to an appropriate authority yet to be determined. Clearly, however, this proposal needed to be more closely addressed by lawyers. It was believed important that it be a regional levy, and not a national one, which could not be attributable to any individual country or state.

Would the cruise lines be willing to participate in this exercise?
The cruise lines gave early notice that they would seek to ensure that this levy was never imposed and in fact began immediately to develop

and implement a strategy of putting pressure on individual countries to secure their rejection of the proposal.

How could the cruise lines be made to comply?
Based on legal advice, the participating member states needed to find legal mechanisms, one regional, that bound the cruise lines to comply and another, national, which provided each state with the legal authority to enforce compliance. Under the legal regimes under which several of the member states operate signature of an international agreement is not by itself a sufficient condition for a local court to enforce compliance. There needs to be local legislation as well, legislation which is supportive of the demands of the international agreement.

What were the challenges to implementation?
An immediate difficulty was that CTO member states operate under a number of different systems of law. Examples include the French Departments, the Netherlands Antilles, and the British colonies, all of which are subject to European legal systems. American territories such as Puerto Rico and the US Virgin Islands operate under American systems. The Commonwealth Caribbean independent states operate within the Caribbean Community. Therefore, enabling them as a group to work together legally on the matter presented a significant challenge.

Would the proposed levy itself be legal or in violation of any of the requirements of, for example, the General Agreement on Trade in Services, the Free Trade Area of the Americas, African, Caribbean, and Pacific Group of States/European Union agreements, and the CARICOM Single Market and Economy?
The proposal and legal opinion were considered yet again by the Council for Finance and Planning meeting in October 2003 and later the meeting of heads of government in November 2003 where it was said to have been approved in principle.

CARICOM decision

In February 2004, the secretary general of CTO was informed by CARICOM by letter that "a broad measure of consensus about the levy on each cruise ticket sold by cruise liners sailing into the ports of CTO member states is unlikely to be achieved at this time".

The year 2004 therefore ended with the per capita levy initiative unresolved and each country left to pursue its own salvation with the cruise lines. There the matter of a sustainable regional fund stood until 2008 when the world faced the worst economic crisis since the Great Depression and fears surfaced once again for the collapse of Caribbean tourism.

Funding initiative resurrected in 2008

In July 2008 as the price of oil reached over US$147 and a global recession witnessed the collapse of companies everywhere, the Caribbean public and private sectors feared once more for the collapse of their tourism industry. The almost knee-jerk reaction was to resurrect the idea of a regional tourism fund. It was put on the agenda of CARICOM heads of government meeting in July in St John's, Antigua. At the end of the meeting the following agreements were announced:

- That the heads supported the proposal for the establishment of a US$60 million marketing fund to promote the Caribbean as a single destination.
- That CARICOM countries would contribute US$21 million towards the fund, while the remainder would come from the CHA, the CTO and other stakeholders.
- That a Caribbean regional tourism brand should be adopted and a timely and comprehensive information gathering system established which would adequately reflect the contribution of tourism to the national economies.
- That a special meeting of the CARICOM Council for Trade and Economic Development (COTED) should be convened, with a tourism and air transportation agenda, to examine the regional marketing fund and related modalities and report to a meeting of the COTED bureau of heads of government within sixty days.
- That tourism ministers would in future be able to participate in meetings of COTED, the second highest decision-making body of CARICOM.

- That other discussions about fund contributions would be held with the Dutch Antilles, the French Antilles, the American territories, the Spanish-speaking countries and the cruise industry.

The Council for Trade and Economic Development follow-up meeting, September 2008

Once again there were high expectations that agreement on the fund reached in principle in July 2008 would be followed by effective action. At the meeting of COTED convened in Port of Spain in September 2008 to follow up on the consensus reached by the heads in July, agreement seemed further away than ever. No mention was now being made about a contribution by the CTO or the CHA. The focus was on placing a tax on airlines flying into the region. However, some delegations, which had supported such an idea in Antigua in July 2008, now declared themselves unable to agree to the airline tax on the grounds that airlines serving their countries were already carrying too heavy a tax burden. They offered instead to contribute to the regional fund from within their own budgets.

Delegations, however, which remained in favour of raising the regional funds by imposing more taxes on airlines, began to think that the opposition of some to the airline tax would place those who agreed to impose it, in an uncompetitive position with respect to attracting airline services. Furthermore, no one at the COTED meeting seemed able to confirm what would be the position on the tax of those CTO states which were not members of CARICOM. The meeting ended with the matter still unresolved and it remained so as of 2013.

It is highly unlikely that the regional land-based public and private sector entities will ever reach a consensus which involves adding to the already heavy tax burden on hotels, land-based amenities and airlines. Agencies such as the International Air Transport Association remain strongly opposed and vocal in their opposition to more airline taxes. Speaking at the association's annual general meeting in Berlin in June 2010, Secretary General Giovanni Bisignani launched a broadside attack in which he referred to global distribution companies as "leeches", labour unions as "out of touch with reality", and Germany's government as "shortsighted" for announcing a new aviation tax.

As of 2013, it does not appear likely that Caribbean governments and private sector tourism entities will reach a consensus, any time soon, on the means of creating a significant regional fund from a sustainable source, for building their regional tourism efforts. While this remains the case, the governments of the United States, the United Kingdom and other European states are themselves imposing increasingly more taxes, both on their own respective outward-bound populations and on incoming visitors, in serving the interests of their own tourism industry.

As can be seen from the CTO tourism statistics attached as appendix 5, 2008 and 2009 were difficult years for Caribbean tourism, although 2010 saw some signs of recovery with respect to arrivals, if not to expenditures. Given the difficulty, up until now, in creating the regional fund, much of which was intended to be spent on regional marketing, it has become even more important that the region find ways of diversifying its product if it is to improve its competitiveness.

Chapters 11 and 12 are devoted to the exploration of the possibilities for developing two major niche markets, first that of sports tourism and second that of the cultural and heritage industries. These are both markets in which the Caribbean can be shown to have a decided advantage.

11
Developing the Sports Tourism Niche Market

The Regional Strategic Development Plan broke new ground when it redefined and expanded the concept of sustainable tourism development. One of the foundations on which sustainability was posited was the diversification of the Caribbean tourism product through the development of a variety of niche markets. Given the Caribbean's year round salubrious climate and attractive natural environment, it was an obvious course of action to expand a world-famous sun, sea, and sand product by exploring the possibilities offered by sports tourism.

Sports tourism defined

Academia loves a debate, and therefore it has wrestled with whether sports tourism should refer only to competitive, formally organized physical activities or should also include physical activities that are not governed by rules, time and competition. The reality is that, whereas massive numbers are drawn to national or international events like the Olympics and The World Games, on a daily basis people selecting a holiday will take into consideration the opportunities offered at the destination or the hotel for physical exercise, recreation and restorative treatments, whether or not competitive and organized. The term "sports tourism" should therefore be inclusive of both types of activity.

The role of sports in social development

Sports have long played a legitimate and important role in the social development of communities. Perhaps no better measure of this reality can be adduced than the role already mentioned in chapter 1 that was played by the Olympic Games in Greece. Few enterprises created by man have lasted so long. Few have been accorded such international importance. In the Ancient World a sacred truce was declared and enforced to permit warring participants to travel unmolested to the Games. Huge crowds travelled to the event. Time in ancient Greece was measured by the four year interval between games, known as an Olympiad, and the greatest honour then to be attained by any Greek was the winning of the simple branch of wild olive given to a victor in the games. Kings competed alongside commoners, and winners became national heroes. Musicians sang praises to the winners, sculptors preserved their strength in marble, and their feats of skill and courage were recorded by the poets and writers of the time. A debate that took place in Barbados a long time ago about whether or not cricketing icon Sir Garfield Sobers, claimed to be the world's most complete cricketer, should be included among those accorded the status of national hero, would have taken an entirely different form, if it had taken place in Ancient Greece. The argument then would have been, Who besides Sir Garry deserved to be honoured as a national hero?

The question is sometimes asked, Why should the world's most brilliant sports figures be accorded heroic status? One answer is, because near impossible demands are made of world famous sportsmen. Many people who have been honoured in various ways and in various fields have done their work behind closed doors and have reputations they have not necessarily earned. In contrast, top sports personalities perform their feats in the middle, before the critical gaze of thousands, and even millions on television. Excellence is expected on every occasion. Success or failure is transparent and applause lasts only as long as the most recent good performance.

Condemnation is public and can be brutal. A sportsman who both succeeds and endures at the top is therefore a unique phenomenon, and deserves to be treasured and honoured.

Sport has been variously described. George Orwell described sport as "war minus the shooting". This is the case, possibly, because few activities of human endeavor create more fierce passions in the breasts of mankind than competitive sport, and if there is one thing fans understand about sport, it is that it is serious business. Sport, then, is a rather more complex activity than it might at first seem. At the individual level it is said to provide deep satisfaction to human beings in their realization of the desire to be self-complete through testing and extension of the body. This tension is said to have a special attraction for the spectators who identify with the contestants, causing a release of energy which affects performance. At the level of the society, sport has become a social phenomenon of considerable magnitude. It has been described as permeating any number of levels of contemporary society, touching upon and deeply influencing such disparate elements as status, race relations, business life, automotive design, clothing styles, the concept of the hero, languages and ethical values.

In fact, with the exception of technology, communications, and tourism itself, probably no other activity had done more to bring countries and continents together, irrespective of distance, culture and language. United Nations secretary general Kofi Annan was moved to remark in 2008 that what the UN was unable to do, the Olympics had done successfully: bring together for peaceful interaction several nations actively at war. It is entirely possible that the name of Usain Bolt, the Jamaican sprinter who broke several records at the 2008 Olympics in Beijing, was better known across the world at that time than many of the political leaders of the world's most important countries.

Contrasting views on the economic impact of international sporting events

As is to be expected, there are differing views on the economic impact, from a tourism perspective, of the major international sporting events of which, perhaps the most famous are, the Summer Olympics and the International Federation of Association Football (FIFA) Soccer World Cup. Two contrasting views are presented below.

European Tour Operators Association negative report

In 2006, as Britain began planning for the 2012 Summer Olympics in London, there were two surprisingly negative reports about the tourism economic impact of world sporting events. The first negative report, which related to the Olympics, was from the European Tour Operators Association. It made the following comments:

- There is no strong link between hosting sporting events and increased tourism.
- The Olympics deter regular tourists, who perceive the city will be full, disrupted, congested and over-priced. The Sydney and Barcelona Olympics were cited as examples of this situation.
- While hotels are full during the Games, the effect is of short duration only.
- Olympic visitors are not major consumers of excursions, of visits to museums and monuments, and of other tourist attractions.
- Action needed to be taken to prevent London's growth as a tourism city being disrupted by the 2012 Olympics.
- There was need prior to 2012 for a strong marketing campaign to counteract any fears that may be held by prospective visitors regarding the Olympics as disruptive to their enjoyment of the city.

Lastminute.com report

The second negative report, which was about World Soccer, was from Lastminute.com. The argument was that, after the defeat of England in the 2006 Soccer World Cup in Germany, English visitors had no interest in remaining in Germany. There was consequently a 35 per cent hike in late bookings from returning British soccer fans looking for an additional holiday. The suggestion here was that the English had gone to Germany for the soccer and to support their team and had no real interest in a German holiday per se.

Counter-arguments of tourism authorities

The British, Spanish and German tourism authorities were, however, quick to counter these views. VisitBritain responded as follows:

- The 2012 Olympics would in fact bring *additional* visitors spending some £2 billion in tourist revenues.
- Preparations were already transforming northeast London.
- Five hundred and ninety thousand visitors came to Manchester for the Commonwealth Games in 2002 versus 550,000 in 2001. In 2003 the number climbed to 750,000.
- In 2012, 40,000 beds would be available for the Olympics in three-star hotels, with 60,000 remaining for other visitors.

The Spanish newspaper *El Pais* rejected the report by the European Tour Operators Association, pointing to the world attention, improved infrastructure and general regeneration of Barcelona that resulted from the Barcelona Olympics.

The German National Tourist Board replied in more detail, citing a survey carried out by them in 2006 which showed the following:

- Forty-three per cent of those surveyed were first-time visitors to Germany, although clearly attracted there because of the World Cup.
- Sixteen per cent were combining attending the World Cup with a holiday in Germany.
- Ten per cent were also visiting family and friends.
- Ninety per cent stated that they were prepared to recommend Germany as a tourism destination.
- Ninety-one per cent said they felt welcome in Germany.
- Around the world the offices of the board reported great enthusiasm for Destination Germany.
- The British fans returning home reported that Germany had proved itself an excellent host.
- Regarding public relations, Germany emerged from the World Cup with a more endearing personality than it had previously.
- After the English team was eliminated, the British supported Germany to win the Cup.

The negative EOTA report should not be rejected in its entirety. There are certainly a number of pitfalls that host countries for major Games should take steps to avoid up front. (These pitfalls will be described later.) Periodically, when major sporting events or festivals are taking place in a country, some local residents look to escape to a quieter place. This situation, it was thought, might present a marketing opportunity in the summer of 2012 for Caribbean countries to target those English persons who would rather enjoy the quiet and tranquility of the Caribbean while the Olympics are on in London.

Perhaps however, two comments may be made in considering the EOTA criticisms. First, the distinction it seems to be making between sporting fans and tourists is not really valid. Secondly, it needs to be questioned whether all or most sports fans can justifiably be stereotyped as lacking an interest in things cultural and in attractions generally.

But even if this were true, the motivation of the hosts is to influence them to spend money at the destination. Certainly revenues lost at museums may be recovered in other ways. With the International Cricket Council (ICC) Cricket World Cup and other international cricket tournaments held in the Caribbean there is abundant evidence that beer sales increase significantly.

Finally, it should be noted that regular tour operators are often replaced by specialist sports tour operators by the organizers of world sporting events, and the regular tour operators may tend to see such events as displacing their normal business.

Sports tourism synergies

Writers on sports tourism, do not, generally speaking, share the pessimistic view about world sporting events, and in fact argue that, not only is there an enormous synergy between tourism and sport, but also that the economic and social impacts extend far beyond those persons and bodies directly involved in the events themselves.

Allen Guttmann, author of *From Ritual to Record: The Nature of Modern Sports* (1978), remarks in the book that "in an age of relatively easy inter-regional and international travel, sports events are able to generate substantial gatherings of peoples to collective rituals. The historical religious pilgrimages have been replaced by modern international flows, to such rites as the Olympic Games, the soccer World Cup, national championships, cup finals and even smaller events." To these events can be added, among others, the ICC Cricket World Cup, the Rugby World Cup, and the US Super Bowl, the scale and costs of each of which are extraordinary.

The considerable economic benefits of such movements of people are listed. These benefits include transportation, construction, renovation of facilities, creation of employment, cultural exchanges, advertising campaigns, specific services and a range of commercial activity, including sports cruises, tours, attractions, and the use of resorts. Furthermore, sport is perceived as providing stimuli for local entrepreneurs, civic leaders and the community at large, for more touristic-oriented skills. Sport also encourages the bringing of various levels of society – organizers, volunteers and entrepreneurs – to work together towards common goals.

Economic impact statistics of sports tourism

Some of the figures given by credible sources for the economic impacts of sports tourism are indeed impressive. In 2003 *Sports Travel Magazine* estimated that the sports-related travel and tourism market in the United States alone is worth some US$118.3 billion. This number included travel by sports spectators and by the families of participants, by sports adventure and sports fantasy camp travellers, and by travellers participating in sports-related corporate incentive projects. It all begins with the event organizers and travel planners who, through their work, create a reason for millions of people to travel to sports events or to take sports-related vacations. The magazine reckoned that its readers alone spend US$6.1 billion on travel each year.

The planning and budget office of the governor of Utah executed a study on the economics of the Olympic Winter Games that were planned for 2002. It estimated that US$2.8 billion would be produced in economic output, 23,000 one-year full-time jobs created, and US$972 million generated in income to Utah workers and business owners. It was further estimated that even after public safety and other government services had been paid for, the state and local governments in Utah would be left with as much as US$140 million in new revenue to invest in, for example, schools, streets, parks and human resources.

Australia, which is big in sports tourism, holds over four hundred sporting events each year, many of which are world championships, as well as international tournaments, all of which are promoted as tourism events. New Zealand assesses that the sport and leisure industry supports 23,000 full-time jobs, contributes US$2.2 billion to the economy and pays US$417 million in taxes. With a population of 3.45 million people, New Zealand has more than four hundred golf courses – that is, more per capita than any other country in the world – and twenty-five ski fields.

The sports tourism opportunity for the Caribbean

It can be argued, therefore, that sports presents the Caribbean with an excellent opportunity for developing one of the fastest-growing niche markets in the tourism sector, and that the Caribbean, with its near-perfect year-round weather, suits itself to almost every kind of land and water sport. It is an opportunity which should be embraced.

The Caribbean, which is four times more dependent on the tourism industry for its foreign exchange earnings and job creation than any other region of the world, faces stiff and growing competition at a global level for market share. In addition to the traditional competition from exotic warm weather destinations, it is encountering increasingly more competition from the other developed countries, which are not only intensifying their promotion of both international and domestic tourism, but are also enhancing their product offers to meet changing consumer preferences. This is a new world of event-marketing and changing distribution systems, and those who are going to stay in business must change with it.

Dealing with seasonality

The commitment of society to the goal of sustainable development requires that jobs not only be created, but also sustained. Adequate returns on investment are most likely to be realized by year-long earnings. The tourism industry is therefore challenged to provide year-round jobs for its employees, and an even stream of revenue. This challenge means that empty hotels in the Caribbean after May, financial droughts in September and October, and layoffs of staff for significant periods, need, if possible, to be avoided.

To fill these "shoulder periods" and "off-seasons" – the two terms share the same meaning – many new events are already being marketed, such as carnivals, music festivals and sports tournaments, all of which have made a difference in dealing with the problem of seasonality. Of all these events, those connected to sports may have attracted the greatest number of international audiences to date.

Existing sports tourism activities in the Caribbean

In the area of significant sporting events targeted at increased tourism flows, considerable progress has been made in the Caribbean with such activities as the Aruba Hi-Winds Pro-Am Windsurfing Championships, Jamaica's Johnnie Walker World Golf Championship, Antigua's Sailing Week, the Rolex Cup Regatta in St Thomas, the Cayman Islands Super Fish Bowl, the Nikonos Shootout in Bonaire, the Tour de la Martinique, the Sandy Lane Gold Cup in horse racing, the Barbados Tourism Authority Charity Golf Tournament and polo in Barbados, motor racing in a number of countries, and cricket at Test, 50-Over One-Day level, and 20/20 overs level, in the countries of the Commonwealth Caribbean. In some cases, it has taken a relatively small investment by the country and good support from sponsors to mount these events with a high level of success.

These examples suggest that the region has merely tapped into a rich economic vein, one which has the potential to yield considerable dividends, whether in marketing to those persons who wish to come to the Caribbean acting as players or officials, to those persons who attend as spectators, or to those persons who come to perform some duty resulting from the sport, such as sports journalists, public relations experts and sponsors.

For visitors to the Caribbean, especially at all-inclusive hotels, already on offer are such activities as water skiing, jet skiing, cricket, athletics, basketball, windsurfing, fishing, soccer, hockey, volleyball, surfing, diving, golf, horse racing, sailing and other water sports, tennis, polo and horseback riding. There are, however, other sporting activities that can be either created or developed for the entertainment of visitors, activities which may in fact seem routine and uninteresting to locals. Road tennis in Barbados is one such example. This sport demands a level of innovation which is not necessarily restricted to those engaged in tourism. Where a level of professionalism – with respect to organization, infrastructure, research, marketing, sponsorship and the buying in of expert advice – has been utilized, impressive economic gains have been achieved. It must be understood, however, that the precondition for successful marketing is a good product, one developed with well-executed research.

The need for sound research of niche markets

The CTRC, from its very beginning in 1974, has tried to impress upon those persons engaged in the tourism sector the critical importance of research. When in 1989 the research and development institution was merged with the CTA to form the CTO, the then-secretary general of the CTO restated the case, for those members who seemed not to understand the matter, that tourism marketing not based on sound research is likely to be ineffective, especially when dealing with niche markets. There is the need to know what are the size and characteristics of the markets in question, where they are to be found, how they are to be reached in terms of communications, and by what means the relevant visitors can be transported to the pertinent destinations. This kind of pre-investment is required to determine where, when, and how much money should be spent, in a targeted manner, in trying to attract the markets in question.

In the 1980s CTRC did some useful research work, seeking to identify the size of the sports markets. In one of its studies on golf it was indicated that there were some 21.7 million golf players in the United States, 12 million in Japan, 300,000 and rising in Germany and 1 million in Canada. Because of a 2003 study of the German market by the CTO, far more information was discovered about the size of the German sport and leisure market than was known previously – at that time, for example, there were 1.5 million surfers, 2 million divers, 250,000 who canoe, 1.2 million anglers, and that hiking was the most popular holiday activity of German holidaymakers.

There is currently a growing market of persons who wish to travel to the Caribbean both to play and watch sports, especially if their own celebrity players are involved. Those Caribbean countries which have had such a difficult time achieving growth in the US market should be reminded that Americans are almost obsessed with sport. Some sixteen million Americans are members of sports clubs. As always the specialist magazines and travel specialists in the marketplace are the best marketing partners and should be identified and utilized accordingly.

Marketing reach

The benefits of hosting highly professional sporting events go far beyond the immediate local economic impact, and include enormous positive long-term publicity and tourism promotion for the country. Some 151 million Americans, half the population, were estimated by the Nielson ratings as having watched the 2009 US Super Bowl football game. Two hundred and sixty million persons world-wide are estimated to have watched the Italy–France Soccer World Cup final in 2006. The Johnny Walker Professional Golf Tournament in Jamaica has aired in eighty-three countries with an estimated total audience of over 300 million viewers, and television news reports went to more than two hundred broadcasters in 130 countries.

FIFA Soccer World Cup 2010 in South Africa

In 2010 the Soccer World Cup took place in South Africa where for only the third time in the history of the World Cup attendance surpassed 3 million. The US tournament in 1994 had drawn 3.59 million fans and that in Germany in 2006 some 3.36 million.

According to press reports in July 2010, the FIFA 2010 World Cup was expected to be the most watched television event in history. Hundreds of broadcasters, representing about seventy countries, transmitted the cup games to a television audience that FIFA officials expected to exceed a cumulative 26 billion, an average of approximately four hundred million viewers per match. Some 700 million viewers were expected to watch the World Cup Final alone.

Overall, it was a great social and economic success for South Africa despite the fears expressed prior to the tournament that fans would be at risk from crime in South Africa and that the massive organization required might be beyond the ability of the country. Of course there were some issues, like those of eviction and resettlement which seem to follow developing countries engaged in putting their best foot forward in preparation for the tournament, but even the worst critics of South Africa as the site selected, could not deny that the tournament was a huge success socially, politically and economically for the country.

Direct economic impact of Test cricket in West Indian countries

ICC Cricket is to the West Indies what World Cup soccer is to the rest of the world and while it has not been promoted as such, Test cricket and, more recently, One-Day and T20 cricket, have been a great tourism niche market for the Commonwealth Caribbean with significant economic impact.

The CTO did a study, at the request of the Barbados Tourism Authority, of the economic impact of one cricket test match between England and the West Indies played in Barbados during the 1998 cricket series between the West Indies and England. During the week immediately after the game approximately 8,300, or 15 per cent, of departing visitors captured in a CTO-conducted survey, indicated that they had come to Barbados for cricket. Some 6,474 or 78 per cent of those visitors were from the United Kingdom. With an average stay of ten days, these visits, associated with one game, translated into some US$24 million to the Barbados economy. It is important to remember that, in these matters, even when the organizers lose money, the economy can gain, which is the best case to be made for government subsidies to sport when a major economic objective has been set.

With respect to cricket in Barbados and golf in Jamaica, we have seen the tourism and the sports people working together, each with an understanding of the economic importance of the event, beyond the immediate respective objectives of the contests themselves. One lesson learned is that it is advisable that research be done both in advance of the event to test its potential, and after, to capture its impact and the lessons learned.

Cricket: A source of social cohesion and pride in the Caribbean

The small territories comprising the Commonwealth Caribbean have had a distinguished history in world cricket, and in fact were world champions for a significant period of time, proving that population size is not as important as some observers suppose in providing world leadership.

Any book on tourism written in the CARICOM region at this time has not only to chronicle the history of West Indian cricket, but also to address the concept of cricket as a tourism niche market and a contributor to Caribbean social and economic development beyond the game. The geographical reach of cricket is considerable. While it is played to date mainly in countries which were former British colonies (and Britain itself), it has a potential audience of two billion people, and it is beginning to be played in some European countries, in North America, and in Asia, including China.

Many claims are made for West Indies cricket by a number of important persons. Clive Lloyd, a former West Indies cricket captain, in his introduction to Michael Manley's book *A History of West Indies Cricket* (1988), has this to say: "All our experiments in Caribbean integration either failed or have maintained a dubious survivability; but cricket remains the instrument of Caribbean cohesion – the remover of arid insularity and nationalistic prejudice. It is through cricket and its many spin offs that we owe our Caribbean consideration and dignity abroad. It is the musical instrument on which we orchestrate our emotions from the extremes of wild enthusiasm to the depths of despair." Regrettably much of that dignity has been forfeited by the dismal performance of Caribbean cricket teams in the first decade of the twenty-first century.

In the same book Manley also writes:

> At a political level, the University of the West Indies apart, cricket is the most completely regional activity undertaken by the people of the member states of CARICOM. It is also the most successful cooperative endeavour and as such, is a constant reminder to a people of otherwise wayward insularity, of the value of collaboration. The West Indies have played at international level for sixty years. For twelve of those they have been virtual or official champions of the world.

Success or failure apart, cricket has a profound implication for the West Indies. Indeed, as C.L.R. James divined with sure instinct and unmatched descriptive flair, West Indian cricket is like a metaphor for social history. Perhaps his most famous cricket quotation – it is from his book *Beyond the Boundary* (1963) – is, "What does he know of cricket, who only cricket knows"?

Books on cricket have been written by persons who have been associated with the game as players or commentators. However, one would be challenged to find a publication in any country which deals with the sport from the perspective of being one of the greatest tourist attractions in the West Indies, and a major economic driver, due to the consumption of goods and services by local and foreign crowds who spend money both at the venue of the game and in the wider society of the country in which the game is played.

Cricket, while not so recognized, has been a sports tourism niche from as early as 1846 when, according to Manley, the first inter-colonial match was played, specifically between British Guiana and Barbados. The first foreign team to tour the West Indies was an American side in 1888, and the first triangular inter-colonial tournament took place in 1891 between Barbados, Trinidad and British Guiana.

Except for breaks during the First and Second World Wars, these tournaments were played and watched by significant and enthusiastic crowds. The tournaments continued from 1893 and 1894 into modern times, sometimes involving Jamaica. In 1895 an English team toured the West Indies for the first time and played in Barbados, Trinidad, Jamaica and British Guiana.

The book *The First West Indies Cricket Tour: Canada and the United States in 1886* (edited by and with an introduction by Hilary McD. Beckles, 2006) records that the West Indies Cricket team made its first overseas tour, specifically, to Canada and the United States, in 1886. It was not until 1900 that the Marylebone Cricket Club, the governing body of cricket, agreed that the West Indies team had reached the standard to be allowed to tour England, though not yet with the status of a "first class side".

The West Indies team – which in 1933 was described in a cartoon in an English newspaper as saying "we have come to learn, sah" – returned in the 1950 tour to defeat comprehensively the English side. That tour marked the rise of the West Indies cricket to the highest heights of world cricket and, beginning with the 1960s, the team established a brand the equal of which for flair and excitement had never been seen before. Full recognition of the West Indies claim to be cricket leaders may be said to have finally come when they were chosen by the ICC to host the Cricket World Cup from 13 March to 28 April 2007.

ICC Cricket World Cup, 2007: Legacy and impact

The Cricket World Cup is the premier international championship of men's One-Day International Cricket. The tournament is the world's fourth largest sporting event viewed by more than a billion people. First organized in England in 1975, it was won four times by Australia (1987, 1999, 2003, 2007), twice by the West Indies (1975, 1979), twice by India (1983, 2011), once by Pakistan (1992) and once by Sri Lanka (1996).

When hosting the 2007 tournament was allocated to the West Indies, serious doubts were immediately raised in a number of quarters, including some of the other countries bidding for the games, as to the Caribbean's ability to host the tournament successfully. The fact that the tournament had to be staged across seven sovereign, but developing Caribbean countries, was seen as a major challenge. People recalled that the staging of matches in the 2002 Soccer World Cup between Japan and Korea, countries which had far greater resources and administrative capacity than the West Indies, had presented major difficulties. It was assumed therefore that the air transport logistics of moving teams, officials, sponsors and their baggage efficiently around the region would defeat regional air carriers. There were serious doubts expressed about the region's ability to find the resources needed to expand, upgrade or build the cricket stadia and bring them up to international standards. Finally, and importantly, few observers thought that the Caribbean people could cope at the various administrative and technical levels required to mount the tournament successfully.

The West Indian countries proved all the doubters wrong. Having made themselves aware of the various standards set by the ICC in the Bid Book, they set about to stage the tournament in a most professional manner at regional and national levels.

A board of directors, comprising fifteen persons from across the region with extensive administrative and managerial experience, was established to oversee the planning process and work closely with national boards established in all the countries where games were scheduled to be played. These boards, although comprising largely private sector personnel, worked closely with governments, the input and assistance of which were critical.

Although some mistakes were made, there can be no doubt that the planning for the 2007 ICC Tournament created standards to be met and an important blueprint for any subsequent tournament of such magnitude. The first task was to identify the challenges and opportunities involved and the skills required to deal with them. Some of the challenges involved:

- delivering on accommodation, ground, sea, and air transportation, airport capacity, facilitation at customs and immigration and airport handling

- ensuring the availability and accessibility to sports fans of recreational services, including restaurants and attractions
- guaranteeing that support services, such as banks, medical services and shopping, were in place to meet the needs of the visitors

The opportunities identified included the following:

- event management legacy, especially in the area of tourism
- cricket development as part of the tourism product
- creative use post-2007 of the stadiums built
- a cultural and entertainment legacy
- the strengthening of auxiliary services
- inter-regional linkages
- improved tourist infrastructure
- additional long-term employment in the tourist sector
- stimulation of new investment and entrepreneurial activity
- global tourism marketing
- collaboration between normally competing entities

At 2013, it is six years since the ICC 2007 cricket tournament has taken place and therefore possible to assess adequately its successes and failures.

The following aspects of the hosting of the tournament can be seen as negatives:

- The crowds were not as large as expected at all venues because India and Pakistan – two teams which normally draw large crowds to cricket – were unexpectedly eliminated early in the tournament by teams which had been perceived as competition minnows.
- The attendance factor was made worse by a combination of high ticket prices and an ICC ban on certain popular local cultural practices normally enjoyed by local sports enthusiasts.
- Scheduling of the tournament during the Caribbean tourist high season led to pressure on hotel room capacity and high accommodation room rates, both of which negatively affected the foreign fans.
- In terms of future tourism business, it can also be argued that the opportunities for major global marketing to attract new business from

non-traditional markets were not fully taken by the region's tourism authorities.
- Plans to measure, through a scientific study, the economic and social impact of the tournament, were not followed through.
- Finally, it was thought by some observers that the best features of travel and airport facilitation – introduced by sunset legislation especially for the tournament – should have been kept in place beyond the event. There were, however, counter-arguments to this position, driven largely by security considerations.

These were all lessons to be learned with profit. Despite all the above, however, there were many positive results:

- There was undoubtedly significant economic impact which could only be attributed to the event.
- As a result of the preparations for 2007 tournament, the region now had some of the best cricket stadiums in the world.
- In the area where confusion was expected to reign – that is, with respect to transportation of teams, officials, media, sponsors and fans – the Caribbean carriers did an excellent and seamless job.
- The success of the West Indies as host can be seen as being recognized in this way: in 2010 the ICC awarded the region the hosting of the ICC 20/20 World Cricket Tournament. This conferment gave the Caribbean region a chance to prove that it had learned many important lessons about hosting major world events.
- While the West Indies team failed to cover itself with glory on the field, the management of the tournament was successful and none of the mistakes of 2007 were repeated.

The ongoing challenge for the region in the future will be to demonstrate that the investment in major infrastructure for international cricket can be put to good and productive use, not only for cricket tournaments, but also for other events capable of attracting large gatherings of people willing and able to consume local goods and services.

Tourism and athletics

Athletics now seem to present another major tourism niche market opportunity for the Caribbean. For some time Jamaica has dominated the sprinting track and field events in international athletics. A few other Caribbean countries, such as Cuba, the Bahamas, Barbados, Grenada and St Kitts, have had some successes. This good fortune has also been good financially for the individuals concerned, and has certainly been of value in promoting the destinations from which they come.

A matter for thought, however, is this: how could the Caribbean exploit its track and field superiority by staging major events at home? If Caribbean stars are major drawing cards in international meets, why could the Caribbean not bring the world to the region to watch its stars in international tournaments? It would take finance, organization, adequate infrastructure and sponsorship, but this should not be beyond the capabilities of a region which now has proven experience in major event planning for world cricket tournaments.

Sports/manufacturing linkages

Finally and importantly, it is being suggested that the region should pay more attention to linkages between sports and manufacturing. In highly industrialized countries there is a considerable spin-off from sports with the development of the manufacturing leisure market. This is one of the fastest-growing sectors of the economy in both Canada and the United States, with some US$13.4 billion being spent on sport and recreational equipment, and some US$14 billion on sports supplies. Despite a lower level of industrial development, Caribbean entrepreneurs must be sufficiently innovative to seize similar opportunities as a number of them did during the ICC World Cup. The entrepreneurs were forced to do so because it was one of the ICC preconditions of the awarding of the games that attention be paid to linkages and legacy. This connection needs to be continued.

12
Developing the Culture/Heritage Tourism Niche Market

It is now generally accepted that another means of implementing the product diversification called for by the regional strategic plan is to develop, expand and promote the cultural and heritage industries of the Caribbean. To do so with any sense of honesty and authenticity brings us face to face with a colonial past: its legacy of slavery, class and racial discrimination; the various influences from the New World, Europe, Africa and Asia; and how these factors have contributed to what is Caribbean culture. These matters have been dealt with from a historical perspective in the introduction and in chapter 2.

It is worth repeating however, that on the long historical road – three centuries – from sugar to tourism in the Caribbean, there have been harsh experiences which have brutalized and confused the psyches of both colonizers and the colonized, causing many doubts to be formed and many questions to be raised about who Caribbean people are, what Caribbean culture is, and even if the entity actually exists.

Concepts of culture

It was inevitable that concepts of culture in the Caribbean would be defined by the colonizers. In many of the territories the ruling classes were, for many years, absentee landlords who received their respective cultural experiences, as they defined them, in the European mother countries. Certainly this situation would have been true for the visual, literary and performing arts. The West Indian territories, with a few exceptions, were thought of by such persons largely as places to exploit for commercial profit, rather than as places to settle and live. For many years as well, formal education was denied the slave population and only reached them through the persistence of religious groups like the Methodists and Moravians – in the face of strong opposition from the established Anglican Church. Such education, even with the best of intentions, would inevitably have been Eurocentric, likely to denigrate any African retentions and to reinforce ideas about white superiority. Nevertheless, even legal prohibition could not prevent areas of survival of African religion, music, secular ritual, language, oral literature and herbal medicines, *inter alia*. The advent of Chinese and Indian immigration in the nineteenth century would have brought new cultural strains, fashioning the various elements into something *sui generis*. Our reality is that, however painful the process, it provided the region with rich and varied experiences which gave birth to a new Caribbean civilization.

For that civilization to flourish, however, there needed to be the self-realization that came with levels of political and constitutional advancement, signed posted along the way by full adult suffrage, the phasing out of white political dominance in societies that were largely black, and ending with independence for most of the territories from the 1960s to the 1980s.

No radical change in the social pecking order followed immediately upon independence. Wealth and skin colour continued to be highly correlated. But the movement towards both political independence and independence itself resulted in a search for identity, and in a debate among the people of the region about indigenous culture. This debate was led by the region's own historians, sociologists, anthropologists, writers and cultural activists, all of whom seemed to have been energized by the movements for independence that were affecting every part of the globe during the 1950s and 1960s. This period was indeed one of the most fertile of the creativity of local Caribbean people, and its importance was not lost on the region's more enlightened political leaders.

Barbados's national hero and the father of independence Errol Walton Barrow wrote the following in the independence issue of *New World Magazine* (November 1966):

It is my sincere hope that independence will release in our people a sense of deep pride in their country, a feeling of being one people, and a self-confidence that we can overcome all obstacles that stand in the way of personal realization of national development.

Our total commitment now, and for the future, is nothing less than the social and cultural upliftment of our nation. In this challenging task, we must know, who we are, whence we came, and where we are heading. A searching analysis of our heritage and traditions must be conducted, if our cultural identity is to be established. Our novelists, poets and short story writers have for some time now been holding a mirror up to our society and interpreting our customs, mores and personality traits. So far, much has been accomplished. I trust that our new political status will stimulate much greater activity in the arts.

May our people draw deeply on our cultural heritage. May we use independence not as an end in itself, but as a turning point in time when we discovered new energies for a massive and successful assault on the problems facing a small community.

Caribbean cultural fragility

Caribbean thinkers and writers, while excited by the new dawn of independence, could not help but be concerned about the fragility of the cultural fabric of societies which had experienced the kind of social trauma discussed earlier. As the tourism industry began to grow rapidly in the 1950s and 1960s, fears were expressed about the ability of the society to withstand the shock of what was seen as invading hordes of white tourists – tourists with notions and practices that were thought by many observers to be reinforcing the inequalities of the past. In those early days the new industry, tourism – like the old one, sugar – was largely owned by foreign white people. It was a service industry, and it involved, for the most part, blacks serving whites.

Clash of indigenous and foreign cultures

Not surprisingly, the region's preoccupation with culture in the period following independence was largely about issues of cultural diffusion, a fact that suggests that, when two cultures come into contact with each other, that of the weaker society is more likely to be diluted by that of the stronger one. Certainly postcolonial societies qualified as the weaker, since colonial people had been taught, by both formal and informal education introduced by the European colonizers, that African heritage was inferior to that of the colonizers. Moreover, during slavery, those persons with an African heritage were forbidden by law to practise certain vestiges of their African past. Part of the region's colonial inheritance has therefore been to undervalue African cultural retentions and to set the mark of cultural excellence by the extent to which the society imitated aspects of the culture of the colonial masters.

The clash of cultures brought fears that the self-concept of the local population would be diminished, the institution of the family weakened, social health and integration threatened, and indigenous culture and social values diluted. As tourism began to take hold in the Caribbean, there was a great deal of evidence that, even in simple instances like speech and dress, indigenous ways of behaving were giving way to those of the tourists, ways which were thought to be more desirable. Some developing countries at the time sought to solve this problem by creating "enclave tourism" which, in effect, isolated tourists from the rest of the society in specific geographical areas. However, this process only succeeded in creating two different societies in the same country. In any case, in practical terms, given the small land masses of most Caribbean countries, it is difficult to practise enclave tourism in this region.

The six decades that have passed since 1950 have permitted Caribbean people to live through a period in which almost every country in the world has gained political independence. Only a tiny minority, mostly Caribbean, loiter on the steps of the premises of their colonial masters. Independence has been accompanied by an assertion of nationalism and self-identity through processes of re-education by which people have taken positive steps to correct some of the worst distortions of colonialism and colonial education. This journey is, however, one which has not yet been completed.

Discovering one's roots has now become fashionable, and attempts to demonize everything of African origin is now regarded as evidence of an impoverished education. Since the 1950s, empires, including the British Empire, have fallen, but other empires, however called, have arisen and exerted their influence over extensive parts of the world. Small states need therefore always to be vigilant for the forces of cultural penetration to the extent that they seek to replace all things indigenous.

Owen Arthur, the prime minister of Barbados from 1994 to 2008, in an address on 9 April 2003 to the opening of the World Commission on the Social Dimensions of Globalization, expressed his own concerns about the continuing threats to Caribbean culture in a post-independence period:

The Caribbean's unique contribution to the development of the global society has to date taken the form of the products of the creative imagination of its people and its contribution to good global governance, drawing upon its superior example of political stability and maturity.

It is vital that in a world where cultural homogeneity is fast becoming the norm, the Caribbean should not yield an iota in expressing our confidence in the value of our cultural norms and the essential aspects of the Caribbean way of life, which has made us, despite our smallness and vulnerability, such a resilient and resourceful people.

Obviously we cannot close our societies. But it has to be clear that the most insidious aspect of the workings of the social dimensions of globalization in the Caribbean, has been in the sphere of cultural penetration, and the effect of such cultural penetration in shaping the perspective, expectations and behaviour especially of our youth.

We ignore our cultural development at our peril.

Whether Caribbean people accept this fact, Caribbean cultural norms are those which were fashioned by the crucible of African slavery, European colonization and Asian indentured labour, during the period that stretches from the seventeenth century until now.

If culture is the totality of man's beliefs, values and ways of doing things (Elliott Parris, "Tourism and Culture: Why Seek a Stronger Linkage", 1983), then it is not possible for a country to be without a culture. We are the product of the sum of our experiences. We cannot pick and choose. We are what we have become and we must do what we can to preserve those aspects of our way of life which have come to identify us as a new civilization and give us our uniqueness in the world. Our artists in their various genres of artistic endeavour have given a great deal of thought to what is Caribbean culture and sought to portray images of that reality. If therefore we are to develop our arts commercially in the service of tourism, and develop a cultural tourism niche, the least we can do is consult with our artists and our cultural experts about how this can best be done and at the least cost to authenticity.

What, then, is cultural tourism?

Definition of cultural tourism

Cultural tourism may be defined as a subset of tourism concerned with a country or region's culture, specifically the lifestyle of the people in its various geographical areas, the history of those people, their art, architecture, religion and other elements that helped to shape their way of life. Cultural tourism includes tourism in the urban areas, particularly historic or large cities, and their cultural facilities, such as museums and theatres. Cultural tourism can also include tourism in rural areas showcasing the traditions of indigenous cultural communities (that is, festivals and rituals) and their values and lifestyle. This form of tourism is becoming generally more popular throughout the developing world and a recent Organisation for Economic Co-operation and Development report has highlighted the role that cultural tourism can play in regional development in different world regions (*The Impact of Culture on Tourism*, 2009).

The problem of defining cultural tourism led the European Association for Tourism and Leisure Education to launch the Cultural Tourism Research Project in 1991. This project was led by Greg Richards, professor of of leisure studies at Tilburg University and professor of events at NHTV in the Netherlands. The research resulted in two definitions of cultural tourism, one conceptual and the other technical. The conceptual definition is as follows: "The movement of persons to cultural attractions away from their normal place of residence with the intention to gather new information and experiences to satisfy their cultural needs"; the technical definition is, "All movements of persons to specific cultural attractions such as heritage sites, artistic and cultural manifestations, arts and drama outside their normal place of residence" (*Cultural Tourism in Europe*, 1996).

Many European countries often cannot offer a competitive sun, sea, and sand product and therefore the core of their tourism product is cultural tourism. They are proud of their historical and societal achievements, and therefore they invite people from throughout the world to learn about them and to enjoy them at a price.

First Caribbean conference: "Cultural Patrimony and the Tourism Product", 1983

One of the areas of focus of the Caribbean Tourism Research and Development Centre from its establishment in 1974, under the leadership of Jean Holder, had been the impact of tourism on Caribbean culture. It therefore joined forces in 1983 with the OAS, and the Caribbean

Conservation Association to bring together tourism practitioners and cultural experts in a seminar in Barbados from 18 to 22 July to discuss, as it was called, "Cultural Patrimony and the Tourism Product: Towards a Mutually Beneficial Relationship". Among the many participants were two prominent Barbadian cultural experts, Cynthia Wilson and Elombe Mottley. The conference produced many learned papers, much discussion and several valuable recommendations. It may therefore be useful to re-examine thirty years later certain of the views therein expressed, when some aspects of the environment will have changed, and when the necessity for tourism product diversification has made cultural tourism an urgent and desirable option.

The organizers invited six cultural experts to address a seminar attended by both tourism and cultural practitioners. The experts were asked to speak to the question of how a strong and beneficial linkage could best be forged between tourism and culture. The following presentations were made:

- "Tourism and Culture: Why Seek a Stronger Linkage?", Elliott Parris
- "Tourism and Historical Architecture in the Caribbean", David Buisseret
- "CARIMOS, Culture, Tourism and Historic Monuments in the Caribbean Region", by Eugenio Perez Montas
- "Tourism and Craft Development", by Jerry Craig
- "Folklore, Folk Art and Craft in the Caribbean: Their Role in Tourism Product Development", by J.D. Elder
- "Performing and Literary Arts: Their Role in Cultural Patrimony and Possibilities for Tourism Incorporation", by Elliott Parris
- "Performing, Visual and Literary Arts: Their Role in Cultural Patrimony and Possibilities for Tourism Incorporation", by Alwyn Bully

These papers, the discussion that followed and the recommendations made may be found in a report published in 1983 by the international trade and tourism division of the department of economic affairs of the OAS. The book contained a wealth of ideas on the subject of culture and tourism linkage, and certainly deserved and deserves detailed study. The papers themselves provided a long list of ideas that can be explored in seeking to develop cultural tourism. A selection of these ideas is presented below.

A definition of culture

Elliott Parris in his paper defined culture as "the totality of man's beliefs, values and ways of doing things". Culture was seen as shared behaviour, resulting from man's living in groups. Parris argued that, since tourism is an industry that sees one group of people playing host to another, promoting tourism without taking into account the culture of both host and guest would be exceedingly reckless, given the potential impacts that guest and host may have on each other. It is especially reckless on the part of the host who may be playing host for all seasons, unlike the guest who visits only for a short time.

Tourism and historical architecture

David Buisseret, who dealt with tourism and historical architecture, sought in his paper to identify some historic sites, largely in Jamaica and the Lesser Antilles, which had been successfully exploited in the interests of tourism, and other sites which seemed to have been neglected, but offered much scope for development in a touristic sense. Buisseret analysed the architectural patrimony under five different headings:

- domestic buildings
- commercial architecture
- industrial structures
- military works
- public buildings

Domestic buildings

Under the heading of domestic buildings Buisseret discussed small buildings, such as Arawak huts and slave quarters, as well as medium-sized houses from the eighteenth and nineteenth centuries, which are still in private hands. He also mentions some examples of entire towns in Puerto Rico (Old San Juan) and the Dominican Republic that exemplify this kind of architecture, which are well preserved (often with government support) and a few areas in the English-speaking Caribbean which, regrettably, more often than not, have been allowed to fall into disrepair. It may be that people do not quite appreciate the touristic value of maintaining such towns as they were and believe that new glass towers everywhere represent modernity and development. Last, but by no means least, he speaks of the abundance of great houses across the Caribbean owned by wealthy landowners and therefore well maintained and preserved.

Commercial buildings

Next, a look is taken at several Caribbean cities with outstanding examples of commercial architecture, many of which have been well restored and are maintained by such bodies as the chambers of commerce. Those places selected for special mention were Willemstad, Curaçao, where the merchants' houses of the eighteenth and nineteenth centuries still fulfil their original function, but now cater largely to the tourist trade; the shops and cafes of Charlotte Amalie in the US Virgin Islands; and the commercial areas in St George's, Grenada, and Nassau, Bahamas.

It was suggested that Kingstown, St Vincent – which was set out about 1765, with houses built in a charming and characteristic style, with arcades facing the street on the lower floors, and shaded sash windows on the upper floors – has great touristic potential, which has never been recognized nor exploited.

Industrial structures

The various industries concerned in the Caribbean with the production of sugar, cocoa, coffee, lime and indigo, have also left the region a wealth of examples of historical industrial structures with good tourism possibilities. None more than sugar, where many examples still remain of the buildings that were used for the various processes of crushing cane, boiling the juice and curing sugar. Cane was crushed by windmills, watermills and mule mills, and whereas there may be only one example of a fully restored windmill in working order (which is situated at Morgan Lewis in Barbados), the Caribbean landscape is covered with relics of the windmills, which could be restored after some fashion.

The remains of many boiling houses are also to be found in the Caribbean, and these could be restored to demonstrate the process of boiling from one cauldron to another, as sugar was crystallized. Sugar could even be sold on a small scale to visitors. There are also curing houses, which little has been done so far to preserve. It is of interest however, that one such building has been converted to an unusual use: the chapel of the University of the West Indies at Mona, Kingston.

There has been a great deal of emphasis placed on buildings connected with sugar because of its dominance. However, coffee has also left some examples of its characteristic architecture, although it seems that only in Clydesdale, in the parish of St Andrew in Jamaica, has a coffee complex been retained and preserved as a popular centre for tourists. In some islands barbecues which take the shape of rolling platforms used for drying cocoa are on display and there is a good example at Griveliere in Guadeloupe which forms part of a tourist visit. It is also suggested that lime kilns and indigo works of a bygone age may be restored and used with profit as places of interest for tourism.

Military works

The category of military works largely refers to the impressive military forts which are to be found in great abundance across the Caribbean. The forts select themselves as products to be marketed to the people of European countries, since, to protect their military interests in the Caribbean, European governments were responsible for their establishment. But, as impressive structures, they have an appeal to most visitors regardless of place of origin. Their use as tourism objects, however, depends on their restoration, historical presentation and marketing.

The outstanding fortifications at Charlotte Amalie in the US Virgin Islands, at Brimstone Hill in St Kitts, at Fort James in Antigua, at Fort Charlotte in St Vincent, at Fort George in Grenada, and at the Cabrits in Dominica, and those in St Lucia and the French Islands, are already well known. Those in Old San Juan in Puerto Rico and in Havana, Cuba, are among the most impressive in the world. The guns, howitzers and mortars that decorate Caribbean forts are held to be much rarer and more interesting than is generally realized.

Other important military architecture includes naval bases built by the British, who based their fleet in the Caribbean during the eighteenth century. English Harbour in Antigua is an example of a well-restored naval base, while the base at Bridgetown seems somewhat neglected, and the one at Port Royal in Jamaica was destroyed. The superb royal naval hospital at Port Royal, built in the eighteenth century, has been preserved, and is both the headquarters of the Jamaican archaeological service and a museum complex.

Other examples of military buildings are the signal stations – of which there are excellent examples at Fort George in Port of Spain and Gun Hill in Barbados – and the magazines for power and shot, many dating also from the eighteenth century.

Public buildings

An outstanding example of those public buildings in the Caribbean which have continued to be of interest to visitors are the several magnificent churches. The churches are British, Dutch and French, and are in good condition because they have been maintained through the ages by their respective congregations. Both their walls and graveyards are a source of interesting historical information, and by North American standards provide an impressive sense of antiquity.

Other public structures of interest are old bridges, many made of stone. But of special interest is the old iron bridge at Spanish Town in Jamaica, a bridge which was constructed in the nineteenth century. Early examples of masterpieces of engineering are some of the Caribbean lighthouses, which are monuments of the industrial revolution, but a number of them regrettably in bad states of repair.

Buisseret ends his paper with reference to the splendid monumental squares to be found in a number of Caribbean capitals which are in good condition through being maintained by government.

Caribbean Plan for Monuments and Sites

In his paper Eugenio Perez Montas, the coordinator of the Caribbean Plan for Monuments and Sites (CARIMOS), explains that the plan was born with the aim of strengthening the conservation of Caribbean monuments and sites, of revitalizing old centres, and of initiating a movement towards a collective consciousness in which a shared heritage is converted into an instrument for economic and social development. Montas takes a rather pragmatic view of the relationship between culture and tourism, and quotes several international and regional sources which suggest that the best prospect of cultural assets surviving lie in their linkage with the tourism industry.

In 1963 the United Nations Conference on International Travel and Tourism not only recommended that high priority be given to investment in tourism within the national plans, but also highlighted the fact that, from a tourist point of view, the cultural, historical and natural patrimony of the nations constituted a substantially important value. The conference therefore urged the adoption of adequate measures to ensure the conservation and protection of the said patrimony.

The Quito Standards, a pan-American convention signed in 1967, again made a strong statement about the relationship between culture and tourism as follows:

> Cultural values are not denaturalized nor compromised when they are linked to the interests of tourism, and far from it, the great attraction of the monuments and the growing affluence of the foreign admirers contribute to strengthen the awareness of the national importance and significance....
>
> If the monuments and sites of the cultural patrimony play an important role in promoting tourism, it is logical to think that the investments required for restoring and equipping them within their specialized technical framework, should be done simultaneously with the investments needed for meeting the facilities required by the tourists and moreover, should both be integrated into one sole economic plan for regional development.

The "International Seminar on Contemporary Tourism and Humanism" was held in Brussels in November 1976 and agreed on a "Charter of Cultural Tourism". Among the declarations from delegates attending was that they were "unanimous in their concern for the protection of the cultural patrimony, which is the basis of international tourism; they undertake to help in the fight initiated on all fronts against the destruction of said heritage by all known sources of pollution; and they appeal to the architects and scientific experts of the whole world so that the most advanced resources of modern technology be used for the protection of monuments".

There is a great deal of evidence that, on the one hand, the growth of mass tourism throughout the world has been an indispensable source of income for all nations possessing magnificent natural sites and distinguished and unique man-made treasures. In fact, tourism has guaranteed the survival of most of these assets because they have attracted countless visitors.

On the other hand there is, admittedly, also the threat of the growing erosion of landmarks and natural features. This threat is posed largely to the coastal zones, small villages and minor architecture, all of which suffer damage and a reduction to uniformity at the hands of developers, a callous local population and uncommitted foreigners. Great landmarks, such as cathedrals, and natural sites like the Grand Canyon, are less vulnerable.

Craft, folklore and folk art

The areas of craft, folklore and folk art were addressed by Jerry Craig and J.D. Elder as they sought to address the question, How can tourism help to promote the rescue, restoration and conservation, and give meaning to cultural patrimony?

Craig made the important point that tourism could only provide a market and a stage on which to display Caribbean culture and to promote among Caribbean nationals a willingness to use local crafts, to preserve traditional architecture and to listen to local music. When this attitude to development becomes action, Craig argued, the rest of the commercial process will be rooted in an understanding and appreciation of Caribbean culture. Craig provided some practical guidelines for success among which were:

- The tourist industry should know where crafts are for sale, where it is made, what are the specialties of each district. The industry should also arrange bus tours to local craft markets.
- Tourism should promote among tourism staff an attitude of cooperation with their colleagues in the craft industry.
- An awareness and understanding of craft should be a central part of the education system, and trained craftspeople, regardless of their academic skills, should be invited into the education system to share their expertise.
- Since most folkloric craft is functional, the objects made should function properly. For example, jugs should not leak, spouts should pour properly, covers for baskets should fit snugly, and table mats should lie flat and not curl around the edges.

- Items should match: a beautiful handmade leather bag should not have a cheap plastic clasp, and linings for straw baskets should not be made of ugly material that ruins the look of the bag.

Craig urged craftspeople to experiment, and suggested that, when they were looking for new designs and new applications for traditional crafts, history, local theatre, the flora and fauna could provide new ideas. Craftspeople, he argued, should not be inhibited in blending historical and contemporary culture with the use of indigenous material to produce attractive, richly textured craft. Craftwork should be a highly visible part of the tourism environment. It should be used in hotels, and workers should be educated about their craft so that they could answer questions fully and encourage tourists' interest in knowing more about the craft.

Craig expressed fears that craft materials, especially straw work, were being used up and not adequately replaced, and suggested the need for collaboration between craftspeople and the ministries of agriculture. Be prepared, Craig suggested, to try new colours, new shapes and new materials, to push for local use of craft in homes, hotels, and public buildings, and to keep pricing reasonable and be flexible about production.

Creating tourism products from folklore, folk arts and crafts

Elder in his paper set out a catalogue of nine types of tourism products which, in his opinion, could be provided from folklore, folk arts, and crafts to be consumed in a variety of ways by the visitor, whether consumed on the spot, listened to, observed, or taken away for a price. Below are some examples of these products, by no means exhaustive, broken down as follows:

- people of the region – their way of life, language, clothes and food
- the physical environment, including natural configurations, such as mountains, volcanoes and waterfalls; man-made infrastructural objects, such as bridges, castles, houses; dwellings of heroes; legendary sites; and military sites, including forts and fortifications
- verbal vernacular arts of the region, including folklore, folktales, riddles, proverbs, beliefs, superstitions and folk poetry
- dramatic arts of the people, such as folk theatre; plays; mimes; rituals; annual ceremonies; folk dances; traditional costumes; masks;

dramatic and folk theatre houses; icons and puppetry figures; and dolls of the region
- ceremonies, including anniversaries, tournaments, carnivals, fetes, wakes and vigils, and such celebrations as crop overs, first fruit festivals and cocoa dance
- child lore, and children's games, among them skip rope rhymes and tongue twister games
- religious activities, including pilgrimages; processions; public initiatory rites; obituary customs; with Spiritual Baptists, thrones of grace; in Cuba, Santeria; and in Trinidad and Tobago, jumbie dance
- culinary arts of the region – these arts would include brule jol, sweet meats and salt meats; native beverages, including ginger beer; and folk cuisine and recipes as well as traditional food taboos, and rituals used to ensure success in hunting and fishing; other culinary arts would be techniques for the preservation of food staples, such as roasting, sun-drying, and the smoking of meat
- music and music making, including musical performances of a wide variety, including traditional forms of music, and folk orchestras and their instruments; aspects of music could embrace techniques for crafting instruments, and processing raw materials for making drums, fiddles and other chordophones, such as hides, fibres, wood, shells of the sea, wire-like metals, bush rope, oil drums for steel band instruments, and pottery for tabors

Elder observed that modern electronic technology had removed the difficulty of transforming audio-visual material of folk derivation into commodities. He further argued:

- Folk songs and folk dances could be packaged for sale.
- Instant photography could package scenery and sights.
- The dialect and speech of the storytellers and poets could be captured on tape.
- Folk craft or handiwork, including articles made by traditional artisans, could be sold in the marketplace.
- Traditional medicines – dried leaves, barks, roots, catalogues of medicines, dried flowers, and pressed oils from medicinal plants, such as musk, rose oil, bay leaf oil – could be made available for sale.

Elder also argued that ceremonies and festivals could be exploited in a number of ways. Examples would include recorded music and drama; miniatures carved in wood, papier mache or plaster of Paris; costumes from Carnival; travelling exhibitions of festival regalia; and documentaries of native ceremonies.

Such events are not, however, only excellent entertainment. According to Elder, most festivals, carnivals and pilgrimages have a deep moral and religious background and base, both of which constitute the devotees' belief system, morals and values. Most of these annual ceremonies project the cultural history of the people, and correspond, in terms of culture, to the lifestyles of peoples in other parts of the world. In countries like the Caribbean the ceremonies have roots stretching backward in time to Europe, Africa and Asia, and can be easily shown to link the New World communities with those of the Old World. For example, performers in the John Canoe Festival have their origins in the Mummers Parade (Swedes of Pennsylvania) or the Morris Dancers of England. The Tobago Reel dance includes the Scottische, the Lancers, the Quadrille and the Polka of Europe. The maypole dance (the Sebucan), common among Caribbean people, came to the Caribbean from Spain.

Elder noted that the handicrafts of the Caribbean fall into two types: native crafts of Amerindian origin, such as Indian basketry made from tirite palms; and European crafts such as crochet, knotting and hardanger, all of which require commercial threads, including wool. He suggested that it is the traditional crafts that use the native local vegetable and mineral-type materials that seem to have most value for any scheme of cultural tourism. Tourism should therefore emphasize aboriginal crafts and encourage the use of the raw materials unique to the region.

The literary, performing and visual arts as a tourism product

Finally, we come to the literary, performing and visual arts with which the word "culture" has become almost synonymous. Colonial peoples have looked for centuries to the capitals of Europe and, in modern times, to certain capitals in North America, for examples of excellence in this field. This fact explains why Caribbean peoples have been known to speak of their region, which has no long nor major tradition of these arts, as being devoid of culture.

In respect of the relationship between culture and tourism, those tourists who visit the West End of London, Broadway in New York and other centres of entertainment are aware that the theatre, which often brings together all three arts, is certainly one of the principal tourist attractions of these cities. It can also be said that in all the major cities in the world, museums, with their exquisite collections of fine art, are great attractions for both locals and visitors. Certainly, no self-respecting city in the developed countries would be without a museum of either greater or lesser significance. It is therefore important that Elliott Parris and Alwyn Bully have addressed the subject of the development of the arts in the Caribbean, and have discussed how the arts can best be used in forming the linkage between culture and tourism.

Until the twentieth century, literature in the Caribbean meant European works. One of the better colonial inheritances was a sound primary and secondary education that ensured that Caribbean children were as versed in the history, prose and poetry of European writers as were their counterparts in the metropole. During the twentieth century, Caribbean writers with names like Price-Mars (Haiti), Aimé Césaire (Martinique) and Leon Damas (Cayenne), began to intrude upon Caribbean attention and in the post–World War Two period, the English-speaking Caribbean produced a flood of authors almost simultaneously, each of whom left his mark outside the region even before he was accepted by his own people. These included writers like Edgar Mittleholzer (Guyana), Roger Mais (Jamaica), George Lamming (Barbados), Samuel Selvon (Trinidad), V.S. Naipaul (Trinidad), Derek Walcott (St Lucia), Andrew Salkey (Jamaica), Edward Brathwaite (Barbados), Austin Clarke (Barbados) and Wilson Harris (Guyana).

Parris stated: "Nowhere else is the cultural patrimony of the Caribbean so thoroughly analysed, presented and evaluated than in the works of its creative writers. The views presented in their work give the whole range of ideas that have circulated or are circulating in our society about who we are as a people." A number of these writers have received international acclaim and recognition, with Walcott and Naipaul each receiving the Nobel Prize for literature for their work.

At the time when most of that Caribbean literature was being written, there was little or no Caribbean readership at home willing and able to support the authors by purchasing and reading their works. These writers, however, became famous by living, writing and publishing their works abroad, which suggests that there was a receptive foreign audience.

That audience has been widened by some of the literature being used as a resource for courses being taught in institutions of higher learning both at home and abroad.

Bringing that literature in some form to an expanded audience comprising tourists in the Caribbean would continue the process of education about who Caribbean people are, and hopefully, help to provide a better living for those writers whose creative efforts have never been adequately rewarded materially. How can this be done? It is ironic that several of the authors concerned have not been strong advocates of the tourism industry, which they have traditionally seen as weakening the fabric of our cultural foundations.

Parris has argued that the way to bring literary works to the attention of a wider audience is by performance. He cited as an example seeing George Lamming's novel *In the Castle of My Skin* being sensitively adapted for the stage at Carifesta '81 in Barbados, and goes on to observe that much of Caribbean literature is capable of theatrical presentation. This needs to be done by playwrights, however, of which to date there are not many in the Caribbean. Some Caribbean playwrights, such as Derek Walcott and Trevor Rhone (Jamaica), have made their mark, but there has been no abundance of riches in this area. Bully admitted that, with the exception of one or two territories, the formal presentation of the performing, visual and literary arts is still relatively young and disorganized. An interesting development in Barbados at the end of the first decade of the twenty-first century was the work of Barbadian historian Hilary McD. Beckles, which has converted historical works about Barbados's national heroes into plays which seem to resonate well with local theatre audiences.

It can therefore be argued that the first step must be to build a theatre audience among the local population. To date, this has been difficult to achieve in most Caribbean countries, and could be helped by governments investing more in both the cultural human resources and the physical infrastructure needed to support cultural industries. It is unlikely that the theatres of London and New York were first built to attract foreign tourists.

Alwyn Bully endorses fully the view that theatre can be an important tool for sensitizing the tourist about the country he or she is visiting:

> The role of drama has long been established as being to teach and to entertain. Theatre therefore is the one art form which, in an evening's entertainment, can

present an accurate picture of a country's national identity – its values, customs, traditions and its unique qualities. At the same time it can utilize music and dance in all their forms, it can produce a faithful impression of the visual arts and craft through its sets and costumes, and, by oral means, give a clear indication as to the standard of the literature of the country.

He adds, however: "The theatre people go about their own particular way with no thought of utilizing tourism as a support area for their own survival of artists, while the hotel and tourist authorities continue to present one-dimensional entertainment with no consideration for the kind of tourist who wants to find out where he really is, and who the people he sees around him in the street really are."

Seminar recommendations

The seminar presentations were followed by a robust debate on the way forward, and certain of the recommendations – general, as well as specific to the different subject areas presented in the seminar papers – are reproduced below.

General recommendations

- The CTRC, the Caribbean Conservation Association and the OAS should continue the dialogue between tourism practitioners and cultural activists by hosting annual meetings between the parties and including such activities within their own programmes.
- Participation in the seminars should be widened to include hotel representatives, business representatives, street vendors, the police, taxi operators, educators, the Caribbean Examinations Council, and high school representatives.
- Countries should pass legislation to ensure protection of cultural objects.
- The CTRC, the Caribbean Conservation Association and the OAS should compile an annotated bibliography of works originating in the Caribbean on subjects relating to cultural and tourism development, and assist in the publication of same.
- Research should be undertaken on the existing requirements and restrictions within the wider Caribbean governing the movement of

people engaged in cultural expression, and action taken to remove same in the interest of fostering cross-fertilization of culture within the Caribbean.
- Legislation should be passed with a view to stopping cultural plagiarism and the emigration of cultural objects, and seeking their repatriation or compensation for same.
- Governments should consider the integration of tourism within cultural patterns and establish a committee charged with this responsibility.
- The OAS should undertake wide distribution of its inventory methodology covering tourism and culture in the region and that the CTRC, the Caribbean Conservation Association and the OAS assist in the undertaking of such inventories through workshops and short courses.
- Libraries should be asked to support the objectives of strengthening the links between tourism and culture by incorporating into the libraries all materials which constitute an authentic record of Caribbean thought and way of life, whether books or graphic materials, such as slides, films, microfilms, periodicals and conference papers.
- A preliminary survey should be undertaken about the potential and experiences in the field of educational tourism and international student exchanges in the Caribbean region.
- A seminar should be organized about educational tourism and international student exchanges, with the participation of educators and student leaders of each country, the governments' cultural and tourism departments, the youth tourism organizations, with the technical cooperation of the International Student Travel Conference, the International Youth Hostels Federation and other international organizations like the WTO and UNESCO, related to or interested in this topic.
- The interrelationship between culture and tourism should be reflected in the teaching of tourism in our public and private schools, and steps be taken to influence the Caribbean Examinations Council to include in its curriculum study of the indigenous culture of the region.
- Each territory, bearing in mind the need to create a more realistic impression of the Caribbean region and the varied elements of culture exhibited in the respective territories, should seek to communicate an identity which is relevant to its culture, and to highlight this identity in its marketing.

- Tourist boards should become more informed about the cultural offerings available, with a view to encourage actively the hoteliers to make use of same.

Specific recommendations related to subject areas

With regard to monuments, sites and vernacular architecture, it was recommended that

- professional studies be made of historic and prehistoric sites to ensure that any use made or work done on the sites follow carefully researched and properly planned guidelines
- CARIMOS, the CTRC and the Caribbean Conservation Association develop a series of maps and a list of places of cultural importance for tourism
- CARIMOS promote publication of all the international conventions and charters relating to monuments, sites and tourism to be used as a basis of information, particularly for secondary schools and universities
- tourism authorities recognize the importance of the preservation of significant forms of vernacular, historic and other architectural forms as an important resource for tourism attractions
- tourism authorities present major historic sites in a manner in which the benefit of tourist visits will accrue to the broadest possible sector of the population, in terms of guides, vendors and craftsmen
- sites be planned and utilized in a manner in which the population is both involved and interested in the activities taking place
- tourism authorities create programmes which heighten, among visitors, the general public and the school and university populations, awareness of the importance of the sites
- sites and buildings, while respecting their original nature, be used, as far as possible, as part of the socio-economic life of the population (for example, centres for displays, craft workshops, exhibits of living history and ecomuseums)
- efforts be made to encourage student tourism whereby student-tourists would assist, where possible, on projects for restorations of sites

- tourist authorities target those special interest groups in foreign countries – such as architects, historians and teachers – who would have an interest in historic buildings
- the appropriate ministry establish the mechanism for protecting monuments, sites and vernacular architecture against the loss of cultural patrimony which results from the use of these sites or through commercialization

With regard to folklore, folk art and handicrafts, it was recommended that

- the education of artisans be seen as part of the movement of adult education
- the state and non-state educational agents take maximum advantage of the human potential of the artisans in educational development
- the final document of the Seminar on Social and Economic Problems of Artisans, held in Cuenca, from 19 to 23 January 1982, be recommended as a framework for the training of craftspeople
- training in the sector be aimed at all craftspeople, and integrate traditional technologies with the requirements of contemporary society; respect the tradition, history and customs of the artisans; leave the artisans free to choose the technologies that seem to them most suitable to their art; prepare the artisans to respond to external demands without losing their identity; and provide support based upon a careful study of the sector, including a census of its most urgent needs in financial credit, availability of raw materials and existence of fair prices
- the artisans be made aware of the need to improve their general, technical and management training, and be provided with training in arithmetic, measurements, reading, writing, forms of communication, cooperative administration, accounting, sales, marketing, human relationships, and the figuring of costs
- training be placed in an institutional framework, with special emphasis on the organization of the artisans themselves and on the attainment of national legislation that will regulate craft activity
- hotels be encouraged to present folk performers as part of their regular entertainment

- tourist authorities be encouraged to take an active part in the promotion of national festivals, such as carnival and independence anniversary celebrations
- exhibition centres for local folk arts and crafts be developed where craftspersons can demonstrate their skill and vision, and visitors can appreciate the art forms being demonstrated
- to avoid the exhaustion and extinction of the flora and fauna used in crafts, the materials be protected from over harvesting, and governments, in their respective agricultural policies, include the allocation of land for the growth of native fibre plants and other facilities for the rearing of species associated with handicrafts, such as molluscs and shellfish

With regard to the performing, literary and visual arts as a tourism product, it was recommended that

- the countries commit themselves to a public awareness campaign directed at strengthening the relationship between tourism and culture by organizing seminars, lectures and meetings among tour planners, hotel managers, tourism and culture officials, the media and other interested parties
- the tourism and cultural sectors and artists be involved in the production of video and audio-visual slides of cultural and artistic presentations as educational and promotional tools
- tourist authorities be encouraged to allocate, for use in the tourism product, funding specifically earmarked for cultural development
- the tourist be exposed to a greater variety of forms of Caribbean performing arts to gain a better understanding of the art form and the skills of the performers
- hotels and tourist authorities redouble their efforts at utilizing theatre as a tourist attraction, providing practitioners with adequate facilities and making available support material for effective presentation
- scholarships provided in the fields of drama, dance, art and music be made available to artists of the Caribbean, preferably at the Cultural Training Centre in Jamaica
- workshops in the performing arts be held in the various territories to teach the disciplines of performance related to tourism

- in each country where "hotel theatre" facilities do not exist, one hotel be provided with the equipment and facilities to enable it to be used as a model for other hotels
- a group of artists be brought together to prepare a model hotel show, one to be taken as a prototype to a specified number of Caribbean countries for display to tourists, hoteliers and local performers. The show is to be videotaped
- research be carried out on the entertainment existing in hotels, as well as what is available in the country, the reasons why such entertainment is used, and that the findings be published in a book
- public art galleries specializing in indigenous art be set up in countries where they do not presently exist
- tourist authorities be encouraged to include, within their information centres at ports of entry, information on cultural activities or information on cultural events taking place each month in their country
- cultural authorities be encouraged to publish and distribute information of cultural events each month
- teachers of the arts be made available in training colleges in the region and that the education authorities be encouraged to utilize fully these skills in the school system
- governments ensure that the work of the visual artists and artisans of their respective countries be prominently displayed in public places, such as hotel rooms, lobbies and foyers, airports, schools, institutions of tertiary education, so that both visitors and the citizens of that country may be reminded constantly of the cultural heritage of the host country.

Conclusions

The seminar that took place in 1983 was a historic event that underscored the added value that the Caribbean Tourism Research and Development Centre, established in 1974, brought to the tourism industry which up until then was largely focused on marketing a sun, sea and sand product. The seminar sought to send several messages; one was that the preservation of the material and non-material elements of culture is a task no less important than development and technological progress; that while tourism can be a cause of the disintegration of the traditional culture, if properly planned, it can help to rescue, preserve and strengthen important cultural values; that community participation in development programmes and the strengthening of self-image will lead to its valuing its traditions and customs, beginning with vernacular architecture which is a component of the landscape and blends with it; that both governments and people must be concerned about the authenticity of cultural expressions offered the tourist; that protection, strengthening and development of cultural forms is not a matter for tourism alone, but is the responsibility of the entire society; that since the tourism sector needs the socio-cultural patrimony as part of its supply of goods and services, it must work jointly with government sectors responsible for protection and development of these resources and contribute to a better socio-cultural relationship.

The cultural maturing of the Caribbean, 1983 to 2010

When the seminar we have been discussing took place in 1983 only two decades had passed since the independence of Jamaica (1962), Trinidad and Tobago (1962), Barbados (1966) and Guyana (1966). Countries like Antigua and Barbuda (1981), Dominica (1978), St Lucia (1979), St Kitts–Nevis (1983) and St Vincent and the Grenadines (1979) had each only been independent for a relatively brief period of time. Certain of the issues discussed at the seminar therefore reflected the concerns about the culture of those people of the English-speaking Caribbean who were in transition from colonialism to self-government and self-discovery.

Much has happened in the CARICOM countries during the past three decades, not only in cultural development, but also in several other areas. Not least is that a new generation of Caribbean men and women has been born, one which was not required to sing "God Save the Queen" at the beginning of each school day. That generation now studies Caribbean literature and Caribbean history written by Caribbean historians. Most of their countries now have ministries of culture and academic institutions which teach the literary, performing and visual arts to tertiary level. There has also been a marked improvement in the infrastructure for hosting cultural events, examples of this improvement being concert halls and theatres. There is, however, still much progress to be made in this area.

At the national level, in several countries there are now institutions like the Edna Manley College of the Visual and Performing Arts in Jamaica and the Barbados Community College, both of which are developmental institutions providing training in the visual and performing arts. At the regional level, the University of the West Indies has created a Centre for the Creative Arts.

Jamaican reggae music has now spread to almost every continent of the globe. Local dance theatre companies are performing a wide range of dance types to professional levels. Caribbean singers and musicians have become international stars, and some visual and performing artists have received international acclaim. With the notable exceptions of possibly two countries, drama and live theatre in the CARICOM states seem to be lagging behind other art forms, both in terms of actors, productions and audience, although a nascent Caribbean film industry is beginning to establish itself, and in some countries soap operas on television have already created a cadre of professional actors. In every country more and more competent authors and poets appear every year but have the greatest difficulty in getting their work published, distributed or both. One change that might help with the distribution would be the organization around the Caribbean of more professionally organized book fairs to assist writers to make their work known and sold. In the final event, it must become easier to have work published in the Caribbean, as self-publishing is an expensive and difficult exercise. In any case, a country which lays claim to First World status but has no publishing house as a vehicle for promoting the creative writing of its citizens is making a hollow claim.

The CARICOM governments have created CARIFESTA (the Caribbean Festival of Arts), which is a multicultural event, the purpose of which is to bring together artists, musicians and authors to exhibit the folkloric and artistic manifestations of the region. Since it was first held in Guyana in 1972, it has taken place in several other Caribbean countries including Jamaica (1976), Cuba (1979), Barbados (1981), Trinidad and Tobago (1992, 1995 and 2006), St Kitts–Nevis (2000), Surinam (2003) and Guyana (2008). Whereas the event is designed for the benefit of Caribbean artists and their community, it could certainly be positioned also as a major tourist event. In several countries national cultural foundations (however called) are performing excellent work in the schools in promoting culture and fostering cultural development. The foundations are very involved in organizing and promoting annual festivals and carnivals, whatever the origins of the events. These festivals and carnivals have become major tourist events and are marketed annually as such.

In the second decade of the twenty-first century, the Caribbean cultural environment has changed somewhat from what it was in colonial times. With new generations born in independent societies, Caribbean people are more confident about who they are. Tourism has had an opportunity to demonstrate that, with all its faults, no other industry has proven, at this time, to be a more solid base for our economic and social development. This reality should render our artists, especially our writers, more willing to embrace tourism than formerly, and to use it as one of the mediums for promoting Caribbean culture to the external world.

Next steps

Perhaps this is the time for the CTO – which, as described earlier in the book, evolved out of a merger of the CTA and the CTRC – or some other institution, to bring together once again, in collaboration with the relevant national, regional and international agencies, the leaders of the private and public sector tourism institutions. This meeting should take place with the leaders of the artistic community, and would be for a determination of where the Caribbean now stands regarding the linkage between tourism and culture. It would be appropriate to review the recommendations of 1983 to determine what has been implemented and what now needs to be done to enlarge the beneficial impacts of tourism for the greater good of the total community.

13

From Sugar to Tourism: The Shift to Services

Chapters 1 to 12 have traced the history and performance of Caribbean tourism from the nineteenth century to the present. This evolution has included attempts to transform Caribbean tourism from a meet-and-greet industry to a development sector framed within a strategic plan, with ambitious goals and objectives to be achieved by the end of the first decade. Considerable progress has been made, but the first decade of the twenty-first century has been a tumultuous one, and it comes as no surprise that the region has fallen short of reaching the tourism targets the setting of which was described in chapter 9.

Chapter 13 begins with a look at how tourism itself is viewed in a twenty-first-century world – a world now dominated by service economies and regulated by international trade in services agreements. It discusses the need for changes in direction and in local and foreign policy required to address the new situation. It also argues the need for an enlarged role for the Caribbean as the negotiations in trade in services resume and continue.

A changing World Bank perspective on tourism in 2005

In the 1970s, institutions like the World Bank seemed to share the 1972 CARIFTA development perspectives, which set the priorities for Caribbean sectoral development, in descending order of importance, as agriculture, manufacturing, tourism. However, comments made in the World Bank Report of 2005 – *A Time to Choose: Caribbean Development in the Twenty-first Century* – suggest a revision of that view. The report made the following claims about the development strategies pursued by Caribbean states since independence:

- Both Europe and the United States have provided preferential access to their markets for a number of commodities that include sugar, bananas, rice and export commodities. However, new international trading rules mandated by the World Trade Organization (WTO) are outlawing that system, and in 2010, such market arrangements are likely to be over, since the region is expected to compete for market access in other countries for those commodities.
- Empirical evidence shows that trade preferences do not help overall trade performances, even as they can affect the pattern of trade, and this has been seen in the specific case of the Caribbean. The Caribbean exports of apparel, sugar, bananas and several other agro-based products have been dependent on preferences, and have suffered as preferences have eroded.
- Despite preferences, quotas have often not been filled; instead, preferences have diverted energy and attention away from sectors that could have been more competitive; dependence of exports on preferences appears to have negatively affected the growth, volume and dynamism of overall exports, and also now gives rise to concerns for future exports. On the other hand, tourism, which for many countries has been the mainstay of exports and growth, has not relied on any preferences from other countries.
- Preferences steer resources to sectors that are not necessarily the most competitive internationally and, since entrepreneurship is limited in small countries, that directing is wasteful, and prevents developing countries from developing abiding sources of comparative advantage.

- Once resources have shifted to these sectors, political will is consequently geared towards maintaining preferences, making these economies less dynamic than they otherwise would be.
- Because these economies have been left out of the reciprocity-based system, their own trade liberalization may in fact have lagged accordingly.

While it has not been stated explicitly, the comments by the World Bank nevertheless seem to suggest that the Caribbean has paid a high price for relying on those commodity exports which were not sustainable in the absence of preferences, and did not recognize, as early as it should have, the value of tourism and of services industries, which grew and prospered without benefit of preferences.

The shift to services: A world-wide phenomenon

Much of this book has dealt with the shift of the Caribbean, for some sixty years, from dependency on sugar to dependency on tourism and other services. Tourism in particular encountered initially much opposition because it displayed many of the more negative social characteristics of the sugar plantation. But, as will also be seen, steps have been taken to address many of these issues.

The shift to services like tourism, as well as to international finance, which has also developed rapidly in the region, is not peculiar to the Caribbean and other developing regions. It is now a feature of the economic strategies of the world's most highly developed countries. What is more, manufacturing has increasingly migrated from places such as the United States, once the greatest of manufacturing countries, to countries such as China, India and Brazil, where labour costs are still competitive. This observation is being stated as a fact without begging the question of the rights and wrongs of this shift – a major point of contention in the 2012 US presidential election campaign.

The Caribbean reality, however, is that the region has moved largely from dependence on sugar to dependence on tourism and other services. There is therefore a serious need for the Caribbean countries to avoid once again becoming monocrop societies. The question to be asked and answered, therefore is, what is to be done, and this includes what role should the all-pervasive tourism sector play in assisting the region to deal with these issues. A major concern is that of food security, given declines both in local agriculture and manufacturing, and the need to feed both the local population and the tourists.

A number of courses, none of which are exclusive, have been recommended:

- Transform the nature of the agricultural industry with a focus on domestic food supply, export of crops desired by the Caribbean diaspora and, where possible, diversify and save the sugar cane industry to create products other than sugar.
- Develop new linkages between tourism and traditional agriculture, and between tourism and manufacturing.
- Rethink Caribbean policies with respect to international trade negotiations, placing services at the top of the Caribbean agenda.
- Develop new international alliances that support the new priorities.

The need for food security

In 2008, as the price of fuel escalated to the unprecedented height of US$147 per barrel of crude oil, the price of food rose to crisis levels, placing millions of people in danger of starvation. This situation was exaggerated by the conversion of crops such as corn and sugar cane into ethanol to supplement the energy resources derived from fossil fuels. In a number of developing countries riots broke out as a result. The situation eased in 2009 as the price of oil fell, but an unstable situation exists in which fluctuations in oil prices have to be anticipated. Now, US$100 per barrel has come to be regarded as the new low in oil prices.

In 2011 the world's oil supply was once more endangered by political chaos in the Middle East, and the spectre of escalating food costs returned. It was then predicted by the Food and Agriculture Organization of the United Nations that many millions of persons would again face poverty and even starvation.

The Caribbean, dependent as it is on expensive food imports to feed both itself and visitors, is already labouring under the load of massive fiscal debt. In 2008, a small country like Barbados – specifically, of 166 square miles and 270,000 people – had a food import bill of a quarter of a billion US dollars, a cost which can be expected to escalate as fuel prices and transport costs rise. The CARICOM heads of government need therefore to make feeding the region's people and their visitors, largely from within national and regional resources, a priority. (This should be a priority on what is admittedly an already overcrowded agenda.) This situation calls for serious planning by both public and private sector agriculturalists. This initiative will also require a campaign to change a number of prejudices which have evolved in the Caribbean because of the history of agriculture in the region. Time is not on the side of this change.

With respect to revenue and to costs connected to agriculture, the emphasis must be on new economic approaches, ones that involve the creation of new types of export agricultural products, and of new areas of domestic agriculture, both of which can be linked with tourism in ways either not previously considered or not fully exploited. Most importantly, these ways must be devoid of the old associations with sugar plantation agriculture.

The agricultural legacy of the slave plantation

The slave plantation has given agriculture a bad name in the Caribbean. In any case, a new generation of Caribbean people who have other options, no longer seem willing to engage in the kind of hard labour associated with the old methods of growing and reaping of sugar cane and cotton. This situation is especially the case, since in the Caribbean region the mechanization of sugar cane harvesting has not yet entirely replaced manual labour.

In 2007, then-prime minister of Trinidad and Tobago, Patrick Manning, while campaigning for national elections, believed strongly enough about a return to the sugar industry and its practices in his country to say that the return to the cutting of sugar cane in Trinidad and Tobago would be a return to slavery and would not happen under his administration. This view suggests the need for a major re-education process to show agriculture as a noble profession – which it is – and to offer the prospect of Caribbean people seeing themselves also as agricultural entrepreneurs and not only as labourers.

Sugar production uneconomic

With respect to the production of sugar from sugar cane, the industry in the Caribbean is threatened in 2013 by being totally uneconomic. From the perspective of the planters, a point has been reached where it is difficult to produce cane sugar without substantial subsidies from government. The cost of production is now far higher than the revenues earned by its sale and the WTO rules now make it illegal for those who import sugar to pay, under special preference arrangements, a higher-than-market price.

The call, however, is not for abandoning agriculture or even the sugar cane industry where it continues to exist, but for maximizing agriculture's role of guaranteeing national food security, reducing import costs, and finding new products, certain of which can be enhanced by linkages with the tourism industry.

Environmental considerations

It is important that those tourism destinations where sugar cane is still grown do not underestimate its value in both conserving the soil and presenting an environmental aspect which is appealing both to locals and visitors. This second need is best understood when one visits islands once covered with fields of waving sugar cane and which have since been replaced by bush, presenting unattractive landscapes. However, unless reasons can be found for growing sugar cane profitably, the beautiful sugar cane plant could well disappear altogether, as has already happened in a number of Caribbean countries. This fact strengthens the case for the production of additional sugar cane products, such as ethanol, which serves the dual purpose of continuing to enhance the environment as well as helping to meet energy needs.

Linkages between agriculture and tourism as part of the national tourism development plan

The existing tourism and agriculture linkage strategies consist largely of individual hotels buying meat and vegetable products from local farmers, in certain cases under special arrangements, where the farms are contracted to produce goods specifically for the hotels. However, it is necessary to widen these efforts so that the linkages between agriculture and tourism take place as part of the national development planning process. These efforts must also become part of the agenda of the relevant organs of CARICOM ministers and ultimately heads of government.

The opportunity for these linkages should not be underestimated. In 2008, there were over 261,000 rooms in tourist accommodation in thirty-three CTO member states, and just over 72,000 of these were in the Commonwealth Caribbean CARICOM states. Over the course of one year almost twenty-one million tourists stay in the CTO tourist accommodation rooms, and there is an equal number of cruise visitors who need to receive supplies both at sea and on land. It would be entirely appropriate if, in the future, the region, at both the public and private sector level, could create new strategies, linking agriculture and tourism to each other – strategies which not only ensure a brighter economic future for the Caribbean, but also, by transforming the way Caribbean people perceive agriculture, help to reverse some of the psychological damage suffered in the past.

New directions for agriculture

In seeking new directions for agriculture, opportunities may exist in supplying some of the beauty and health needs of both tourists and locals from our agricultural products. The world's malls and department stores are now replete with beauty and spa products that boast of agricultural origins.

The Inter-American Institute for Cooperation on Agriculture has led the way in suggesting other opportunities which we have not sufficiently exploited. These opportunities are in the areas of horticulture, processed foods, bottled water – now a multi-billion dollar industry – herbals and medicinals, craft, farm and agro-based sites and tours – including cultural and scientific sites and attractions – recreational tours, adventure, fishing, hiking, biking, hunting, caving, camping, culinary tourism, health and wellness tourism – including visits to herbal gardens – and hot springs. Of course providing transportation to all these activities represents another industry in itself.

None of this is likely to happen by itself, however. What is needed are national and even regional mechanisms which are given specific responsibility for the creation of these linkages, and entrepreneurs with the vision and investment capital similar to those who created the Body Shops throughout Europe.

Selling old products to new customers

In chapter 2 it was seen how the trade in bananas, beginning in the late nineteenth century, had led to the creation of the tourism industry in certain Caribbean countries. It would be entirely appropriate if, in the twenty-first century, tourism was able to return the favour for bananas and other agricultural products by creating new regional customers among the tourism fraternity, making it unnecessary to have to ship all or most of the Caribbean bananas to Europe or to North America.

An expanded role for the Caribbean Regional Negotiating Machinery

The Caribbean Regional Negotiating Machinery – which has since been renamed the Office of Trade Negotiations, and which initially was confined to negotiating in hemispheric and international forums about agricultural and merchandizing trade – later turned its attention to negotiating in trade in services. Its expertise in its restructured form should now be utilized in the region to negotiate with both the locally based tourism enterprises and the cruise lines about strengthening the tourism's linkages with agriculture and the manufacturing industries. Not much imagination is required to envisage an expansion of the industrial products that could be sold to the local tourism industries if the necessary effort were applied by the two sectors.

The implementation of some of these ideas requires a quantum leap in thinking about which aspects of agriculture and manufacturing are seen as closely allied to the services sector. Such a shift calls for the respective ministries to be equally committed to making it happen. It would lead to the creation of a new breed of entrepreneurs, and perhaps projects like the Youth Entrepreneurship Scheme in Barbados could play a part in encouraging youth involvement.

Such ventures, however, need to be supported, not only by technical assistance but also by research which identifies the needs to be met and the opportunities that exist, and it may be that far more attention needs to be paid to strengthening the research arms of our tourism institutions and giving them a wider mandate than bringing tourists to the Caribbean. These efforts also need to be underpinned by a banking and finance system that would be willing to take some risks in supporting operations that follow new directions.

New foreign policy directions required

In its 2005 World Bank report, described earlier in this chapter, the point was made that the existence of preferences leads countries to shift all their resources towards maintaining those preferences. It is certainly the case that, since independence, the focus of the Commonwealth Caribbean's foreign policy and of much of the time and energies of its diplomatic staff have been deployed in negotiating and preserving, for as long as possible, the preferential arrangements for agricultural and manufactured products being sold to both Europe and North America. This focus has skewed the respective foreign policies of the Commonwealth Caribbean to the extent that little effort has been made in the past to develop trading and other economic relationships with countries even as close as those in Latin America, far less those in the Middle East, Africa and Asia. The focus has also negatively affected the trade in services with those countries in the Middle East, Africa and Asia. If there are now changes on the horizon, it is because Europe has now unilaterally ended the major preferential arrangements which existed.

The region's foreign policy – which often seems to have been designed to preserve links with former colonial masters, and which was born out of colonial trading relationships – now needs to be adjusted to reflect the major shift to dependence on services and in the policies of former colonial masters. The world has changed radically. Metropolitan patronage to former colonies has been replaced by demands for reciprocity in all areas of trade and where the region displays a comparative advantage in anything – for example tourism or international financial services – it can expect the developed world to bring the full brunt of competition against it. This situation calls for new foreign policies and the development of new foreign alliances with countries with which there is a commonality of interests.

The rest of this chapter is therefore devoted to reviewing some of the international trading agreements under which CARICOM states have operated for decades, and identifying the steps needed to be taken in the future for their economic survival.

Review of Lomé and Cotonou agreements and Economic Partnership Agreement negotiations

In the post-independence era, trade between Europe and some seventy-eight former colonial countries in Africa, the Caribbean and the Pacific (ACP), which had proceeded in the colonial period, was regulated under various agreements known first as Lomé agreements, and later as the Cotonou Agreement, names of places in Africa, where they were signed. These arrangements had to be reviewed in the light of agreements reached in various trade and service negotiations within the WTO with a view to being in consonance with them. For this purpose, a series of trade negotiations began between the European Union and ACP states, negotiations which came to be known as Economic Partnership Agreements (EPAs).

The old trade agreements had recognized the disparities in resources between the colonies and the Metropole as trading partners, and various accommodations were consequently made in the form of special prices for certain products from the developing countries, and preferential access to European markets.

A number of objections to these accommodations were made within the WTO by both small and large countries, countries which were outside of these arrangements between Europe and its former colonies. These objections led to the setting of a timetable for the dismantlement of the accommodations.

Even before the EPA negotiations began, however, Europe had begun to dismantle the arrangements for critical ACP exports, exports such as sugar, rice and bananas. It was therefore not surprising that the EPA talks began in a less-than-friendly atmosphere. The European Union was insisting that unless the ACP states concluded the EPAs, including services, by the 31 December 2007, preferential access to its markets for the seventy-eight ACP states would be ended.

Given the new directions in the development of a services sector – including tourism – by many developing countries, the insistence by Europe that the ACP countries open up their economies to the EU service companies and EU investment was scary. What was even more scary was that eventually all other member countries of the WTO would claim access to the ACP markets.

The first EPA talks were between Europe and the Caribbean. An assumed objective of the European Union was that whatever was agreed in these talks would set a precedent for the African and Pacific country negotiations to follow.

EPA initialled

On 16 December 2007, over the objections of at least one country – Guyana – the negotiators from the European Union and from the CARICOM states initialled their EPA, with the intention of signing it early in 2008. The negotiators from the CARICOM also included the Dominican Republic, and together formed a group called the Caribbean Forum (CARIFORUM).

The region had been forced to negotiate against a deadline of 31 December 2007 imposed by the European Union, the penalty for missing which was the threat of the imposition on Caribbean exports into Europe of the Generalized System of Preferences standards. In short, had CARIFORUM not signed, its members faced possible exposure to a wide range of tariffs the countries had never had to pay before.

In an article published on www.caribbean360.com ("The Caribbean Should Prepare Now for Implications of EPA with Europe", 22 December 2007), business executive and former diplomat Sir Ronald Sanders detailed the following three negative consequences of signing the agreement as it was:

1. The European Union would now be able to compete with local companies and receive national treatment in bidding for government contracts in the Caribbean.
2. Eighty per cent of imports from the European Union would enter the Caribbean markets at lower duties than is now the case. In some cases there would be no duties at all.

3. The European Union service companies in such areas as tourism and banking would also have access to Caribbean markets to compete with local companies.

In an article called "The Commonwealth Caribbean and the New Colonialism: Risks and Resistance in an Age of Globalization", Sanders's views about the signing of the EPA are more fully expressed. Excerpts from the article are attached as appendix 6.

In October 2008, five days after thirteen CARIFORUM countries and the European Union signed the EPA, Guyana also signed the document in Brussels. This signing took place after the parties had agreed that "in the implementation of the agreement, they will take account of the Revised Treaty of Chaguaramas". The parties had also agreed to the insertion of other clauses, including agreement to review the agreement every four years. The first review will take place in 2013.

The impact on tourism of signing the EPA

Trade negotiations, whether bilateral, hemispheric or international, have for centuries been about trade in goods, and not in services. There has therefore been a steep learning curve for both developed and developing countries in hemispheric and international negotiations in services, whether in the Free Trade Area of the Americas (FTAA), the Doha Round or the WTO. This situation would seem to present the Caribbean – which is now largely dependent on tourism, of which it has a long and successful experience – and international financial services, with an opportunity to take a leadership position in such negotiations.

The general provisions, described in chapter 1 of the EPA agreement and section 7, which specifically covers tourism, seem to have recognized a number of the travel and tourism concerns advanced by the Caribbean. These sections of the document deal with anti-competitive practices; access to technology; the facilitation of small and medium-sized enterprises; the mutual recognition of requirements, qualifications and licences; increasing the impact of tourism on sustainable development, compliance with environmental and quality standards; development cooperation; technical assistance; and the exchange of information, including consultation.

Much of the success of the agreement will, however, depend on how these articles are implemented and whether CARIFORUM and the European Union each understand these provisions in the same way. The language used, for example, in respect of transfers of technology, speaks of "*endeavouring* to facilitate the transfer of" (emphasis added). Certain of the extreme calls in Europe by environmentalists for restriction of air travel because of air pollution would decimate the region's tourism industry and therefore harm its development. These and other uncertainties have led, in some quarters, to demands for further clarifications to be had on EPA matters, clarifications which should probably have been the subject of wider public discussion and explanation before signing took place.

Hemispheric and international negotiations in services

The Caribbean's bilateral negotiations with the European Union about services must be placed in the context of what has been happening with the FTAA, the Doha Round and the WTO negotiations generally. There have been breakdowns and pauses in international trade negotiations during periods when bilateral or hemispheric negotiations have been taking place. The challenge for small Caribbean developing states is to ensure that nothing agreed to in bilateral negotiations with any country will return at a later date to haunt them in the wider international arena. In dealing with services, the Caribbean developing states need to take extra care, because this is where their future economic development currently appears to lie, and because there is a certain complexity and lack of familiarity with service issues.

The world's economic reality is that services now account for at least 20 per cent of recorded world trade, as well as the majority of the domestic services in most economies. This proportion is expected to reach 50 per cent of world trade by 2020.

Until the suspension of the Doha Round, and what must be viewed as a pause in the FTAA negotiations, the Caribbean was involved in services negotiating on five different fronts simultaneously. These efforts were divided between the CARICOM Single Market and Economy; the FTAA; the

ACP–EU negotiations; the CARICOM–Canada negotiations; and the WTO negotiations. In these talks the Caribbean has been engaged in negotiating

- offensive and defensive positions with developed countries possessing negotiating resources many times greater than its own
- against deadlines, for example those set by the European Union and the FTAA, before it was able to set its own house in the CARICOM Single Market and Economy in order
- in the context of agendas largely established by developed countries with their own interests in mind

A leading role for the Caribbean in services negotiations

Given the importance of tourism and air transportation to the socio-economic health and survival of the Caribbean region, it is highly recommended that far more attention be paid by Caribbean negotiators in world trade to the services issues, and in particular to tourism and travel issues, than has been paid in the past. This development requires greater interaction between Caribbean governments and private sector agencies operating service industries in their countries.

There are concerns to be borne in mind as follows:

- The benefits of deregulation, liberalization and privatization are often not the solution for the economic problems of developing countries which they are so widely touted to be. Often, even when greater market access is achieved for such countries by liberalization, it is a two-way street that leads to decimation of the domestic market. The negotiating stance for poor developing countries should always be for one-way liberalization, at least for a specified period.
- In the past, international negotiations have been about the European Union and United States jockeying for advantages with respect to each other's position on subsidies – mainly agricultural subsidies – and countries like Brazil, India and China ensuring that their agricultural

sectors would not be harmed in the struggle between the European Union and United States. Small developing countries are in danger of being crushed by these struggles about both agricultural and non-agricultural goods.

- With respect to non-agricultural goods, industrial countries want developing countries to cut their tariffs by 60 to 70 per cent, while they cut theirs by 20 to 30 per cent. These tariff losses would result in serious losses of revenue for the developing countries, with no means of replacement save the introduction of new taxes – taxes which the World Bank and the International Monetary Fund have often advised to be necessary.

Therefore, when in the future Caribbean people participate in hemispheric and international trade negotiations, they should indeed be knowledgeable about the issues relating to agricultural and other products, but they must also be conscious at all times of this fact: most of the Caribbean countries are small islands, and are dependent on tourism and other services. In brief, Caribbean people should not ignore other sectors, especially where this secures them allies for their cause, but they should pay far more attention, than is now the case, to gaining advantages in the service industries.

The Caribbean has certain strengths derived from its intimate knowledge of the tourism industry and, unlike in many other areas, almost every country, developed and developing, is starting from a platform of unfamiliarity with respect to trade in services.

Until 1995 no multilateral agreement existed on rules for the trade in services. To quote the *Business Guide to the General Agreement on Trade in Services*:

> Economists generally viewed services as not tradable, or even worse, non-productive economic activities, and therefore, unworthy of policy focus. Academic studies had concentrated on employment patterns in services as supports to manufacturing – ignoring the direct contributions service industries made to domestic production and foreign exchange earnings. Government export development planning tended to target goods, and so government agencies were largely unfamiliar with the activities of their own services exporters. As national statistical agencies did not collect trade statistics on services, few accurate and comprehensive data sets existed.

As Caribbean people bring tourism to the centre of the negotiations in trade in services, we return to the subject of making people understand yet another aspect of tourism: exactly how it functions as an export industry.

The complexity of services negotiations

People have been accustomed to a form of external trade, comprising an exchange of goods between residents and non-residents, where the producers stay in one country and the goods travel across borders to another. In such circumstances tariffs and non-tariff barriers at the borders are easy to understand.

In James L. Heskett's book *Managing in the Service Economy* Leonard Berry is quoted as observing that, to people to whom a "good" is an object, imagination is called for to grasp the concept of a form of trade which might be, for example, a deed, a performance or an effort. With these forms the essence of what is being bought is intangible. In tourism one speaks of selling "an experience" and even "a memory", a concept to which the traditional economist is likely to be unaccustomed.

Negotiators in services may find doing so more complicated than negotiations in trade in goods. The barriers to trade in services are much more subtle, and mistakes made in liberalizing markets could lead to negating, across a multiplicity of areas, the protection which national policies often seek to put in place to defend the respective cores of their economies.

Trade in services has forced international negotiators to invent completely new concepts. In doing so, negotiators have come up with four possibilities for trade in services:

1. where the service itself moves across borders
2. where the customer moves across the border to receive the service, as in the case in which a visitor comes to the Caribbean
3. where the producer of the service moves across the border to provide that service through establishing a commercial establishment
4. where the producer moves across the border, only temporarily, to provide the service

Understanding these four "modes of supply", as they are called, is fundamental to understanding what needs to be negotiated from the perspective of the tourism industry.

Defining a role for the Caribbean in services negotiations

The Caribbean should seek to carve out for itself a significant role in the various trade negotiations in services. To begin with, the Caribbean can help to achieve a better and more accurate definition of tourism than that currently obtaining under the General Agreement on Trade in Services, which limits the definition to hotels, restaurants, travel agencies and tour operator services. Such a definition excludes air transportation and cruise shipping, thereby placing them outside the tourism services negotiations.

With respect to the FTAA negotiations, which are still stalled at 2013, tourism is apparently mentioned only once, and that is in a footnote. Every opportunity needs to be taken to determine the acceptable definition of tourism, and to seek to include tourism language, when and if the talks resume.

The tourism agenda: Equality between equals and proportionality between unequals

The Caribbean should take the lead in defining what the tourism agenda in these negotiations should be for developing countries. A study issued in August 2003 and mandated by the Caribbean Regional Negotiating Machinery has assisted in clarifying what some of the agenda points are:

- enhancing the capacity of small service suppliers to participate in the tourism sector
- removing restrictions imposed by third countries on their residents visiting the Caribbean to consume services
- increasing the direct market access of their services to the main tourist originating markets such as Europe, the United States and Canada

- reducing the costs of tourism inputs in terms of the goods and services that the tourism sector consumes
- promoting the sustainable tourism development of the tourism industry
- encouraging a pro-competitive international trading environment for Caribbean tourism – provided air transportation and cruise tourism are explored by these tourism negotiations, this particular objective should offer some protection for the region's own efforts in these areas

Certain of these goals were provided for in the General Agreement on Trade in Services, and it is a welcome development that a number of these have found their way into the EPA agreement on tourism. They were set out as follows:

Section 10.4.1 of article 4 speaks to:

1. strengthening domestic services capacity and its efficiency and competitiveness *inter alia* through access to technology on a commercial basis
2. improvement of their access to distribution channels and information networks
3. liberalization of market access in sectors and modes of supply of export interest to them
4. establishment in developed countries of contact points to facilitate the access of developing countries members' service suppliers to information related to the respective markets – this information would concern commercial and technical aspects of the supply of services, the availability of services technology, and the registration for and obtaining of professional qualifications

Article 5, section 10.4.2, dealing with economic integration, allows countries, on a number of specified conditions: "to be party to an agreement liberalizing trade in services between or among the parties, (such as the CSME group), without having to comply with the Most-Favoured-Nation Treatment [MFN] of Article 11, which under normal circumstances requires according immediately and unconditionally to services and services suppliers of any member of WTO, treatment not less favourable than it accords to like services and services suppliers of any other country".

Article 19, section 10.4.3, dealing with negotiation of specific commitments, states that

> the process of liberalization shall take place with due respect for national policy objectives and the level of development of individual members, both overall and in individual sectors. There shall be appropriate flexibility for individual developing country members for opening fewer sectors, liberalizing fewer types of transactions, progressively extending market access in line with their development situation and, when making access to their markets available to foreign service suppliers, attaching to such access conditions aimed at achieving the objectives referred to in article IV.

For the reasons set out below, vigilance is needed to ensure that the protection promised under the above articles will in fact be achieved:

1. To increase their capacity, developing countries constantly need to obtain aid from the same countries with which they are seeking to gain an advantage in negotiations.
2. The liberalizing of access to their markets can at one and the same time lower the cost of imports needed to make tourism less costly and therefore more competitive, but decimate the cadre of local suppliers who, if not given special protection, will find it difficult to compete with the inward flow of cheaper goods.
3. Governments face a reduction in the amount of revenue they would normally earn from a variety of tariffs.

Liberalization is a two-edged sword, and if it takes place between unequals, it spells certain death for the weaker brethren. If the developed world honestly wishes to entertain a development agenda for small, poor states, it is necessary that liberalization should be a one-way street, where the truly poor can gain market access without having to open up their markets in a manner that decimates their industries. According to the principle enunciated by Aristotle, "equality between equals, and proportionality between unequals".

For all the reasons given above and more, the suspension of the Doha Round talks was probably not a bad development since that suspension gave the Caribbean region some time to review its positions and to make the appropriate alliances necessary for its survival.

The CARICOM Single Market and Economy: A CARICOM priority

That being said, it has to be recognized that, in the future, much of the energy of foreign ministers of the developing world will be focused on examination of the items of merit of the failed Doha Development Round, formation of meaningful new alliances with people of similar interests, and pursuit of bilateral negotiations in the area of liberalization of trade in services. It should be noted that Venezuela has promoted a new alliance named the Bolivarian Alliance for the Americas, seen as an alternative to the FTAA, which has already been joined by Antigua and Barbuda, Dominica, and St Vincent and the Grenadines. (The formation of the Bolivarian Alliance for the Americas was mentioned earlier, in chapter 5.) No doubt other CARICOM countries will consider becoming members of the alliance. They need, however, to ensure that new alliances do not negatively affect existing negotiations within CARICOM and the Organisation of Eastern Caribbean States, which should continue to be seen as the priority relationship.

It is important that the member states of CARICOM press on, with speed, both to form the CARICOM Single Market and Economy and consolidate the internal alliance, recognizing in their regional foreign policy initiatives that the Caribbean countries have become, to a large extent, service economies.

14
The Major Factors Determining How Global Tourism Performs

Chapter 13 dealt with the implications for the tourism sector of the shift by many of the world's leading economies to services, and the role which Caribbean countries must play, in their own interests, in the bilateral and international services negotiations.

Chapter 14 takes a closer look at what are the major factors that affect the tourism performance of a country or region, and what policies and actions need to be taken by Caribbean countries to protect, promote and enhance their own tourism industries. It has become clear that if there is not a substantial amount of creative thinking on their part and a willingness to change the strategies and policies applied to their tourism in the past, the future will be bleak.

The following five factors are among the most critical that influence tourism performance:

1. the state of the economy of the source markets
2. the global air transportation situation
3. the environment in which business is done, such as the presence or absence of political or civil strife

4. the likelihood of natural disasters occurring, for example, hurricanes, earthquakes and tsunamis
5. the changing and competing tourism policies in those countries which form the major source markets

Lessons learned from international trade negotiations

For at least three reasons, the outcome of international trade negotiations recounted in chapter 13 was an awakening for Caribbean countries. First, the countries would now increasingly be expected to rely on their own resources. Second, the countries needed to change economic direction from dependence on commodity preferences to exploitation of their advantages in tourism and financial services. Third, and probably most importantly, the countries needed to court new economic and political friends, and to diversify their markets in every form of trade.

Having lost the advantages in commodities and some manufactures, the Caribbean region had nevertheless gained by special relationships with its former colonial masters. The countries in the Caribbean are now very dependent on obtaining their tourists from those same countries in Europe and North America with which they had always traded. It will later be shown that those same countries are now in competition with their former colonies for tourists. Furthermore, the global economic recession that had started in 2008 and continued unabated suggested a need to contemplate seriously the diversification of the traditional European and North American source markets. As the first decade of the twenty-first century was ending and the second decade beginning, the Caribbean's twin hopes for early recovery of the global economy and an environment in which tourism could grow again were both threatened by the world's continuing economic woes. The Caribbean therefore watched, not without some level of anxiety, to see whether the varying stimuli applied in 2010 by the governments of North America and Europe to their ailing economies would have the desired effect of enabling them to recover from the recession.

Even before 2008, as the Caribbean's dependence on tourism became almost chronic, some countries in the region had begun to look beyond western Europe and North America for tourism business. The economic troubles of those countries since 2008 and the economic growth of the new emerging economies of the BRIC countries – Brazil, Russia, India and China – and others in Latin America, Europe, Asia and Africa demanded new thinking about how and where the Caribbean needed to spend its tourism marketing dollars.

What follows is, first, a brief analysis of the economic performance of the traditional source markets in 2010 and 2011, followed by a similar analysis of the new emerging economies of those countries just described. The other critical factors mentioned above are therefore also examined in the process.

United States

In August 2010 US Federal Reserve chairman Ben Bernanke launched a plan which was intended to create growth within the US economy, prevent prices from falling and push markets higher through the purchase of government bonds. This involved pumping US$600 billion into American treasuries at the rate of US$75 billion per month, a programme that ended in June 2011.

The programme enjoyed some success. In August 2010, US stock prices took off and rose some 18 per cent through the end of the year; the unemployment rate which had hovered between 9.8 per cent and 9.4 per cent during the last quarter of 2010, fell to 8.8 per cent by April 2011, although some seven million people, who had been employed three years before, were now out of work. However, Americans had now started to spend more, and consumer spending had climbed seven months in a row, growing during the last quarter of 2010 at the fastest pace in three years.

As 2011 progressed, however, prominent new issues emerged. Higher prices for commodities and energy demands now threatened to reverse the economic gains described as taking place in the United States. One set of problems resulted from droughts, severe weather and increased energy demands from China, which helped to keep the price of oil high. A second set of problems was created by the expanding chaos that followed revolutions in certain of the oil-producing North African and Middle Eastern countries. These revolutions had begun in Tunisia, then spread to Egypt, Bahrain, Yemen, Libya and Syria.

As March 2011 began, West Texas Intermediate oil reached US$98.63 per barrel, and in London Brent crude was US$114.22 per barrel. Fears existed that, in addition to the rises in oil prices connected to those countries where revolts were taking place, similar rumblings in Iran and Algeria, and even in Iraq and Saudi Arabia, might erupt into matters of considerably greater seriousness. The concern at the time was less about day-to-day oil supplies – which could be compensated through increased production by those oil countries where those political problems just described were in fact under control – but about the decline in spare capacity, which would in turn affect negatively future demand. The US stock market reflected instantly these developments by falling some 150 per cent.

Meanwhile old problems persisted domestically, examples of which included falling house values, and a decline in credit card usage, usage which directly affects the travel and tourism sector. Questions also arose about how the proposed end of the Fed stimulus in June 2011 would affect the market.

The message Bernanke delivered when he addressed the American Congress on 1 March 2011 was this. A prolonged rise in oil prices would indeed hurt the US economy, but runaway inflation was nevertheless unlikely. He predicted that the most likely outcome of the rise in commodity prices would be at most a temporary and relatively modest increase in US consumer price inflation. The impression given by the chairman was, however, that he would do whatever was required to keep the US economy progressing.

The forecast for the American economy drawn from a number of sources in January 2011 was that it was continuing its slow and steady march to recovery, despite continued unemployment and weak economic growth.

In January, Michael Youngman, author of the CTO executive brief, quoted a United States Tour Operators Association poll as supporting the view that 87 per cent of American tour operators were cautiously optimistic about the growth of the US economy in 2011. This position was similar to the one supported through the findings of his own survey, that of key wholesalers and agency chains important to the Caribbean.

However, the developments in the Middle East continued to have special implications for the US government, burdened as it is with the role of being the world's policeman, and urged to intervene in every dispute that threatens the peace of the world or the human rights of citizens of other countries.

As the 2012 US presidential elections drew nearer, in a country even more starkly divided politically in 2011 than it was in 2008, it was thought that US president Barack Obama's government would have to walk a delicate line between seeming not to abandon America's role of world policeman while also giving the economic recovery of his own country the attention that it needed. In July 2011 approximately nine million persons were still unemployed in the United States, with the rate of unemployment standing at 9.2 per cent.

By July 2011, serious consideration was therefore being given in the United States to reintroducing a second financial stimulus.

Canada

In 2010 and 2011, Canada remained the economic bright spark in North America, with deficit and debt ratios much lower than in the United States or any of the other G8 countries. Although unemployment remained at 8 per cent, Youngman was of the opinion that Canada's economic stability was assured, since it was mainly commodity-based and heavily influenced by global commodity prices. These, including oil, were at a high level in 2011.

The prospects for Canada's oil production and export continued to be excellent because the oil sands of Alberta represent the second-largest recoverable reserve behind Saudi Arabia, and because oil production was expected to double over the next ten years.

Canada had become the largest exporter of oil to the United States, ahead of both Saudi Arabia and Mexico. In theory, therefore, Canada seemed a good prospect as a tourism source market for the region and, in 2010, a number of Caribbean countries experienced increased arrivals from Canada.

Growth in traffic had been linked to the arrival of a low-cost carrier, WestJet, which was in competition with Air Canada. However, as WestJet raised its introductory fares to sustainable levels and expanded into other Caribbean and Latin American destinations, the number of visitors from Canada, ever price-sensitive, fell.

United Kingdom

The British economy began to experience considerable difficulty as early as 2007 when problems with repayment of subprime mortgages in the United States triggered financial disasters around the world. British house prices began to fall rapidly, with the first dramatic sign of trouble being the collapse of Northern Rock Bank in September 2007, which was rescued in February 2008 through being nationalized.

Throughout 2008 there was a surge in the price of all commodities, resulting in surging inflation. As recession deepened the government fought back with massive bailouts estimated to have reached £1.5 trillion. By January 2009, the United Kingdom was in the longest recession since British records began, with a 6.2 per cent falloff in output. The economy then shrunk by 5 per cent for the full year of 2009.

Chancellor of the exchequer George Osborne of the Conservative-Liberal coalition government – which took office after elections in May 2010 promising to balance Britain's financial books within five years – introduced a budget to Parliament in June 2010 that BBC political editor Nick Robinson described as "a massive gamble economically and politically" because of the severity of the cuts proposed. The budget included increasing the value added tax from 17.5 per cent to 20 per cent; freezing both child benefits and public sector pay; and cutting over a four-year period 25 per cent from public service spending, except in health and foreign aid.

As 2010 continued, the economy in Britain was thought to be recovering, but there was a contraction of 0.5 per cent in the last quarter of the year, one that left a growth figure for the entire year of only 1.4 per cent. Bad weather was identified as the chief cause. Fears of double-dip recession were, however, erased by positive news in February 2011 in the manufacturing, building and services sectors.

The level of unemployment – which in January 2010 was put at 7.9 per cent – remained a major area of concern. For sixteen- to twenty-four-year-olds, its level was 20.3 per cent. Overall male unemployment was 1.4 million and female unemployment 1.02 million. Analysts expected that the unemployment figure would continue to rise, an increase that would be largely due to the spending cuts aimed at cutting the budget deficit. There was no doubt that the draconian budget cuts in 2010 would continue to reduce household income as costs in basics like heating oil, petrol, and bus and train fares, continued to increase.

All these factors – combined with the promotion of staycations, where people are encouraged to holiday at home in the United Kingdom – resulted in a decline in the number of Britons taking holidays in the Caribbean in 2010. A continuing source of concern to the Caribbean tourism industry was the UK APD, which, following increases in 2010, had risen a massive

275 per cent above 2007 rates for all cabin classes to the Caribbean – surely a deterrent to travel. Research by Cheapflights Media, published in July 2011, showed that there was a 51.3 per cent drop in traffic to Barbados and a 25 per cent drop in traffic to Jamaica since the higher rate four-band APD was introduced. By May 2012 Britain had once more slipped into recession.

Other Europe, except Germany

Although Europe as a whole both receives and generates the world's largest number of tourists, the potential for many Caribbean countries out of mainland Europe has always been somewhat stymied by the shortage of direct air connections. In more recent times deteriorating economic circumstances in Europe have led to a trend of decrease in the number of European visitors to the Caribbean: in 2007 there were 5.5 million visitors; in 2008, 5.4 million; in 2009; 5.0 million; and in 2010, 4.9 million. This drop is not surprising because, except for Germany, the economic indicators of a number of European countries – indicators such as unemployment, growth in the GDP, the percentages of debt to GDP, and fiscal deficits to GDP – since the global meltdown that began in 2008 look more like those of developing countries than of developed ones. Table 14.1 relating to five of the major tourist producing countries is instructive.

Table 14.1 European Economic Indicators

Country	Unemployment 2009	Debt as 2010	Fiscal Deficit % GDP	GDP Growth % GDP	2009
France	8.8	10.1	78.1	7.5	−4.9
Germany	7.6	7.3	73.4	3.0	−4.7
Italy	6.9	8.8	116.0	5.3	−5.0
Netherlands	2.8	4.1	53.3	5.4	−3.9
Spain	17.4	19.1	53.3	11.1	−3.7

Germany

The German economy contracted in 2009 but, unlike many others in Europe, steamed ahead in 2010 with an overall improvement of growth of

3.6 per cent. Such progress was fuelled by strong exports of luxury cars and manufactured goods to China and other Asian countries. Youngman in the CTO executive brief of January 2011 painted a positive picture of a Germany as a country with the smallest budget deficit of all the developed countries except Canada. Germany in Youngman's brief was also shown to maintain lower levels of household debt relative to other European countries, and to be experiencing little pressure for increased personal and business taxes or new curbs to public spending – taxes and curbs which are in force in many other eurozone countries. He reported growth in the German travel market in 2010 with good prospects for 2011 as winter bookings to warm-weather destinations included growth in double digits, with cruise bookings showing equally strong growth. Gross sales in the German market totalled approximately €21 million from 40.4 million customers. Unfortunately, the Caribbean remains small players in this market, being unable to match the competition on price, and without much direct scheduled air service from Germany.

The Caribbean

By 2010 the intra-Caribbean market had become a major tourism source market, representing 20 per cent or more of business for many of the countries of the eastern Caribbean. The state of the economies of Caribbean countries is therefore a major factor in the levels of visitor traffic, although this fact seems to be seldom taken into consideration by Caribbean analysts.

In 2010 and 2011 a number of Caribbean countries remained in economic recession, with some undergoing International Monetary Fund restructuring programmes, as they laboured under unsustainable burdens of debt and soaring unemployment. This situation therefore continued to affect negatively the disposable incomes of Caribbean people, and was an important contributor towards the decrease in the numbers of intra-Caribbean travellers.

Latin America

Several Latin American countries that had been prosperous at the beginning of the twentieth century subsequently suffered economic decline, and up until the end of the 1990s were not seen by CARICOM countries as major tourism source markets. This situation has now radically changed, and in 2011 a number of Latin American economies were outperforming some of those of western Europe and North America. Those Latin American countries are now therefore seen as major prospects as tourist markets for the Caribbean, but exploiting the opportunities will depend on whether problems of poor air connections between them and the Caribbean can be solved and other basic preconditions for tourist exchange put in place.

In 2010, there was a general economic growth of 6 per cent in GDP in Latin America, with even higher rates in some individual Latin American countries such as Brazil. More importantly there were prospects of this overall growth trend continuing in 2011.

Brazil

Brazil, the world's eighth-largest economy, has both thriving agricultural and manufacturing sectors and new prospects for oil production. The Central Bank of Brazil reported a GDP growth of 8.8 per cent in 2010 with predictions for further growth of 7.3 per cent in 2011. Unemployment in Brazil fell to 6.7 per cent in August 2010 and reached the unexpectedly low level of 6.1 per cent in January 2011.

The Brazilian outward-bound travel market is forecast to grow annually by 4.5 per cent up until 2020. The one constraint on this rise might be air service connections with the rest of the world. This situation is, however, a changing one. Travel by air between the Caribbean and Brazil, for example, formerly had to be performed via Miami, which meant a journey of approximately thirteen hours. In 2011, the Brazilian carrier GOL maintains direct services between São Paulo and such destinations as Aruba, Columbia, Venezuela, the Dominican Republic, Barbados and St Maarten, reducing travel time to six hours or less, depending on the destination.

These flights will not only open up the Brazil tourist market, but will also provide access to destinations further south, such as Chile and Argentina, which are mature tourist markets. Columbia and Mexico are also of interest to the other CTO member states.

Other air transport initiatives into Central and South America are bound to follow. Non-stop service connecting the Bahamas to Panama – seen as the "Hub of the Americas" – was started by Copa Airlines on 15 June 2011. The service will link Nassau to Copa's network of forty-nine destinations in twenty-seven countries across North America, South America and the Caribbean region. According to the *Nassau Guardian* (21 January 2011), there are four flights a week scheduled for Monday, Wednesday, Thursday and Saturday. Each flight departs from Panama City at 9:18 a.m. and arrives in Nassau shortly after 1:00 p.m. The flight will then leave Nassau at 3:25 p.m. and arrive in Panama at 5:02 p.m. Copa currently also flies to Jamaica, Cuba, Trinidad and Tobago, St Maarten, Puerto Rico and the Dominican Republic. On 8 July 2011 Barbados and Panama signed a memorandum of understanding on air services that provided the framework for airlines from both countries to operate flights between the two states.

Russia

The Russian economy experienced growth of 5.6 per cent in 2008, but suffered its worst performance in 2009, contracting by some 7.9 per cent. This drop took place largely because oil exports, which had underpinned growth, had been affected by a falling demand for energy. However, in 2010, the economy recovered by about 3.9 per cent after the recession of 2008 and 2009, largely due to rising energy demand and prices, the reversal in the trend in global markets and the rise in commodity prices generally.

In 2011, the Russian government started large-scale privatization, involving some 5,500 businesses with the intention of modernizing the private sector and improving the investment climate. It is also seeking to gain membership in the World Trade Organization. Given the extent of restructuring that still needs to take place in the economy, only moderate growth was achieved in 2011, as compared with the other three member countries of the BRIC group, specifically and as noted earlier, Brazil, India and China. However, wealthy Russians are already showing interest in high-quality real estate purchases in the Caribbean, and have been spending their holidays there in increasing numbers. Both the Dominican Republic and Cuba received large numbers of Russian visitors in 2012.

China and India

China and India each enjoy prospects of economic growth of some 8 to 9 per cent. These countries are already producing increasingly more tourists to Asia and Europe, and are gaining a reputation for the purchase of luxury goods. China is, however, a major prospect for the Caribbean because of its growing political and economic links with the region.

China

In the 1990s Japan was seen as the country in Asia with the greatest potential to provide tourists to the Caribbean. However, the flow of Japanese tourists to the Caribbean has now in fact dried up because of the difficulties which have continued to assail the Japanese economy. This situation has been made worse by the earthquake, tsunami, and nuclear explosions which occurred in the country in March 2011, and seem likely to damage the Japanese economy even further over an extended period of time.

The prospects of China generating tourists to the Caribbean have been enhanced by increasing aid activity of China in the region and the fact that more and more Caribbean countries have diplomatic relations with China, some with resident ambassadors. In 2013 China promised the Caribbean US$3 billion in aid.

Chinese leisure trips have grown considerably since the Chinese government first sanctioned overseas leisure trips in 1997. The *Economist* in June 2006 reported that, in the previous calendar year, more than thirty-one million Chinese travelled outside of China; the United Nations World Tourism Organization had projected that the number would reach fifty million by 2010 and one hundred million by 2020 (*UNWTO Highlights*, 2010).

Currently, the majority of Chinese tourists are characterized as frugal, travelling mainly to neighbouring Asian countries or to Russia, staying largely in cheaper hotels and showing a preference for Chinese food. It is estimated, however, that about five to six million could be characterized as international tourists travelling as far afield as Europe and North America. Chinese tourists, it should be noted, save their money for shopping on luxury goods.

However, this profile is one that is changing constantly, and where the Chinese travel in future will depend to a large extent on the development of air services between China and the rest of the world.

African countries

Like Latin America, Africa has not been to date a productive tourist market for the Caribbean. This situation has been the case for two reasons. First, despite what seems to be a shared ethnicity between the Caribbean and certain parts of Africa, few of the preconditions for tourism development, such as family relationships, trade and colonial ties, do in fact exist. Second, the routing for travel between Africa and the Caribbean over either North America or Europe presents African travellers with a long, tedious and expensive journey.

With respect to economic issues and available disposable income, there are many misconceptions about these issues based on negative portrayals of Africa by the international media. The true situation is that different African countries have varying economic abilities, and there are sections of the populations with considerable disposable income. Currently, the economies of many African countries, which tend to be commodity-based, are improving as the prices of commodities escalate. With respect to travel between Africa and the Caribbean, the current routes by air could be cut by more than half in terms of time and distance if the matter were seriously addressed.

If one takes the distance between Barbados and Senegal, for example, it will be seen that this is a six-hour flight directly across the Atlantic Ocean. The fact that no such direct flights exist, has, however, as much to do with history as with economics.

Spasmodic efforts to fly directly from places like Barbados or Jamaica to West Africa and South Africa have failed because of the non-existence of certain of the basic conditions for sustaining air traffic between countries. Missing conditions include acceptable trade, business and diplomatic relationships; ethnic populations needing to visit friends and relatives; communications in general; and the structures needed to facilitate and promote tourism business. This situation can of course change, but much effort on both sides is required for it to do so.

North Africa is currently a growth area, one linked to the economies of the Middle East and of Europe. Potential tourism business always requires air links between the countries involved and strong airlines. Currently, airlines such as Air Arabia Egypt, Air Arabia Maroc and Ethiopian Airlines are thriving, while air transport development in Central and West Africa has been minimal. This situation for Central and West Africa has been due to a number of problems, including political conflicts.

However, it has been predicted by the International Monetary Fund that the economies of sub-Saharan Africa will grow by 4.9 per cent in

2011, following economic growth of 2.9 per cent in 2010. The reason given for this shift is that Africa is less integrated with the global economy, has been less affected by the recession, and has been benefiting from the worldwide economic recovery in 2010, as demand for African exports increased.

Summary

The review of the economic prospects of the traditional and emerging tourism source markets is a useful exercise. But economic factors are not by themselves a sufficient condition of developing a prosperous tourism trade between countries. Often the prospects for good tourism business fall apart because adequate air transportation connecting services at an affordable price are not available.

The global air transportation situation

However significant the economic performance of the source market country, and however great the potential demand, the success or failure of the international tourism sector depends on the availability of air transportation services at affordable costs. For many reasons these services do not now exist between the Caribbean and the potential markets identified above, and it is a matter of urgency that they in fact be created. However, it has been demonstrated many times over that the performance of air transportation services depends on the vagaries of the world economy, and even more specifically on what happens to the price and availability of one of the commodities on which air transportation is most dependent. That commodity is aviation fuel. How therefore can air transportation be expected to perform in the second decade of the twenty-first century?

Our best source for such forecasts is the International Air Transport Association (IATA), but, in these difficult times, it has to be recognized that even IATA has often been forced to review many of its forecasts, mostly downwards, in the face of the fluctuating fortunes of oil and other natural and man-made disasters visited upon mankind.

Looking backwards and forward by the International Air Transport Association

In his report to its annual general meeting, held in Berlin in 2010, the director general and CEO of IATA, Giovanni Bisignani, outlined the performance of global air transportation during the first decade: US$50 billion was lost, and globally, the years 2008 and 2009 were two of the worst for the sector. A major cause of this performance, he argued, was the volatility of the price of fuel, which fell from US$147 in July 2008 to less than US$40 in 2009, with an average for the year of US$62. In 2009, US$9.9 billion had been lost. Passenger traffic fell by 2.1 per cent, cargo 9.8 per cent, average yields 14 per cent and industry revenues 15 per cent. By April 2010, the price of oil had inched back to US$85.

All of these shifts had a negative impact on travel and profits. In 2009, premium travel which generates a disproportionate amount of airline profits and is a function of business travel, international trade and financial activity fell by 25 per cent, although economy travel fell by only 9 per cent. One is therefore able to compare the slow and relatively weak resurgence of travel business in Europe and North America with that of Asia, South America and the Middle East where economic recovery from the recession was robust.

However, by mid-2009, air travel markets were beginning to turn upwards, a product of the huge fiscal and monetary stimulus measures taken by governments globally. Cargo too rose sharply towards the end of 2009, as countries emerged from the recession. Various regions did, however, perform differently, as described below.

Airline performance in selected regions and countries, 2010

Europe: Recovery of air transportation in Europe in 2010 was slow. In April 2010 European airlines were forced to shut down for a six-day period because of the eruption of the Icelandic volcano Eyjafjallajökull. This resulted in an industry loss of US$1.7 billion for European carriers, 70 per cent of the flights of which were affected.

United States: In the United States, where airlines had experienced considerable financial difficulties in 2008 and 2009, revenue in 2010 grew some

15 per cent over 2009, 7 per cent over 2008 and 3 per cent over 2007, which had been a boom year. Even challenges in the last quarter of 2010, such as stormy weather in Northeastern hubs and as far south such as Atlanta, failed to derail the growth of 2010. The exception to this success was American Airlines, which lost US$389 million.

The upward trend continued in 2011. The Air Transport Association of America – the industry trade organization for the leading US airlines – reported on 11 March 2011 that passenger revenue had risen 13 per cent in February 2011 over February 2010, continuing the fourteenth consecutive month of revenue growth.

This rise could be explained by significant decreases in the price of fuel in 2009, cuts in capacity through mergers and other consolidations, and fare increases and other forms of revenue generation, all of which placed the industry on a footing for growth in 2010.

Asia: In 2010, China was reported by IATA to have had the highest compound annual growth rate: 13.9 per cent. Other countries in Asia with double-digit growth were Vietnam with 10.9 per cent, India with 10.5 per cent and the Philippines with 10.2 per cent.

Latin America: The news from Latin America about airline performance in 2010 was positive, and in line with the economic successes of the countries. In 2010, the leading airlines of Latin America carried 136.4 million passengers, some 11 per cent more than in 2009, with a load factor of 73.3 per cent, up 3.2 per cent over 2009.

In March 2011, the Air Transportation and Caribbean Air Transport Association (ALTA) announced that its member airlines had carried 12.4 million passengers in January 2011, an increase of 3.5 per cent on the previous year. Traffic – measured in terms of revenue passenger kilometres – grew by 2.8 per cent, capacity – measured in terms of available seat kilometres – by 1 per cent, and the load factor was 78.8 per cent or 1.4 per cent above the previous year. The reporting carriers were Aerolineas Argentinas, Aeroméxico, Avianca, Copa Airlines, GOL Transportes Aéreos, the LAN Group, Mexicana, MexicanaClick, Pluna, Grupo TACA, TAM, Varig Log and Volaris.

The executive director of ALTA, Alex de Gunten, expressed the view that Latin America had re-emerged significantly as a success story of efficiency growth and positive changes in aviation, and that ALTA expected the trend in increased passenger demand to continue well into 2011 and after.

Predictions on air transportation in various regions

Asia: IATA predicted that by 2014, China, Japan and Hong Kong would be the biggest international passenger markets in Asia, with China being the largest international and domestic market on the continent. The association predicted further that

- Asia would enjoy the highest growth rate for international freight at 9.8 per cent, with Hong Kong, Japan, China, South Korea and Chinese Taipei composing the region's top five markets
- China would contribute the most new travellers, some 360 million or 45 per cent of the 800 million additional persons expected to travel by 2014
- by 2014, one billion people will travel by air in the Asia-Pacific region, representing 30 per cent of the global total and a 4 per cent increase over 2009
- Asia Pacific would represent 28 per cent of global cargo

The Middle East: IATA predicted that the Middle East would have the fastest commercial aviation growth rate of 9.4 per cent, with the United Arab Emirates, Kuwait and Jordan among the top ten fastest-growing countries. The United Arab Emirates was ranked seventh for international passengers at 82.3 million, and was seen as leading the region in the area of cargo, handling some 2.7 million tonnes.

Africa: It was predicted that Africa, which is the second-fastest growing region of the world in terms of commercial aviation, would see an international passenger growth of 7.7 per cent over the next three years. International cargo demand was expected to be 5.8 per cent. African carriers experienced growth rates of 12.6 per cent for October 2010 and 16.4 per cent for November 2010, and in fact moved 11 per cent more people in November 2010 than during the pre-recession peak in 2008.

In 2010, the African Airlines Association predictions were very much in synchronization with those of IATA, projecting that African traffic growth will, for the foreseeable future, be higher than the world average. This difference is the case because, during the first half of 2010, African airlines showed a 3.4 per cent higher passenger traffic rate than was the global average for the same period. South Africa experienced a 10.6 per cent growth in 2010.

IATA revises its predictions

However, addressing some seven hundred aviation leaders at the IATA Annual General Meeting on 6 June 2011 in Singapore, Bisignani, now the outgoing director general, reported that the airline industry in 2011 was down 78 per cent year-on-year. He downgraded the 2011 airline industry profit forecast to US$4 billion. This drop is a 54 per cent fall compared to the US$8.6 billion forecast made in March 2011, and a 78 per cent drop compared with the US$18 billion net profit recorded in 2010. Bisignani stated:

> Natural disasters in Japan, unrest in the Middle East and North Africa, plus the sharp rise in oil prices have slashed industry profit expectations to $4 billion this year. That we are making any money at all in a year with this combination of unprecedented shocks is a result of a very fragile balance. The efficiency gains of the last decade and the strengthening global economic environment are balancing the high price of fuel. But with a dismal 0.7% margin, there is little buffer left against further shocks.

The continuing cause of greatest concern was the price of fuel. The IATA forecast in June 2012 was that the global airline industry bill for 2012 would total US$207 billion, accounting for 33 per cent of operating expenses at US$110 per barrel of Brent oil. In 2011 it had been US$176 billion, or 30 per cent of operating expenses at US$111.20 per barrel of Brent. The 2012 bill was five times that of 2005, some US$44 billion, representing 14 per cent of operating expenses at US$28 per barrel of Brent. The association estimated that for each US$1 increase in the average annual oil price, airlines faced an additional US$1.6 billion in costs. In addition, higher travel costs were now weakening price-sensitive demand, and the airlines were not expected to be able to offset higher costs with increased revenues.

Bisignani suggested that the greatest risk posed was whether there would be a weakening of the global economy. The situation was poor: the high price of oil was continuing, although economic recessions were less easily triggered by energy costs than in the 1970s. The situation was also good:

the global corporate sector was wealthy in cash, business confidence was high and world trade continued to expand at around 9 per cent annually. In these circumstances the International Monetary Fund had raised global economic growth projections, suggesting a recovery to historic levels of 5.6 per cent for the rest of 2011. In an update to predictions made in October's 2012 World Economic Outlook, the IMF indicated that the upturn in 2013 would be more gradual than previously anticipated. Its current forecast is that the world economy will grow by 4.1 per cent in 2013, up from 3.5 per cent in 2012 but 0.1 per cent lower than the forecast in October 2012.

Needless to say, in the Caribbean, the corporate sector was not wealthy in cash, currently had low business confidence, and there were few prospects of major trade expansion. IATA's revised regional airline growth projections for 2011 were:

- Asia-Pacific carriers were to earn US$2.1 billion, down from US$10 billion in 2010.
- North American carriers were to earn US$1.4 billion, down from US$4.1 billion in 2010.
- European carriers were to earn US$500 million, down from US$1.9 billion in 2010.
- Middle Eastern carriers were to earn US$100 million, down from US$900 million in 2010.
- Latin American carriers were to earn US$100 million, down from the US$900 million in 2010 (however, this figure nevertheless represented a third consecutive year of growth, which no other region had achieved).
- African carriers were expected to make a loss US$100 million in 2011 due to the dampening of demand that resulted from major political unrest. Poor infrastructure, restrictive government regulations and limited capacity growth were three of the factors that affected overall growth negatively, despite economic growth.

The need for a tranquil tourism business environment

Positive predictions made by IATA and UNWTO in 2010 in respect of air transportation were made before the political and civil unrest in North

Africa, the Middle East and elsewhere. As was seen, these predictions consequently had to be revised.

Political unrest

Before the first quarter of 2011 had come to an end, the world was plunged into a period of great uncertainty. Political unrest in the Middle East and North Africa began with an uprising in Tunisia on 16 January 2011. The uprising then spread to Egypt, Yemen, Bahrain, Libya and Syria, and threatened the status quo even in Jordan and Saudi Arabia.

By mid-March civil war had come to Libya, and the United States, France and Britain – in pursuit of resolution 1973, passed on 17 March 2011 by the United Nations Security Council – started air strikes on Libyan targets two days later. The stated objective was to establish a no-fly zone to prevent attacks from the air by Colonel Gaddafi on his own people. By 20 March 2011, the zone had been established. Notable abstentions to the council vote were Brazil, China, Germany, India and the Russian federation.

By 21 March, oil production in Libya had almost ground to a halt, and there was little doubt that a combination of war and international sanctions would keep the country's oil exports of some 1.3 million barrels per day out of the global market for some time. No one knew for certain how the conflict would end or when. By mid-April, the international consensus was that the situation in Libya was deadlocked.

What was not in doubt was that these events were driving the price of oil upwards with the common and expected negative consequences for the travel and tourism industry. Certain pundits were predicting civil war in Libya would be long and, and frustrated NATO powers, convinced that affairs in Libya would not be settled to their satisfaction while Gaddafi remained in office, were considering seeking a change of mandate from the Security Council regarding Libya.

By September 2011, however, the Libyan rebels, aided by NATO forces, seemed very much in charge of the country, with Gaddafi in flight, and few pockets of resistance loyal to him remaining. On 20 October, Gaddafi was shot to death, bringing his forty-one year dictatorship to an end, and greatly improving the prospects of Libyan oil once more flowing freely to the Western countries that had assisted in his overthrow.

Looming of new food crisis

In 2011, the spectre of a new food crisis recalled memories of the global situation of 2008. In that year, as the price of fuel reached US$147 per barrel and increasingly more agricultural products were being converted into energy products – this conversion was part of an effort to supplement the shortages of fossil fuels – food supplies became both high-priced and scarce. This situation regarding food led to riots among the poor and deprived in several countries around the world. In February 2011, the World Bank reported that the costs of food items were once more spiraling globally, and were having a negative impact upon the Caribbean region (*Barbados Advocate*, 21 February 2011).

The history is summarized as follows. Since February 2009, international food prices had risen by more than 30 per cent, and agricultural raw material prices by more than 6 per cent. Since June 2010, forty-four million people globally had been added to the ranks of the poor, following the sharp spike in food prices. Certain South American countries, such as Chile, Peru, Colombia and Brazil – all of which are large producers and exporters of commodities – benefited greatly from this situation. The respective prices of maize, soybean oil and palm oil, for example, rose from September to November 2010 by over 7 per cent per month, while the respective prices of gold, sugar, copper and coffee experienced price increases of over 5 per cent. As was stated earlier, this situation identified these countries as potential emerging tourism markets for the Caribbean.

However, countries in Central America and the Caribbean have been excluded from the – as it has been called – "bonanza" of rising commodity prices, as several of these countries are highly vulnerable to a potential food crisis because of their extreme dependence on food imports, coupled with high poverty rates. Countries specifically identified were El Salvador, Haiti, Jamaica, Suriname, and St Vincent and the Grenadines. But the list was expanded to such countries as Mexico, Guatemala, Nicaragua, Guyana and Belize. This expansion was due to such considerations as the rates of poverty, and the combination of the greater poverty with limited abundance of commodity exports.

The World Bank called for the betterment of social programmes in the short term and the improvement in the production and distribution of food items in the long term. What was not mentioned is that the deterioration of the social and economic condition of the poor masses can lead to conditions of social unrest, conditions which in turn are the enemy of the tourism industry on which the countries of the Caribbean are heavily dependent.

Natural disasters

On 11 March 2011, Japan experienced an earthquake of 9.0 magnitude and a resulting devastating tsunami. The nuclear power plant at Fukushima Daiichi was struck, and there were fears that damage to the electrical components and coolant pumps of reactors one and two might result in the release of harmful radiation. A race against time therefore began to limit the damage.

On 22 March, Yukiya Amano, director general of the International Atomic Energy Agency, told the board of governors of the United Nations nuclear watchdog that "the crisis has still not been resolved and the situation at the Fukushima Daiichi power plant remains very serious".

By 18 April, the number of people being reported dead were 13,843 with 14,030 still missing, the situation a result of both the earthquake and the tsunami. There were 136,481 people displaced by the disasters. The destruction of property was major, with the costs of rebuilding in Japan estimated by the International Monetary Fund at US$235 billion.

All these developments put further pressure on already high oil prices, as Japan sought to supplement lost nuclear energy supplies by importing more oil. At 20 March 2011, the price of West Texas Intermediate was US$101.07 and Brent Crude Oil US$116.34.

It was therefore impossible for anyone to predict, with any certainty, how tourism would be affected for the remainder of 2011, and what the remainder of the second decade would bring for the industry. In fact, both IATA and UNWTO hurried to revise their earlier predictions.

Changing and competing tourism policies in the traditional source markets

The fourth, but by no means least important, of the factors likely to affect the future of tourism is the changing tourism policies of the traditional tourism source-market countries. The highly developed countries of Europe and

North America have been magnets for ever-increasing numbers of visitors. Their respective central governments, however, have historically tended to treat tourism as a private sector activity, and to take a somewhat "hands off" attitude to the industry. It was unusual for there to be a minister of tourism in a cabinet, and if tourism was assigned to a ministry, it was certainly not seen as a major portfolio. This situation was the case prior to the global economic meltdown of 2008 and 2009.

This situation is now either changed or is changing. As the global economy deteriorated after 2007, and the developed countries found themselves now burdened with massive debt, they began to recognize the ability of tourism to be a major part of their export drive. They therefore created the kind of government tourism apparatus that seemed most suited to deal with tourism as such, and to demonstrate greater aggression in their marketing. Another negative side of this development for the Caribbean can be seen in the plans of developed countries to expand their domestic tourism at the expense of those countries that had become highly dependent on them as tourism source markets. Perhaps the two best examples of this change in tourism policy is to be seen with respect to the American and British governments.

The United States

In former times, the US government could not be said to have a tourism policy. In 1996, its department dealing with tourism, the US Travel and Tourism Association, was closed. Matters are quite different now. In 2010, with a view to creating more jobs and doubling by 2015 the current level of exports, the US Government launched a major National Export Initiative. US Secretary for Commerce Gary Locke informed a meeting of the Travel and Tourism Advisory Board – which, meaningfully, operated out of the Commerce Department – that, through November 2010, total US exports had increased by 17 per cent, and that travel and tourism was on track to contribute to significant growth. Locke stated: "Travel and tourism continues to be one of the bright spots in the US economy. With a US$28.3 billion trade surplus in the first eleven months of 2010, this industry has a huge role to play in helping our country answer President Obama's call to double our exports by 2015 and win the future."

Locke announced a 47 per cent increase in the travel and tourism trade surplus in 2010. More than 55 million international visitors travelled to the

US during the first eleven months of 2010 – some 11.4 million more than in 2009 – and between them spent US$122.7 billion, a spending increase of 10 per cent over 2009. In 2010, the tourism industry was employing 8 million people in the United States and accounting for 2.6 per cent of the total US GDP.

In 2011, as the US government struggled to create new jobs, the US Department of Labor reported that the travel industry had added 14,900 jobs in April of that year and, in the first four months of 2011, had expanded employment payrolls by 59,300 persons, accounting for 8 per cent of all jobs created thus far in 2011. A report released on 12 May 2012 by US Travel indicated the intention to add, through a series of visa policy recommendations, 1.3 million jobs to help the United States achieve the goal of becoming more competitive in the global travel market and so to expand US exports and drive economic growth. A target has been set of reaching 37.7 million visitors by 2015, and members of the Travel Facilitation Working Group have presented ten recommendations to the board. These recommendations addressed key visa and customer service issues with a view to increasing overseas international visitors. In fact, in 2011 visitors to the United States were already noticing a more welcoming attitude from immigration officers at the US borders. This aggressive tourism strategy to win international visitors to the United States is definitely a new development, and is a sign of the times.

This new US policy is a definite departure from its predecessor when Florida, Hawaii and New York were seen as the Caribbean's major competitors in the United States. But even so, these old competitors are also increasing their efforts. Such efforts are producing strong results. Miami, for example, experienced significant growth in international and domestic visitors and visitor expenditure in 2010. Overnight visitors grew by 5.6 per cent to a record number of 12.6 million in 2010 and domestic visitors by 4.7 per cent to 6.5 million. The growth in the number of domestic visitors reflects the increase in the number of staycations being promoted in the United States as well as in the Caribbean and elsewhere.

The spending by international visitors was approximately US$12.4 billion, with US$6.4 billion spent by domestic visitors. This on-land performance was complemented by record cruise numbers. In 2010, the Port of Miami welcomed 4.3 million cruise passengers, an increase of 9.3 per cent over 2009, as well as two new passenger cruise ships, the Norwegian Cruise Line Epic and the Celebrity Eclipse.

On 24 April 2012, New York mayor Michael R. Bloomberg and NYC and Company announced that New York had set a new goal to generate US$70 billion in economic impact by 2015. In 2011 a goal had been set of attracting fifty million visitors by 2012. It is estimated that the tourism industry will by 2015 contribute US$45 billion in direct spending to the city and add 30,000 new jobs to the city's workforce, bringing the tourism workforce to upwards of 350,000 jobs across the five boroughs of New York.

In 2009, the US House of Representatives approved the Travel Promotion Act, an act which included a charge of US$10 to be levied on visitors from countries not currently required to have an entry visa to the United States. Travellers would pay once in a two-year period, however often they visited the United States. The money would be used to create a company to market the US as an attractive destination for tourists, business travellers and students. The company needed, however, to raise up to US$100 million in matching funds from the private sector. It would then operate as a partnership between the private and public sectors, overseen by Congress and the secretary of commerce.

This act imitates the policy the Caribbean governments approved in 1992 to create a Caribbean-wide marketing fund to promote the region as a single destination. But by 2013, little success has been achieved in creating a sustainable Caribbean marketing fund, apart from an isolated effort in 2002 that followed the terrorist events of 9/11 in the United States.

Inevitably, those countries, especially those in Europe, which would be affected by the US$10 tax oppose the measure. However, they can hardly object with any credibility to the US government taxing of travel and tourism when there has been an explosion of taxes on the industry by European governments. Both the local British travel industry and those countries receiving British tourists have been waging a hard battle since 2008 against the onerous British APD on passengers departing from Britain. To make matters worse, in 2011 the European Union decided to bring aviation into its Emissions Trading System, a shift which, if implemented, would result in increased taxes on aviation even before any global approach to tourism taxation has been agreed upon. Fortunately, in 2012 a decision was taken to postpone this measure in the face of objections from a number of countries.

The United Kingdom

Even before the economic meltdown of 2008 and 2009 there were signs that the British Labour government recognized the importance of the economic role of tourism. It was the first British government to appoint a minister of tourism – called the minister for tourism, film and broadcasting – but during its term of office there were several changes of minister. The first minister, Janet Anderson, appointed in 1997, was then followed by Tom Clarke, Kim Howells, Richard Caborn, James Purnell, Shaun Woodward, Margaret Hodge and Barbara Follett, respectively.

In 2008, Graham Boynton interviewed Barbara Follett about Labour's policy on tourism, which he described as an £85 billion industry. He described her answers as "rather vague, politically correct and little more than white noise" (*Daily Telegraph*, 24 October 2008). When, however, the British Conservative Party in 2010 formed its coalition government with the Liberal Democrats, it appointed John Penrose as minister of tourism and heritage, and immediately signaled its intention to give greater recognition to the importance of tourism as a development sector.

On 12 August 2010, David Cameron, in what was probably the first tourism policy speech by a British prime minister, made the pronouncement that tourism, as the third largest contributor to the UK economy, must be integrated into every aspect of government policy. It was a speech that every tourism public or private sector entity in the Caribbean would wish to hear from its own prime minister. Cameron stated:

> For too long, tourism has been looked down on as a second class service sector. That's just wrong. Tourism is a fiercely competitive market, requiring skills, talent, enterprise and a government that backs Britain. It's fundamental to the rebuilding and rebalancing of our economy.
>
> It's one of the best and fastest ways of generating the jobs we need so badly in this country. And it's absolutely crucial to us making the most of the Olympics and indeed a whole decade of great international sport across Britain.

It is therefore understandable why Britain was most upset when it did not succeed in being allocated the hosting of the FIFA World Cup games of 2018.

Having declared that tourism was Britain's third-highest export industry after chemicals and financial services, the prime minister indicated that tourism was also a huge domestic market with the British making 126 million overnight domestic trips in 2009 and spending £22 billion. Cameron estimated that tourism contributed £115 billion to the British economy each year, and that for every 0.5 per cent increase in the United Kingdom's share of the world market, tourism could add £2.7 billion (US$4.4 billion) to the British economy and more than 50,000 jobs.

Cameron's statement about the role of his government with respect to tourism needs to be read and understood by Caribbean governments. He also claimed:

> We're going to be a government that understands the huge potential of our tourism industry, that gets tourism and that gives the industry the backing that it needs. A successful tourism policy needs an active and engaged government. But taking Britain up the league table of tourist destinations isn't something that we in government will do alone. It is something that we will all do together.
>
> Industry in the lead but with government – and society as a whole – standing behind you every step of the way.

Given his commitment, the controversial British APD, which has been described by the British government as an environmental tax, was being viewed by many observers as part of a strategy to support domestic tourism, which its prime minister had expressed a desire to see grow by 50 per cent at the expense of outward-bound tourism.

Caribbean governments, Caribbean public and private sector tourism organizations, British tour operators and some British airlines all lobbied the British government throughout 2010 either to have the APD reduced or to change aspects of its application which discriminated against the Caribbean.

In the budget delivered on 23 March 2011, the chancellor of the exchequer, George Osborne, announced a freeze on the current level of the tax until April 2012. He did not, however, respond to the charge that it was unfair that persons travelling from Britain to the Caribbean would continue to be taxed more heavily than those persons travelling from Britain to more distant parts of the United States, such as Hawaii or California. The tax is based on distance, but the distance is calculated between London and the capital city of the country to which one travels, rather than on the distance between the points actually travelled. Osborne simply promised further consultation on the existing bans, which he admitted had been arbitrarily imposed by the previous outgoing Labour government.

Rumours in September 2011 that the UK government would proceed with plans to increase the APD were confirmed when it was announced on 29 November 2011 that by April 2012 the APD would be increased by 8 per cent. There was, however, also a promise that, on 6 December 2011, the government would publish its response to the consultation on APD reform, setting out its views on the representations that have been made by the Caribbean, its airline partners, the West Indian community in the United Kingdom and others.

Far from responding to tourism interests, both at home and abroad, to reduce the level of APD or to change the system of bands to a more equitable level, the British government has taken the following decisions with respect to the APD:

- to further increase the APD rates effective from 1 April 2013
- to extend the APD to business jets from April 2013 – this includes all flights on aircraft with an authorized take-off weight of 5.7 tonnes or more; flights on aircraft of over 20 tonnes but with fewer than nineteen seats will have to pay a new premium rate of APD which will be double the standard rate for each band
- effective 1 January 2013, the APD rates for long haul flights departing Northern Ireland were set at zero

The APD is expected to provide receipts of £2.9 billion for 2012/2013 and £3.8 billion by 2016/2017.

15

The Second Decade
Whither Caribbean Tourism?

This book has looked at how tourism developed in the Caribbean, from the nineteenth century until the start of the second decade of the twenty-first, in the context of the Caribbean's complex social and economic history. We have seen how tourism replaced sugar as the driver of Caribbean economies in several countries, surviving many of the challenges of race and class that were a principal part of a colonial past. Ultimately, tourism established its validity as a genuine economic sector, embraced by both the major developed countries of Europe and North America and by the developing world.

It is reasonable to ask, therefore, what does the future hold for global tourism, and therefore for Caribbean tourism? A good starting point would be to see what global organizations like IATA and the UNWTO have to say on the subject, although even they have had, on a number of occasions, to revise their forecasts in the light of turbulent and ever-changing global economic and political circumstances.

IATA global predictions for tourism performance

In step with its predictions for air transportation mentioned in chapter 14, IATA made some predictions for global tourism by 2014:

- International passengers will rise from 952 million in 2009 to 1.3 billion in 2014, representing an annual compound growth rate of 5.9 per cent.
- The fastest growing markets will be China with 10.8 per cent, the United Arab Emirates with 10.2 per cent, Vietnam with 10.2 per cent, Malaysia with 10.1 per cent and Sri Lanka with 9.5 per cent.
- With respect to number of arrivals, the top five countries with the most international passengers will be the United States with 215 million persons (up 45 million), the United Kingdom with 198 million (up 33 million), Germany with 163 million (up 29 million), Spain with 123 million (up 21 million) and France with 111 million (up 21 million).
- Latin America will continue to grow healthily, with international passenger demand increasing at a rate of 5.7 per cent. International freight demand will increase 6.4 per cent, with Peru leading the region's freight growth with 9 per cent. North American international passenger demand will grow 4.9 per cent and freight at 7.6 per cent.
- There will be a decided shift in the industry eastwards to Asia.

UNWTO predictions for global tourism performance

The positive predictions for tourism made by IATA were also supported by UNWTO, which forecast that international tourism would grow by between 4 and 5 per cent in 2011. Its optimism was based on signs of tourism growth in 2010, as many of the source market countries seemed to be emerging from recession in response to policies of economic stimulation that had been applied to their faltering economies.

According to UNWTO, international tourism, having declined by 58 million persons or 4 per cent in 2009, grew by 6.7 per cent to 935 million persons in 2010. The vast majority of destinations posted positive results, sufficient to offset recent losses or bring them close to this target. Recovery, however, came at different speeds and was driven primarily by emerging economies. While tourism growth in advanced economies was 5 per cent, it was 8 per cent in emerging ones.

In 2010, international tourism receipts had reached US$919 billion, up 5 per cent from US$851 billion in 2009. For those who see China as a potential market and a future major player in tourism, it is worthy of note that it now ranks third in the world in terms of arrivals, after France and the United States, and fourth in tourism receipts.

In May 2011, UNWTO again assessed the state of international tourism and was still optimistic. Its report, published on 11 May 2011, indicated that international tourist arrivals grew by close to 5 per cent during the first months of 2011, consolidating the 7 per cent registered in 2010. Growth was in fact positive in all world subregions during January and February 2011, with the exceptions of the Middle East and North Africa. These exceptions were to be expected, however, given the political turmoil and even armed struggles taking place in certain of the countries of that region. It was nevertheless believed, however, that the high performance in arrivals in Europe and South America were far in advance of expectations and would compensate for the decrease in arrivals in North Africa, the Middle East, and also in Japan caused in that case by the respective man-made and natural disasters. In any case, the view was also expressed that the decreases in business in Tunisia, Egypt and Japan would bottom out by the end of 2011, and recovery would take place there also.

During the first half of 2011, South America and South Asia led growth in arrivals with +15 per cent, followed by sub-Saharan Africa with +13 per cent, and Central and Eastern Europe with +12 per cent.

The secretary general of UNWTO therefore predicted boldly that international tourist arrivals would increase by some 4 to 5 per cent in 2011, with emerging economies continuing to grow at a faster rate of +6 per cent. He was especially positive about emerging economies and developing countries, and singled out Africa where, in particular, tourism is increasingly recognized as a driver of development, exports and jobs.

Poll on tourism potential of Brazil, Russia, India and China

Much has also been claimed about the emerging respective markets of the BRIC countries – Brazil, Russia, India and China – and the possibilities for developing new tourism business with them. A 2010 World Travel Market poll of 1,300 exhibitors revealed that almost half of the industry perceives the BRIC economies as one of the biggest growth opportunities of the next five years. In fact, one in three respondents indicated that the BRIC tourism potential is the biggest tourism opportunity for the next five years, and a further 55 per cent stated that the business conducted with the BRIC countries in the past year had resulted in a positive impact on their businesses over the previous twelve months. In 2011, the World Travel Market focused on the BRIC countries and dedicated its first headline session to discussing their travel and tourism potential.

It needs to be clarified, however, that the BRIC countries should not, at this stage, be perceived as replacing North America and Europe as the Caribbean's major tourism markets. Economic recovery in the world's developed countries may be somewhat delayed, but everything is currently being done to ensure a return to growth. The latest effort in this regard is the decision by certain of the world's most important central banks – including the Federal Reserve and the European Central Bank – coming to the rescue of Europe. The banks did so by acting, on 30 November 2011, to make it cheaper for banks around the world to borrow US dollars – the currency in which most financial transactions are done – and so avoid the credit crunch of 2008. What is therefore being spoken of here is of the need to diversify Caribbean tourism markets and to make serious efforts to exploit the BRIC markets.

Recommendations for these new thrusts were supported by the positive reports coming out of Latin countries in 2011 about air transportation performance. (These reports were in addition to those emerging from Brazil in the same year.) In July 2011, ALTA announced that its member airlines carried 11.2 million passengers in May 2011, up 6.7 per cent on the same period of the previous year. Traffic, as expressed as revenue passenger kilometres, grew by 9.2 per cent, capacity, expressed as available seat kilometres, by 0.4 per cent and the load factor jumped to 73.3 per cent. The number of passengers carried between January to May 2011 were 57.1 million, an increase of 5.4 per cent as compared with the same period of the past year, with a load factor of 75.2 per cent.

Meanwhile, GOL, Brazil's second largest carrier – which had recently expanded its services into the Caribbean islands – confirmed in July 2011 that it was in talks about purchasing 100 per cent of Webjet, the country's fourth largest airline.

News about the economic performance of Latin America continued to run counter to the bad news in other places. The Economic Survey of Latin America and the Caribbean released its report for 2010 and 2011 in July 2011. In the report the survey predicting continuing economic recovery, with Latin America growing by 4.7 per cent, Central America by 4.3 per cent and the Caribbean by 1.9 per cent in 2011. Further, Latin America was expected to grow by 4.1 per cent in 2012.

The 2012 Economic Survey of Latin America issued by Economic Commission for Latin America and the Caribbean, indicated that the economic growth of the region slowed in the second quarter of 2012, although several of the region's economies maintained their momentum. The GDP growth rates for Latin America in 2012 were in fact 3.2 per cent, with a forecast for 2013 of 4.0 per cent. Growth in the Caribbean in 2012 was 1.6 per cent with a forecast for 2013 of 2.2 per cent.

An article in the *Latin Business Chronicle* (12 April 2012) by Mark Chesnut, later reproduced by David Lewis of *Manchester Trade*, states: "Airlines in Europe, as well as one particular airline in the Middle East, see opportunity in Latin America's fast growing economies and increasingly mobile populations." Chesnut quotes Marta Sánchez Oquillas, the head of sales of Iberia for Latin America, as saying: "More foreign investment, trade and tourism are behind this trend. This is boosting the size of the middle classes and their purchasing power, and, as a consequence, the demand for travel, which is somehow compensating for the weak demand in Europe, especially in Spain." Air France–KLM, Emirates and even LAN in Chile are increasing their services to Latin America which they see as a productive growth market.

Already Barbados, Jamaica, and Trinidad and Tobago have announced separate initiatives for developing a relationship with Brazil, and have either commenced or are in discussions about airline services. It is being suggested here that to exploit fully the opportunities for two way business and tourism traffic and cargo, the time is ripe for a full-fledged Caribbean approach to the Brazilian and other BRIC country markets. Certainly LIAT, which currently flies to twenty-one different Caribbean destinations, is well placed to feed traffic from all over the region to hubs in the southern Caribbean, from which there are long haul services both to and from Brazil and other countries further south.

Disappointing news on economic recovery in developed countries 2011

As 2011 continued, however, prospects of an early recovery from recession by the developed countries did not materialize. On the contrary, economic reports about those countries, which comprise the traditional major tourism source markets, continued to speak of slow and jobless growth. Importantly, Britain and the United States continued to labour under vast amounts of debt, and several countries in the eurozone, such as Portugal, Ireland, Greece and Spain, experienced serious economic difficulties, surviving only by massive bailouts, as junk-bond status threatened.

On 11 July 2011 European officials met in Brussels amid fears that the Greek debt crisis was spreading to Italy, the eurozone's third largest economy. There were concerns that Italy could be the next victim of a regional debt crisis following the sharp sell-off of Italian assets on 8 July. Italy had the highest sovereign debt ratio relatively to its economy in the eurozone after Greece – its debt was 119 per cent of GDP and the annual deficit was 4.6 per cent. This means that the total debt stood at 2.5 trillion euros, and there were fears that, should the country default, the eurozone's existing rescue mechanism, the European Financial Stability Facility, would not have sufficient funds to help it out.

Reports emerging from the International Monetary Fund and World Bank meetings of the early autumn of 2011 about global recovery were far from optimistic, and global air transportation and tourism agencies such as IATA and UNWTO were once more forced to review downwards their earlier predictions of recovery and growth. IATA reported in October 2011 that total passenger traffic fell by 1.6 per cent in August compared to July, and that airlines were expected to see profitability fall from US$6.9 billion to US$4.9 billion going into 2012.

Despite major bailouts by eurozone countries, fears about a default on its debt by Greece, with serious consequences for the rest of the area, returned. Thousands of Greeks filled the streets of Athens in October 2011 in protest at the severity of the economic measures proposed by the government. To cap it all, by November 2011, as a final testimony to the fact that finding a solution was beyond the capabilities of their politicians, the elected prime ministers of Greece and Italy were replaced by technocratic unelected prime ministers. The Greek economic crisis continued well into 2012, with the possible fallout from Greece leaving the eurozone being prepared for by other European countries.

From several quarters the consensus arose that the global recession that had started in 2008 had witnessed many fits and starts of recovery, but was likely to persist for five years or more. The one consolation was that the rest of Europe, in its own best interests, believed that it could not afford to allow

Greece and Italy to fail. Every small improvement in the world economy was greeted with a fanfare, and when at the end of November 2011 the US unemployment rate had fallen to 8.6 per cent, it was cheered as a major achievement.

Performance of intra-regional carriers 2010 and 2011

Turning now specifically to the Caribbean, it would be instructive to see how the region was performing in 2010 and 2011, both in respect of air transportation – which is a critical factor in an archipelago dependent on tourism – and with respect to the tourism industry in general. It has been shown earlier that in 2010 there were clear signs of recovery throughout the world in respect to air transportation. However, Caribbean airline performance in 2010 went against the trend with a series of losses, and an attempt is made here to explain why this was the case. Caribbean carriers operate in a region of low demand and are sensitive to increased prices and additional competition and capacity from any quarter.

The major carriers involved in servicing intra-Caribbean routes were American Eagle, Air Jamaica, Bahamasair, Cayman Airways, LIAT Airline, and Caribbean Airlines, which replaced BWIA International Airways as the national carrier of Trinidad and Tobago at the beginning of 2007.

American Eagle

Since 1966, the American Eagle jet-prop service has operated from the Puerto Rico hub in San Juan to several Caribbean islands, certain of which have airports that cannot as yet accommodate larger planes, and which depend on connecting services over various hubs to transport customers from long-haul destinations.

Both American Airlines and American Eagle are owned by AMR Corporation. The major role in the Caribbean of the Eagle is to distribute to other Caribbean destinations passengers brought by American Airlines to San Juan from several gateways in mainland America. The largest segment of the Eagle's other traffic, which originates in the Caribbean, has traditionally comprised persons travelling to San Juan for business or to shop. The shopping market has, however, been somewhat reduced because of the baggage limitations which are currently in force on all the carriers.

American Airlines was the dominant carrier to the region for many years. It launched its Caribbean service in 1971 when it bought Trans Caribbean Airways. It was at that time that Peter Dolara, an employee of Trans Caribbean Airways, moved over to American Airlines where, during some forty years, he became almost a legendary figure in determining what services American would offer in the Caribbean and across Latin America. He was been appointed senior vice president in 1989, and after having presided over the development of the Miami hub as the largest international gateway in American's network with over nine thousand employees, he retired in June 2012.

The Luis Muñoz Marín International Airport in San Juan had served as a hub for Pan Am, Trans Caribbean Airways and Eastern Airlines. It had also been a hub for Prinair, Puerto Rico's international airline, from 1966 until 1984, which became bankrupt and went permanently out of business. It was in 1986, however, that American opened its connecting hub in San Juan, and by 2001 the number of flights operated by American Airlines and American Eagle into the Caribbean had grown to 135 flights.

American's position as the major legacy carrier in the Caribbean has been greatly challenged by the arrival of low-cost carriers like JetBlue, Spirit Airlines and Air Tran Airways, and it is finding it increasingly difficult to compete with them at a time when, as a result of an unsettled world economic and political situation, airline costs keep rising.

At the height of the economic crisis in 2008, with fuel at US$147 per barrel, American announced its intention to cut domestic capacity by 11 to 12 per cent, and overall capacity, including international flights, by 8 per cent. The airline further announced that, starting in September 2009, it would cut the daily number of American Eagle flights out of San Juan from ninety-three to fifty-one flights. Among the flights identified were those to Santo Domingo, Antigua, St Maarten, Aruba, and Samana in the Dominican Republic. Certain of the flights were later restored, but in September 2010, further cuts were announced to take place by April 2011. These cuts would affect service to Anguilla, La Romana, Port of Spain and Puerto Plata, and bring down the number of Eagle flights into the Caribbean from fifty-eight to thirty-six flights.

On 1 April 2011, the American Airlines director of corporate affairs for Latin America and the Caribbean, Martha Pantin, announced that the American Eagle flight from San Juan to Barbados would cease to operate, but that American would be continuing service to Barbados out of Dallas/

Fort Worth International Airport and non-stop flights to New York and Miami. However, it was announced on 8 August 2011 that the service between San Juan and Barbados would be restored by the end of 2011 and, starting 18 November 2011, a twice-weekly service would begin with a sixty-four-seater ATR 72 aircraft.

Since 2007, AMR, the parent company of American Eagle, had been testing the idea of selling it. In July 2010, the idea was advanced again, this time to Republic Airways Holdings. However, on 18 November 2011, a news item was carried in Sky Talk that plans to divest American Eagle were being pushed ahead to 2012 to wait for pilots working for Eagle to vote on a tentative agreement.

In his book *Don't Burn Our Bridges: The Case for Owning Airlines*, Jean Holder had written that the problem dogging American Airlines, which continued year after year to suffer continuous losses, was this: unlike its major competitors among the legacy carriers in the United States, American had not gone into bankruptcy, an event which would have allowed it to shed debt, cut labour costs, restructure its operations, possibly look for a suitable US partner with which to merge, and find its way back to profitability. Instead, under the weight of its costs, which included expensive pensions and surging fuel prices, it lost more than US$11 billion since 2001.

It finally took the plunge on 28 November 2011 and filed for bankruptcy – a filing that included American Eagle – while assuring the world that it had enough cash to continue its operations as usual and would emerge a stronger and reborn airline. There were two rumours abroad about American Airlines: one was that after emerging from bankruptcy, it would seek to merge with US Airways; the other was that it is likely to become a target for a takeover by one of the other major US legacy carriers. In the final event, a decision was taken in 2013 to enter into a merger with US Airways.

On 19 April 2012, however, a plan was announced to phase out American's base in San Juan as part of a network overhaul in the Chapter 11 restructuring of the company. The ATR fleet of American Eagle was phased out in April 2013, representing the end of a forty-one year old era.

Air Jamaica and Caribbean Airlines

After many years of accumulated losses estimated in 2008 to have reached US$1.3 billion, Air Jamaica was put up for sale by its owner, the Government of Jamaica, and agreement reached for its purchase by Caribbean Airlines (CAL) of Trinidad and Tobago. The negotiations that ensued ended with agreement for a merger between the two carriers under which Jamaica would own 16 per cent of CAL and would be represented by one director on its board. In return, CAL would take over the "profitable" routes of Jamaica and would promote two distinct brands, that of CAL and Air Jamaica. CAL was also given the right, until 30 April 2011, to pull out of the agreement without penalty.

However, there were general elections in Trinidad and Tobago in May 2010 in which the government that negotiated the agreement lost office. There was then substantial immediate public discussion about whether the incoming government would honour the agreement. A committee established by the new government proposed that the agreement be honoured and CAL continued to operate the two brands. CAL, which was in receipt of a government subsidy equal to any money paid for fuel over US$50 per barrel, also extended that subsidy to the Air Jamaica operation.

In 2010 the CEO of CAL announced that the airline had made a small profit in 2008, that the results for 2009, when finally signed off by the board, would show a profit, and that the results for 2010 were expected to be even better.

On 1 March 2011, however, the *Jamaica Observer* speculated that the first year of operation of the Jamaica routes in fact resulted in a loss to CAL of some US$50 million, even with the fuel subsidy in place. The *Observer* therefore reopened speculation about whether the agreement between CAL and Air Jamaica would hold or whether CAL would walk away from it before 30 April 2011. On 27 May 2011, however, Jamaica's minister of finance, Audley Shaw, and his counterpart in Trinidad and Tobago, Winston Dookeran, signed the shareholder agreement representing the formal merger of Air Jamaica and Caribbean Airlines.

The arrival of low-fare carrier REDjet in May 2011, which, by the end of 2011, was competing on the Antigua, Jamaica, Guyana, Trinidad, and St Lucia routes, drove down airfares in the Caribbean, forcing other competing carriers to do the same. CAL, with its fuel subsidy and backed by the resources of the Government of Trinidad and Tobago, responded with an aggressive campaign of highly competitive fares and expanding capacity.

In November 2011, CAL announced a profit of TT$200 million but later in the month, on 27 November, questions were asked by the media about whether this figure made allowances for the receipt by the carrier of a fuel subsidy of TT$279 million. Their interpretation was that CAL had in fact suffered losses, despite flying full to most of its destinations.

At the beginning of May 2012, finance minister Winston Dookeran announced in Parliament that in 2011 CAL had lost US$52.8 million and Air Jamaica US$38.1 million. Transport minister Devant Maharaj urged in explanation of these developments that the Air Jamaica operations were hemorrhaging and the Trinidadian taxpayers had been paying for the luxury of Jamaicans flying on a fuel subsidy. He blamed former People's National Movement prime minister Patrick Manning, whom he said had "attempted to become the colonial master of the Caribbean". In the meantime CAL announced plans to return to London, with flights from Jamaica to London, and from Trinidad and Barbados to London, in mid-2012. At March 2013 CAL was operating three flights a week from Port of Spain to London but had not restarted any services from Jamaica.

Bahamasair

Bahamasair, created on 18 June 1973, has had a history of struggle. According to its audited financial statements for the year ending June 2006, the company suffered a net loss of US$19.9 million, had up to that time accumulated losses of US$398 million and liabilities in excess of total assets of US$70 million. Its operations have always been subsidized in the annual budget of the Bahamas, and in 2008 it received a supplementary US$11.3 million.

In the manner of certain other government-owned Caribbean carriers, Bahamasair has been overstaffed due to the reluctance of governments to make staff redundant and the insistence by some unions of maintaining employment levels despite the level of costs. The number of staff, however, had declined through attrition from 709 in January 2009 to 667 by April 2010. What was more, the minister of public works and transport, Neko Grant, called in 2010 for industrial agreements to be negotiated to reflect significant reductions in labour costs – one of the few costs, as opposed to fuel and maintenance, over which the company had any control.

In the budget for 2009 and 2010 a subsidy of US$17 million had been requested, but an additional sum of US$3.5 million needed to be provided during the year. In the fiscal year for 2009 and 2010 the losses reached US$23.6 million.

In the face of much criticism, Bahamasair instituted a number of cost-saving measures in 2011. Grant claimed that these measures had cut costs substantially. However, with 2011, the accumulated debt was US$473 million.

In the budget for 2011 and 2012 the government increased the Bahamasair subsidy by US$2.6 million to US$18.6 million. Henry Woods, the managing director, remarked that, despite the problems of the airline, it is still faring well against competition. Because of its safety record, competitive price scale, and improved service, Bahamasair has its loyal customers, and is still able to attract new business.

When in May 2012 the Progressive Liberal Party, led by Perry Christie, defeated the Free National Movement Party of Hubert Ingraham at the polls, the new deputy prime minister and minister of works and urban development, Philip Brave Davis, indicated certain of the new policies proposed for Bahamasair. He confirmed that the carrier's average deficit was US$21 million per year, and that it had recently requested a US$22 million subsidy. Davis indicated that issues affecting employees would be prioritized, as the government plotted the airline's revitalization as the carrier of choice among local and international markets. He promised to look at demoting certain local routes to smaller carriers, and to address the issues of an aging fleet. Davis also claimed that the airline was never expected to make a profit, but that there were ways to make the deficit more manageable. Speaking of its domestic role, Davis stated that Bahamasair "was designed to ensure that there would be adequate transportation between the islands and it was thought then, and as I think has been the case, that some subsidy would be required for some of the far flung islands". In reports carried in the *Nation* (16 March 2013), there was an announcement by the deputy prime minister and minister of works and urban development, Philip Davis, that Bahamasair had lost US$11.7 million in 2012, as opposed to US$9.8 million in 2011. The loss was attributed mainly to the challenges associated with an aging fleet and increases in airport and fuel charges.

Cayman Airways

Governments of the Cayman Islands have always maintained a special relationship between its airline, Cayman Airways, the department of tourism

(CIDOT) and the tourism sector generally. This relationship has therefore led to what may be regarded as an enlightened view for a country heavily dependent on tourism and financial services. The return on investment of the carrier is not seen merely in terms of the bottom line, but in terms of the totality of the contribution of the travel and tourism sector to the GDP of the country.

CIDOT currently provides marketing, promotions, and public relations services for Cayman Airways, a situation which allows significant economies of scale and cost savings to be realized at a national level. Certain specific services are as follows:

- *media planning and buying*: CIDOT strategically purchased television in key markets with a special consideration placed on Cayman Airways markets.
- *print advertising*: When applicable, Cayman Airways is used as the call to action in print advertising in gateway cities.
- *television advertising*: CIDOT works closely with designated wholesalers to ensure Cayman Airways is identified as the call to action on all television advertisements in designated cities.
- *interactive and direct marketing*: CIDOT builds customized web sites for Cayman Airways to promote special offers to consumers and drive business through to caymanairways.com.
- *public relations*: CIDOT public relations develops and distributes press releases, feature articles and the like and maintains a high level of awareness of Cayman Airways in the international media.
- *regional sales promotions*: CIDOT promotes Cayman Airways routes at consumer events, travel trade shows, blitzes and sales calls along with "hot happenings" – as they are called – and consumer and trade newsletters.

Former premier McKeeva Bush expressed his commitment to the carrier both in his budget speech in June 2010 and in his address to the legislature in February 2011. The following is a quotation from the budget speech ("Partnership for Recovery", 15 June 2010):

> From its inception, Cayman Airways has received funding annually from the government, with the intent to cover the airline's operating costs. The level of funding

has always been less than what was actually required to cover the airline's operating costs.

In the last ten years, this funding shortfall from the government has forced the airline into just over 50 million dollars in debt, with 19 million dollars of this debt owed to non-bank counter parties. The debt owed to banks has grown to a level that demands approximately a half-million dollars each month to service.

The level of bank debt combined with the additional level of non-bank debt, is now of a magnitude which is unsustainable and severely threatens the continued operations of the national airline.

This is one of the issues that we, as a government, have to face and fix.

In this regard, the airline has managed to reduce its expenditure in fiscal year ending June 2010 by between ten and twelve million dollars. The final number will depend largely on the fluctuations in fuel prices when compared to what obtained in the fiscal year ending June 2009.

Amongst the measures taken, Cayman Airways proactively commenced reductions in staffing levels in August 2009 and has achieved an 11 per cent reduction, from just over 400 employees in mid-2009 to 355 in April this year.

The annualized cost savings of this staff reduction, along with other staff related reductions such as work permit fees and overtime payments is currently projected to be near two million dollars.

Other examples of significant cost reduction include the successful re-negotiation of aircraft leases, which have resulted in annualised savings of over 1.2 million dollars. Strategic reductions in scheduled flying have also been implemented to better align capacity with demand, without any negative impact on revenue.

Significant cost reductions have been achieved in almost every expense category and will be permanent in nature. This assures Cayman Airways a solid and effective cost structure as the airline continues to improve its revenue management processes.

LIAT Airline

In 2013, LIAT is in its fifty-seventh year and serving twenty-one countries in the Caribbean Basin, having dropped one of its destinations in 2011. It had generally operated about one thousand flights a week, although it did sometimes make adjustments to the schedule for various reasons. In 2009 it carried over one million passengers, but since then has lost some market share, transporting 913,803 persons in 2010; 859,266 in 2011; and 809,937 in 2012.

As with other Caribbean carriers, LIAT was undercapitalized from its beginning and has struggled financially for most of its existence. By 2004, it had built an accumulated debt of US$115 million. In 2006 it suffered an operating loss of US$12.6 million and in 2007 of US$1.7 million.

It was in 2007 that LIAT took over the assets of Caribbean Star and wiped out its debt, thanks to a capital investment by its shareholders of US$60 million. This feat was accomplished through a loan from the Caribbean Development Bank and LIAT's negotiation of debt forgiveness from Export Development Canada, thanks to the generosity of that agency. In 2008 LIAT made a small operating profit of US$746,945 (EC$2.01 million) and in 2009 a net profit of some US$3.26 million (EC$8.8 million).

As with all the other airlines operating in the Caribbean, LIAT's fare levels to the customer have been greatly increased by a regime of government taxes and airport charges, twin charges which can represent as much as 40 per cent of the fare. However, by operating after 2007 in an environment of reduced competition, the company was able to keep fares high and therefore survive. These high fares, however, brought diminishing returns, as they were unpopular and affected travel flows negatively.

In 2010, somewhat overwhelmed by high fuel prices, high maintenance costs and its inability to secure the agreement of its ten unions to cut staff and related costs, LIAT returned to a loss-making situation of US$7.48 million (EC$20.2 million).

The year 2011 continued to present even greater challenges for LIAT as new competition arose on its routes from CAL, Air BVI and from low-fare carrier REDjet. Cutting costs and increasing revenues therefore became necessary as a matter of survival. After protracted negotiations in 2011, agreement was finally reached, with all but one union, to close the City Ticketing Offices on 31 August 2011. Throughout 2011, LIAT was engaged on a major restructuring plan, based on a number of studies, which included renewal of its fleet and revamping its route structure. The struggle to cut costs and raise revenues continued throughout 2011, and LIAT still ended 2011 with losses of EC$45.9 million (US$17 million) and 2012 with losses of EC$23.9 million (US$8.8 million).

REDjet

In 2007 the news first broke that an Irish-owned carrier, called Airone, was seeking authorization to be based in and to fly out of Jamaica to the United States and Caribbean destinations. The Government of Jamaica did not approve its application, but in 2010 it sought and was given permission to be based in Barbados with the stated intention to begin operations to Guyana, Jamaica, and Trinidad and Tobago.

In 2011 an Air Operating Certificate was awarded REDjet by the Barbados Civil Aviation Department, and the Barbados Air Transport Licensing Authority approved its routes and fares to operate. The fares advertised by that airline were as low as US$9.99 one way, plus taxes.

There were, however, an array of taxes payable even on REDjet. Leaving from Barbados to Trinidad and Tobago there was the airport security charge of US$2.50, a passenger service charge of US$27.50, a Barbados sales tax charge of US$1.75, and from Trinidad and Tobago to Barbados there were the airport terminal charge of US$1.50, the concourse fee of US$7.50, the passenger user charge of US$15.70 and the Barbados sales tax of US$1.75 for a total of US$51.70.

There were also other REDjet costs. There was a US$5.00 charge for all website bookings, per passenger, per flight. Carry-on handbags and a laptop could be carried free, but a small bag weighing up to fifteen kilograms would cost US$10.00, one weighing 22.5 kilograms, US$17.50, and a large bag up to thirty kilograms over US$25.00. Priority boarding would also cost US$10.00.

Despite these other charges, REDjet's lowest return fare from Barbados to Trinidad and Tobago was about US$119.18, as opposed to the regular LIAT fare of US$250.50.

In view of the pending competition, both LIAT and CAL launched special fares for a restricted period. LIAT offered a return fare of US$44.00 with taxes at US$61.55. LIAT did not charge for online booking and there was no charge for a fifty-pound bag. The CAL special was an economy return fare of US$181.60. CAL, however, accepted, at no cost, one checked bag of fifty pounds, one carry-on bag of twenty-two pounds, plus one laptop.

REDjet started services from Barbados to Guyana in May 2011, but although 8 May 2011 was set as the date on which its operations to Port of Spain would begin, a snag arose when the Government of Trinidad and Tobago announced that no application had been made to, and no approval given by its appropriate authorities, for REDjet to operate into and out of Trinidad and Tobago. The then-minister of works and transport, Jack Warner, made it clear, however, that the national carrier CAL was not afraid of competition, and that the application, when received, would in fact be duly considered. It was made in April 2011 but the delay in receiving approval continued.

The arrival of REDjet as a competitor caused a great deal of excitement and controversy. After years of high fares in the Caribbean, the general public craved low fares, and was not particularly concerned about whether REDjet's fares were sustainable or whether the existing carriers could survive a regime of high costs and low fares.

REDjet argued that its operating model was similar to that of Ryanair and other LCC carriers in North America and Europe, and that by keeping costs low, it would increase the volume of air travellers, not only for itself, but also for other carriers in the region.

Those observers who have studied existing LCC models in other parts of the world know that such models contain costs by flying point to point on heavily trafficked routes, that such airlines fly from secondary airports, where the taxes and other fees payable by airlines are lower than at the major airports, that they are usually free of the demands of unions and the several other obligations for which legacy carriers are liable, and that much of the new traffic for LCCs comes from converting to airline travel passengers who normally in large countries travel significant distances by bus and train.

Since no such possibilities exist in the Caribbean, it remained to be seen if in a Caribbean environment, where the conditions differ markedly from those in Europe and North America, the same positive financial results would be achieved by a low-fare carrier offering à la carte pricing.

By early July 2011, REDjet, despite its best efforts, had not received permission to fly to either Jamaica or Trinidad and Tobago which argued that there were still some safety issues to settle. Matters came to a head at the July CARICOM heads of government meeting in St Kitts, when persons hinted that the Government of Trinidad and Tobago might be preventing REDjet from flying, not so much from concerns about safety, but to protect its carrier CAL from competition. After a hearing in the Port of Spain High Court permission was given to REDjet to fly to Trinidad and Tobago by 28 July 2011, and two days later the carrier received permission to fly to Jamaica as well. REDjet, however, then announced that the Jamaica service would not commence until October 2011.

In August and September 2011, REDjet with services to Barbados, Guyana and Trinidad, suffered some reversals due to mechanical problems, resulting in approximately 953 persons being stranded, bringing home to its owners the reality that operating an airline, especially in the Caribbean, was a challenging enterprise.

In October 2011, REDjet began flying to Jamaica and in November a return service, between Guyana and Antigua, was also launched. Loud objections were, however, raised by REDjet in November 2011 to what it deemed to be delays being experienced in having its application to the Barbados Air Transport Licensing Authority to fly several routes in the Eastern Caribbean approved. The routes mentioned were from Barbados to St Lucia, Grenada, St Kitts, Antigua and St Maarten, and there was suggestion that the delays were intended to protect LIAT, a corporation in which the Barbados government has the largest shareholding.

In November 2011, accusations were made that the Government of Barbados was sabotaging the airline, although the blame was later shifted to the Barbadian technocrats. It was also rumoured that the REDjet owners had now lost about US$8 million due to the delays being experienced in flying the routes applied for. The Barbados government, however, contended that, in its original application to operate from Barbados, REDjet had never expressed the intention to fly to the small Eastern Caribbean countries for which applications were now being made, but instead to the larger countries in the outer band of the Caribbean, and to develop *other* routes in South and Central America.

As the end of the year approached, the debate continued, and included whether REDjet would move its base from Barbados. The latest development in December 2011 was that approval was granted for REDjet to operate flights to St Lucia on Fridays and Sundays, starting on 16 December, and that other approvals were likely to be given to REDjet to fly to other Caribbean destinations, including St Maarten.

On 16 March 2012, however, Robbie Burns of REDjet announced, to the great surprise of many in the region, that REDjet was suspending services from 23.59 on that day. LIAT was requested and agreed to assist with facilitating the return of stranded passengers to their respective places of origin.

Summary

As the second decade of the twenty-first century began, Caribbean carriers continued the struggle to survive. Bahamasair and Cayman Airways continued to be assisted in their normal operations by the fact that they were in receipt of annual subsidies in the national budgets of the countries that own them.

CAL, in expectation of an expanded fleet that was initially projected to include nine ATRs announced plans to compete on more Caribbean routes, while also competing with international carriers on North American routes, reopening services to London from Trinidad, Barbados and Jamaica, and exploring new long-haul destinations. An example of such a destination is India. At 2013 services to London from Port of Spain, but not from Jamaica, had resumed. No flights to India had been started and the number of ATRs ordered had been reduced to four.

The fuel subsidy granted CAL seems necessary to the expansionist plans of the company. At 2013 the Government of Trinidad and Tobago continues providing the fuel subsidy which covers both the Air Jamaica and CAL operations. Two related issues are as follows: if the subsidy is maintained, it will need to grow to even larger proportions as services expand, and questions have been raised by its competitor, LIAT, about whether the subsidy is in breach of the provisions of the CARICOM Multilateral Air Services Agreement. At March 2013 LIAT had taken legal advice on the matter but no further steps had been taken.

At May 2012, REDjet had talked of restarting operations, and of awaiting a bailout from the Government of Barbados while also awaiting other sources of funding. Furthermore, it was reported that an Irishman, Geoffrey O'Byrne White – former chief executive officer of the Irish regional airline Cityjet, and a person with over thirty years of experience in the airline industry – had been recruited to manage the day-to-day operations of REDjet, replacing Ian Burns as CEO. The company however faced the challenge of having its cancelled Air Operating Certificate restored by the Civil Aviation Authority of Barbados, which argued that REDjet must first receive the funding it sought before the certificate could be restored. It never therefore resumed operations after March 2012.

LIAT

At March 2013, LIAT's major shareholder governments are not subsidizing its daily operations, but they are making critical capital investments in its programme of replacing its aging fleet by new ATR 42 and 72 aircraft.

Efforts are also being made to expand the number of countries investing in the airline.

One of its major competitors, American Eagle, ceased operating after the spring of 2013, but there will still be competition from other carriers such as CAL, Air BVI, Air Caraibes, Winair, Seaborne Airways, Cape Air and an expanding JetBlue, already operating flights to a number of Eastern Caribbean destinations, both direct and over its San Juan hub. In addition, there are a number of long-haul carriers out of Britain, like British Airways and Virgin Atlantic, which now fly directly to some islands to which their passengers were formerly transferred by LIAT over its hubs at Antigua and Barbados.

LIAT, like all other Caribbean airlines in the region, is currently operating in a market of falling demand and increasing capacity. One solution posed is the creation of one Caribbean airline, owned by the countries of the Caribbean Community and serving both intra-regional and long-haul routes, well-capitalized and managed by experts along commercial lines. This concept is, however, a utopian one, which is easily visualized but difficult to implement.

The option for its own future, which does indeed lie in LIAT's hands, is to create entirely new strategic directions for itself. Given its critical importance to several countries in the Eastern Caribbean, its demise should not be considered an option by its shareholders.

In 2013 LIAT, under the leadership of a new CEO, Captain Ian Brunton, is engaged in implementing a new business plan which seeks to transform the carrier, taking it from a loss making venture to making a profit as early as 2013. There have been several inputs into the business plan as follows:

- a 2011 strategic plan after consultations with its shareholder prime minister, board of directors, management and unions
- an institutional strengthening study carried out by Pricewaterhouse Coopers
- the recommendations of a route analysis study executed by Lufthansa Consulting
- a fleet renewal programme in respect of which Bombardier, Embraer and ATR aircraft manufacturing companies have responded to RFPs

It has been decided that the new fleet for the immediate future will comprise a mix of ATR 42s and ATR 72s and the company is currently in the process of negotiating the required finance. An option also considered has been the acquisition of some regional jets for expanding the current route structure but no decision on this had been taken at March 2013.

The final chapter of the survival of any of the Caribbean-owned carriers is yet to be written. A combination of the fare wars unleashed in 2011 and 2012 and the current overcapacity in the Caribbean region remain a serious threat to the survival of the regional carriers. For the present, the Caribbean will have to accept two existing realities about air transportation in the region: a continuing situation of poor global economic performance leading to reduce demand for travel within our region and the fact that airline profitability continues to be threatened by the persistent high cost of aviation fuel, a cost which now represents as much as 33 per cent of airline operating costs. Despite some short-term fluctuations, the cost of oil seems likely to remain at around US$100 per barrel or higher over the longer term.

Whether they are publicly or privately owned, airline companies must be able to operate fleets of new fuel-efficient planes if they are to have any chance of meeting and exceeding their costs of operations. This fact poses a major challenge for most airline owners in the Caribbean.

In this environment, Caribbean governments, business management, and other social partners in the region need to have, as a matter of urgency, a frank dialogue with each other about what the challenges in fact are, and what cooperative action is needed not only to compete, but also to survive.

Caribbean tourism performance, 2010

In 2010, despite slow economic growth and increasing competition in the Caribbean's traditional source markets, visitor arrival numbers to the Caribbean recovered to 2008 levels. According to the CTO more than 23 million tourists visited the region in 2010, an increase of nearly 5 per cent from the 22.1 million travellers that had come in 2009.

At a press conference on 2 March 2011 held at the CTO headquarters, the organization's director of research and information technology, Winfield Griffith, presented a mostly positive report for 2010, indicating that US arrivals increased by 5.7 per cent to surpass the pre-recession level of 11.5 million. Canadian arrivals had increased by 4 per cent, although arrivals from Britain were down by approximately 1.1 million travellers, compared with the 1.4 million that had come in 2007.

When broken out in terms of subregions, it was seen that the fifteen CARICOM countries had had a 3.6 per cent increase in arrivals, and the countries of the Organisation of Eastern Caribbean States one of 2.9 per cent. The Spanish-speaking Caribbean experienced a 6 per cent increase in arrivals, but the Dutch Caribbean saw a decrease, pulled down by a 6 per cent decrease to Curaçao.

There was some other good news. For the first time in three years, hotel performance in 2010 indicated some improvement: occupancy was up by 3.1 per cent, average daily revenue up by 4.3 per cent, total room revenues up by 7.1 per cent and revenue per room by 7.5 per cent.

Visitor expenditure down

Griffith, however, also reported that average visitor spending was down to the level it was at approximately six years before, a result that was not unexpected, considering the state of the economies in the source markets. People, refusing to give up the needed holiday, were still travelling, but either had less money to spend or decided that it was wise to be frugal in a continuing situation of global uncertainty about the economic future. Overall the director himself was cautiously optimistic about the future of the Caribbean tourism industry, forecasting continuing improvement and about a 5 per cent increase in arrivals to the Caribbean in 2011.

Cruise tourism

Cruise tourism passenger arrivals were also up by 6 per cent in 2010. However, days after Griffith's pronouncement was made, two major cruise lines serving the region announced that certain of their ships that had normally serviced Barbados in both winter and summer were now being transferred to other regions of the world. The apparent cause was the escalating costs of fuel, which had made it uneconomical for the cruise lines to service destinations as far south of Miami as Barbados. Given the global scenario outlined above, the performance of Caribbean tourism as the second decade of this century began may be described as mixed.

Caribbean tourism performance 2011

Early reports on the Caribbean in 2011 confirmed a return to growth in arrivals from external markets (see statistics in appendix 5). Again this finding was not accompanied by increases in visitor expenditure. On several fronts fare wars in hotel prices began, and realists were advising the need to temper optimism in 2011 with considerable caution.

With the arrival of low-fare carrier REDjet in mid-2011, basic airfares of all airlines serving intra-Caribbean routes fell, and the number of intra-Caribbean visitors marginally increased. However, due to the high taxes, duties and other charges on air travel that continued to exist in the region, the costs of travel to the customer in 2011 remained higher than is desirable, preventing even greater expansion in the number of travellers (see appendix 8: LIAT Fares and Taxes Tables). This is an issue that Caribbean governments need to address.

Cruise passengers forecast 2011 and 2012 disappointing

The forecast for cruise passenger arrivals for 2011 and 2012 was this: the region's share of international cruise arrivals was likely to fall to about 35 per cent as cruise lines would transfer more and more ships to both old and new destinations such as the Mediterranean, South America, the Pacific Northeast, Australia and Asia, during the November-to-April period. In earlier chapters it was seen that at one time the Caribbean's share of cruise tourism was over 60 per cent. By 2009 it was about 41 per cent.

2012 performance and forecast for 2013

On 13 February 2013, chairman of the CTO Beverly Nicholson-Doty issued a wide-ranging statement in which she said that Caribbean Tourism with its 5.4 per cent growth in 2012 had outpaced the rest of the world. She cited UNWTO statistics which reported that there were one billion international tourist arrivals in 2012, a number that was 4 per cent above that for 2011. She added that she expected traffic flow to the Caribbean to grow a further 4 to 5 per cent in 2013. Arrivals to the Caribbean from the United States were up 4.1 per cent with increases in all reporting countries.

Canada is the fastest growing market, with a 5.9 per cent growth in arrivals in 2012, marking the fifth straight year of growth. Cause for concern was that those countries that relied heavily on the UK market were hard pressed to recover due to the United Kingdom's ailing economy and its onerous APD tax.

In 2012, an encouraging sign was that visitor spending in the CTO member countries totalled US$27 billion, a 3.6 per cent increase over 2011, marking a return of aggregate spending by visitors to the pre-recession levels. Caribbean hotels also reported improved performance in four key areas; overall occupancy rates for the Caribbean increased by 7.1 per cent; average daily rate went up to 4.8 per cent; total room revenues rose by 8.9 per cent and revenue per available room rose by 12.4 per cent in 2012. The situation with cruise tourism in 2012 was less optimistic. It was described as "flat region-wide for each of the last three years following an intra-regional shifting of cruise schedules resulting in fairly significant increases in the northern Caribbean activity, offset by reductions in that of the south".

The posted results for the region, taken as a whole, are encouraging, signalling a sustained recovery after a long and painful period of recession. It is somewhat misleading, however, since it conceals the fact that the robust growth and recovery is taking place largely in the Spanish and other Caribbean, rather than in the CARICOM/OECS states, a number of which continue to struggle. The situation reflects the plight of those states that are largely dependent on the UK market. An optimistic view suggests that when the UK market recovers their performance will reflect that reality.

However that may be, the CTO report reinforces the position taken throughout this book that economic history over the past sixty years has demonstrated that tourism, both in the Caribbean region and globally, enjoys great resilience. Whatever challenges it has faced, whether from natural or man-made disasters, it has recovered in a short space of time. Our prediction, therefore, is that, provided the region recognizes that change is needed with respect to the industry and where, and what, that change should be, tourism will survive the present recession and continue, as in the past, to be the region's strongest economic sector. That is no reason for the Caribbean to be complacent, however.

Over that same period of time, there have been significant changes in the tourism products that people buy and how they buy them. There must therefore be corresponding changes in the products on offer and how the region both promotes and sells them. Perhaps the minds of our youth should be excited by competitions in which new tourism products are suggested for sale to both visitors and locals, thereby increasing the things to do, see and buy, and expanding the range of recreational activities for all.

The various kinds of social media available as promotional tools should be exploited to the fullest and the skills of staff trained to work in tourism, and especially air transportation, must be upgraded to enable efficient use in pursuit of greater productivity of ever-increasing technology.

One unchanging requirement for a successful industry is quality service, which is not just about being socially pleasant. It is also a result of a standard, set by training, that brands the product and punishes or rewards staff according to failure or success in achieving it. These developments have serious implications for the kind, size and costs of the staff of companies, for the modus operandi of trade unions that represent tourism workers, and indeed for tourism entrepreneurs, who must not only be knowledgeable about what is going on in tourism across the world, but must also be creative in inventing and packaging for sale their new products.

It needs also to be recognized that competition in both the tourism and airline industries has intensified even more since the 2008 global recession began, and companies face the dilemma that, while certain basic costs become progressively higher, customers are seeking lower and lower prices.

Furthermore, while airlines are striving to drive down costs to the consumer, governments, burdened by debt, and in search of new sources of revenue, keep imposing new taxes and duties on airlines, costs which are a serious deterrent to the growth in travel. Sooner, rather than later, governments must face the reality that the onerous nature of these impositions brings diminishing returns and must be addressed. A study released by the World Travel and Tourism Council in early 2012 argues that the British APD, which is the world's highest tax on airlines and rose even higher in April 2012, is actually costing Britain jobs and revenue. It was suggested that its removal would create as many as 91,000 jobs and add £4.2 billion to the economy in twelve months. From April 2012 a family of four flying from Britain to the Caribbean in economy class is paying £440 in taxes alone.

The critical importance of tourism to the Caribbean

The history of Caribbean tourism, as delineated in this book, has revealed that, since the fall of King Sugar, tourism and services, starting with the 1960s, have been the drivers of the economies of the vast majority of the states of the Caribbean. There is no good reason to think that this will change in the immediate future, unless large quantities of oil are found. This claim is not, however, an argument for abandoning efforts to transform the agricultural industry and revitalizing manufacturing. But we must avoid the tendency, every time there is a decrease in Caribbean tourism arrival numbers or visitor expenditure, to engage in self-deception about manufacturing replacing tourism and other services as the leading Caribbean sector. In fact, despite a high level of rhetoric in the United States in 2012 about recovering manufacturing jobs lost to countries like India and China, it is most unlikely that, even there, any reversal of the trend for services to dominate the US economy will take place. It will not happen in the Caribbean. It is, however, recommended that, where in the small Caribbean islands the existing realities of land and soil make certain forms of agriculture possible, realistic and creative steps should be taken to diversify through agriculture the economies of those islands. The same observation obtains for the manufacturing sectors which, with a great deal more effort, creativity and focus, could be expanded far beyond the situation as it now exists. In both cases, however, linkages with the tourism sector are important and some of the suggestions made in chapter 13 of this book should indeed be considered. That argument is, however, a case for further strengthening the Caribbean tourism sector, rather than for shifting the present priorities.

A footnote to the above paragraph is this. The larger islands such as the Dominican Republic, Cuba and even Jamaica, as well as the CARICOM continental states such as Belize, Guyana, Suriname, have the land space to produce significant agricultural and other commodities for both local and external markets. Better opportunities therefore do exist for those countries to develop further those aspects of their economies and to respond to the growing global demand for commodities. Maximum effort should therefore be invested in their exploitation.

In tourism, unlike in the case of the export of sugar and bananas, the region's horizons are not circumscribed, by old connections with former colonial powers that, in any case, no longer carry the burden of guilt caused by colonial exploitation. The tourism world is indeed the Caribbean's oyster. The region must therefore remain focused on maximizing tourism's possibilities on a global scale and not respond to every sound of alarm from those pessimists who never tire of suggesting that tourism is a fickle economic option. Moreover, while advocating the need for balanced growth and respect for the socio-cultural and environmental issues, one must be concerned about the agenda of those persons whose preferences in defence of the status quo seem to favour underdevelopment over progress that could benefit the vast majority of the residents.

David Jessop, in an article of 25 February 2011 in the *Barbados Advocate* called "The View from Europe", places in perspective the importance of tourism to the Caribbean:

> The Caribbean is 13th globally in absolute size; first in its relative contribution to national economies; and 10th internationally in its contribution to long-term national growth.
>
> Moreover, it is the biggest employer after the public sector, the largest single contributor to gross domestic product, and was worth in 2010 some US$39.4 billion, based on an estimated Caribbean travel and tourism demand of US$55.4 billion, less imported goods and services including travel and tourism spending abroad of US$16 billion.

Caribbean governments must internalize the implications of those figures while paying attention to the new aggressive tourism policies and competition coming from the United Kingdom, the United States and other developed countries. It would be ironic for the Caribbean to seek to underestimate the role of tourism as a development sector just when countries such as the United Kingdom and the United States are preaching to their own respective peoples its virtues as an export sector.

Perhaps the time has come for Caribbean prime ministers to convene a second conference on the present and future of Caribbean tourism, as was first done in 1975 after the energy crisis of 1974 and 1975. The agenda should include at least the following items: a regional tourism development plan that sets targets for the region in the second decade of the twenty-first century; clear guidelines on how major inputs from regional agriculture, manufacturing and other sectors, can be received from within the region; finding solutions to creating a sustainable intra-Caribbean transportation system as the foundation on which to build a regionally integrated Caribbean Community; and examining the case for the removal or reduction of many of the existing taxes, duties and fees that currently constitute a barrier to air travel. The conference should be supported by well-researched studies and presentations, with an action agenda in the relevant areas, and should involve not only the usual tourism professionals, but also economists and other technical experts involved in the region's development process.

The need for the Caribbean to work together

Having prioritized the tourism agenda, the next step for the regional leaders should be to strengthen regional approaches to tourism and air transportation. As the twenty-first century progresses, the truth is that the survival of companies and institutions of every kind, even at the global level, has been a function of their ability to cooperate, consolidate or merge. For example, the major legacy carriers, the existence of some of which seemed threatened three years ago, have all improved their chances of survival by mergers or alliance. By the same token, it is arguable that greater cooperation between the Caribbean countries, many of them small and impoverished, but sharing common aspirations, a common region, a common history and common socio-economic goals, is in their best interests.

In 2011, CARICOM countries seemed to be going in an entirely different direction. At a time when these countries are struggling to emerge from a prolonged recession, almost every regional institution seems weaker than before, and fears are being expressed, even by some Caribbean prime ministers, that the CARICOM integration movement is in serious crisis and is facing the possibility of disintegrating completely, unless there is a rescue in some form. Such a collapse would be a disaster for the region and its people.

Sir Ronald Sanders, in an article called "Ambition without Action Is Failure" (*Jamaica Observer*, 4 March 2012) which deals with CARICOM's failure to achieve its targets, concludes:

CARICOM is the only viable instrument open to its member-countries to maintain their identity, strengthen their bargaining capacity in the international community, and collectively improve the quality of life of their people. Individual nations may flirt with this organization or that grouping of nations for the temporary and transient benefits they receive, but at the end of the day, it is CARICOM alone that gives them each an equal voice free of threat, and the real opportunity for mutually beneficial programmes.

Sanders seems to disagree with a *Jamaica Gleaner* editorial of the same date, which argues that CARICOM's survival may depend on widening the fifteen grouping to be truly Caribbean in its ambit, and therefore recommends the inclusion in the group of Cuba and the Dominican Republic. In reality, the argument of deepening, before widening CARICOM, has been made for decades and yielded only scant success. Perhaps the time has come to follow the example of the CTO with its pan-Caribbean membership, and determine whether an infusion of some new blood from the wider Caribbean will revitalize the patient.

However, Sanders's view on the importance of CARICOM is strongly supported by this author, and it is being suggested, with respect to tourism, that there are a number of areas where urgent joint action would pay dividends. These areas include the making of a fresh assault upon old markets; the development of new tourism markets in the BRIC countries and generally exploring other South-South relationships; the exploration of the possibilities for joint action in enriching the Caribbean product offer in the fields of culture and sport and in other niches, all outlined in the previous chapters; the maximizing of the linkages between tourism, agriculture and manufacturing within a strong and integrated single market and economy, one that increases the agricultural land space and expertise to exploit fully both sectors. Much of this was stated as long ago as 1972, but it is feared that, to use a cliché, when all is said and done, more will be said than done.

None of the above improvements will happen, however, without strong and enlightened leadership, some of which was seen in the 1960s and 1970s, when serendipity brought together some outstanding leaders committed to regional integration. These leaders were supported by the intellectual muscle of brilliant technicians, with the result that the region, despite its small size, not only gained respect from the external world, but also was able to make significant progress in meeting major integration targets. It can happen again.

The present generation of leaders is being asked to take us even further, in circumstances in which the challenges of the external environment have become much more difficult than had previously been the case. The sight of developed European states, which inhabit, with a few exceptions, a connected land space, struggling in 2011 to preserve their union, must have challenged the confidence of the leaders of the CARICOM countries, endowed, as those countries are, with far less natural and financial resources. They face a far greater difficulty in bridging the communications gap between themselves, which is exacerbated by large expanses of sea water. Part of the solution, of course, is to be found in an efficient and affordable intraregional transport system. It therefore remains a mystery why this subject has not long ago been elevated to the top of the agenda of Caribbean heads of government.

This situation must change. It must be discussed in the near future in all its aspects and every attempt made to wrestle the problems to the ground until they are resolved to the satisfaction of all the members. The existing situation should not continue where the costs of LIAT, a Caribbean airline serving twenty-one Caribbean countries, is left to be a burden to a few member states, while Caribbean Airlines, the carrier owned by CARICOM's richest member state, Trinidad and Tobago, is heavily subsidized by its government, and seems to be pursuing the ambition of being the only intra-regional carrier left standing. This pursuit seems neither sensitive to the mutuality of the interests of members of the community, nor respectful of the spirit and principles of the CARICOM Multilateral Air Services Agreement, which was completed in 1996 and came into effect in November 1998.

Perhaps one explanation of why little progress is ever made in the Caribbean in matters of air transportation is this: in a region which prides itself on its knowledge of the travel industry, little seems to be known at any level, about the complexity of the finances and operations of air and sea transportation. Hence the plethora of simplistic solutions offered by a variety of sources about an industry where even the most experienced of entrepreneurs, renowned for their successes in other fields, have failed.

It should also be noted that while over a period of fifty years several technical and vocational institutions and later university courses have been created across the region to meet the continuously expanding needs of the hospitality and tourism industry, nothing similar has been done in respect of air or sea transportation. In fact, in 2013, with the exception of the Art Williams and Harry Wendt Engineering School at the Ogle International Airport in Guyana – which was established by the Guyanese Defence Force and which trains and licences aircraft maintenance engineers – there are no tertiary institutions of learning, at least in the Commonwealth Caribbean, which offer general or postgraduate courses or degrees in air transportation and very few texts are available on the subject. One of the reasons for this may be that air services to and from external markets are still supplied largely by foreign carriers with foreign staff and expertise, and to a lesser extent by those few Caribbean carriers, which operate both externally and internally.

There seems therefore to be a case for adding the teaching of air transportation and aviation to the curriculum of Caribbean universities and technical institutions, not only with a view to creating technical expertise in the area, but also to enabling the wider tourism fraternity to be able to study and understand better a subject that affects critically the success of their industry. It is also highly desirable that many of the Caribbean aviation staff, which learned their craft on the job and have practical experience, should now be able to upgrade their various skills at an academic institution to serve better an industry which now operates on the cutting edge of technology.

A press report published on 19 December 2011 credited Ramesh Lutchmedial, director general of the T&T Civil Aviation Authority and chairman of the Caribbean Aviation Safety and Security Oversight System, with calling on his regional aviation colleagues to collaborate in establishing a world class aviation training product to develop the next generation of aviation leaders in the Caribbean. He promised that Trinidad and Tobago would be taking the lead by offering three master's degree programmes in aviation, in partnership with the City University of London, to commence in 2012. An aviation institution was established in 2013.

Need for advocacy in air transportation in the Caribbean

Perhaps air transportation in the Caribbean also suffers from an additional deficiency: the fact that there are no national or regional associations in being to safeguard and promote the interests of the Caribbean air transportation sector. This sad fact should be contrasted with the situation where hotel and tourism associations, both national and regional, constitute powerful lobbies for their interests, including soliciting various types of concessions, marketing support and other incentives.

It is here being suggested that the airlines operating to and in the region establish a separate Caribbean airline association to deliver effective advocacy for their causes and otherwise to circulate information about the sector to create a better understanding of their needs, challenges and accomplishments.

On a global scale, the International Air Transportation Association has lobbied governments and airports around the world to reduce the existing taxes and duties on airlines, on the grounds that such charges frequently lead to diminishing returns for the very governments in question, and also injure airline operations. Its efforts have thus far met with only limited success.

Hopefully, a Caribbean agency of the type suggested above could not only add its voice to those persons and groups lobbying against the APD and other European taxes, but would also seek to persuade Caribbean governments, by producing studies similar to those done by the World Travel and Tourism Council in 2012, that the reduction of the regime of high and onerous taxes, duties, and other add-ons on Caribbean air travel, will in fact lead to creating jobs and increasing revenue.

There is good reason to believe that when we can resolve the issues and challenges that face air transportation to and within the region, the future of Caribbean tourism will be a great deal brighter than it is today.

Appendix 1
International and Caribbean Tourist Arrivals, 1970 to 2010

Table A1.1 International and Caribbean Tourist Arrivals, 1970–2010 (millions)

All Countries			Caribbean		
Year	Tourists	% Change	Year	Tourists	% Change
1970	165.8	–	1970	4.2	–
1971	172.2	3.9	1971	4.6	9.5
1972	181.9	5.6	1972	5.1	10.9
1973	190.6	4.8	1973	5.4	5.9
1974	197.1	3.4	1974	5.7	5.6
1975	214.4	8.8	1975	5.5	−3.5
1976	220.7	2.9	1976	5.8	5.5
1977	239.1	8.3	1977	6.2	6.9
1978	257.4	7.7	1978	6.6	6.5
1979	274.0	6.4	1979	6.8	3.0
1980[n]	276.7	–	1980	6.9	1.5
1981	276.9	0.1	1981	6.7	−2.9
1982	276.7	−0.1	1982	6.9	3.0
1983	280.3	1.3	1983	7.3	5.8
1984	304.8	8.7	1984	7.6	4.1

(continued)

Table A1.1 International and Caribbean Tourist Arrivals, 1970–2010 (millions) (*continued*)

	All Countries			Caribbean	
Year	Tourists	% Change	Year	Tourists	% Change
1985	317.9	4.3	1985	8.0	5.3
1986	327.8	3.1	1986	9.6	20.0
1987	357.6	9.1	1987	10.9	13.5
1988	384.1	7.4	1988	11.3	3.7
1989	406.2	5.8	1989	12.0	6.2
1990	434.5	7.0	1990	12.8	6.7
1991	432.7	−0.4	1991	13.0	1.9
1992	471.5	9.0	1992	14.0	7.1
1993	486.1	3.1	1993	15.0	7.1
1994	507.6	4.4	1994	15.7	4.7
1995	527.6	3.9	1995	16.2	3.4
1996	560.5	6.2	1996	16.7	3.2
1997	586.3	4.6	1997	17.9	7.0
1998	601.9	2.7	1998	18.3	2.0
1999	625.4	3.9	1999	19.1	4.7
2000	673.6	7.7	2000	20.3	6.3
2001	673.0	−0.1	2001	19.6	−3.4
2002	692.5	2.9	2002	19.0	−3.0
2003	683.7	−1.3	2003	20.3	6.9
2004	754.1	10.3	2004	21.8	7.0
2005	798.7	5.9	2005	22.2	2.0
2006	844.0	5.7	2006	22.2	0.0
2007	899.0	6.5	2007	22.9	3.1
2008	917.8	8.7	2008	22.9	3.3
2009	882.8	−3.8	2009	22.1	−3.8
2010	939.5	6.4	2010	22.8	3.3

	Percentage Increase			Percentage Increase	
Period	Total	Average	Period	Total	Average
2000–2010	39.5	3.4	2000–2010	12.1	1.2
2005–2010	17.6	3.3	2005–2010	2.6	0.5

[n]New series (Includes tourist arrivals in Cancun and Cozumel)
Source: World Tourism Organization; Caribbean Tourism Organization

Figure A1.1 International Arrivals vs Caribbean Arrivals (% change)

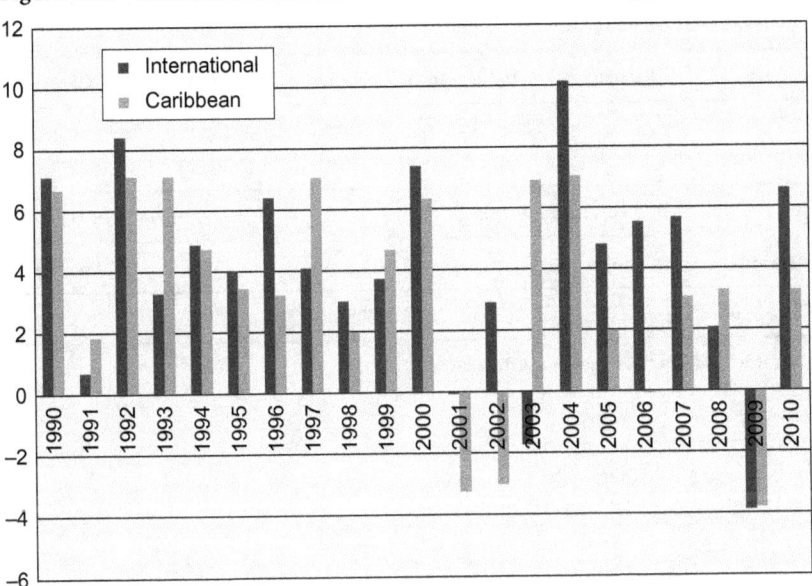

Table A1.2 Cruise Passenger Arrivals in the Caribbean, 1980–2010 (thousands)

Year	Passengers	% Change	Year	Passengers	% Change
1980	3,805	–	1994[n]	9,776	–
1981	3,590	-5.7	1995	9,881	1.1
1982	3,455	-3.8	1996	10,954	10.9
1983	3,550	2.7	1997	12,089	10.4
1984	3,720	4.8	1998	12,434	13.5
1985	4,300	15.6	1999	12,154	0.5
1986	5,000	16.3	2000	14,542	19.6
1987	5,600	12	2001	14,892	2.4
1988	6,340	13.2	2002	15,945	7.1
1989	6,710	5.8	2003	18,003	12.9
1990	7,750	15.5	2004	19,877	10.4
1991	8,700	12.3	2005	18,753	-5.7
1992	9,400	8.0	2006	18,931	0.9
1993	9,610	2.2	2007	19,363	2.3
			2008	18,830	-2.8

(*continued*)

Table A1.2 Cruise Passenger Arrivals in the Caribbean, 1980–2010 (thousands) (*continued*)

Year	Passengers	% Change	Year	Passengers	% Change
			2009	18,911	0.4
			2010	20,515	8.5

| Period | Percentage Increase | | Period | Percentage Increase | |
	Total	Average		Total	Average
2000–2010	41.1	3.5	2005–2010	9.4	1.8

[n]New series (includes cruise passenger arrivals in Haiti)
Source: Caribbean Tourism Organization

Appendix 2
Key Information on Various Aspects of the Cruise Industry: Caribbean Cruise Survey, 2000

Table A2.1 Costs: Port Charges and Head Taxes

		Costs Per Passenger (US$)		Costs Per Ship Call (US$)		
Rank	Destination	Port Charges	Head Tax	Total	Head Taxes	Other Costs
1	St Croix	0.00	0.00	0	0	0
2	St Martin	0.13	0.00	266	0	266
3	Dominican Republic*	2.00	2.00	3,900	3,900	n/a*
4	Martinique	3.36	0.00	6,545	0	6,545
5	Aruba	4.57	3.50	8,911	6,825	2,086
6	Grenada	4.98	3.00	9,713	5,850	3,863
7	St Lucia*	5.00	n/a	9,750	9,750	n/a*
8	St Maarten*	5.05	5.00	9,862	9,750	112.50+*
9	Curaçao	5.22	3.50	10,180	6,825	3,355
10	St Barts	6.00	6.00	11,700	11,700	0
11	St Kitts	6.44	5.00	12,550	9,750	2,800

(*continued*)

Table A2.1 Costs: Port Charges and Head Taxes (*continued*)

Rank	Destination	Costs Per Passenger (US$)			Costs Per Ship Call (US$)	
		Port Charges	Head Tax	Total	Head Taxes	Other Costs
12	Barbados	6.85	6.00	13,365	11,700	1,665
13	Dominica	6.76	5.00	13,185	9,750	3,435
14	British Virgin Islands	7.08	7.00	13,813	13,650	163
15	Key West	7.26	7.00	14,150	13,650	500
16	Trinidad & Tobago	7.45	5.00	14,533	9,750	4,783
17	Antigua & Barbuda*	7.50	7.50	14,625	14,625	n/a*
18	St Vincent & Grenadines	7.71	7.36	14,932	14,352	684
19	Guadeloupe	8.54	2.50	16,648	4,875	11,773
20	St Thomas	9.51	7.50	18,544	14,625	3,919
21	Cayman Is.	11.27	2.00	21,982	3,900	18,082
22	Puerto Rico	12.30	10.30	23,980	20,085	3,895
23	Nassau	15.69	15.00	30,604	29,250	1,354
24	Jamaica	17.59	15.00	34,309	29,250	5,059
25	Freeport, Bahamas	17.77	15.00	34,655	29,250	5,405

Cost per pax: The total cost per passenger, including head tax and other fees but excluding optional charges for such items as fresh water and waste disposal.

Total cost/call: The total cost of one ship call by a vessel with the dimensions of the *Sun Princess*, excluding optional charges.

Total head taxes: The overall head tax fee for a vessel with the passenger capacity of the *Sun Princess*. This set of figures assumes double occupancy.

Total other costs: All other costs, excluding ship's agent fees and all optional fees, for a ship with the dimensions of the *Sun Princess*.

*Destinations where additional fee information was unavailable.
Actual price ranking may be slightly higher than shown.

See *Cruise Industry News*.

Table A2.1 uses the *Sun Princess* – a ship of 77,000 gross registered tonnes, 856-foot length, 26-foot draft, 1,950 passengers – as the sample vessel. It shows that the average cost per call for a ship the size of the *Sun Princess* is US$14,530, or US$7.45 per passenger. However, these figures do not take volume discounts into account, nor are they statistically weighted to count the fees of highly visited islands more so than fees of infrequently visited ones.

Overview of purchasing issues based on information from cruise line purchasing executives

The cruise companies are large consumers* of a wide range of goods and services to run their operations. The companies operate centralized and efficient purchasing systems. Items are purchased in bulk and placed in a centrally located warehouse. Containers of supplies are then shipped to specific ports to meet their ships.

Cruise ships operating in the region are usually provisioned at their base port – mainly Miami or San Juan – for the outward trip. Supplies for the return leg of the journey are either stored on board or shipped to a Caribbean port where they can be taken on board. St Thomas has emerged as an important supply point for ships based in the region because of its easy access from Miami, lower storage costs than in San Juan and port facilities which are considered ideal for loading.

Due to the need to ensure freshness of supply, the cruise lines are interested in sourcing supplies of fresh produce elsewhere in the Caribbean, particularly such items as fresh fruit and vegetables, flowers, and dairy products. This situation especially applies to the return leg of the cruise journey, where some cruise lines now have arrangements to ship containers of supplies – including fruit, vegetables, dairy products and other provisions – to Caribbean ports in order to replenish their supplies.

Items with good potential for sale to cruise lines

Based on discussions with cruise line purchasing executives, the following items appear to have good potential for sourcing in the Caribbean on a continuing basis.

Food and Beverage Items	Hotel Items
Fresh fruit	Cigarettes
Vegetables	Fresh flowers
Dairy products (ice cream, eggs, cheese, etc.)	Towels
Fish (preferably frozen)	Linens
Beverages (soft drinks, beer, spirits, etc.)	Uniforms
Coffee	Soap

Bottled water
Juices

Spices
Jams/jellies
Other specialty food items

Port and Marine Items
Bulk water
Petroleum products
Stevedoring
Warehousing
Repairs and services
Port dues (pilotage, tendering, etc.)

Paper products
Other toiletries (e.g., nature care products, etc.)

Services
Laundry (crew and passengers)
Dry cleaning (crew)
Video rental (crew)
Mail services
Extermination/pest control
Garbage collection/disposal
Entertainment services

Regional performance

Cruise tourism for the period of 1990 to 2000 has been the fastest growing segment of the Caribbean tourism sector. In that decade, cruise passenger visits to Caribbean destinations grew by 5.9 per cent per annum, compared with 4.5 per cent for tourist arrivals – that is, stay-over arrivals. Cruise passenger visitation to CARICOM member countries grew faster than for the region as a whole during the period, although tourist arrivals grew somewhat more slowly.

Table A2.2 Tourist and Cruise Passenger Arrivals (thousands), 1990–2000

	Caribbean			CARICOM Countries		
Type of visitor	1990	2000*	Average annual growth	1990	2000*	Average annual growth
Tourists	13,710	21,230	4.5%	3864	4811	2.2%
Cruise passengers	7,750	13,965	5.9%	5546	3271	6.4%

*provisional
Source: Florida-Caribbean Cruise Association.
*Royal Caribbean, the second largest cruise line, described its 1998 operation as equivalent to 45 hotels of 400 rooms each. Its food and beverage operation was equal to that of 783 restaurants with seating for 125 persons each.

Table A2.3 Share of Cruise Business by Bed Days and Regions

Region	Bed-days (*thousands*)			Average annual growth 1987–2000	% share		
	1987	1991	2000		1987	1991	2000
Caribbean**	11,892.3	17,045.0	25,698.9	6.1	58.4	60.1	47.7
Mediterranean	841.1	1,949.3	6,277.1	16.7	4.1	6.9	11.7
Alaska	1,715.2	1,972.9	4,197.3	7.1	8.4	7.0	8.0
Other Destinations	5,928.4	7,374.5	17,689.5	8.8	29.1	26.0	32.6
Total	20,377.0	28,341.7	53,862.8	7.8	100.0	100.0	100.0

Source: Cruise Lines International Association (CLIA), 2001.
**includes Bermuda, which received 2.1 per cent of total bed-days in 2000.

Leading region for cruise tourism

In 2000, the Caribbean was the world's premier cruising region, accounting for 48 per cent of all bed-days marketed out of North America. While our share of this business has declined over the years as the cruise industry sought to add new itineraries for its burgeoning capacity, there seemed little doubt that the Caribbean would retain its position as the leading cruising region into the foreseeable future.

Interestingly, as the table below shows, the region's share peaked at 60 per cent in 1991, when the Gulf Crisis led to a significant repositioning of capacity to the Caribbean from other cruising regions. The turmoil in the travel market resulting from the 9/11 terrorist attack in New York led to a similar repositioning.

Expansion of the North American cruise sector

Over the decade 1990 to 2000, the number of cruise berths marketed out of North America has grown from 83,500 to 155,500, an average increase of 6.4 per cent per annum. This cruise capacity was expected to grow even faster over the next few years: according to the Cruise Lines International Association (*Cruise Industry News*, 2001), contracts had already been signed for

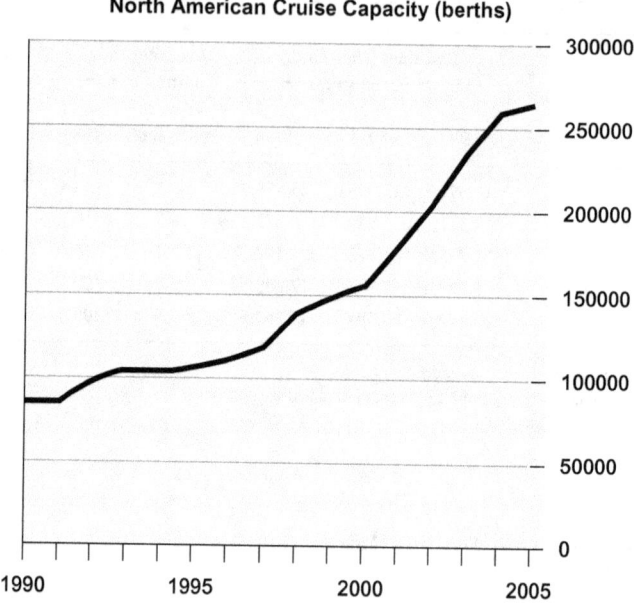

North American Cruise Capacity (berths)

another 94,000 berths by 2005, with another 14,000 berths planned but not yet contracted. This translated into an average 11 per cent annual growth in cruise capacity through 2005.

Dominance by a few major players

Through a series of mergers and acquisitions during the period of 1990 to 2000, a few large cruise companies emerged and dominated the industry. Carnival Corporation and Royal Caribbean Cruises together accounted for just over 60 per cent of the cruise capacity deployed in the region in 2000. Carnival is also a part owner, with Star Cruises, of Norwegian Cruise Line, which itself accounted for 5.7 per cent of total capacity in 2000. The Florida-Caribbean Cruise Association member lines represented 90 per cent of total capacity in the region in 2000.

Trend towards bigger ships in the Caribbean

One of the most significant developments, since the mid-1980s, was the increasing size of the cruise ships visiting Caribbean destinations. While

Table A2.4 Caribbean Cruise Capacity,* 2000

Major Cruise Line	Capacity (*thousands*)	% Share
Carnival Cruise Lines (including Holland America)	1,666.3	36.3
Royal Caribbean Cruise Lines (including Celebrity Cruises)	1,257.6	27.4
Other cruise lines	1,574.2	38.0
Total	4,598.1	100.0

Source: *Cruise Industry News.*
*Passenger capacity, based on double occupancy.

all of the new ships built between 1980 and 1984 held under 1,500 berths, more than 80 per cent of the new berths added between 2000 and 2005 were on ships with more than 1,500 berths.

Most of these newer, larger ships were assigned to itineraries within the Caribbean while the older ships which they replaced were sent to destinations outside the region. As a result of this development, most destinations now received a growing number of cruise passenger arrivals on a declining number of ships. This situation placed greater pressure on existing plant and created a demand for new or expanded facilities to handle these larger ships.

Cruise-related expenditures

The CTO estimated that the passengers on cruise ships spent some US$1.9 billion at Caribbean destinations in 1999, or 10.3 per cent of the US$18.7 billion total expenditure by all visitors to the region. Total expenditure by tourists – stay-over visitors – stood at an estimated US$16.8 billion.

Average expenditure by cruise passengers varies considerably between destinations, due primarily to the amount spent on shopping, with St Thomas in the US Virgin Islands routinely recording the highest per capita spending levels.

It should be noted, however, that these expenditure figures often do not take into account the commission retained by cruise ships for tours presold on board ship. And some national estimates of total expenditure are made on the assumption that all cruise passengers disembark at the destination, which is seldom the case, even though it is generally agreed that the vast majority do go ashore at most ports of call.

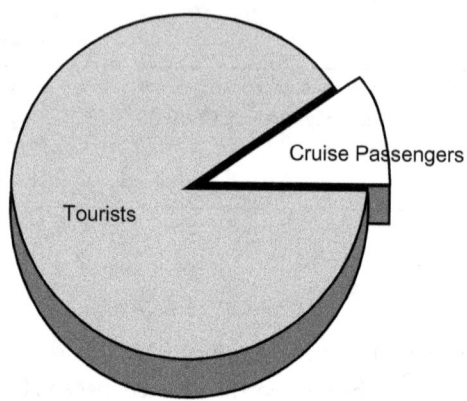

Total Visitor Expenditure - 1999

On the other hand, these cruise passenger figures do *not* include estimates for the money spent by crew members or for the expenditures made directly by the cruise lines.

Statistics from a 1999 study carried out by PricewaterhouseCoopers (PwC) place total spending by crew members at ports of call at US$97 million.*

The PwC study estimates that the typical cruise ship carrying 2,000 passengers and 900 crew members generated almost US$259,000 in passenger and crew expenditure during a port of call visit.

Cruise Industry News estimates that average costs at a Caribbean port to a ship similar to the *Sun Princess* was US$14,530.00 per call in 2000, or US$7.50 per passenger.* These figures were inclusive of head taxes and other port fees but excluded ships agent and other optional fees, such as fresh water and waste disposal.

Within CARICOM, this cost varied from US$3,863 in Grenada to US$34,655 in Freeport, Bahamas, to US$30,604 in Nassau.

Note

*Cruise Industry's Economic Impact on the Caribbean, conducted by PwC on behalf of FCCA member cruise lines.

Appendix 3
Tourism Taxes in Five Selected Caribbean Societies (Executive Summary, 1994 PwC Study for CTO)

This report documents a number of current fiscal policies of five selected Caribbean countries (Aruba, Bahamas, Barbados, Jamaica and St Lucia) as they apply to the tourism sector. Both taxes and applicable incentives are examined. It contrasts these with the fiscal policies as they pertain to another economic sector such as agriculture or retailing, and with common practices outside the Caribbean. A number of recommendations are provided to simplify and/or improve the tax code. Both the various types of taxes and fiscal incentives are examined.

Caribbean fiscal policies

As tourism is the major earner of foreign revenue, as well as a major employer in many Caribbean countries, governments have tended to grant a number of fiscal incentives to promote the sector. There is some question, however, as to the real effectiveness of the non-fiscal important conditions that an investor would like to see fulfiled (such as product quality, political and economic stability, long-term viability, good infrastructure, trained and available personnel and others) as well as the specific attributes of typical incentives that are available in most countries (they are discretionary as opposed to automatic, and possibly benefit the investor less on a net basis than would be expected from a cursory review). Finally, many incentives now exist that promote new construction; these should be carefully evaluated as they may in the long run lead to over-capacity. These types of incentives should be carefully coordinated with the level of development of tourism in each country.

A number of taxes apply to the tourism industry specifically, while the tourism industry is also subject to general taxes such as profit taxes and land taxes that are applicable to other economic sectors. A summary of the most common taxes imposed on the tourism sector are:

- Room tax, occupancy tax or hotel tax is essentially a sales tax on hotel occupancy and is a moderate generator of income in all countries surveyed (in Jamaica no separate room tax exists but a general consumption tax is applied instead).
- Departure tax is levied on departing visitors and is also a moderate income generator (high in the Bahamas).
- Casino tax, only applicable in Aruba and the Bahamas, is a moderately strong generator of government revenue.
- Jamaica is the only country in our study having introduced a General Consumption Tax. It offers preferential rates to the tourism sector. Barbados is set to introduce a value-added tax in 1996 while Aruba is contemplating either a sales tax or VAT.*
- Import duties form a major source of revenues for governments in the Caribbean; in the Bahamas, it is the principal source in the absence of direct taxes such as income tax or profit tax. Unfortunately, this tax is extremely difficult to analyse by economic sector, as data are registered by product category rather than by sector. Therefore, the contribution of the tourism sector is very hard to measure. In general, it must also be remarked that legislation surrounding import duties and levies tends to be quite complex.
- Property taxes and other fees form a major source of revenue in the Bahamas and a low to moderate source of revenue in other countries.
- Corporate profit taxes from the tourism sector are a small contributor to government revenues, due to poor profitability of the hotel sector

and numerous exemptions that have been granted. The Bahamas tax system does not have a profit tax at all.

Fiscal policy as related to ancillary sectors in the tourism industry, such as food and beverage, taxis, and duty-free shops, appears to be much less coordinated and practices vary significantly by country. There appears to be no coherent fiscal policy with regard to these sectors, with the exception of new legislation being introduced now in St Lucia. Isolated incentives are available in some countries, such as lower duties on taxis and rental cars (Jamaica, Barbados) or duty free importation of food & beverage equipment (Barbados). Counterbalancing the few incentives is the fact that these sectors are not targeted by specific taxes either.

It is interesting to compare the tax regime in the tourism sector to a different sector, preferably one which is also a foreign exchange generator. If the fiscal regime as applicable to the tourism sector is compared to that of the agriculture sector in Barbados, Jamaica or St Lucia, three main differences stand out:

- While in both sectors tax incentives are available on *investment*, agriculture also offers investment for *operational inputs* such as fertilizer.
- While in tourism *outputs* are taxed through room tax or GCT, in agriculture outputs are taxed.
- Tax incentives in the tourism sector are of a limited duration while some tax incentives in agriculture are automatic and ongoing.

Furthermore, there are structural costs incurred by the nature of tourism, for example higher property taxes (due to high-value land for tourism versus farms) and higher utility consumption. The conclusion is that the tax regime in agriculture tends to lower costs for this sector more on an ongoing basis, thereby creating a structural advantage, for the agriculture industry.

Selected Non-Caribbean fiscal policies

We contrasted the taxation regime that the tourism sector in Caribbean countries is subjected to, with that in selected non-Caribbean countries. For this analysis, we reviewed policies in Malta, Mauritius, Fiji, Cyprus,

Portugal, Greece, Spain, Ireland, and New Zealand. Our major findings were:

1. Unlike the Caribbean, VAT or sales tax is utilized in each of the countries that we surveyed. This is relevant to the Caribbean insofar as several Caribbean nations are not introducing or contemplating introduction of a sales tax or VAT. Many of the Caribbean countries take the form of a reduced sales tax. This implies that selective reduction of sales tax rates in those countries which decide to introduce one can become a new method in the arsenal to stimulate tourism in the Caribbean.
2. Incentives in the tourism area are more general than only the hotel sector. They tend to also include the food and beverage, entertainment and touristic attraction areas. In the Caribbean, we noticed that the primary attention area of incentives has been in the hotel sector while other ancillary tourism sectors are the beneficiary of incentives more sporadically.
3. Incentives outside the Caribbean typically do not include a full exemption of profit tax. Most often, incentives are in the area of reduced VAT, reduced profit tax, and accelerated depreciation. In contrast, Caribbean states tend to grant total or near total exemptions on a number of taxes to encourage investment; the question is whether this is necessary. We have referred earlier to the fact that the appropriate intensity of fiscal incentives can be higher in the initial stages of development but should be evaluated critically once an infrastructure of established hotels and ancillary services has developed. Most Caribbean countries are now beyond the "infancy" stage of their tourism development. Caribbean countries, like their competitors elsewhere, should not only consider the use of more non-fiscal incentives as opposed to purely fiscal ones, but also should also evaluate whether the totality of fiscal incentives (e.g., exemption versus reduction of tax rates) is still appropriate.
4. Non-Caribbean states not only provide incentives to new investors, but also to ongoing businesses. In contrast, Caribbean states mostly provide incentives that stimulate development of new capacity. This policy should be evaluated in light of the available capacity, tourism growth and occupancy rates, in order to avoid overcapacity.
5. A separate room tax is quite rare outside the Caribbean, only Cyprus and Mauritius charge room tax. VAT is charged instead in other countries. To the extent that Caribbean may move to incorporate VAT or

general sales taxes in their fiscal regimes, room tax may be phased out and replaced by VAT or sales tax.
6. Departure tax for airline passengers is fairly common in non-Caribbean countries although they are not universally applied. Given the fact that this tax is also relatively easy to administer and collect, as well as the fact that it represents a relatively small expenditure on the part of the tourist, we would favour maintenance of some type of departure tax in any restructured tax system. We would, however, argue in favour of a more user-friendly implementation of this tax through incorporation of the levies in the price of an airline fare, as is commonly the case in the United States or has been recently introduced in the United Kingdom.
7. The average rates utilized for taxes which are paid directly by tourists, such as room tax/VAT and departure tax, are not significantly different on the whole when the group of non-Caribbean and Caribbean countries is compared. More significant differences exist between countries of each group, although the range of rates that are applied is limited. The commonality and similarity of these taxes, paired with their low budgetary implications, implies that they should not be a major factor on the planning process of the tourist. This assumption is only valid within certain limits: an exorbitantly high tax rate in one of these categories will of course have a detrimental effect.
8. Tax on cruise passengers levied directly on passengers is rare outside the Caribbean, only in Cyprus is this tax applied. In contrast, taxing cruise passengers is a fairly common practice in the Caribbean. In our sample of 5 nations, only Aruba did not tax cruise passengers. Quite significant tax revenue is derived from this type of taxation in those countries with a high number of sea arrivals such as the Bahamas. Restructuring of this type of levy would not be without controversy.

Recommendations

From the considerations above, it can be concluded that there is room for a simplification or reorganisation of some of the characteristics of the tax code as it applies to the Caribbean tourism sector. Tempting as it may be, we are of the opinion however, that it is not possible to arrive at a single model for taxation that can be applied throughout the Caribbean. The exercise to arrive at such a uniform model needs to account for the significant differences that exist among Caribbean nations, along five major parameters:

- The overall economic and fiscal objectives of the government
- The overall structure of the fiscal regime
- The level of development and profitability of the tourism sector
- The overall tourism development strategy
- The cost-competitiveness of the destination

There are nonetheless a number of areas of improvement and simplification possible in both the tax structures themselves and the incentive systems. These are summarized in the following points.

1. We recommend that governments carefully evaluate the intended purpose of available fiscal incentives. Many incentives are still focussed on direct expansion of hotel room capacity. Declining growth rates in tourism arrivals and moderate occupancy rates in several Caribbean countries call this policy into question. We therefore recommend that the desirability to offer incentives tied to new construction or expansion must be evaluated.
2. Fiscal incentives can instead be oriented towards lowering the input costs of the hotel and ancillary sectors. Concretely, this implies lowering import duties, fixed fees and other costs related to the daily operations of the industry. The net result will be a continued incentive for both existing industry players to upgrade and improve through increased profitability, and to possible new entrants as well offering continued lower operating costs. Specific ways that the lowering of input costs can be realized are:

   - lowering of import duties on principal inputs such as food and beverages for the tourism sector
   - reduction of fixed charges such as property taxes and licence fees
   - offering preferred electricity rates to companies in the tourism sector, particularly hotels
   - offering tax credits for training and upgrading personnel, which has the beneficial side effect of upgrading the tourism product as a whole.

3. A simple method to achieve the above would be to grant certain tax credits to the companies in the tourism sector directly, based on the amount of qualifying purchases they have made. In effect, the tourism sector would receive a credit for the import duties that were charged implicitly in the price of their purchases. Provided this system is kept simple, it would not create a major administrative overhead.
4. Incentives should be planned more holistically, with the entire tourism sector in mind. Although we did not review the St Lucia Tourism Incentive Bill specifically, we applaud the concept behind legislation that considers the overall economic sector rather than only the hotel industry.
5. Incentives must become more transparent. Concrete points where our research found improvements are warranted are:

    - Conditions to qualify for an incentive should be stated as explicitly as possible.
    - Incentives should be automatically available to any investor who qualifies, and should not depend on a lengthy approval process.
    - Incentives should not require contact with many different government agencies or the submission of endless forms. Ideally, government should create an agency specifically charged with aiding potential investors.

6. In general, import duties provide a mechanism that is easier to administer and control than a reliance on sales taxes or direct taxes on profits. By shifting the point of assessment and collection to the point where goods cross the border rather than when the ultimate consumer purchases the goods, administration of a tax system can be coordinated with the Customs function and is greatly simplified.
7. We find that the legislation surrounding import duties and levies is extremely complex in all countries. Simplification of this sector is extremely complex. It would require detailed data on the revenues by product category and data, now absent, or revenues by economic sector. The consequences of new rules implied by a simplified code would need to be considered for each sector. However, a simpler system of import duties and levies would benefit government and the private sector by the lowering of administrative processes on both sides, by creating a more predictable and transparent environment and by opening new and simple incentive opportunities.

8. The long-term viability of relying primarily on import duties needs to be evaluated also in light of the General Agreement for Trade and Tariffs (GATT) and the worldwide movement to reduce import barriers. In the case of small Caribbean nations with limited resources and limited local production, a case can be made in favour of taxing goods at the border regardless of the above considerations. The relatively limited amount of local value-added and high reliance on imports (even local processing industries that must in many cases be taxed through a sales tax or VAT) are primarily imports or derived thereof in the first place. Therefore, the added administrative burden of taxing goods at a later point in the cycle weighs significantly against the simplicity of taxing goods at the border.
9. Non-fiscal incentives are utilized much more in other regions than is apparently the case in the Caribbean. Frequently observed measures that are not extremely difficult to implement are among others: the availability of capital at preferential rates, government guarantees on loans, training grants or facilities, elimination of currency exchange restrictions and liberal granting of currency exchange restrictions and liberal granting of work permits.
10. Fiscal incentives need not imply the total exemption from a category of taxes. A stimulus can also be provided by reductions rather than complete exemption of certain tax categories (profit tax, land tax). This may be an area where Caribbean countries can coordinate their efforts to avoid competing against one another by refusing to implement such changes or competing with different levels of reductions.
11. In general, we believe that the private sector is more benefited by reductions in fixed charges such as land tax and business fees than by reductions in profit taxes. Reduction of fixed charges reduces risk.
12. A specific issue that is currently of importance in a number of Caribbean nations (among which are Barbados and Aruba) is the introduction of a value-added tax or general sales tax. In the context of this study, we would like to pose two important reservations that should be considered in these discussions.

    - The administration of either a general sales tax or (especially) a value-added tax imposes an additional administrative burden on both the business community and the government.
    - The introduction of a VAT or sales tax may be detrimental to the development of tourism, as shown by the experience of several

European countries. We would recommend countries that do implement a VAT or sales tax to offer preferential rates to tourism activities.

13. Two taxes, namely room tax and departure tax, are commonly charged specifically to the tourism sector. As these are relatively simple taxes, there are a number of advantages to incorporating them in a tax code and particularly departure tax is a common phenomenon.

    It can be correctly argued that two separate taxes which are aimed specifically at the tourism sector unnecessarily complicate the tax code and are unfair in that they are not charged to other economic sectors. However, governments derive moderate to significant revenue from these taxes and we believe that it will be difficult to convince governments to the restructuring of these two taxes, considering their advantages and revenue generating possibilities.
14. The above does not apply to countries which have or choose to implement a general sales tax. Since room tax is essentially a sales tax on hotel revenue, a separate room tax should be eliminated in these cases and the lost revenue should be made up for by the sales tax – possibly at reduced rates as discussed before.
15. For the sake of "user friendliness" as far as the tourist is concerned, it is desirable not to create the impression in the tourist's mind that he or she is being overtaxed. It should be possible to incorporate certain taxes, particularly departure tax, in the price of a package or ticket so that they are less "visible" to the tourist.
16. This study has specifically excluded from consideration a prime source of revenue for many Caribbean countries (except the Bahamas), namely the wage, income and social security taxes derived from the salaries of the employees in the tourism sector. While this source of revenue is significant, it has not been studied in any detail as we can safely assume that it would socially and politically not be viable to offer fiscal incentives specifically for the *individuals* working in the tourism sector. To our knowledge, no country currently differentiates these individual taxes based on the industry sector that employs that individual.

---

*Since this study was completed in 1994 several Caribbean countries have added VAT and included the departure taxes in the ticket price to be collected by the airlines.

Appendix 4
Draft Inter-Governmental Agreement for the Regulation of Cruise Shipping in the Caribbean

The Contracting Parties:-

Recognizing that the cruise shipping industry offers considerable potential as an instrument for the promotion and development of the economy of the Caribbean countries;

Aware of the need to ensure that the operations of cruise ships should be conducted as to preserve the integrity of the Caribbean environment;

Convinced of the desirability of providing a forum for the coordination of the member states' policies in relation to cruise shipping;

Desiring to enhance the level of services that their countries offer to the cruise shipping industry by improving the channels;

Agree as follows:

Article 1
Meaning of Terms
   In this Agreement:
   "Authority" means the Caribbean Cruise Shipping Authority established under Article 2;
   "Caribbean state" includes any state in the Caribbean region and any member state of the Caribbean community;
   "Competent Authority" means the official designated by a Contracting Party under Article 12;
   "Depositary" means the depositary under Article 23;
   "Fund" means the Environmental Fund established under Article 16;
   "United Nations Convention on the Law of the Sea" means the United Nations Convention on the Law of the Sea done at Montego Bay on December 10, 1982.

Article 2
Establishment of the Authority
   The Contracting Parties hereby establish a Caribbean Cruise Shipping Authority with such functions as set out in this Agreement:

Article 3
The functions of the Authority
The functions of the Authority shall be to:

(a) Provide a forum for the coordination of the Contracting Parties' policies in relation to cruise shipping;
(b) Settle the levels of taxes and other charges to be uniformly applied to cruise shipping by Contracting Parties subject to the grading of facilities offered, and the permitted exemptions from and discounts on those charges which may be offered;
(c) grade the facilities offered by Contracting Parties to cruise ships for the purpose of settling appropriate levels of taxes and other charges;
(d) provide a reservoir of technical assistance for the Contracting Parties in their cruise shipping management, assisting with:

(i) the drafting of regulations for adoption by individual countries for application to cruise ships;
(ii) the establishment and maintenance of procedures for the inspection of ships for safety and environmental compliance;
(iii) the provision of legal and managerial technical expertise in negotiations with cruise ship operators and flag states of cruise ships;
(iv) the upgrading of visitor reception facilities;
(v) the provision of training for persons concerned with cruise shipping;
(vi) study and conduct research into the problems of the coastal states relating to cruise shipping;
(vii) promote the joint marketing of the Contracting Parties' countries as cruise shipping destinations:
(viii) provide the cruise ship industry with a channel of communication with relevant authorities in its Contracting Parties on matters relating to cruise shipping.

Article 4
The Council

1. The principal organ of the Authority shall be the Council, which shall comprise all the member countries of the Authority.
2. The Council shall at the commencement of each meeting choose one member country to provide a Chairman of the Council.
3. The country elected under Article 4.2 to provide the Chairman of the Council shall enjoy the right to designate the Chairman to hold office until the commencement of the meeting next subsequent to the meeting at which that chairman's nominating country was elected.
4. The country nominating a Chairman may not be chosen again for the purpose at the first meeting after the expiry of one year's continuous tenure of office of a Chairman or Chairmen nominated by that country.

Article 5
The Governing Board

1. The Council of the Authority shall at its first meeting elect a Chairman of the Governing Board and not more than fourteen other persons who

shall together with that Chairman constitute the Governing Board of the Authority.

2. The Council shall pay due regard, in the election of members of the Governing Board of the Authority, to the principles of equitable geographical and language distribution. In submitting the names of candidates for election to the Board, members of the Authority shall bear in mind the need to nominate candidates of the highest standard of competence, with qualifications in tourism, shipping and port administration in particular.

3. Members of the Governing Board shall serve in their personal capacities. In the performance of their duties they shall neither seek nor receive instructions from any Government, whether of the Contracting Parties or otherwise, or from any other authority. They shall refrain from any action which might reflect on their position as officials of the authority, and shall be responsible only to the Council of the Authority.

4. The tenure of membership of any member of the Governing Board shall be four years. A member of the Governing Board may be re-elected at the end of any period of tenure, but due regard shall be paid to the principle of rotation of membership.

Article 6
Functions of the Governing Board

The Governing Board shall supervise the day-to-day operations of the Authority, and may exercise the powers of the Council between meetings of the Council.

Article 7
Voting in the Council

1. Each member of the Council shall have one vote.
2. Procedural questions shall be decided by a majority of members present and voting.
3. Substantive questions, including the question whether any question is substantive or procedural, shall be decided by a two-thirds majority of members present and voting, provided that a majority of members of the Council concur in the decision.

Article 8
Voting in the Governing Board

1. Each member of the Governing Board shall have one vote.
2. Procedural questions shall be decided by a majority of members present and voting.
3. Substantive questions, including the question whether any question is substantive or procedural, shall be decided by a two-thirds majority of members present and voting provided that a majority of the members of the Governing Board concur in the decision.

Article 9
The Headquarters of the Authority

1. The Headquarters of the Authority shall be in Barbados.
2. The Council may establish offices of the Authority in other Contracting States or elsewhere for the better discharge of its functions.

Article 10
The Administrative Office

1. There shall be an Administrative Office of the Authority comprising an Executive Director and such staff as the Authority may require.
2. The Executive Director shall be appointed by the Council for a term not exceeding five years and may be reappointed.
3. The Executive Director shall be the chief executive officer of the Authority, and shall be charged with the responsibility of ensuring the due performance by the Authority of its functions under this Agreement.
4. The Executive Director shall make an annual report to the Council on the work of the Authority.
5. In the performance of their duties the Executive Director and his staff shall neither seek instructions from any Government, whether of the Contracting Parties or otherwise, or from any other authority. They shall refrain from any action which might reflect on their position as officials of the authority, and shall be responsible only to the Authority.
6. Each Contracting Party undertakes to respect the exclusively international character of the responsibilities of the Executive Director and

his staff and shall not seek to influence them in the discharge of their responsibilities.
7. The Council shall approve the Staff Regulations governing the operation of the Administrative Office.

Article 11
The Budget of the Authority

1. The Council shall determine the budget of the Authority, and shall be guided in so doing by the need for the Authority to carry out its functions with due regard to economy.
2. The Executive Director shall keep proper accounts of the Authority's revenue and expenditure and its assets and liabilities, which accounts shall be prepared up to such accounting date and to cover such period as the Council shall determine and shall be circulated to the Governments of the Contracting Parties within twelve months of the accounting date.
3. The Contracting Parties agree to contribute to the Authority for the support of its budget such sum in Barbados dollars as shall constitute the equivalent of one United States dollar for each cruise ship passenger visiting its ports in the calendar year preceding the date on which contributions are due.
4. The sum in Article 11.3 may be varied by the decision of the Council from time to time.

Article 12
The Competent Authority
Each Contracting Party undertakes to designate a Competent Authority who shall be responsible for monitoring and supervising the operation of this Agreement in its territory and in areas over which it exercises jurisdiction and control.

Article 13

1. The Council shall determine the minimum level of taxes and charges to be applied to cruise ships visiting destinations in the territory of the Contracting Parties or in areas over which they exercise jurisdiction and control.

2. The Council may in the discharge of its obligations under Article 13.1 set differing levels of taxes and charges:

   (a) to be applied to different destinations based on a grading of the facilities provided to cruise ships and cruise ship passengers at such different destinations;

   (b) to be applied to different ships visiting a single destination according to the grading of different levels of facilities provided at such destination to different ships at such destination.

3. The Council may in the discharge of its obligations under Article 13.1 set maximum levels of discounts or other reductions of or exemptions from the minimum level of taxes and charges there recommended for particular circumstances which, in the opinion of the Council may justify the application of such discounts, reductions or exemptions.

4. The Council shall give to Contracting Parties at least three months' notice of the date of coming into effect of any decision taken under this Article.

5. The decisions of the Council under this Article shall be published by the Council in a Schedule of Cruise Shipping Charges of the Authority, which shall be revised as frequently as the Council considers practicable to reflect the decisions of the Council currently in force.

6. The Council shall establish procedures providing an opportunity for formal consultation with cruise shipping interests on the level of taxes and charges to be applied under this Article.

Article 14
Implementation by Contracting Parties of the Schedule of Cruise Shipping Charges

1. The Contracting Parties agree:

   (a) with effect from June 1st 1995 or the beginning of the calendar month which follows the expiration of six months from the first decisions of the Council under Article 13;

   (b) to give timely information to the Authority on any taxation and charges, additional to those required to be applied under Article 13, which they intend to apply to cruise ships visiting their countries;

   (c) in the event that they are in any instance unable to comply with Article 14.1. (b), to honour representations made by the Authority on their behalf concerning the levels of taxation and charges to be applied to cruise ships visiting their countries.

2. In the event that any Contracting Party has, at the date of the coming into force of this Agreement, given undertakings that levels of charges and taxation will be applied to such cruise ships or their passengers, which levels would not conform with the obligations of that Contracting Party under Article 14, that Contracting Party shall be exempted from the obligations under Article 14 to the extent necessary, to enable that Contracting Party shall be exempted from the obligations under Article 14 to the extent necessary, but no more than is necessary, to enable that Contracting Party to honour such undertakings.

Article 15
Protection of the Marine Environment

1. The Council shall:
   (a) promote the adoption of common measures of environmental protection to be applied by the Contracting Parties to cruise shipping in their territorial seas and internal waters; and
   (b) assist the Contracting Parties in ensuring that their legislation meets general international standards in relation to the environmental protection measures to be applied to cruise shipping in their maritime zones.
2. For the purposes of Article 15.1, the Council shall prepare model legislation suitable for adoption by the Contracting Parties.
3. The Council shall establish procedures providing an opportunity for formal consultation with cruise shipping interests in the process of preparing model legislation under Article 15.2, with a view to applying co-operative arrangements under Article 211.3 of the United Nations Convention on the Law of the Sea.
4. The Council shall keep the International Maritime Organization and operators of cruise ships visiting destinations in the countries of the Contracting Parties informed of of the co-operative arrangements applied under Article 15.4.
5. The Contracting Parties shall provide the Council at all times with current information on their legislation in force which applies measures

of environmental protection to cruise shipping in their internal waters, territorial waters and maritime zones.
6. The Council shall keep the International Maritime Organization and operators of cruise ships visiting destinations in the countries of the Contracting Parties informed of the legislation in Article 15.6.

Article 16
The Environmental Fund

1. Contracting Parties hereby establish a Fund for the promotion of the protection and preservation of the marine environment of the Caribbean.
2. Contributions to the Fund shall be made by Contracting Parties in such amounts as the Council shall decide, such amounts being a percentage of charges payable by cruise ships under Article 13.1.
3. The Management Committee of the Fund may, subject to such conditions as the Council may require, invest the contributions to the Fund and may use the resources in the Fund to assist member countries which suffer or are in imminent danger of suffering loss on account of any environmental casualty or disaster.
4. The Fund shall be administered by a Management Committee appointed by the Governing Board.
5. It shall be the responsibility of the Executive Director to carry out the decisions of the Management Committee in its administration of the Fund and to maintain accounts for the Fund. The accounts for the Fund shall be included in the Executive Director's accounting under Article 11.2.
6. Should the Council determine that the resources in the Fund at any time exceed what would be required for the purposes of Article 16.3, the Council may authorise the Management Committee to use the surplus to support other activity, whether or not conducted by the Authority, for the benefit of the environment of any or all of the Contracting Parties.

Article 17
Settlement of Disputes

1. Any dispute arising between any of the Contracting Parties relating to the operation of this Agreement shall in the first instance be the subject of negotiation between the Parties concerned.

2. If negotiation fails to produce an amicable settlement of the dispute, the dispute may at the option of any party thereto, by written notification addressed to the other party or parties to the dispute, be submitted to the arbitral procedure under Articles 18 to 20.

Article 18

1. A list of arbitrators shall be drawn up and maintained by the Secretary General of the Caribbean Tourism Organization. Every Contracting Party shall be entitled to nominate a maximum of three arbitrators, each of whom shall be a person experienced in either commercial, tourism or shipping matters and enjoying the highest reputation for fairness, competence and integrity. The names of the persons so nominated shall constitute the list.
2. An arbitrator's name may be withdrawn by a nominating Contracting Party at any time, provided that an arbitrator who has commenced the hearing of a dispute may continue in that capacity until the dispute is finally determined.
3. A Contracting Party may nominate an additional member of the list of arbitrators at any time when, on account of omission to nominate or the occurrence of a vacancy, the total number of arbitrators nominated to the list by that Contracting Party, including the person to be nominated, will not exceed three. For the purposes of this calculation an arbitrator whose name has be withdrawn shall not be included, notwithstanding that such arbitrator is continuing to function under the proviso to Article 18.2.

Article 19
Composition of the Arbitral Tribunal

1. The arbitral tribunal shall consist of at least three members.
2. The party instituting the proceedings shall appoint one member of the tribunal to be chosen from the list referred to in Article 18.1. The appointment shall be included in the notification under Article 17.2.
3. Any other party to the dispute shall, within 30 days of receipt of the notification under Article 17.2, notify the party instituting the proceedings of its appointment of one member of the tribunal to be chosen

from the list under Article 18.1. If the appointment under this subparagraph is not made within the period of 30 days, the party instituting the proceedings may, within two weeks of the expiration of that period, call for the appointment to be made under Article 19.5.

4. The President of the arbitral shall be appointed by agreement between the parties from the list under Article 18.1. If agreement on the appointment of the President is not reached within 60 days after the institution of proceedings under Article 17.2, the President shall be appointed under Article 19.5.

5. Where an appointment has not been made within the time limits prescribed by Article 19.3 and 19.4, the first person in the following list who is not a national of either party, and who is willing to act, shall make the appointment from the list under Article 18.1:

   (i) the President of the International Court of Justice;
   (ii) the President of the International Tribunal for the Law of the Sea;
   (iii) the Vice-President of the International Court of Justice;
   (iv) the Vice-President of the International Tribunal for the Law of the Sea;
   (v) the Secretary-General of the United Nations;
   (vi) the Secretary-General of the International Maritime Organization;
   (vii) the Secretary-General of the Organization of American States;
   (viii) the Secretary-General of the Caribbean Tourism Organization.

6. Any appointment under Article 19.5 shall ensure that the person appointed to the tribunal is not of the same nationality as any other member of the tribunal.

7. Where the tribunal would consist of an even number of members under the other provisions of this Article, an additional member of the tribunal shall be appointed in the same manner as the President of the tribunal is appointed.

8. Where more than one party to the dispute shares the same interest with another Party, the other parties to the dispute shall be entitled jointly to appoint sufficient other members of the tribunal to achieve equality in the membership of the tribunal between members of the tribunal by parties in opposed interests.

9. Any dispute as to the applicability and implementation of Article 19.8 shall be determined by the President of the tribunal.
10. Any vacancy in the tribunal shall be filled in the same manner as the initial appointment.

Article 20
Arbitral Procedure
The provisions of Articles 5 to 11 and Article 12.1 of Annex VII of the United Nations Convention on the Law of the Sea shall apply *mutatis mutandis* to an arbitration under this Article.

Article 21
Legal Capacity
The Authority shall enjoy under the law of each Contracting Party such legal status and legal capacity as may be necessary for the fulfillment of its objectives and the exercise of its functions, in particular the capacity to contract, to acquire and dispose of moveable and immovable property, and to institute legal proceedings.

Article 22
Privileges and Immunities

1. The privileges and immunities to be recognized and granted to the Authority by the Contracting Parties shall be set out in a Protocol to be concluded to this Agreement.
2. The Authority shall conclude with the Government of Barbados an agreement relating to the privileges and immunities to be recognized and granted to the Authority.

Article 23
Depositary
The Secretary General of the Caribbean Tourism Organization shall be the Depositary of this Agreement.

Article 24
Reservations
No reservations shall be permitted to this Agreement.

Article 25
Parties
The Agreement shall be open for signature by any Caribbean state.

Article 26
Mode of Entry into Force

1. This Agreement shall be subject to ratification.
2. Instruments of ratification shall be deposited with the Depositary, who shall transmit certified copies to the Government of each Contracting Party.

Article 27
Date of Entry into Force
This Agreement shall enter into force on the deposit of instruments of ratification by six Member States mentioned in Article 25.

Article 28
Amendments to this Agreement

1. The Council may at any time recommend to the Contracting Parties any amendment to this Agreement.
2. An amendment proposed under Article 28.1 shall enter into force one month after the date on which the last of the instruments of ratification is deposited.

Article 29
Denunciation

1. Any Contracting Party may denounce this Agreement by giving notice in writing to the Depositary who shall promptly notify the other Member States. Denunciation shall take effect twelve months after the notice is received by the Depositary.
2. A party which denounces this Agreement shall not thereby become entitled to any refund of contributions paid to the Authority or to the Fund.

Appendix 5
Caribbean Tourism Arrivals 2008–2011

Table A5.1 Tourist (Stop-over) Arrivals in 2008

Destination	Period	Tourist Arrivals	% Change Overall	Winter[#]	Summer[#]
Anguilla	Jan–Dec	68,282	−12.1	−13.9	−10.8
Antigua & Barbuda[*]	Jan–Dec	265,841	1.5	9.4	−3.2
Aruba	Jan–Dec	826,774	7.1	15.9	2.7
Bahamas	Jan–Dec	1,462,404	−4.3	1.6	−7.6
Barbados[P]	Jan–Dec	567,667	−0.9	−1.0	−0.9
Belize	Jan–Dec	245,027	−2.6	−0.9	−3.8
Bermuda[*]	Jan–Dec	263,613	−13.7	−10.1	−14.9
Bonaire	Jan–Dec	74,342	0.0	9.6	−5.0
British Virgin Islands[P]	Jan–Dec	345,934	−3.4	−1.1	−5.0
Cancun (Mexico)[**]	Jan–Dec	2,165,320	7.1	9.5	5.6
Cayman Islands	Jan–Dec	302,879	3.9	9.5	0.3
Cuba	Jan–Dec	2,348,340	9.1	14.6	5.2
Curaçao	Jan–Dec	408,942	36.4	42.9	33.6
Dominica	Jan–Dec	78,481	2.6	−13.6	10.9
Dominican Republic[*]	Jan–Dec	3,979,672	0.0	5.6	−3.4
Grenada[P]	Jan–Dec	123,770	−4.1	−10.6	−0.4
Guyana[P]	Jan–Dec	132,776	1.0	1.9	0.6

(continued)

Table A5.1 Tourist (Stop-over) Arrivals in 2008 (*continued*)

Destination	Period	Tourist Arrivals	% Change Overall	% Change Winter[#]	% Change Summer[#]
Jamaica	Jan–Dec	1,767,271	3.9	10.1	0.7
Martinique[P]	Jan–Dec	479,933	−4.6	−4.6	−4.6
Montserrat	Jan–Dec	7,360	−5.0	−8.4	−3.3
Puerto Rico[**]	Jan–Dec	1,320,905	−2.6	−3.3	−2.2
Saba	Jan–Dec	12,043	3.2	1.2	4.4
St Lucia	Jan–Dec	295,761	2.9	9.4	−0.6
St Eustatius	Jan–Jul	7,146	4.0	1.6	7.4
St Kitts & Nevis[P]	Jan–Dec	106,408	–	−11.1	−15.3
St Maarten[*]	Jan–Dec	475,410	1.3	5.1	−1.3
St Vincent & the Grenadines	Jan–Dec	84,101	−6.2	−15.7	−0.4
Suriname	Jan–Jul	89,397	−8.1	−6.0	−10.4
Trinidad & Tobago	Jan–Dec	430,513	−4.2	5.2	−9.0
US Virgin Islands	Jan–Dec	678,904	−2.1	5.0	−6.5

[*]Non-resident air arrivals
[**]Non-resident hotel registrations only
[P]Preliminary figures
[#]Winter: January to April; summer: May to December.
Note: Figures are subject to revision by reporting countries.
Source: Data supplied by member countries.

Table A5.2a Tourist Arrivals by Month, 2008

Destination	January		February		March		April		May		June	
	Tourists	% change	Tourists	% change	Tourists	% change	Tourists	% change	Tourists	% change	Tourists	% change
Anguilla	6,108	-17.6	7,177	-6.4	8,446	-14.6	6,442	-16.7	6,322	-8.5	5,177	-14.0
Antigua & Barbuda*	25,119	11.1	28,614	22.7	28,241	-3.5	25,259	10.8	20,885	6.7	18,634	4.6
Aruba	71,262	20.8	73,004	22.0	81,204	19.1	69,889	3.0	63,612	22.8	61,370	4.4
Bahamas	110,503	6.6	129,001	6.8	174,681	-0.8	146,273	-3.3	140,943	2.0	153,249	-4.6
Barbados[P]	48,958	4.2	54,224	10.0	56,027	18.3	46,330	-27.4	45,342	-2.0	43,540	3.7
Belize	23,130	7.4	25,803	0.7	30,818	-1.4	21,361	-9.5	20,209	1.4	22,261	-0.7
Bermuda*	9,320	-13.1	13,524	2.5	18,885	-13.8	23,557	-12.1	31,102	-9.8	32,796	-14.5
Bonaire	6,453	12.4	7,089	2.4	7,292	1.8	7,261	24.8	5,898	5.3	6,075	6.1
British Virgin Islands[P]	34,221	9.8	35,355	-0.3	45,103	2.3	34,302	-14.2	32,713	8.1	31,469	-0.7
Cancun (Mexico)**	189,184	8.5	202,595	11.6	231,349	11.6	205,562	6.1	183,377	10.0	200,400	2.8
Cayman Islands	25,845	8.9	30,380	8.7	38,425	9.3	29,978	11.0	25,722	9.8	27,971	8.3
Cuba	248,446	12.3	259,832	19.2	286,145	14.3	232,668	12.7	158,824	17.4	153,727	13.9
Curaçao	29,317	33.5	33,646	54.4	35,321	55.2	30,997	29.3	26,602	31.4	26,123	28.8
Dominica	5,561	-2.0	5,157	-39.4	6,877	23.6	4,859	-22.2	7,077	-0.1	4,827	-5.3
Dominican Republic*	391,310	4.1	413,841	11.0	435,779	5.6	353,782	1.4	289,402	8.1	331,871	1.2
Grenada[P]	11,415	-8.8	10,338	-5.1	11,531	15.0	9,487	-34.1	9,592	3.3	10,314	25.2
Guyana	9,062[P]	1.4	8,885[P]	49.9	12,626[P]	-9.7	12,139[P]	-7.2	8,286	-18.1	9,244	-23.4
Jamaica	142,861	10.1	156,831	18.0	184,267	12.0	152,199	1.1	141,236	7.0	161,958	3.5
Martinique[P]	48,622	-3.1	46,709	-4.9	53,399	0.5	46,170	-10.9	37,580	6.8	29,084	-5.8

(*continued*)

Table A5.2a Tourist Arrivals by Month, 2008 (*continued*)

Destination	January Tourists	January % change	February Tourists	February % change	March Tourists	March % change	April Tourists	April % change	May Tourists	May % change	June Tourists	June % change
Montserrat	516	-10.3	581	14.8	719	-14.8	495	-17.1	481	-10.4	555	5.1
Puerto Rico**	121,215	1.4	130,546	-0.9	147,790	-4.0	121,561	-9.1	107,755	-1.3	108,420	-2.1
Saba	1,101	2.2	1,132	-3.5	1,193	7.3	1,114	-0.9	1,124	39.8	883	-1.9
St Lucia	24,958	14.0	29,088	18.2	31,982	20.4	24,197	-12.7	27,782	10.2	23,223	6.4
St Eustatius	1,212	21.3	1,023	-1.5	959	-11.5	940	-0.6	1,098	9.6	854	-6.2
St Kitts & Nevis[P]	10,255	-16.6	10,801	4.6	12,686	-13.8	9,623	-15.8	8,216	-18.9	10,556	-5.4
St Maarten*	48,688	13.5	49,498	5.1	55,595	4.9	43,992	-2.5	37,878	15.3	33,707	-3.9
St Vincent & the Grenadines	6,370	-24.2	7,976	-4.8	7,664	-19.0	6,567	-14.0	6,131	-6.8	8,020	6.4
Suriname	12,309	23.7	11,916	-15.9	8,947	-25.2	14,832	-1.0	11,470	-1.6	10,471	-15.0
Trinidad & Tobago	46,577	39.5	34,999	-26.1	40,780	17.0	37,733	4.6	29,278	-15.1	30,002	-15.0
US Virgin Islands	64,431	7.7	66,305	10.9	81,280	2.2	67,121	0.7	58,859	5.3	62,779	1.7

*Non-resident air arrivals
**Non-resident hotel registrations only
[P]Preliminary figures
Note: Figures are subject to revision by reporting countries.
Source: Data supplied by member countries.

Table A5.2b Tourist Arrivals by Month, 2008

Destination	July Tourists	July % change	August Tourists	August % change	September Tourists	September % change	October Tourists	October % change	November Tourists	November % change	December Tourists	December % change
Anguilla	6,964	0.4	6,441	-7.0	1,675	-11.3	2,230	-18.5	4,866	-19.7	6,344	-13.7
Antigua & Barbuda*	23,883	1.8	20,972	-1.3	12,211	-8.8	17,159	-10.4	20,662	-5.9	24,022	-11.1
Aruba	70,713	4.5	76,614	5.6	55,007	-5.1	58,956	-6.2	66,161	-2.5	78,982	1.6
Bahamas	158,836	0.1	128,137	-4.9	44,297	-37.1	73,383	-8.4	91,685	-15.1	110,916	-11.1
Barbados[P]	55,005	1.3	45,309	-2.9	34,166	5.7	40,168	-3.4	45,232	-5.4	53,366	-2.1
Belize	22,146	-2.5	18,655	3.0	8,957	-20.7	11,129	-9.5	17,170	-9.2	23,388	-2.4
Bermuda*	33,422	-10.8	32,048	-14.4	18,993	-17.3	21,314	-17.9	15,970	-23.1	12,182	-18.3
Bonaire	6,223	-2.6	5,687	2.3	4,510	-11.0	5,512	-16.7	6,056	-9.2	6,186	-10.6
British Virgin Islands[P]	34,805	1.7	20,817	-3.6	7,949	-18.5	14,209	-19.9	23,125	-14.9	31,866	-8.8
Cancun (Mexico)**	206,242	0.5	174,701	4.7	106,713	1.1	121,341	5.5	151,356	5.5	192,500	14.9
Cayman Islands	30,008	11.6	21,629	11.0	10,330	-9.8	14,710	-2.6	19,731	-21.8	28,150	-7.0
Cuba	185,585	8.2	167,826	8.8	104,098	-12.4	124,512	-0.3	180,613	-1.3	246,064	5.4
Curaçao	28,325	20.6	30,135	17.9	25,698	10.3	33,192	23.8	46,728	43.7	62,858	69.4
Dominica	9,062	1.2	7,422	-1.5	3,782	-8.3	12,025	54.2	4,674	29.3	7,158	13.5
Dominican Republic*	386,690	-3.6	329,636	-2.0	194,248	-10.0	209,616	-10.7	268,469	-5.8	375,028	-6.4
Grenada[P]	13,294	7.9	14,713	-3.3	5,828	-14.6	7,978	-3.9	7,999	-15.3	11,281	-3.4
Guyana	16,027	-10.8	14,430	3.8	8,591	2.7	9,556	-0.7	9,465	6.2	14,465[P]	68.0
Jamaica	185,447	-5.1	142,467	4.2	92,037	2.6	106,104	-1.9	122,250	-1.8	179,614	-0.2
Martinique[P]	42,079	-9.4	50,902	-5.6	27,321	-8.1	24,410	1.7	29,623	1.2	44,034	-10.8

(*continued*)

Table A5.2b Tourist Arrivals by Month, 2008 (continued)

Destination	July Tourists	July % change	August Tourists	August % change	September Tourists	September % change	October Tourists	October % change	November Tourists	November % change	December Tourists	December % change
Montserrat	763	13.4	478	-13.1	340	-16.3	473	8.7	507	-14.9	1,452	-3.1
Puerto Rico[**]	113,490	0.7	114,260	4.0	63,690	-8.2	83,986	-2.6	97,589	-8.0	110,603	-2.4
Saba	1,534	6.4	928	5.8	532	-3.1	619	2.5	874	2.3	1,009	-12.8
St Lucia	29,095	-2.2	25,315	8.9	15,149	-11.2	18,996	-3.1	19,803	-10.6	26,173	-5.8
St Eustatius	1,060	18.7	—	—	—	—	—	—	—	—	—	—
St Kitts & Nevis[P]	9,492	-10.1	7,840	-14.0	5,261	-15.0	5,422	-15.0	7,112	-27.8	9,144	-23.5
St Maarten[*]	43,162	9.7	41,291	12.6	19,273	-13.0	24,409	-13.8	35,596	-3.7	42,321	-15.1
St Vincent & the Grenadines	10,171	-7.6	7,257	-2.8	3,800	-3.4	4,832	120.2	5,388	-16.3	9,925	-6.3
Suriname	19,452	-12.4	—	—	—	—	—	—	—	—	—	—
Trinidad & Tobago	47,948	12.8	36,414	-6.1	26,900	-7.7	30,980	-3.2	29,772	-17.7	39,130	-19.9
US Virgin Islands	62,455	-1.5	54,045	-3.5	24,400	-18.9	26,607	-36.9	46,879	-10.9	63,743	-2.8

[*]Non-resident air arrivals
[**]Non-resident hotel registrations only
[P]Preliminary figures
Note: Figures are subject to revision by reporting countries.
Source: Data supplied by member countries.

Table A5.3 Tourist Arrivals by Main Market, 2008

Destination	Period	United States Tourists	% change	Canada Tourists	% change	Europe Tourists	% change	Other Tourists	% change
Anguilla	Jan–Dec	40,202	-12.6	2,074	-13.3	8,962	-17.0	17,044	-7.8
Antigua & Barbuda*	Jan–Dec	84,032	6.8	13,189	25.7	110,265	-4.5	58,355	2.1
Aruba	Jan–Dec	537,860	3.4	32,496	26.6	73,144	8.6	183,274	15.5
Bahamas	Jan–Dec	1,176,683	-6.9	114,947	14.6	93,799	7.6	76,975	0.6
Barbados[P]	Jan–Dec	131,795	-1.6	57,335	8.2	251,778	0.4	126,759	-6.6
Belize	Jan–Dec	147,655	-3.2	17,693	6.2	34,265	0.3	45,414	-5.9
Bermuda*	Jan–Dec	189,388	-17.5	27,207	-2.3	35,003	-2.6	12,015	-2.1
Bonaire	Jan–Dec	32,267	0.6	2,024	17.9	30,768	-2.1	9,283	2.2
Cancun (Mexico)**	Jan–Dec	1,679,848	6.9	130,509	11.5	213,077	1.8	141,886	14.3
Cayman Islands	Jan–Dec	240,462	3.7	18,544	6.9	21,271	5.0	22,602	2.7
Cuba[#]	Jan–Dec	—	—	818,246	23.9	909,086	-1.6	621,008	9.4
Curaçao	Jan–Dec	43,680	-5.5	7,244	5.0	136,747	12.6	211,271	76.7
Dominica	Jan–Dec	20,458	-4.7	3,310	26.8	13,179	22.7	41,534	-0.4
Dominican Republic*	Jan–Dec	1,092,240	1.1	635,933	8.3	1,345,290	-3.0	906,209	-2.0
Grenada[P]	Jan–Dec	21,479	-20.8	6,211	3.2	43,047	3.0	53,033	-2.1
Guyana[P]	Jan–Dec	67,924	-1.4	22,297	14.3	9,208	-4.9	33,347	-0.3
Jamaica	Jan–Dec	1,150,942	1.6	236,193	23.9	284,700	-1.5	95,436	7.6
Montserrat	Jan–Dec	1,922	-8.9	395	1.8	2,333	-1.4	2,710	-6.0

(continued)

Table A5.3 Tourist Arrivals by Main Market, 2008 (*continued*)

Destination	Period	United States		Canada		Europe		Other	
		Tourists	% change	Tourists	% change	Tourists	% change	Tourists	% change
Puerto Rico[**]	Jan–Dec	1,184,769	-1.4	15,936	-4.8	28,673	-19.7	91,527	-10.5
Saba	Jan–Dec	4,456	-0.2	757	1.7	5,605	6.0	1,225	4.2
St Lucia	Jan–Dec	108,596	-4.3	26,279	41.0	96,871	9.1	64,015	-3.8
St Eustatius	Jan–Jul	1,663	-95.0	165	-94.4	3,754	-47.9	1,564	-90.5
St Kitts & Nevis[p]	Jan–Dec	62,769	-8.5	6,812	-3.7	9,458	-35.3	27,369	-16.8
St Maarten[*]	Jan–Dec	257,912	1.6	34,055	5.3	102,713	6.6	80,730	-7.1
St Vincent & the G'dines	Jan–Dec	24,042	-9.8	6,882	2.0	22,302	-4.9	30,875	-5.9
Suriname	Jan–Jul	3,026	21.3	723	5.2	60,055	-5.8	25,593	-15.5
Trinidad & Tobago	Jan–Dec	186,695	3.4	53,404	3.9	62,399	-24.4	128,015	-5.2
US Virgin Islands[**#]	Jan–Dec	672,870	9.9	8,922	48.3	15,679	5.3	34,029	-26.7

[*] Non-resident air arrivals
[**] Non-resident hotel registrations only
[p] Preliminary figures
[#] US total included in Other

Note: Figures are subject to revision by reporting countries; USVI reported figures in this table are hotel registrations and their reported stay-over totals are air arrivals.
Source: Data supplied by member countries.

Table A5.4 Cruise Passenger Arrivals, 2008 and 2007

Destination	Period	2008	2007	% change
Antigua & Barbuda	Jan–Dec	580,853	672,788	−13.7
Aruba	Jan–Dec	556,090	481,775	15.4
Bahamas	Jan–Dec	2,861,140	2,970,659	−3.7
Barbados	Jan–Dec	597,523	616,354	−3.1
Belize	Jan–Dec	597,370	624,128	−4.3
Bermuda	Jan–Dec	286,409	354,024	−19.1
Bonaire	Jan–Dec	175,702	97,635	80.0
British Virgin Islands	Jan–Dec	571,749	575,211	−0.6
Cayman Islands	Jan–Dec	1,553,053	1,715,666	−9.5
Cozumel (Mexico)	Jan–Dec	2,569,433	2,488,190	3.3
Curaçao	Jan–Oct	239,208	255,985	−6.6
Dominica	Jan–Dec	380,941	354,515	7.5
Dominican Republic	Jan–Dec	417,685	384,878	8.5
Grenada[P]	Jan–Dec	292,712	270,323	8.3
Jamaica	Jan–Dec	1,088,901	1,179,504	−7.7
Martinique	Jan–Dec	87,079	71,683	21.5
Montserrat	Jan–Dec	251	273	−8.1
Puerto Rico	Jan–Dec	1,392,624	1,437,239	−3.1
St Lucia	Jan–Dec	619,680	610,343	1.5
St Maarten	Jan–Dec	1,345,812	1,421,906	−5.4
St Vincent & the Grenadines	Jan–Dec	116,709	144,555	−19.3
Trinidad & Tobago	Jan–Dec	44,042	76,741	−42.6
US Virgin Islands	Jan–Dec	1,757,067	1,917,878	−8.4

[P] Preliminary figures
Note: Figures are subject to revision by reporting countries.
Source: Data supplied by member countries.

Table A5.5 Tourist (Stop-over) Arrivals in 2009

Destination	Period	Tourist Arrivals	% Change Overall	% Change Winter[#]	% Change Summer[#]
Anguilla	Jan–Dec	57,891	−15.2	−21.8	−10.6
Antigua & Barbuda[*]	Jan–Dec	234,410	−11.8	−13.6	−10.6
Aruba[P]	Jan–Dec	812,623	−1.7	−6.8	1.1
Bahamas	Jan–Dec	1,327,005	−9.3	−14.2	−6.2
Barbados[P]	Jan–Dec	518,564	−8.7	−7.2	−9.5
Belize	Jan–Dec	232,247	−5.2	−7.1	−3.9
Bermuda	Jan–Dec	235,860	−10.5	−21.8	−6.8
Bonaire	Jan–Dec	66,998	−9.9	−16.3	−6.0
British Virgin Islands	Jan–Dec	308,793	−10.7	−16.3	−6.5
Cancun (Mexico)[**]	Jan–Dec	1,891,448	−12.6	1.0	−21.1
Cayman Islands	Jan–Dec	271,958	−10.2	−12.5	−8.6
Cuba	Jan–Dec	2,429,809	3.5	1.9	4.7
Curaçao[P]	Jan–Dec	366,703	−10.3	−3.1	−13.7
Dominica[P]	Jan–Dec	74,923	−6.8	−1.4	−9.1
Dominican Republic[*]	Jan–Dec	3,992,303	0.3	−4.8	3.7
Grenada[P]	Jan–Dec	113,370	−12.5	−11.4	−13.2
Guyana[P]	Jan–Dec	141,053	6.2	−1.9	10.1
Jamaica	Jan–Dec	1,831,097	3.6	2.0	4.5
Martinique[P]	Jan–Dec	443,202	−7.9	−16.9	−2.3
Montserrat	Jan–Dec	6,311	−14.3	−11.4	−15.5
Puerto Rico[**]	Jan–Dec	1,300,783	−1.6	−7.3	2.2
Saba	Jan–Dec	11,957	−0.7	1.4	−2.0
St Eustatius	Jan–Apr	4,025	−2.6	−2.6	–
St Lucia	Jan–Dec	278,491	−5.8	−8.8	−4.1
St Maarten[*]	Jan–Dec	440,185	−7.4	−13.7	−2.9
St Vincent & the Grenadines	Jan–Dec	75,446	−10.3	−8.1	−11.4
Suriname	Jan–Dec	150,396	−0.2	−31.6	14.4
Trinidad & Tobago	Jan–Oct	342,091	−5.4	−10.5	−1.4
US Virgin Islands	Jan–Dec	666,051	−2.5	−10.0	2.6

[*]Non-resident air arrivals
[**]Non-resident hotel registrations only
[P]Preliminary figures
[#]Winter: January to April; summer: May to December.
Note: Figures are subject to revision by reporting countries.
Source: Data supplied by member countries.

Table A5.6a Tourist Arrivals by Month, 2009

Destination	January Tourists	January % change	February Tourists	February % change	March Tourists	March % change	April Tourists	April % change	May Tourists	May % change	June Tourists	June % change
Anguilla	4,958	-18.8	5,489	-23.5	5,714	-32.3	5,861	-9.0	4,354	-31.1	4,340	-16.2
Antigua & Barbuda*	22,657	-9.8	24,471	-14.5	23,272	-18.1	22,416	-11.3	17,048	-18.4	16,365	-12.2
Aruba[P]	69,225	-2.9	67,107	-8.1	67,456	-16.9	71,621	2.5	61,479	-3.4	63,117	2.8
Bahamas	93,679	-15.2	110,078	-14.7	143,453	-17.9	133,767	-8.5	122,475	-13.1	131,192	-14.4
Barbados[P]	45,455	-7.2	49,838	-8.1	50,237	-10.3	45,277	-2.3	38,665	-14.7	34,377	-21.0
Belize	22,580	-2.4	22,600	-12.4	26,499	-14.0	22,210	4.0	17,855	-11.6	20,118	-9.6
Bermuda	7,703	-17.3	10,013	-26.0	14,519	-23.1	18,810	-20.2	25,456	-18.2	30,713	-6.4
Bonaire	5,488	-15.0	6,266	-11.6	6,365	-12.7	5,409	-25.5	5,301	-10.1	4,566	-24.8
British Virgin Islands	29,514	-13.8	27,080	-23.4	33,880	-24.9	34,230	-0.2	28,034	-14.3	27,350	-13.1
Cancun (Mexico)**	212,323	12.2	216,449	6.8	223,945	-3.2	184,331	-10.3	63,606	-65.3	134,501	-32.9
Cayman Islands	23,404	-9.4	26,482	-12.8	31,194	-18.8	27,973	-6.7	21,438	-16.7	24,149	-13.7
Cuba	268,115	7.9	262,985	1.2	279,199	-2.4	236,301	1.6	164,652	3.7	164,941	7.3
Curaçao	32,379	10.4	31,658	-5.9	30,001	-15.1	31,178	0.6	26,329	-1.0	28,19[P]	7.9
Dominica[P]	6,008	-7.4	6,853	30.9	4,414	-35.9	5,876	20.9	6,640	-18.7	3,946	-18.4
Dominican Republic*	382,055	-2.4	387,487	-6.4	406,270	-6.8	342,398	-3.2	296,374	2.4	331,373	-0.2
Grenada[P]	12,987	-2.6	9,688	-19.6	9,949	-25.5	10,451	6.0	7,408	-22.8	7,094	-31.2
Guyana[P]	8,132	-10.3	8,400	-5.5	11,876	-5.9	13,507	11.3	8,941	7.9	11,012	19.1
Jamaica	148,886	4.2	160,282	2.2	175,929	-4.5	164,090	7.8	153,443	8.6	168,561	4.1
Martinique[P]	40,678	-11.2	38,066	-17.9	35,618	-32.9	40,221	-1.0	35,242	-9.6	30,116	-1.6

(continued)

Table A5.6a Tourist Arrivals by Month, 2009 (*continued*)

Destination	January Tourists	January % change	February Tourists	February % change	March Tourists	March % change	April Tourists	April % change	May Tourists	May % change	June Tourists	June % change
Montserrat	468	-9.3	502	-13.6	617	-14.2	460	-7.1	395	-17.9	392	-29.4
Puerto Rico**	115,719	-4.5	118,027	-9.6	128,609	-13.0	120,576	-0.8	107,630	-0.1	105,505	-3.0
Saba	1,178	7.0	1,119	-1.1	1,193	0.0	1,115	0.1	1,013	-9.9	936	6.0
St Eustatius	1,154	-4.8	862	-15.7	1,008	5.1	1,001	6.5	–	–	–	–
St Lucia	23,051	-7.6	25,262	-13.2	25,938	-18.9	26,326	8.8	25,292	-9.0	19,706	-15.1
St Maarten*	44,647	-8.3	42,521	-14.1	41,878	-24.7	41,601	-5.4	33,566	-11.4	31,464	-6.7
St Vincent & the Grenadines	6,444	1.2	6,049	-24.2	7,065	-7.8	6,704	2.1	4,676	-23.7	6,137	-23.5
Suriname	8,173	-33.6	8,300	-30.3	7,393	-17.4	8,987	-39.4	6,397	-44.7	12,007	-8.4
Trinidad & Tobago	30,620	-34.3	46,085	31.7	32,005	-21.5	34,641	-8.2	32,048	9.5	33,126	10.4
US Virgin Islands	60,679	-5.8	62,225	-6.2	62,585	-23.0	65,738	-2.1	57,571	-2.2	58,110	-7.4

*Non-resident air arrivals
**Non-resident hotel registrations only
P Preliminary figures
Note: Figures are subject to revision by reporting countries.
Source: Data supplied by member countries.

Table A5.6b Tourist Arrivals by Month, 2009

Destination	July Tourists	July % change	August Tourists	August % change	September Tourists	September % change	October Tourists	October % change	November Tourists	November % change	December Tourists	December % change
Anguilla	5,537	-20.5	5,374	-16.6	1,706	1.9	2,985	28.7	4,874	0.2	6,699	5.6
Antigua & Barbuda*	22,538	-5.6	17,410	-17.0	11,141	-8.8	15,279	-11.0	18,510	-10.4	23,303	-3.0
Aruba[P]	75,231	6.4	75,220	-1.8	55,162	0.3	63,252	7.3	67,848	2.5	75,905	-3.9
Bahamas	144,226	-9.2	109,130	-14.8	53,822	21.5	76,568	3.6	93,264	1.7	115,351	4.0
Barbados[P]	48,046	-12.7	39,034	-13.8	28,892	-15.4	38,757	-3.5	46,251	2.3	53,735	0.7
Belize	21,291	-3.9	17,461	-6.4	9,994	11.6	11,547	3.8	15,927	-7.2	24,165	3.3
Bermuda	32,837	-1.8	27,877	-13.0	19,233	1.3	22,391	2.6	14,800	-7.3	11,508	-5.5
Bonaire	6,594	6.0	4,885	-14.1	4,442	-1.5	5,740	2.3	5,680	-6.2	6,262	1.2
British Virgin Islands	32,331	-7.1	17,849	-14.3	8,195	3.1	15,137	6.5	24,382	5.4	30,811	-3.3
Cancun (Mexico)**	157,966	-23.4	139,029	-20.4	96,832	-9.3	120,800	-0.4	151,318	0.0	190,348	-1.1
Cayman Islands	25,775	-14.1	19,231	-11.1	9,115	-11.8	13,018	-11.5	20,614	4.5	29,565	5.0
Cuba	196,990	6.1	163,875	-2.4	119,914	15.2	142,544	14.5	182,778	1.2	247,515	0.6
Curaçao[P]	29,815	5.3	30,923	2.6	27,334	6.4	32,406[P]	-2.4	33,382	-28.6	33,107	-47.3
Dominica[P]	9,028	3.1	7,715	3.9	4,358	15.1	7,703	-36.5	4,260	-9.2	8,122	13.5
Dominican Republic*	393,452	1.7	325,863	-1.1	204,522	5.3	229,388	9.4	284,824	6.1	408,297	8.9
Grenada[P]	12,025	-9.5	12,287	-16.5	5,735	-1.6	7,894	-1.1	7,795	-2.6	10,057	-10.9
Guyana[P]	19,370	20.9	15,056	4.3	8,613	0.3	9,900	3.6	10,191	7.7	16,055	11.0
Jamaica	195,940	5.7	152,573	7.1	95,263	3.5	108,820	2.6	125,494	2.7	181,816	1.2
Martinique[P]	44,674	0.3	55,263	3.8	28,043	0.1	26,314	1.4	28,451	-5.8	40,516	-7.3

(continued)

Table A5.6b Tourist Arrivals by Month, 2009 (continued)

Destination	July Tourists	July % change	August Tourists	August % change	September Tourists	September % change	October Tourists	October % change	November Tourists	November % change	December Tourists	December % change
Montserrat	557	-27.0	395	-17.4	278	-18.2	398	-15.9	435	-14.2	1,414	-2.6
Puerto Rico**	111,014	-2.2	110,613	-3.2	77,459	21.6	89,206	5.6	103,165	5.7	113,260	2.6
Saba	1,267	-17.4	886	-4.5	487	-8.5	716	15.7	805	-7.9	1,242	23.1
St Eustatius	–	–	–	–	–	–	–	–	–	–	–	–
St Lucia	26,794	-7.9	23,304	-7.9	14,675	-3.1	19,031	0.2	21,777	10.0	27,335	4.4
St Maarten*	39,546	-8.4	37,549	-9.1	19,183	-0.5	27,045	10.8	36,005	1.1	45,180	6.8
St Vincent & the Grenadines	8,454	-16.9	6,670	-8.1	3,392	-10.7	4,851	0.4	5,404	0.3	9,600	-3.3
Suriname	20,023	2.9	17,532	9.0	10,641	56.6	15,262	48.7	14,237	31.7	21,444	46.6
Trinidad & Tobago	43,450	-9.4	35,112	-3.6	25,442	-5.4	29,562	-4.6	–	–	–	–
US Virgin Islands	61,144	-2.1	50,834	-5.9	28,410	16.4	39,108	26.2	52,724	12.5	66,923	5.0

*Non-resident air arrivals
**Non-resident hotel registrations only
ᵖPreliminary figures
Note: Figures are subject to revision by reporting countries.
Source: Data supplied by member countries.

Table A5.7 Tourist Arrivals by Main Market

Destination	Period	United States Tourists	United States % change	Canada Tourists	Canada % change	Europe Tourists	Europe % change	Other Tourists	Other % change
Anguilla	Jan–Dec	34,073	-15.2	2,032	-2.0	7,475	-16.6	14,311	-16.0
Antigua & Barbuda[*]	Jan–Dec	82,068	-2.3	12,947	-1.8	93,442	-15.3	45,953	-21.3
Aruba	Jan–Dec	528,104	-1.8	33,856	4.2	75,000	2.5	175,663	-4.2
Bahamas	Jan–Dec	1,068,725	-9.2	107,041	-6.9	78,816	-16.0	72,423	-5.9
Barbados[P]	Jan–Dec	122,306	-7.2	63,751	11.2	220,704	-12.3	111,803	-11.8
Belize	Jan–Dec	139,560	-5.5	17,211	-2.7	29,604	-13.6	45,872	1.0
Bermuda	Jan–Dec	172,652	-8.8	24,854	-8.6	28,960	-17.3	9,394	-21.8
Bonaire	Jan–Dec	25,236	-21.8	1,799	-11.1	30,234	-1.7	9,729	4.8
Cancun (Mexico)[**]	Jan–Dec	1,503,183	-10.5	122,881	-5.8	157,364	-26.1	108,020	-23.9
Cayman Islands	Jan–Dec	215,037	-10.6	17,254	-7.0	19,117	-10.1	20,550	-9.1
Curaçao[P]	Jan–Dec	35,953	-17.7	6,483	-10.5	149,276	9.2	174,991	-20.9
Cuba[#]	Jan–Dec	—		914,884	11.8	838,340	-7.8	676,585	9.0
Dominica[P]	Jan–Dec	18,193	-11.3	2,618	-21.4	11,591	-15.8	42,521	-0.7
Dominican Republic[*]	Jan–Dec	1,148,533	5.2	646,285	1.6	1,245,925	-7.4	951,560	5.0
Grenada[P]	Jan–Dec	21,111	-3.3	6,295	-0.7	35,650	-19.0	50,314	-12.4
Guyana[P]	Jan–Dec	76,151	12.1	23,802	6.7	8,252	-10.4	32,848	-1.5
Jamaica	Jan–Dec	1,172,844	1.9	290,307	22.9	276,799	-2.8	91,147	-4.5
Montserrat	Jan–Dec	1,606	-16.4	367	-7.1	2,031	-12.9	2,307	-14.9
Puerto Rico[**]	Jan–Dec	1,173,176	-1.0	16,210	1.8	28,060	-2.1	83,337	-8.9

(continued)

Table A5.7 Tourist Arrivals by Main Market (*continued*)

Destination	Period	United States		Canada		Europe		Other	
		Tourists	% change	Tourists	% change	Tourists	% change	Tourists	% change
Saba	Jan–Dec	3,784	-15.1	942	24.4	6,179	10.2	1,052	-14.1
St Eustatius	Jan–Apr	829	-16.3	91	-18.0	2,213	4.2	892	-1.9
St Lucia	Jan–Dec	98,685	-9.1	28,563	8.7	86,819	-10.4	64,424	0.6
St Maarten*	Jan–Dec	240,431	-6.8	32,277	-5.2	98,341	-4.3	69,136	-14.4
St Vincent & the Grenadines	Jan–Dec	20,159	-16.2	6,820	-0.9	19,097	-14.4	29,370	-4.9
Suriname	Jan–Dec	4,950	-0.5	1,295	8.5	87,799	-7.9	56,352	14.4
Trinidad & Tobago	Jan–Oct	158,203	2.1	39,212	-11.3	48,985	-8.4	95,691	-12.2
US Virgin Islands**	Jan–Dec	724,910	6.5	10,412	14.3	16,479	3.9	35,348	2.3

*Non-resident air arrivals
**Non-resident hotel registrations only
PPreliminary figures
#US total included in Other

Note: Figures are subject to revision by reporting countries; USVI reported figures in this table are hotel registrations and their reported stay-over totals are air arrivals.
Source: Data supplied by member countries.

Table A5.8 Cruise Passenger Arrivals, 2009 and 2008

Destination	Period	2009	2008	% change
Antigua & Barbuda	Jan–Dec	712,792	580,853	22.7
Aruba	Jan–Dec	606,768	556,090	9.1
Bahamas	Jan–Dec	3,255,780	2,861,140	13.8
Barbados	Jan–Dec	635,746	597,523	6.4
Belize	Jan–Dec	705,219	597,370	18.1
Bermuda	Jan–Dec	318,528	286,409	11.2
Bonaire	Jan–Dec	213,191	175,702	21.3
British Virgin Islands	Jan–Dec	530,327	571,749	−7.2
Cayman Islands	Jan–Dec	1,520,372	1,553,053	−2.1
Cozumel (Mexico)	Jan–Dec	2,221,729	2,569,433	−13.5
Curaçao	Jan–Dec	423,088	352,897	19.9
Dominica	Jan–Dec	530,332	386,414	37.2
Dominican Republic	Jan–Dec	374,284	348,923	7.3
Grenada[P]	Jan–Dec	339,752	292,712	16.1
Jamaica	Jan–Dec	922,349	1,088,901	−15.3
Martinique	Jan–Dec	69,749	87,079	−19.9
Puerto Rico	Jan–Dec	1,179,022	1,392,624	−15.3
St Lucia	Jan–Dec	699,306	619,680	12.8
St Maarten	Jan–Dec	1,215,146	1,345,812	−9.7
St Vincent & the Grenadines	Jan–Dec	149,464	116,613	28.2
Trinidad & Tobago	Jan–Dec	119,600	48,666	145.8
US Virgin Islands	Jan–Dec	1,582,264	1,757,067	−9.9

[P] Preliminary figures
Note: Figures are subject to revision by reporting countries.
Source: Data supplied by member countries.

Table A5.9 Tourist (Stop-over) Arrivals in 2010

Destination	Period	Tourist Arrivals	% Change Overall	Winter[#]	Summer[#]
Anguilla	Jan–Dec	61,998	7.1	9.3	5.8
Antigua & Barbuda[*]	Jan–Dec	231,305	−1.3	−1.7	−1.1
Aruba	Jan–Dec	825,451	1.6	3.7	0.5
Bahamas	Jan–Dec	1,368,053	3.1	0.7	4.5
Barbados[P]	Jan–Dec	532,180	2.6	−0.5	4.4
Belize	Jan–Dec	238,158	2.5	1.6	3.2
Bermuda[*]	Jan–Dec	232,262	−1.5	−8.1	0.3
Bonaire	Jan–Jun	35,173	5.3	7.1	1.1
British Virgin Islands	Jan–Dec	330,343	7.0	13.6	2.5
Cancun (Mexico)[**]	Jan–Dec	2,106,485	11.4	−0.6	20.9
Cayman Islands	Jan–Dec	288,272	6.0	5.6	6.2
Cuba	Jan–Dec	2,531,745	4.2	0.7	6.8
Curaçao	Jan–Dec	341,656	−6.8	−11.6	−4.4
Dominica[P]	Jan–Dec	76,517	2.1	9.2	−1.0
Dominican Republic[*]	Jan–Dec	4,124,543	3.3	2.3	3.9
Grenada[P]	Jan–Dec	106,156	−6.4	−6.6	−6.2
Guyana	Jan–Dec	150,141	6.3	7.1	5.9
Jamaica[P]	Jan–Dec	1,921,678	4.9	7.3	3.6
Martinique	Jan–Dec	476,492	7.9	17.4	2.8
Montserrat	Jan–Sep	4,015	−1.2	−6.2	3.9
Puerto Rico[**]	Jan–Dec	1,369,814	5.2	9.8	2.6
Saba	Jan–Dec	12,327	3.1	9.1	−0.6
St Lucia	Jan–Dec	305,937	9.9	8.9	10.4
St Eustatius	Jan–Jun	6,699	11.6	18.3	−1.0
St Maarten[*]	Jan–Dec	443,136	0.7	4.8	−1.9
St Vincent & the Grenadines	Jan–Dec	72,478	−3.9	−2.9	−4.5
Suriname	Jan–Oct	165,806	–	–	–
Trinidad & Tobago	Jan–May	158,117	−9.9	−8.7	−15.1
US Virgin Islands	Jan–Dec	691,194	3.8	11.5	−0.9

[*]Non-resident air arrivals
[**]Non-resident hotel registrations only
[P]Preliminary figures
[#]Winter: January to April; summer: May to December.
Note: Figures are subject to revision by reporting countries.
Source: Data supplied by member countries.

Table A5.10a Tourist Arrivals by Month, 2010

Destination	January Tourists	January % change	February Tourists	February % change	March Tourists	March % change	April Tourists	April % change	May Tourists	May % change	June Tourists	June % change
Anguilla	5,207	5.0	5,892	7.3	6,969	22.0	5,998	2.3	5,286	21.4	4,384	1.0
Antigua & Barbuda[*]	22,230	-1.9	22,378	-8.6	25,908	11.3	20,586	-7.7	17,719	3.9	15,597	-4.7
Aruba	71,396	3.1	67,710	0.9	77,258	14.5	69,192	-3.4	64,383	4.7	60,243	-4.6
Bahamas	91,260	-2.6	104,913	-4.7	157,863	10.0	130,309	-2.6	127,176	3.8	145,603	11.0
Barbados[P]	48,336	6.3	48,585	-2.5	51,570	2.7	41,357	-8.7	46,813	21.1	35,179	2.3
Belize	22,380	-0.9	23,763	5.1	29,680	12.0	19,547	-12.0	19,208	7.6	21,010	4.4
Bermuda[*]	6,327	-17.9	8,674	-13.4	13,864	-4.5	18,067	-4.0	28,027	10.1	31,418	2.3
Bonaire	6,720	22.4	6,587	5.1	6,504	2.2	5,388	-0.4	5,576	5.2	4,398	-3.7
British Virgin Islands	31,410	6.4	32,618	20.5	41,974	23.9	35,707	4.3	27,553	-1.7	31,415	14.9
Cancun (Mexico)[**]	209,831	-1.2	206,450	-4.6	221,519	-1.1	194,333	5.4	168,824	165.4	195,581	45.4
Cayman Islands	25,006	6.8	27,193	2.7	35,642	14.3	27,355	-2.2	21,824	1.8	25,050	3.7
Cuba	255,612	-4.7	257,548	-2.1	298,347	6.9	242,876	2.8	171,447	4.1	164,102	-0.5
Curaçao	28,065	-13.3	26,912	-15.0	29,773	-0.8	25,988	-16.6	26,558	0.9	23,067	-18.2
Dominica[P]	6,302	4.9	7,338	7.1	6,007	36.1	5,631	-4.2	8,139	22.6	3,790	-4.0
Dominican Republic[*]	404,264	5.8	395,779	2.1	421,829	3.8	331,521	-3.2	297,019	0.2	348,375	5.1
Grenada[P]	12,063	-7.1	9,655	-0.3	10,484	5.4	8,035	-23.1	6,254	-15.6	6,178	-12.9
Guyana	9,284	13.9	7,716	-8.5	13,506	13.6	14,484	7.0	9,660	7.8	11,651	5.6
Jamaica	161,094	8.2	167,462	4.5	201,378	14.5	166,955	1.7	149,775	-2.4	164,205	-2.6
Martinique	41,997	3.3	46,347	21.8	52,578	47.7	40,478	0.7	34,280	-2.0	28,713	-3.8

(continued)

Table A5.10a Tourist Arrivals by Month, 2010 (*continued*)

Destination	January Tourists	January % change	February Tourists	February % change	March Tourists	March % change	April Tourists	April % change	May Tourists	May % change	June Tourists	June % change
Montserrat	438	-6.4	425	-15.3	590	-4.4	467	1.5	367	-7.1	399	1.8
Puerto Rico[**]	125,749	8.7	131,728	11.6	145,373	13.0	127,172	5.5	104,989	-2.5	107,629	2.0
Saba	1,239	5.2	1,276	14.0	1,346	12.8	1,161	4.1	950	-6.2	829	-11.4
St Lucia	26,083	13.2	27,867	10.3	29,580	14.0	25,984	-1.3	30,349	20.0	22,993	16.7
St Eustatius	1,175	1.8	1,373	59.3	1,122	17.0	962	2.3	1,065	-5.2	1,002	4.0
St Maarten[*]	46,546	4.3	45,070	6.0	46,423	10.9	40,723	-2.1	34,545	2.9	30,369	-3.5
St Vincent & the Grenadines	5,935	-7.9	6,401	5.8	7,627	8.0	5,534	-17.5	4,732	1.2	6,504	6.0
Suriname	14,773	–	16,323	–	16,308	–	16,302	–	14,482	–	12,586	–
Trinidad & Tobago	34,118	11.4	33,858	-26.5	33,740	5.4	29,203	-15.7	27,198	-15.1	–	–
US Virgin Islands	66,212	9.1	66,391	6.7	80,980	29.4	66,526	1.2	57,316	-0.4	59,710	2.8

[*]Non-resident air arrivals
[**]Non-resident hotel registrations only
[p]Preliminary figures
Note: Figures are subject to revision by reporting countries.
Source: Data supplied by member countries.

Table A5.10b Tourist Arrivals by Month, 2010

Destination	July Tourists	July % change	August Tourists	August % change	September Tourists	September % change	October Tourists	October % change	November Tourists	November % change	December Tourists	December % change
Anguilla	6,398	15.5	4,643	-13.6	1,763	3.3	2,956	-1.0	5,213	7.0	7,289	8.8
Antigua & Barbuda[*]	22,029	-2.3	17,027	-2.2	9,936	-10.8	14,679	-3.9	18,472	-0.2	24,644	5.8
Aruba	75,369	0.2	73,230	-2.6	58,460	6.0	67,034	6.0	63,388	-6.6	77,788	2.5
Bahamas	156,713	8.7	119,960	9.9	57,264	6.4	74,169	-3.1	93,370	0.1	109,453	-5.1
Barbados[P]	51,499	7.2	41,882	7.3	30,065	4.1	39,030	0.7	44,838	-3.1	53,026	-1.3
Belize	23,046	8.2	17,927	2.7	8,966	-10.3	11,538	-0.1	16,920	6.2	24,173	0.0
Bermuda[*]	33,839	3.1	28,429	2.0	16,538	-14.0	21,014	-6.1	14,783	-0.1	11,282	-2.0
Bonaire	—	—	—	—	—	—	—	—	—	—	—	—
British Virgin Is.	33,539	3.7	18,810	5.4	7,837	-4.4	14,529	-4.0	22,650	-7.1	32,301	4.8
Cancun (Mexico)[**]	193,195	22.3	160,771	15.6	109,645	13.2	120,545	-0.1	144,742	-4.3	180,949	-4.9
Cayman Islands	29,203	13.3	19,097	-0.7	9,564	4.9	13,796	6.0	23,151	12.3	31,391	6.2
Cuba	206,347	4.8	172,820	5.5	134,539	12.2	164,577	15.5	200,338	9.6	263,092	6.3
Curaçao	29,845	0.1	30,772	-0.5	26,784	-2.0	32,120	-0.9	29,435	-11.8	32,337	-2.3
Dominica[P]	8,831	-2.2	7,207	-6.6	3,788	-13.1	7,342	1.8	3,930	-7.7	7,712	-5.0
Dominican Republic[*]	417,699	6.2	333,110	2.2	219,292	7.2	247,254	7.8	297,036	4.3	411,365	0.8
Grenada[P]	11,429	-5.0	12,016	-2.2	5,347	-6.8	7,947	0.7	7,503	-3.7	9,245	-8.1
Guyana	21,208	9.3	16,807	11.5	9,222	7.0	10,031	1.1	10,738	5.2	15,834	-1.5
Jamaica	204,526	4.4	159,408	4.5	97,010	1.8	114,699	5.4	134,320	7.0	200,846	10.5
Martinique	46,084	3.5	54,489	-1.1	28,453	2.6	26,996	3.0	29,977	6.1	46,100	13.8

(*continued*)

Table A5.10b Tourist Arrivals by Month, 2010 (*continued*)

Destination	July Tourists	July % change	August Tourists	August % change	September Tourists	September % change	October Tourists	October % change	November Tourists	November % change	December Tourists	December % change
Montserrat	455	-18.3	386	-2.3	488	75.5	–	–	–	–	–	–
Puerto Rico**	116,515	5.4	111,158	0.5	81,693	4.5	95,009	6.6	99,632	-4.0	123,167	8.7
Saba	1,223	-3.5	850	-4.1	551	13.1	870	21.5	855	6.2	1,177	-5.2
St Eustatius	–	–	–	–	–	–	–	–	–	–	–	–
St Lucia	34,186	27.6	29,589	27.0	17,393	18.5	20,624	8.4	14,741	-32.3	26,548	-2.9
St Maarten	41,242	4.3	33,358	-11.2	18,249	-4.9	28,329	4.7	35,363	-1.8	42,919	-5.0
St Vincent & the Grenadines	7,897	-6.6	6,485	-2.8	3,207	-5.5	3,973	-18.1	5,149	-4.7	9,034	-5.9
Suriname	23,949	–	20,373	–	13,535	–	17,175	–	–	–	–	–
Trinidad & Tobago	–	–	–	–	–	–	–	–	–	–	–	–
US Virgin Islands	65,475	7.1	50,941	0.2	27,881	-1.9	38,426	-1.7	48,064	-8.8	63,272	-5.5

*Non-resident air arrivals
**Non-resident hotel registrations only
ᵖPreliminary figures

Note: Figures are subject to revision by reporting countries.
Source: Data supplied by member countries.

Table A5.11 Tourist Arrivals by Main Market, 2010

Destination	Period	United States Tourists	United States % change	Canada Tourists	Canada % change	Europe Tourists	Europe % change	Other Tourists	Other % change
Anguilla	Jan–Dec	38,882	14.1	2,403	18.3	7,558	1.1	13,155	-8.1
Antigua & Barbuda*	Jan–Dec	81,529	-0.7	17,759	37.2	86,101	-7.9	45,916	-0.1
Aruba	Jan–Dec	535,814	1.5	37,702	11.4	76,362	1.8	175,573	-0.1
Bahamas	Jan–Dec	1,095,272	2.5	119,230	11.4	78,018	-1.0	75,533	4.3
Barbados[P]	Jan–Dec	134,969	10.4	72,351	13.5	212,276	-3.8	112,584	0.7
Belize	Jan–Dec	145,080	4.0	17,892	4.0	28,548	-3.6	46,638	1.7
Bermuda*	Jan–Dec	166,016	-3.8	30,402	22.3	28,498	-1.6	7,346	-21.8
Bonaire	Jan–Jun	14,494	5.7	1,417	40.6	15,273	3.7	3,989	1.0
Cancun (Mexico)**	Jan–Dec	1,661,768	10.5	126,587	3.0	141,162	-10.3	176,968	63.8
Cayman Islands	Jan–Dec	228,461	6.2	19,499	13.0	19,850	3.8	20,462	-0.4
Cuba[#]	Jan–Dec	—	—	945,248	3.3	809,514	-3.4	776,982	14.8
Curaçao	Jan–Dec	48,672	35.4	7,600	17.2	163,546	9.6	121,838	-30.4
Dominica[P]	Jan–Dec	19,266	5.9	2,858	9.2	10,724	-7.5	43,669	2.7
Dominican Republic*	Jan–Dec	1,226,367	6.8	659,063	2.0	1,184,269	-4.9	1,054,844	10.9
Grenada[P]	Jan–Dec	20,038	-5.1	6,187	-1.7	33,452	-6.2	46,479	-7.6
Guyana	Jan–Dec	82,182	6.8	25,058	5.2	8,217	-0.7	34,684	7.6
Jamaica	Jan–Dec	1,242,943	6.0	325,191	12.0	271,315	-2.0	82,229	-9.8
Montserrat	Jan–Sep	1,134	6.7	279	18.2	988	-19.7	1,614	5.1
Puerto Rico**	Jan–Dec	1,231,748	4.9	19,216	18.6	28,802	5.5	90,048	7.5

(continued)

Table A5.11 Tourist Arrivals by Main Market, 2010 (*continued*)

Destination	Period	United States		Canada		Europe		Other	
		Tourists	% change	Tourists	% change	Tourists	% change	Tourists	% change
Saba	Jan–Dec	3,775	-0.2	1,065	13.1	6,335	2.5	1,152	9.5
St Lucia	Jan–Dec	129,085	30.8	32,154	12.6	85,695	-1.3	59,003	-8.4
St Eustatius	Jan–Jun	1,245	-7.3	125	-8.1	3,952	24.5	1,377	2.2
St Maarten	Jan–Dec	236,379	-1.7	33,498	3.8	101,118	2.8	72,141	4.3
St Vincent & the Grenadines	Jan–Dec	21,551	6.9	7,208	5.7	17,665	-7.5	26,054	-11.3
Suriname	Jan–Oct	5,124	–	1,402	–	88,951	–	70,329	–
Trinidad & Tobago	Jan–May	74,229	-4.6	19,510	-9.3	23,524	-17.9	40,854	-13.9
US Virgin Islands**	Jan–Dec	696,878	-3.9	6,601	-36.6	14,446	-12.3	31,104	-12.1

*Non-resident air arrivals
**Non-resident hotel registrations only
ᵖPreliminary figures
#US total included in Other

Note: Figures are subject to revision by reporting countries; USVI reported figures in this table are hotel registrations and their reported stay-over totals are air arrivals.
Source: Data supplied by member countries.

Table A5.12 Cruise Passenger Arrivals, 2010 and 2009

Destination	Period	2010	2009	% change
Antigua & Barbuda	Jan–Dec	557,635	712,792	−21.8
Aruba	Jan–Dec	569,424	606,768	−6.2
Bahamas	Jan–Dec	3,803,122	3,255,780	16.8
Barbados	Jan–Dec	664,747	635,212	4.6
Belize	Jan–Dec	764,628	705,219	8.4
Bermuda	Jan–Dec	347,931	318,528	9.2
Bonaire	Jan–May	154,016	148,055	4.0
British Virgin Islands	Jan–Dec	501,451	530,327	−5.4
Cayman Islands	Jan–Dec	1,597,838	1,520,372	5.1
Cozumel (Mexico)	Jan–Dec	2,911,146	2,221,729	31.0
Curaçao	Jan–Dec	383,036	423,088	−9.5
Dominica	Jan–Dec	517,979	532,352	−2.7
Dominican Republic	Jan–Dec	352,539	496,728	−29.0
Grenada	Jan–Dec	333,556	342,852	−2.7
Jamaica[P]	Jan–Dec	909,619	922,349	−1.4
Martinique	Jan–Dec	74,634	69,749	7.0
Puerto Rico	Jan–Oct	955,329	949,798	0.6
St Lucia	Jan–Dec	670,043	699,306	−4.2
St Maarten	Jan–Dec	1,512,618	1,215,146	24.5
St Vincent & the Grenadines	Jan–Dec	110,955	149,464	−25.8
Trinidad & Tobago	Jan–May	71,802	83,709	−14.2
US Virgin Islands	Jan–Dec	1,858,946	1,582,264	17.5

[P]Preliminary figures
Note: Figures are subject to revision by reporting countries.
Source: Data supplied by member countries.

Table A5.13 Tourist (Stop-over) Arrivals in 2011

Destination	Period	Tourist Arrivals	% Change Overall	% Change Winter[#]	% Change Summer[#]
Anguilla	Jan–Jul	44,937	12.0	11.2	13.1
Antigua & Barbuda[*]	Jan–Nov	217,261	5.1	6.5	4.0
Aruba	Jan–Nov	789,861	5.6	5.0	6.0
Bahamas	Jan–Oct	1,121,789	−3.7	−0.6	−5.9
Barbados[P]	Jan–Nov	512,783	7.0	9.9	5.1
Belize[P]	Jan–Nov	223,319	3.0	4.3	1.9
Bermuda[*]	Jan–Sep	191,203	3.3	9.3	1.2
British Virgin Islands	Jan–Oct	276,872	0.5	3.9	−3.1
Cancun (Mexico)[**]	Jan–Sep	1,671,710	0.7	−2.5	3.9
Cayman Islands	Jan–Nov	275,738	7.3	8.2	6.6
Cuba	Jan–Nov	2,440,306	7.6	11.9	3.8
Curaçao	Jan–Nov	352,417	13.9	16.3	12.6
Dominica[P]	Jan–Nov	65,976	−4.1	−1.5	−5.6
Dominican Republic[*]	Jan–Nov	3,862,045	4.0	5.2	3.1
Grenada[*n]	Jan–Oct	94,770	–	–	–
Guyana	Jan–Oct	126,313	0.8	−4.8	4.1
Jamaica	Jan–Sep	1,501,782	2.0	5.1	−0.8
Martinique	Jan–Oct	410,958	2.6	4.1	1.4
Montserrat	Jan–Sep	3,992	−0.6	4.9	−5.6
Puerto Rico[**]	Jan–Oct	1,199,876	4.4	4.6	4.2
St Lucia	Jan–Aug	212,486	−6.2	2.1	−14.1
St Maarten[*]	Jan–Sep	316,155	−6.1	−3.6	−8.8
St Vincent & the Grenadines[P]	Jan–Nov	64,997	2.4	3.7	1.6
Suriname	Jan–Oct	176,817	6.6	5.1	7.6
US Virgin Islands	Jan–Oct	555,273	−4.2	−3.9	−4.6

[*]Non-resident air arrivals
[**]Non-resident hotel registrations only
[P]Preliminary figures
[#]Winter: January to April; summer: May to December.
Note: Figures are subject to revision by reporting countries.
Source: Data supplied by member countries.

Table A5.14a Tourist Arrivals by Month, 2011

Destination	January Tourists	January % change	February Tourists	February % change	March Tourists	March % change	April Tourists	April % change	May Tourists	May % change	June Tourists	June % change
Anguilla	5,707	9.6	6,463	9.7	7,357	5.6	7,230	20.5	6,072	14.9	5,426	23.8
Antigua & Barbuda*	23,813	7.1	23,826	6.5	24,734	-4.5	24,760	19.7	17,346	-2.1	17,025	9.2
Aruba	74,623	4.5	68,755	1.5	76,938	-0.4	79,589	15.0	65,268	1.4	67,999	12.9
Bahamas	84,003	-8.0	106,221	1.2	152,360	-3.5	138,806	6.5	116,919	-8.1	142,053	-2.4
Barbados[P]	52,194	8.0	51,793	6.6	53,257	3.3	51,442	24.4	41,699	-10.9	38,490	9.4
Belize	23,592	5.3	23,854	0.4	28,643	-3.6	23,585	19.8	19,289	-0.9	21,755	2.0
Bermuda*	6,677	5.5	8,907	2.7	15,240	9.9	20,481	13.4	26,913	-4.0	33,068	5.3
British Virgin Islands	32,887	4.7	35,015	7.3	42,233	0.6	37,133	4.0	27,863	1.1	27,373	-12.9
Cancun (Mexico)**	201,672	-3.9	195,888	-5.1	220,111	-0.6	193,867	-0.2	165,944	-1.7	180,397	-7.8
Cayman Islands	26,445	5.8	29,911	10.0	37,466	5.1	30,824	12.7	23,440	7.4	26,960	7.6
Cuba	296,060	15.8	293,047	13.8	315,454	5.7	275,410	13.4	183,818	7.2	174,076	6.1
Curaçao	30,092	7.2	31,342	16.5	33,115	11.2	34,242	31.8	28,044	5.6	28,909	25.3
Dominica[P]	5,951	-5.6	5,124	-30.2	7,478	24.5	6,346	12.7	5,135	-36.9	4,794	26.5
Dominican Republic*	409,539	1.3	407,615	3.0	439,613	4.2	378,009	14.0	297,788	0.3	346,727	-0.5
Grenada*n	11,782	—	9,375	—	10,093	—	9,526	—	7,399	—	8,054	—
Guyana	9,559	3.0	9,365	-1.4	10,087	-25.3	15,516	7.1	10,939	13.2	12,525	7.5
Jamaica	174,144	8.1	175,114	4.6	204,046	1.3	179,444	7.5	146,583	-2.1	166,545	1.4
Martinique	43,805	4.3	45,068	-2.8	53,198	1.2	46,707	15.4	35,169	2.6	29,855	4.0
Montserrat	541	23.5	425	0.0	634	7.5	415	-11.1	342	-6.8	416	4.3

(continued)

Table A5.14a Tourist Arrivals by Month, 2011 (*continued*)

Destination	January		February		March		April		May		June	
	Tourists	% change	Tourists	% change	Tourists	% change	Tourists	% change	Tourists	% change	Tourists	% change
Puerto Rico[**]	127,980	1.8	138,144	4.9	150,584	2.2	139,567	9.7	112,094	6.8	112,993	5.2
St Lucia	27,010	3.6	26,221	-5.9	29,421	-0.5	29,198	12.4	24,033	-20.4	21,518	-6.4
St Maarten[*]	46,929	0.8	42,892	-4.8	44,204	-4.8	38,232	-6.1	29,367	-15.0	28,556	-6.0
St Vincent & the Grenadines	6,200	4.5	6,368	-0.5	6,391	-16.2	7,474	35.1	4,985	5.3	6,960	7.0
Suriname	14,554	-1.5	14,979	-8.2	18,066	10.8	19,344	18.7	14,981	3.4	16,403	30.3
US Virgin Islands	67,196	1.5	63,802	-3.9	74,716	-7.7	63,449	-4.6	49,153	-14.2	56,699	-5.0

[*] Non-resident air arrivals
[**] Non-resident hotel registrations only
[P] Preliminary figures
[n] New series

Note: Figures are subject to revision by reporting countries.
Source: Data supplied by member countries.

413

Table A5.14b Tourist Arrivals by Month, 2011

Destination	July Tourists	July % change	August Tourists	August % change	September Tourists	September % change	October Tourists	October % change	November Tourists	November % change	December Tourists	December % change
Anguilla	6,682	4.4	—	—	—	—	—	—	—	—	—	—
Antigua & Barbuda*	23,522	6.8	18,079	6.2	10,474	5.4	14,974	2.0	18,708	1.3	—	—
Aruba	81,070	7.6	79,687	8.8	63,906	9.3	65,227	-2.7	66,799	5.4	—	—
Bahamas	154,865	-1.2	103,389	-13.8	57,797	0.9	65,376	-11.9	—	—	—	—
Barbados^P	58,237	13.1	49,961	19.3	29,144	-3.1	39,358	0.8	47,208	5.3	—	—
Belize	24,042	2.6	17,735	-3.8	9,823	6.2	12,093	1.4	18,908	8.3	—	—
Bermuda*	33,516	-1.0	28,370	-0.2	18,031	9.0	—	—	—	—	—	—
British Virgin Islands	33,153	-1.2	17,789	-5.4	7,913	1.0	15,513	6.8	—	—	—	—
Cancun (Mexico)**	211,127	9.3	173,821	8.1	128,883	17.5	—	—	—	—	—	—
Cayman Islands	31,407	7.5	20,017	4.8	9,977	4.3	14,356	4.1	24,935	7.7	—	—
Cuba	209,643	1.6	174,359	0.9	142,322	5.8	161,514	-1.9	214,603	7.1	—	—
Curaçao	33,266	11.5	36,408	18.3	31,144	16.3	32,461	1.1	33,394	13.5	—	—
Dominica^P	9,941	12.6	7,314	1.5	3,535	-6.7	7,716^P	-1.6	2,642^P	-32.8	—	—
Dominican Republic*	433,016	3.7	328,344	-1.4	239,706	9.3	265,840	7.5	315,848	6.3	—	—
Grenada*^n	11,553	—	13,297	—	5,446	—	8,245	—	—	—	—	—
Guyana	21,908	3.3	16,154	-3.9	9,408	2.0	10,852	8.2	—	—	—	—
Jamaica	202,493	-1.0	155,133	-2.7	98,280	1.3	—	—	—	—	—	—
Martinique	46,829	1.6	54,770	0.5	28,587	0.5	26,970	-0.1	—	—	—	—
Montserrat	572	25.7	399	3.4	248	-49.2	—	—	—	—	—	—

(continued)

Table A5.14b Tourist Arrivals by Month, 2011 (*continued*)

Destination	July Tourists	July % change	August Tourists	August % change	September Tourists	September % change	October Tourists	October % change	November Tourists	November % change	December Tourists	December % change
Puerto Rico[**]	129,573	11.2	118,547	5.9	80,376	-1.6	90,018	-5.3	–	–	–	–
St Lucia	29,707	-13.1	25,378	-14.2	–	–	–	–	–	–	–	–
St Maarten[*]	37,424	-9.3	30,724	-7.9	17,827	-2.3	–	–	–	–	–	–
St Vincent & the Grenadines	7,366	-6.7	6,247	-3.7	3,488	8.8	4,416	11.2	5,102[P]	-0.9	–	–
Suriname	23,862	-0.4	21,683	6.4	14,976	10.6	17,969	4.6	–	–	–	–
US Virgin Islands	65,113	-0.6	47,460	-6.8	27,816	-0.2	39,869	3.8	–	–	–	–

[*]Non-resident air arrivals
[**]Non-resident hotel registrations only
[P]Preliminary figures
[n]New series
Note: Figures are subject to revision by reporting countries.
Source: Data supplied by member countries.

Table A5.15 Tourist Arrivals by Main Market, 2011

Destination	Period	United States Tourists	% change	Canada Tourists	% change	Europe Tourists	% change	Other Tourists	% change
Anguilla	Jan–Jul	30,147	15.2	1,924	19.6	4,734	4.7	8,132	3.9
Antigua & Barbuda*	Jan–Nov	75,741	2.3	20,001	26.5	83,047	4.9	38,472	2.1
Aruba	Jan–Nov	488,131	-1.0	35,223	7.8	75,202	7.5	191,305	26.0
Bahamas	Jan–Oct	890,227	-5.5	96,713	3.1	64,854	-0.9	69,995	9.3
Barbados[P]	Jan–Nov	128,622	6.1	63,540	-1.1	203,090	6.9	117,531	13.4
Belize[P]	Jan–Nov	139,402	6.8	17,154	9.8	27,189	1.0	39,574	-9.6
Bermuda*	Jan–Sep	142,588	5.5	22,218	-2.6	21,081	-3.1	5,316	-2.0
Cancun (Mexico)**	Jan–Sep	1,307,091	0.6	128,017	34.3	121,886	3.9	114,716	-22.9
Cayman Islands	Jan–Nov	218,850	6.5	21,248	32.1	18,572	6.5	17,068	-4.1
Cuba[#]	Jan–Nov	–	–	899,608	6.6	740,010	1.1	800,688	15.6
Curaçao	Jan–Nov	57,284	29.5	7,272	13.9	154,453	2.9	133,408	22.9
Dominica[P]	Jan–Nov	16,341	-7.1	2,664	3.2	9,820	1.4	37,151	-4.6
Dominican Republic*	Jan–Nov	1,173,773	3.7	581,982	0.9	1,057,605	-1.2	1,048,685	12.3
Grenada*[n]	Jan–Oct	19,119	–	5,247	–	27,640	–	42,764	–
Guyana	Jan–Oct	68,240	-1.3	19,311	-6.9	6,854	-1.6	31,908	11.9
Jamaica	Jan–Sep	954,483	-1.7	285,934	20.6	190,142	-6.7	71,223	18.3
Puerto Rico**	Jan–Oct	1,086,427	4.8	18,260	14.5	22,180	11.6	73,009	-5.4
Montserrat	Jan–Sep	1,150	1.4	221	-20.8	1,154	16.8	1,467	-9.1

(continued)

Table A5.15 Tourist Arrivals by Main Market, 2011 (*continued*)

Destination	Period	United States		Canada		Europe		Other	
		Tourists	% change	Tourists	% change	Tourists	% change	Tourists	% change
St Lucia	Jan–Aug	86,848	−10.2	25,511	4.2	60,236	−1.4	39,891	−10.1
St Maarten*	Jan–Sep	165,305	−10.0	23,260	−3.5	74,606	−1.2	52,984	−0.4
St Vincent & the Grenadines[p]	Jan–Nov	18,313	−2.5	5,717	−4.5	17,986	16.5	22,981	−1.1
Suriname	Jan–Oct	6,365	24.2	1,549	10.5	86,196	−3.1	82,707	17.6
US Virgin Islands**	Jan–Sep	472,187	−15.4	5,296	6.0	12,656	11.8	26,933	15.2

*Non-resident air arrivals
**Non-resident hotel registrations only
[p]Preliminary figures
[n]New series
[#]US total included in Other

Note: Figures are subject to revision by reporting countries; USVI reported figures in this table are hotel registrations and their reported stay-over totals are air arrivals.
Source: Data supplied by member countries.

Table A5.16 Cruise Passenger Arrivals, 2011 and 2010

Destination	Period	2011	2010	% change
Antigua & Barbuda	Jan–Aug	399,490	352,009	13.5
Aruba	Jan–Oct	423,534	398,418	6.3
Bahamas	Jan–Oct	3,320,720	3,089,036	7.5
Barbados	Jan–Nov	535,550	541,728	−1.1
Belize	Jan–Nov	631,177	655,739	−3.7
Bermuda	Jan–Sep	349,198	321,295	8.7
British Virgin Islands	Jan–Oct	368,892	382,847	−3.6
Cayman Islands	Jan–Nov	1,242,024	1,422,245	−12.7
Cozumel (Mexico)	Jan–Oct	2,273,290	2,286,734	−0.6
Curaçao	Jan–Nov	311,366	328,413	−5.2
Dominica	Jan–Nov	276,112	454,568	−39.3
Dominican Republic	Jan–Sep	234,272	239,513	−2.2
Grenada	Jan–Oct	233,921	218,169	7.2
Jamaica	Jan–Oct	848,237	725,782	16.9
Martinique	Jan–Oct	18,303	57,957	−68.4
Puerto Rico	Jan–Jul	735,066	769,938	−4.5
St Lucia	Jan–Aug	414,660	458,486	9.6
St Maarten	Jan–Jun	970,759	850,462	14.1
St Vincent & the Grenadines	Jan–Nov	71,029	93,386	−23.9
US Virgin Islands	Jan–Oct	1,553,192	1,433,645	8.3

Note: Figures are subject to revision by reporting countries.
Source: Data supplied by member countries.

Appendix 6
Excerpts from a Speech by Sir Ronald Sanders in June 2007 at the Watershed Media Centre in Bristol, England

Let it be said first of all that the ACP countries were foolish to allow the European Commission to force them into separate regional negotiations on Economic Partnership Agreements to succeed the Lome and Cotonou agreements.

The strength of the ACP in successfully negotiating the Lome and Cotonou agreements rested firmly on the foundation of their unity; once that unity was untied, the door was open for intrigue, for manipulation and, ultimately for coercion. The Caribbean tried hard to preserve that unity; it was francophone Africa that led the way to fragmentation.

But, the European Commission was morally wrong for insisting upon separate regional negotiations. The advantage that the European Union gains now in trying to force agreements that are unhappily negotiated may come back to haunt it eventually. For, if the terms of the agreement are unfair, they will not long endure.

Indeed, they may promote resistance in other vital areas of international life.

The EU has been pushing ACP countries to conclude Economic Partnership Agreements (EPAs) by the end of the year, claiming that preferences which they now enjoy will not be approved by the WTO come the beginning of next year.

This abdication of preferences for ACP countries would be a contravention of the EU's obligation under the existing Cotonou agreement which requires the EU to provide at least equivalent market access on 1 January 2008.[1] But, it has become obvious that two key elements that were envisaged when the EPAs were proposed are being abandoned by the EU. There are a strong development component and a genuine partnership.

The European Commission negotiators have dismissed pro-development proposals from the ACP group, and have sought to impose upon the negotiations, terms which were rejected by developing countries in the wider trade negotiations in the WTO.

In a publication, entitled "Global Europe: Competing in the World," the European commission states that 'Free Trade Agreements if approached with care, can build on WTO and other international rules by going further and faster in promoting openness and integration, by tackling issues which are not ready for multilateral discussion and by preparing the ground for the next level of multilateral liberalization."

The publication states specifically: "Many key issues, including investment, public procurement, competition which remain outside the WTO at this time can be addressed through FTAs."

It is clear, therefore, that what the EU could not achieve in the failed WTO negotiations, they are ready to impose on ACP States through bilateral bullying.

These issues of public procurement, investment competition are called "the Singapore issues" because they first came up at a meeting in Singapore. And, what the European Commission is demanding is the right, without restriction, for European companies to compete in ACP countries on a equal basis with much smaller and less well resourced local companies for public and private sector projects; and the right to invest in any sector of the economies of ACP countries including the provision of services.

If the EU is successful in these demands, local companies in ACP countries could be faced with competition before they are ready to cope with it and, as a consequence, find themselves squeezed out of their own domestic markets. Local ownership would be minimized, and local populations could be relegated, over time, to the role of workers only.

The EU also wants trade in goods and services opened up on a reciprocal basis. This means that the small ACP countries would be treated as if they were the equals of Europe in trade and investment terms despite the huge differences in the level of their development and their financial capacity.

In short, the ACP countries could be swamped by Europe for despite the talk about "reciprocity," it simply is not possible for ACP companies to compete within their own countries (let alone in Europe) with much larger and well resourced European companies.

It would be a case of giants and dwarves or sharks and sardines.

Indeed, in as much as the European Commissioners may not want to hear it, and they would strenuously deny it, the risk is that these EPAs could well be the start of a new era of colonialism in which the economies of ACP countries are held in thrall to European companies.

Of course, while the EU is banging down doors to Caribbean markets, it is slamming shut its own doors to immigration from outside its own area.

So, effectively, European capital and services would move into Caribbean countries to derive profits for repatriation, but Caribbean labour would be trapped in the confines of economies increasingly controlled by expatriate owners.

Are there not echoes here of a bygone age, and of another kind of confinement? Another kind of bondage?

The trade minister of Barbados, Dame Billie Miller, who is a seasoned campaigner in all of the trade negotiations in which the Caribbean has been involved, particularly with the EU and the WTO made a telling observation recently. She declared that regional negotiators remained firmly convinced that preferential treatment must be given to small vulnerable economies and developing countries, as there is a need to protect sensitive sectors and industries from rapid liberalisation.

She went on to say: "Europe and the other OECD countries gave themselves since the Second World War – virtually the better part of 60 years – to arrive at where they would like us (the Caribbean) to be. And they expect us to do this in 10 to 15 years. It is just a human and physical impossibility."[2]

And what was being said in the Caribbean had resonances in Africa. A Namibian trade analyst, Wallie Roux, lost his job because he suggested that the EU was trying to browbeat southern African governments into signing an EPA before they had a chance to analyse its consequences.

Roux had urged the SADC governments not to capitulate to demands that they sign an EPA swiftly. He wrote: "If you are unwise enough to rush for a deadline without looking at the content of the agreement, then you are signing away your life."

I use Dame Billie's remarks and Mr Roux's observations to point out the growing unease of ACP countries with the hurried pace at which the EU wants to complete the EPAs.

Theirs are not the only expressions of discontent; they are many others – some cast in language more virulent and more vexed, and others couched in the language of scholarship and research but no less indignant. Among them are NGOs such as Christian Aid, Action Aid, Traidcraft and Tearfund. Collectively in a well researched document, they have concluded that "There is overwhelming evidence to show that the European Commission, mandated by EU member states to negotiate on their behalf, is failing to conduct negotiations in a way that will promote development and is abusing the principle of partnership . . . the EC has consistently broken the spirit and the letter of the Cotonou Agreement."[3]

If Commonwealth Caribbean countries acquiesce to EU demands for full reciprocity in trade and for the opening of their markets to European companies for unrestricted competition in the provision of services and for the right to procurement for contracts in the public and private sectors, they will face double jeopardy.

For, in any free trade agreement that the United States might enter with CARICOM countries, US negotiators will demand no less favourable treatment than is accorded to the European Union, and CARICOM countries will have no choice but to give it.

In such circumstances, CARICOM will lose what little control they still have of their economies and they will also lose any semblance of autonomy in their decision making.

A new kind of colonialism will be real.

And, if this new kind of colonialism does materialize, CARICOM governments will have contributed to it by their own failure to band together to resist it.

No one CARICOM government, no one CARICOM country can alone navigate the turbulent sea of today's international economy. Nation-states much larger than the tiny states of the Commonwealth Caribbean have sought economic salvation in larger groupings.

The EU might have been formed to stop the scourge on internecine warfare in Europe, but it evolved to counter the economic dominance of the United States and to secure for its member states a stake in the global economy.

Had they not pooled vital aspects of their sovereignty into the European Union, no one European nation would have matched the power of the United States, coped with the growth of China or rivaled it in the global market place.

If this observation is valid for the large states of Europe, how much more valid it is for the tiny countries of the Caribbean.

The delay by CARICOM of seventeen years in implementing a single market to which they committed themselves in 1986 has set back the region enormously.

Had they acted sooner, Caribbean economies would by now have completed the process of adjustment that is still necessary today; Caribbean borders would have been eliminated for Caribbean people; laws harmonized and capital markets created; businesses would have merged and become more competitive.

CARICOM governments are still to act on a recommendation made in 1992 to establish a CARICOM Commission to oversee a single market, CARICOM's functional cooperation programmes and CARICOM's external relations. The recommendation was made by the West Indian Commission which they charged with charting the road map for CARICOM's future.[4]

Had action been taken on this, CARICOM countries would by now have had a single, effective and well-supported negotiating machinery in the World Trade Organization and in negotiations with the EU, with the US and others.

CARICOM countries could have fielded one team speaking for all – just as the European Commissioners speak with one voice the joint position of their numerous states.

Instead, the negotiations with the EU and in the WTO have had to cater for factional differences and have lacked coherence.

The urge to hold on to as much power as possible has been too strong for national governments to relinquish; such sovereignty as they have ceded to a common pool has been extracted only by their incapacity to cope with the demands of the international environment, and even then only when the demands have reached a crisis.

In conclusion, the risks of a new colonialism for Commonwealth Caribbean countries are here and now.

The present international economic environment in which there is a scramble for control of resources and for advantage in the world markets would have brought these risks in any event.

The sadness for CARICOM countries is that by failing to put in place the much needed structures of unity, they have weakened their own chances of resisting these risks, and made themselves more vulnerable to a new colonialism.

Notes

[1] "Partnership under Pressure: An Assessment of the European Union's Conduct in the EPA Negotiations", May 2007.
[2] Opening statement at a trade policy seminar, University of the West Indies, Cave Hill, Barbados, reported in the *Nation*, Barbados.
[3] "Partnership under Pressure", 5n9.
[4] See *Time for Action: Report of the West Indian Commission* (University of the West Indies Press, Jamaica, 1993).

Appendix 7
LIAT Fares and Taxes Tables

	FARE	FARE	TAXES	TAXES	LIAT FIS	LIAT FIS	TOTAL	TOTAL	TAXES AS A % OF TOTAL FARE/	TAXES AS A % OF TOTAL FARE/	FIS AS A % OF TOTAL FARE	FIS AS A % OF TOTAL FARE	INCREASE / DECREASE % 2011
ORIGIN ANU	2011	2008	2011	2008	2011	2008	2011	2008	2011	2008	2011	2008	OVER 2008
AXA	216.00	156.00	45.00	20.00	25.00	45.00	286.00	221.00	15.73	9.05	8.74	20.36	29.41
BGI	284.00	248.00	106.20	78.70	40.00	27.50	430.20	354.20	24.69	22.22	9.30	7.76	21.46
CUR	516.00	456.00	25.00	35.00	40.00	45.00	581.00	536.00	4.30	6.53	6.88	8.40	8.40
DOM	212.00	152.00	40.90	16.40	25.00	45.00	277.90	213.40	14.72	7.69	9.00	21.09	30.22
EIS	252.00	192.00	52.00	12.00	35.00	45.00	339.00	249.00	15.34	4.82	10.32	18.07	36.14
FDF	290.07	230.00	77.61	35.28	35.00	45.00	402.68	310.28	19.27	11.37	8.69	14.50	29.78
GEO	516.00	456.00	102.40	73.40	40.00	45.00	658.40	574.40	15.55	12.78	6.08	7.83	14.62
GND	376.00	316.00	71.83	53.71	40.00	45.00	487.83	414.71	14.72	12.95	8.20	10.85	17.63
NEV	188.00	128.00	58.90	17.80	25.00	45.00	271.90	190.80	21.66	9.33	9.19	23.58	42.51
POS	376.00	316.00	104.85	59.90	40.00	45.00	520.85	420.90	20.13	14.23	7.68	10.69	23.75
PTP	274.16	214.00	60.70	36.91	25.00	45.00	359.86	295.91	16.87	12.47	6.95	15.21	21.61
SDQ	414.00	345.00	173.84	125.65	40.00	45.00	627.84	515.65	27.69	24.37	6.37	8.73	21.76
SJU	260.00	190.00	44.00	33.95	35.00	45.00	339.00	268.95	12.98	12.62	10.32	16.73	26.05
SKB	188.00	128.00	90.80	22.80	25.00	45.00	303.80	195.80	29.89	11.64	8.23	22.98	55.16
SLU	278.00	218.00	116.05	56.55	35.00	45.00	429.05	319.55	27.05	17.70	8.16	14.08	34.27
STT	274.00	204.00	37.50	24.50	35.00	45.00	346.50	273.50	10.82	8.96	10.10	16.45	26.69
STX	274.00	204.00	37.50	24.50	35.00	45.00	346.50	273.50	10.82	8.96	10.10	16.45	26.69
SVD	300.00	245.00	55.00	12.00	35.00	45.00	390.00	302.00	14.10	3.97	8.97	14.90	29.14
SXM	228.00	168.00	69.35	49.35	25.00	45.00	322.35	262.35	21.51	18.81	7.76	17.15	22.87

							AXA						
	FARE	FARE	TAXES	TAXES	LIAT FIS	LIAT FIS	TOTAL	TOTAL	TAXES AS A % OF TOTAL FARE/	TAXES AS A % OF TOTAL FARE/	FIS AS A % OF TOTAL FARE	FIS AS A % OF TOTAL FARE	INCREASE / DECREASE % 2011
ORIGIN	2011	2008	2011	2008	2011	2008	2011	2008	2011	2008	2011	2008	OVER 2008
ANU	216.00	156.00	66.60	35.60	25.00	45.00	307.60	236.60	21.65	15.05	8.13	19.02	30.01
BGI	430.00	382.00	126.76	95.15	40.00	27.50	596.76	504.65	21.24	18.85	6.70	5.45	18.25
DOM	300.00	245.00	42.50	43.00	35.00	45.00	377.50	333.00	11.26	12.91	9.27	13.51	13.36
EIS	200.00	145.00	47.00	32.00	25.00	45.00	272.00	222.00	17.28	14.41	9.19	20.27	22.52
GEO	680.00	620.00	137.00	183.00	40.00	45.00	857.00	848.00	15.99	21.58	4.67	5.31	1.06
GND	464.00	454.00	74.33	37.51	40.00	45.00	578.33	536.51	12.85	6.99	6.92	8.39	7.79
NEV	220.00	160.00	44.50	26.00	25.00	45.00	289.50	231.00	15.37	11.26	8.64	19.48	25.32
POS	464.00	454.00	113.05	48.10	40.00	45.00	617.05	547.10	18.32	8.79	6.48	8.23	12.79
SKB	220.00	160.00	89.00	31.00	25.00	45.00	334.00	236.00	26.65	13.14	7.49	19.07	41.53
SLU	368.00	308.00	117.79	88.29	40.00	45.00	525.79	441.29	22.40	20.01	7.61	10.20	19.15
STT	230.00	160.00	32.50	29.50	25.00	45.00	287.50	234.50	11.30	12.58	8.70	19.19	22.60
SVD	464.00	454.00	53.39	20.00	40.00	45.00	557.39	519.00	9.58	3.85	7.18	8.67	7.40

							BGI						
	FARE	FARE	TAXES	TAXES	LIAT FIS	LIAT FIS	TOTAL	TOTAL	TAXES AS A % OF TOTAL FARE/	TAXES AS A % OF TOTAL FARE/	FIS AS A % OF TOTAL FARE	FIS AS A % OF TOTAL FARE	INCREASE / DECREASE % 2011
ORIGIN	2011	2008	2011	2008	2011	2008	2011	2008	2011	2008	2011	2008	OVER 2008
ANU	284.00	248.00	84.90	66.30	40.00	27.50	408.90	341.80	20.76	22.22	9.78	8.05	19.63
AXA	430.00	382.00	51.50	66.50	40.00	27.50	521.50	476.00	9.88	13.97	7.67	5.78	9.56
CUR	270.00	222.00	39.00	31.50	40.00	27.50	349.00	281.00	11.17	6.53	11.46	9.79	24.20
DOM	220.00	172.00	48.00	44.40	35.00	27.50	303.00	243.90	15.84	7.69	11.55	11.28	24.23
EIS	392.00	355.00	58.00	38.50	40.00	27.50	490.00	421.00	11.84	4.82	8.16	6.53	16.39
FDF	258.24	210.00	71.42	61.78	25.00	27.50	354.66	299.28	20.14	11.37	7.05	9.19	18.50
GEO	270.00	222.00	72.00	64.80	40.00	27.50	382.00	314.30	18.85	12.78	10.47	8.75	21.54
GND	208.00	178.00	70.83	66.40	35.00	27.50	313.83	271.90	22.57	12.95	11.15	10.11	15.42
NEV	372.00	326.00	83.70	84.10	40.00	27.50	495.70	437.60	16.89	9.33	8.07	6.28	13.28
POS	226.00	178.00	88.85	65.70	35.00	27.50	349.85	271.20	25.40	14.23	10.00	10.14	29.00
PTP	389.19	345.00	67.20	58.41	35.00	27.50	491.39	430.91	13.68	12.47	7.12	6.38	14.04
SDQ	616.00	578.00	214.26	215.23	40.00	27.50	870.26	820.73	24.62	24.37	4.60	3.35	6.03
SJU	486.00	428.00	50.50	50.45	40.00	27.50	576.50	505.95	8.76	12.62	6.94	5.44	13.94
SKB	348.00	300.00	113.30	131.50	40.00	27.50	501.30	459.00	22.60	11.64	7.98	5.99	9.22
SLU	202.00	154.00	116.85	78.25	25.00	27.50	343.85	259.75	33.98	17.70	7.27	10.59	32.38
STT	462.00	414.00	44.00	61.00	40.00	27.50	546.00	502.50	8.06	8.96	7.33	5.47	8.66
STX	462.00	414.00	44.00	61.00	40.00	27.50	546.00	502.50	8.06	8.96	7.33	5.47	8.66
SVD	200.00	152.00	41.50	39.10	25.00	27.50	266.50	218.60	15.57	3.97	9.38	12.58	21.91

							CUR						
	FARE	FARE	TAXES	TAXES	LIAT FIS	LIAT FIS	TOTAL	TOTAL	TAXES AS A % OF TOTAL FARE/	TAXES AS A % OF TOTAL FARE/	FIS AS A % OF TOTAL FARE	FIS AS A % OF TOTAL FARE	INCREASE / DECREASE % 2011
ORIGIN	2011	2008	2011	2008	2011	2008	2011	2008	2011	2008	2011	2008	OVER 2008
ANU	516.00	456.00	76.60	57.80	40.00	45.00	632.60	558.80	12.11	10.34	6.32	8.05	13.21
BGI	270.00	248.00	93.76	49.15	40.00	27.50	403.76	324.65	23.22	15.14	9.91	8.47	24.37
GND	374.00	316.00	54.33	86.00	40.00	45.00	468.33	447.00	11.60	19.24	8.54	10.07	4.77
POS	366.00	316.00	78.35	48.40	40.00	45.00	484.35	409.40	16.18	11.82	8.26	10.99	18.31
SLU	360.00	218.00	97.19	82.69	40.00	45.00	497.19	345.69	19.55	23.92	8.05	13.02	43.83
SVD	360.00	245.00	33.00	70.00	40.00	45.00	433.00	360.00	7.62	19.44	9.24	12.50	20.28

ORIGIN	FARE 2011	FARE 2008	TAXES 2011	TAXES 2008	LIAT FIS 2011	LIAT FIS 2008	TOTAL 2011	TOTAL 2008	TAXES AS A % OF TOTAL FARE/ 2011	TAXES AS A % OF TOTAL FARE/ 2008	FIS AS A % OF TOTAL FARE 2011	FIS AS A % OF TOTAL FARE 2008	INCREASE / DECREASE % 2011 OVER 2008
							DOM						
ANU	212.00	152.00	46.20	20.50	25.00	45.00	283.20	217.50	16.31	9.43	8.83	20.69	0.00
AXA	300.00	245.00	20.00	25.00	35.00	45.00	355.00	315.00	5.63	7.94	9.86	14.29	12.70
BGI	220.00	172.00	70.00	57.30	35.00	27.50	325.00	256.80	21.54	22.31	10.77	10.71	1.57
EIS	318.00	258.00	27.00	22.00	35.00	45.00	380.00	325.00	7.11	6.77	9.21	13.85	0.00
FDF	263.88	204.00	52.61	35.28	25.00	45.00	341.49	284.28	15.41	12.41	7.32	15.83	0.00
GEO	516.00	456.00	92.40	123.40	40.00	45.00	648.40	624.40	14.25	19.76	6.17	7.21	0.00
GND	318.00	258.00	54.33	57.91	35.00	45.00	407.33	360.91	13.34	16.05	8.59	12.47	0.00
NEV	236.00	176.00	38.60	32.60	25.00	45.00	299.60	253.60	12.88	12.85	8.34	17.74	0.00
POS	332.00	272.00	73.25	53.30	40.00	45.00	445.25	370.30	16.45	14.39	8.98	12.15	0.00
PTP	274.16	214.00	35.70	36.91	25.00	45.00	334.86	295.91	10.66	12.47	7.47	15.21	0.00
SDQ	534.00	460.00	168.04	159.85	40.00	45.00	742.04	664.85	22.65	24.04	5.39	6.77	0.94
SJU	390.00	320.00	19.00	33.95	40.00	45.00	449.00	398.95	4.23	8.51	8.91	11.28	0.49
SKB	236.00	176.00	70.60	37.60	35.00	45.00	341.60	258.60	20.67	14.54	10.25	17.40	0.00
SLU	212.00	152.00	86.09	41.59	25.00	45.00	323.09	238.59	26.65	17.43	7.74	18.86	6.99
STT	344.00	274.00	12.50	34.50	40.00	45.00	396.50	353.50	3.15	9.76	10.09	12.73	0.00
STX	344.00	274.00	12.50	34.50	35.00	45.00	391.50	353.50	3.19	9.76	8.94	12.73	0.00
SVD	248.00	178.00	19.90	43.90	35.00	45.00	302.90	266.90	6.57	16.45	11.55	16.86	0.00
SXM	272.00	202.00	44.35	59.35	35.00	45.00	351.35	306.35	12.62	19.37	9.96	14.69	16.52

ORIGIN	FARE 2011	FARE 2008	TAXES 2011	TAXES 2008	LIAT FIS 2011	LIAT FIS 2008	TOTAL 2011	TOTAL 2008	TAXES AS A % OF TOTAL FARE/ 2011	TAXES AS A % OF TOTAL FARE/ 2008	FIS AS A % OF TOTAL FARE 2011	FIS AS A % OF TOTAL FARE 2008	INCREASE / DECREASE % 2011 OVER 2008
							GND						
ANU	376.00	316.00	109.43	53.71	40.00	45.00	525.43	414.71	20.83	12.95	7.61	10.85	26.70
AXA	464.00	454.00	74.33	0.00	40.00	45.00	578.33	499.00	12.85	9.05	6.92	9.02	15.90
BGI	208.00	178.00	107.23	75.30	35.00	27.50	350.23	280.80	30.62	22.22	9.99	9.79	24.73
CUR	374.00	314.00	54.33	99.60	40.00	45.00	468.33	458.60	11.60	6.53	8.54	9.81	2.12
DOM	318.00	258.00	78.19	51.47	35.00	45.00	431.19	354.47	18.13	7.69	8.12	12.70	21.64
EIS	438.00	378.00	81.33	59.10	40.00	45.00	559.33	482.10	14.54	4.82	7.15	9.33	16.02
FDF	350.40	290.00	94.25	122.38	35.00	45.00	479.65	457.38	19.65	11.37	7.30	9.84	4.87
GEO	374.00	314.00	110.43	119.20	40.00	45.00	524.43	478.20	21.06	12.78	7.63	9.41	9.67
NEV	388.00	328.00	100.63	64.90	40.00	45.00	528.63	437.90	19.04	9.33	7.57	10.28	20.72
POS	206.00	146.00	93.68	41.50	25.00	45.00	324.68	232.50	28.85	14.23	7.70	19.35	39.65
PTP	356.04	296.00	90.03	114.01	35.00	45.00	481.07	455.01	18.71	12.47	7.28	9.89	5.73
SJU	414.00	344.00	73.33	41.05	40.00	45.00	527.33	430.05	13.91	12.62	7.59	10.46	22.62
SKB	390.00	330.00	140.33	70.10	40.00	45.00	570.33	445.10	24.61	11.64	7.01	10.11	28.14
SLU	202.00	142.00	132.18	87.96	25.00	45.00	359.18	274.96	36.80	17.70	6.96	16.37	30.63
STT	414.00	344.00	59.33	56.60	40.00	45.00	513.33	445.60	11.56	8.96	7.79	10.10	15.20
STX	414.00	344.00	66.83	56.60	40.00	45.00	520.83	445.60	12.83	8.96	7.68	10.10	16.88
SVD	196.00	136.00	49.13	18.90	25.00	45.00	270.13	199.90	18.19	3.97	9.25	22.51	35.13
SXM	384.00	324.00	91.18	96.45	40.00	45.00	515.18	465.45	17.70	18.81	7.76	9.67	10.68

	PTP												
	FARE	FARE	TAXES	TAXES	LIAT FIS	LIAT FIS	TOTAL	TOTAL	TAXES AS A % OF TOTAL FARE/	TAXES AS A % OF TOTAL FARE/	FIS AS A % OF TOTAL FARE	FIS AS A % OF TOTAL FARE	INCREASE / DECREASE % 2011
ORIGIN	2011	2008	2011	2008	2011	2008	2011	2008	2011	2008	2011	2008	OVER 2008
ANU	274.16	214.00	88.12	58.31	25.00	45.00	387.28	317.31	22.75	18.38	6.46	14.18	22.05
BGI	389.19	345.00	135.31	93.91	35.00	27.50	559.50	466.41	24.18	20.13	6.26	5.90	19.96
DOM	274.16	214.00	56.27	52.97	25.00	45.00	355.43	311.97	15.83	16.98	7.03	14.42	13.93
EIS	356.04	296.00	84.55	53.91	35.00	45.00	475.59	394.91	17.78	13.65	7.36	11.40	20.43
GND	356.04	296.00	90.03	93.61	35.00	45.00	481.07	434.61	18.71	21.54	7.28	10.35	10.69
POS	422.01	362.00	122.45	98.71	40.00	45.00	584.46	505.71	20.95	19.52	6.84	8.90	15.57
SKB	284.43	224.00	111.14	74.31	25.00	45.00	420.57	343.31	26.43	21.65	5.94	13.11	22.50
SLU	342.45	282.00	131.58	83.77	35.00	45.00	509.03	410.77	25.85	20.39	6.88	10.96	23.92
STT	366.32	296.00	48.20	71.41	35.00	45.00	449.52	412.41	10.72	17.32	7.79	10.91	9.00
SVD	331.77	258.00	64.99	59.81	35.00	45.00	431.76	362.81	15.05	16.49	8.11	12.40	19.00
SXM	297.03	236.00	80.05	91.26	35.00	45.00	412.08	372.26	19.43	24.52	8.49	12.09	10.70

	GEO												
	FARE	FARE	TAXES	TAXES	LIAT FIS	LIAT FIS	TOTAL	TOTAL	TAXES AS A % OF TOTAL FARE/	TAXES AS A % OF TOTAL FARE/	FIS AS A % OF TOTAL FARE	FIS AS A % OF TOTAL FARE	INCREASE / DECREASE % 2011
ORIGIN	2011	2008	2011	2008	2011	2008	2011	2008	2011	2008	2011	2008	OVER 2008
ANU	516.00	456.00	76.60	50.60	40.00	45.00	632.60	551.60	12.11	12.78	6.32	8.16	14.68
AXA	680.00	620.00	35.00	90.00	40.00	45.00	755.00	755.00	4.64	11.92	5.30	5.96	0.00
BGI	270.00	222.00	78.76	64.80	40.00	27.50	388.76	314.30	20.26	22.22	10.29	8.75	23.69
DOM	516.00	456.00	53.70	29.20	40.00	45.00	609.70	530.20	8.81	7.69	6.56	8.49	14.99
EIS	688.00	628.00	27.00	2.00	40.00	45.00	755.00	675.00	3.58	4.82	5.30	6.67	11.85
FDF	356.04	296.00	54.92	55.28	40.00	45.00	450.96	396.28	12.18	11.37	8.87	11.36	13.80
GND	374.00	314.00	54.33	103.50	40.00	45.00	468.33	462.50	11.60	12.95	8.54	9.73	1.26
NEV	590.00	530.00	89.00	98.00	40.00	45.00	719.00	673.00	12.38	9.33	5.56	6.69	6.84
POS	366.00	306.00	93.35	48.40	40.00	45.00	499.35	399.40	18.69	14.23	8.01	11.27	25.03
SKB	540.00	480.00	108.50	68.00	40.00	45.00	688.50	593.00	15.76	11.64	5.81	7.59	16.10
SLU	360.00	300.00	112.19	82.69	40.00	45.00	512.19	427.69	21.90	17.70	7.81	10.52	19.76
STT	670.00	600.00	20.00	94.50	40.00	45.00	730.00	739.50	2.74	8.96	5.48	6.09	-1.28
SVD	360.00	300.00	33.00	70.00	40.00	45.00	433.00	415.00	7.62	3.97	9.24	10.84	4.34
SXM	620.00	560.00	44.35	39.35	40.00	45.00	704.35	644.35	6.30	18.81	5.68	6.98	9.31

	FDF												
	FARE	FARE	TAXES	TAXES	LIAT FIS	LIAT FIS	TOTAL	TOTAL	TAXES AS A % OF TOTAL FARE/	TAXES AS A % OF TOTAL FARE/	FIS AS A % OF TOTAL FARE	FIS AS A % OF TOTAL FARE	INCREASE / DECREASE % 2011
ORIGIN	2011	2008	2011	2008	2011	2008	2011	2008	2011	2008	2011	2008	OVER 2008
ANU	290.07	230.00	104.31	35.28	35.00	45.00	429.38	310.28	24.29	11.37	8.15	14.50	38.38
BGI	258.24	210.00	116.62	78.70	25.00	27.50	399.86	316.20	29.17	24.89	6.25	8.70	26.46
GEO	356.04	296.00	148.33	73.40	40.00	45.00	544.37	414.40	27.25	17.71	7.35	10.86	31.36
GND	350.40	290.00	94.25	53.71	35.00	45.00	479.65	388.71	19.65	13.82	7.30	11.58	23.40
POS	356.04	296.00	129.47	59.90	35.00	45.00	520.51	400.90	24.87	14.94	6.72	11.22	29.84
SKB	313.94	254.00	131.00	22.80	35.00	45.00	479.94	321.80	27.30	7.09	7.29	13.98	49.14
SLU	150.97	182.00	121.44	56.55	25.00	45.00	297.41	283.55	40.83	19.94	8.41	15.87	4.89

	SJU												
	FARE	FARE	TAXES	TAXES	LIAT FIS	LIAT FIS	TOTAL	TOTAL	TAXES AS A % OF TOTAL FARE/	TAXES AS A % OF TOTAL FARE/	FIS AS A % OF TOTAL FARE	FIS AS A % OF TOTAL FARE	INCREASE / DECREASE % 2011
ORIGIN	2011	2008	2011	2008	2011	2008	2011	2008	2011	2008	2011	2008	OVER 2008
ANU	260.00	190.00	70.00	52.75	35.00	45.00	365.00	287.75	19.18	18.33	9.59	15.64	26.85
BGI	486.00	428.00	135.56	114.65	40.00	27.50	661.56	570.15	20.49	20.11	6.05	4.82	16.03
DOM	390.00	320.00	48.26	45.95	40.00	45.00	478.26	410.95	10.09	11.18	8.36	10.95	16.38
GND	414.00	344.00	73.33	78.25	40.00	45.00	527.33	467.25	13.91	16.75	7.59	9.63	12.86
POS	492.00	422.00	116.25	63.10	40.00	45.00	648.25	530.10	17.93	11.90	6.17	8.49	22.29
SKB	278.00	208.00	93.80	59.35	35.00	45.00	406.80	312.35	23.06	19.00	8.60	14.41	30.24
SLU	406.00	336.00	119.65	91.74	40.00	45.00	565.65	472.74	21.15	19.41	7.07	9.52	19.65
SVD	430.00	360.00	40.50	41.95	40.00	45.00	510.50	446.95	7.93	9.39	7.84	10.07	14.22
SXM	266.00	196.00	45.85	88.30	35.00	45.00	346.85	329.30	13.22	26.81	10.09	13.67	5.33

	SDQ												
	FARE	FARE	TAXES	TAXES	LIAT FIS	LIAT FIS	TOTAL	TOTAL	TAXES AS A % OF TOTAL FARE/	TAXES AS A % OF TOTAL FARE/	FIS AS A % OF TOTAL FARE	FIS AS A % OF TOTAL FARE	INCREASE / DECREASE % 2011
ORIGIN	2011	2008	2011	2008	2011	2008	2011	2008	2011	2008	2011	2008	OVER 2008
ANU	414.00	345.00	149.00	125.65	40.00	45.00	603.00	515.65	24.71	24.37	6.63	8.73	16.94
BGI	626.00	578.00	223.66	78.70	40.00	27.50	889.66	684.20	25.14	11.50	4.50	4.02	30.03
DOM	534.00	460.00	122.66	16.40	40.00	45.00	696.66	521.40	17.61	3.15	5.74	8.63	33.61
EIS	474.00	450.00	109.66	12.00	40.00	45.00	623.66	507.00	17.58	2.37	6.41	8.88	23.01
GND	610.00	536.00	136.93	53.71	40.00	45.00	786.93	634.71	17.40	8.46	5.08	7.09	23.98
POS	688.00	614.00	209.25	59.90	40.00	45.00	937.25	718.90	22.33	8.33	4.27	6.26	30.37
SKB	498.00	424.00	174.40	22.80	40.00	45.00	712.40	491.80	24.48	4.64	5.61	9.15	44.86
SLU	544.00	470.00	193.59	56.55	40.00	45.00	777.59	571.55	24.90	9.89	5.14	7.87	36.05
SVD	580.00	506.00	124.29	12.00	40.00	45.00	744.29	563.00	16.70	2.13	5.37	7.99	32.20
SXM	534.00	460.00	126.95	49.35	40.00	45.00	700.95	554.35	18.11	8.90	5.71	8.12	26.45

	STX												
	FARE	FARE	TAXES	TAXES	LIAT FIS	LIAT FIS	TOTAL	TOTAL	TAXES AS A % OF TOTAL FARE/	TAXES AS A % OF TOTAL FARE/	FIS AS A % OF TOTAL FARE	FIS AS A % OF TOTAL FARE	INCREASE / DECREASE % 2011
ORIGIN	2011	2008	2011	2008	2011	2008	2011	2008	2011	2008	2011	2008	OVER 2008
ANU	274.00	204.00	64.90	44.90	35.00	45.00	373.90	293.90	17.36	15.28	9.36	15.31	27.22
BGI	462.00	152.00	124.86	123.10	40.00	27.50	626.86	302.60	19.92	40.68	6.38	9.09	107.16
DOM	344.00	274.00	38.30	55.06	35.00	45.00	417.30	374.06	9.18	14.72	8.39	12.03	11.56
PTP	366.32	296.00	48.20	36.91	35.00	45.00	449.52	377.91	10.72	9.77	7.79	11.91	18.95
SKB	250.00	180.00	98.85	37.50	35.00	45.00	383.85	262.50	25.75	14.29	9.12	17.14	46.23
SLU	404.00	334.00	132.34	94.75	40.00	45.00	576.34	473.75	22.96	20.00	6.94	9.50	21.65
SVD	408.00	344.00	71.60	84.75	40.00	45.00	519.60	473.75	13.78	17.89	7.70	9.50	9.68
SXM	250.00	180.00	56.85	66.85	25.00	45.00	331.85	291.85	17.13	22.91	7.53	15.42	13.71

	SKB											
	FARE	FARE	TAXES	TAXES	LIAT FIS	LIAT FIS	TOTAL	TOTAL	TAXES AS A % OF TOTAL FARE/	TAXES AS A % OF TOTAL FARE/	FIS AS A % OF TOTAL FARE	FIS AS A % OF TOTAL FARE	INCREASE / DECREASE % 2011
ORIGIN	2011	2008	2011	2008	2011	2008	2011	2008	2011	2008	2011	2008	OVER 2008
ANU	188.00	128.00	90.80	22.80	25.00	45.00	303.80	195.80	29.89	11.64	8.23	22.98	55.16
AXA	220.00	160.00	67.00	15.00	25.00	45.00	312.00	220.00	21.47	6.82	8.01	20.45	41.82
BGI	348.00	300.00	139.40	96.50	40.00	27.50	527.40	424.00	26.43	22.76	7.58	6.49	24.39
DOM	236.00	176.00	64.70	33.20	35.00	45.00	335.70	254.20	19.27	13.06	10.43	17.70	32.06
EIS	232.00	172.00	74.00	7.00	25.00	45.00	331.00	224.00	22.36	3.13	7.55	20.09	47.77
FDF	313.94	254.00	99.61	50.28	35.00	45.00	448.55	349.28	22.21	14.40	7.80	12.88	28.42
GEO	540.00	480.00	128.00	92.00	40.00	45.00	708.00	617.00	18.08	14.91	5.65	7.29	14.75
GND	390.00	330.00	93.83	70.10	40.00	45.00	523.83	445.10	17.91	15.75	7.64	10.11	17.69
POS	412.00	352.00	132.25	80.30	40.00	45.00	584.25	477.30	22.64	16.82	6.85	9.43	22.41
PTP	284.43	224.00	82.70	51.91	25.00	45.00	392.13	320.91	21.09	16.18	6.38	14.02	22.19
SDQ	498.00	424.00	204.28	159.09	40.00	45.00	742.28	628.09	27.52	25.33	5.39	7.16	18.18
SJU	278.00	208.00	66.00	48.95	35.00	45.00	379.00	301.95	17.41	16.21	9.23	14.90	25.52
SLU	318.00	258.00	141.05	74.55	35.00	45.00	494.05	377.55	28.55	19.75	7.08	11.92	30.86
STT	250.00	180.00	59.50	29.50	35.00	45.00	344.50	254.50	17.27	11.59	10.16	17.68	35.36
STX	250.00	180.00	83.85	39.50	25.00	45.00	358.85	264.50	23.37	14.93	6.97	17.01	35.67
SVD	326.00	242.00	97.65	32.10	35.00	45.00	458.65	319.10	21.29	10.06	7.63	14.10	43.73
SXM	196.00	136.00	91.35	44.35	25.00	45.00	312.35	225.35	29.25	19.68	8.00	19.97	38.61

	NEV											
	FARE	FARE	TAXES	TAXES	LIAT FIS	LIAT FIS	TOTAL	TOTAL	TAXES AS A % OF TOTAL FARE/	TAXES AS A % OF TOTAL FARE/	FIS AS A % OF TOTAL FARE	FIS AS A % OF TOTAL FARE	INCREASE / DECREASE % 2011
ORIGIN	2011	2008	2011	2008	2011	2008	2011	2008	2011	2008	2011	2008	OVER 2008
ANU	188.00	128.00	58.80	17.80	25.00	45.00	271.80	190.80	21.63	9.33	9.20	23.58	42.45
AXA	220.00	160.00	35.00	20.00	25.00	45.00	280.00	225.00	12.50	8.89	8.93	20.00	24.44
BGI	372.00	326.00	111.60	100.40	40.00	27.50	523.60	453.90	21.31	22.12	7.64	6.06	15.36
DOM	236.00	176.00	32.70	28.20	25.00	45.00	293.70	249.20	11.13	11.32	8.51	18.06	17.86
EIS	216.00	156.00	61.35	22.00	35.00	45.00	312.35	223.00	19.64	9.87	11.21	20.18	40.07
GEO	590.00	530.00	118.50	124.50	40.00	45.00	748.50	699.50	15.83	17.80	5.34	6.43	7.01
GND	388.00	328.00	61.83	64.90	40.00	45.00	489.83	437.90	12.62	14.82	8.17	10.28	11.86
POS	396.00	336.00	97.85	72.90	40.00	45.00	533.85	453.90	18.33	16.06	7.49	9.91	17.61
SXM	380.00	192.00	44.35	59.35	40.00	45.00	464.35	296.35	9.55	18.81	8.61	15.18	16.52

	SLU											
	FARE	FARE	TAXES	TAXES	LIAT FIS	LIAT FIS	TOTAL	TOTAL	TAXES AS A % OF TOTAL FARE/	TAXES AS A % OF TOTAL FARE/	FIS AS A % OF TOTAL FARE	FIS AS A % OF TOTAL FARE	INCREASE / DECREASE % 2011
ORIGIN	2011	2008	2011	2008	2011	2008	2011	2008	2011	2008	2011	2008	OVER 2008
ANU	278.00	218.00	122.99	61.99	35.00	45.00	435.99	324.99	28.21	19.07	8.03	13.85	34.15
AXA	368.00	308.00	90.19	65.19	40.00	45.00	498.19	418.19	18.10	15.59	8.03	10.76	19.13
BGI	202.00	154.00	137.05	89.79	25.00	27.50	364.05	271.29	37.65	33.10	6.87	10.14	34.19
CUR	360.00	300.00	70.19	110.19	40.00	45.00	470.19	455.19	14.93	24.21	8.51	9.89	3.30
DOM	212.00	152.00	86.09	41.59	25.00	45.00	323.09	238.59	26.65	17.43	7.74	18.86	35.42
EIS	372.00	312.00	97.19	57.19	40.00	45.00	509.19	414.19	19.09	13.81	7.86	10.86	22.94
FDF	150.19	182.00	110.11	60.47	25.00	45.00	285.30	287.47	38.59	21.04	8.76	15.65	-0.75
GEO	360.00	300.00	139.19	75.19	40.00	45.00	539.19	420.19	25.81	17.89	7.42	10.71	28.32
GND	202.00	142.00	117.02	91.50	24.00	45.00	343.02	278.50	34.11	32.85	7.00	16.16	23.17
NEV	312.00	252.00	116.39	75.39	35.00	45.00	463.39	372.39	25.12	20.24	7.55	12.08	24.44
POS	268.00	208.00	133.84	68.89	35.00	45.00	436.84	321.89	30.64	21.40	8.01	13.98	35.71
PTP	342.45	282.00	105.89	62.11	35.00	45.00	483.34	389.11	21.91	15.96	7.24	11.56	24.22
SDQ	544.00	470.00	239.83	196.64	40.00	45.00	823.83	711.64	29.11	27.63	4.86	6.32	15.76
SJU	406.00	336.00	89.19	79.14	40.00	45.00	535.19	460.14	16.67	17.20	7.47	9.78	16.31
SKB	318.00	258.00	148.99	80.99	35.00	45.00	501.99	383.99	29.68	21.09	6.97	11.72	30.73
STT	404.00	334.00	82.69	69.69	40.00	45.00	526.69	448.69	15.70	15.53	7.59	10.03	17.38
SVD	196.00	136.00	79.99	36.99	25.00	45.00	300.99	217.99	26.58	16.97	8.31	20.64	38.08
SXM	310.00	250.00	114.54	94.54	40.00	45.00	464.54	389.54	24.66	24.27	8.61	11.55	19.25

ORIGIN	SXM												
	FARE	FARE	TAXES	TAXES	LIAT FIS	LIAT FIS	TOTAL	TOTAL	TAXES AS A % OF TOTAL FARE/	TAXES AS A % OF TOTAL FARE/	FIS AS A % OF TOTAL FARE	FIS AS A % OF TOTAL FARE	INCREASE / DECREASE % 2011
	2011	2008	2011	2008	2011	2008	2011	2008	2011	2008	2011	2008	OVER 2008
ANU	228.00	168.00	92.15	70.15	25.00	45.00	345.15	283.15	26.70	24.77	7.24	15.89	21.90
BGI	408.00	345.00	147.25	127.60	40.00	27.50	595.25	500.10	24.74	25.51	6.72	5.50	19.03
DOM	272.00	202.00	64.75	74.51	35.00	45.00	371.75	321.51	17.42	23.18	9.41	14.00	15.63
EIS	196.00	136.00	71.35	46.35	25.00	45.00	292.35	227.35	24.41	20.39	8.55	19.79	28.59
GEO	620.00	560.00	137.35	163.35	40.00	45.00	797.35	768.35	17.23	21.26	5.02	5.86	3.77
GND	384.00	324.00	98.68	108.85	40.00	45.00	522.68	477.85	18.88	22.78	7.65	9.42	9.38
NEV	252.00	192.00	86.05	78.55	25.00	45.00	363.05	315.55	23.70	24.89	6.89	14.26	15.05
POS	438.00	378.00	133.50	123.55	40.00	45.00	611.50	546.55	21.83	22.61	6.54	8.23	11.88
PTP	297.03	236.00	80.05	91.26	35.00	45.00	412.08	372.26	19.43	24.52	8.49	12.09	10.70
SDQ	534.00	460.00	212.39	197.85	40.00	45.00	786.39	702.85	27.01	28.15	5.09	6.40	11.89
SJU	266.00	196.00	63.35	88.30	35.00	45.00	364.35	329.30	17.39	26.81	9.61	13.67	10.64
SKB	196.00	136.00	110.95	57.95	25.00	45.00	331.95	238.95	33.42	24.25	7.53	18.83	38.92
SLU	310.00	250.00	137.80	163.30	40.00	45.00	487.80	458.30	28.25	35.63	8.20	9.82	6.44
STT	258.00	188.00	56.85	58.85	25.00	45.00	339.85	291.85	16.73	20.16	7.36	15.42	16.45
STX	250.00	180.00	56.85	58.85	25.00	45.00	331.85	283.85	17.13	20.73	7.53	15.85	16.91
SVD	380.00	320.00	63.35	80.35	40.00	45.00	483.35	445.35	13.11	18.04	8.28	10.10	8.53

ORIGIN	STT												
	FARE	FARE	TAXES	TAXES	LIAT FIS	LIAT FIS	TOTAL	TOTAL	TAXES AS A % OF TOTAL FARE/	TAXES AS A % OF TOTAL FARE/	FIS AS A % OF TOTAL FARE	FIS AS A % OF TOTAL FARE	INCREASE / DECREASE % 2011
	2011	2008	2011	2008	2011	2008	2011	2008	2011	2008	2011	2008	OVER 2008
ANU	274.00	204.00	64.90	44.90	35.00	45.00	373.90	293.90	17.36	15.28	9.36	15.31	27.22
AXA	230.00	160.00	32.50	29.50	25.00	45.00	287.50	234.50	11.30	12.58	8.70	19.19	22.60
BGI	462.00	414.00	124.86	123.10	40.00	27.50	626.86	564.60	19.92	21.80	6.38	4.87	11.03
DOM	344.00	274.00	38.30	55.06	40.00	45.00	422.30	374.06	9.07	14.72	9.47	12.03	12.90
GEO	670.00	600.00	120.50	184.50	40.00	45.00	830.50	829.50	14.51	22.24	4.82	5.42	0.12
GND	414.00	344.00	59.33	86.00	40.00	45.00	513.33	475.00	11.56	18.11	7.79	9.47	8.07
NEV	286.00	216.00	56.10	56.10	35.00	45.00	377.10	317.10	14.88	17.69	9.28	14.19	18.92
POS	450.00	380.00	103.45	99.00	40.00	45.00	593.45	524.00	17.43	18.89	6.74	8.59	13.25
PTP	366.32	296.00	48.20	71.41	35.00	45.00	449.52	412.41	10.72	17.32	7.79	10.91	9.00
SKB	250.00	180.00	84.50	37.50	35.00	45.00	369.50	262.50	22.87	14.29	9.47	17.14	40.76
SLU	404.00	334.00	112.99	94.75	40.00	45.00	556.99	473.75	20.29	20.00	7.18	9.50	17.57
SVD	414.00	344.00	48.20	56.70	40.00	45.00	502.20	445.70	9.60	12.72	7.96	10.10	12.68
SXM	258.00	188.00	56.85	58.85	25.00	45.00	339.85	291.85	16.73	20.16	7.36	15.42	16.45

	SVD											
	FARE	FARE	TAXES	TAXES	LIAT FIS	LIAT FIS	TOTAL	TOTAL	TAXES AS A % OF TOTAL FARE/	TAXES AS A % OF TOTAL FARE/	FIS AS A % OF TOTAL FARE	FIS AS A % OF TOTAL FARE	INCREASE / DECREASE % 2011
ORIGIN	2011	2008	2011	2008	2011	2008	2011	2008	2011	2008	2011	2008	OVER 2008
ANU	300.00	245.00	70.00	24.00	35.00	45.00	405.00	314.00	17.28	3.97	8.64	14.33	28.98
AXA	464.00	454.00	32.69	0.00	40.00	45.00	536.69	499.00	6.09	0.00	7.45	9.02	7.55
BGI	200.00	152.00	66.50	47.30	25.00	27.50	291.50	226.80	22.81	22.22	8.58	12.13	28.53
CUR	360.00	300.00	15.00	0.00	40.00	45.00	415.00	345.00	3.61	6.53	9.64	13.04	20.29
DOM	248.00	178.00	26.00	8.36	35.00	45.00	309.00	231.36	8.41	7.69	11.33	19.45	33.56
EIS	390.00	330.00	27.00	2.00	40.00	45.00	457.00	377.00	5.91	4.82	8.75	11.94	21.22
FDF	350.00	290.00	47.35	25.28	25.00	45.00	422.35	360.28	11.21	11.37	5.92	12.49	17.23
GEO	360.00	300.00	69.00	40.00	40.00	45.00	469.00	385.00	14.71	12.78	8.53	11.69	21.82
GND	196.00	136.00	39.33	25.70	25.00	45.00	260.33	206.70	15.11	12.95	9.60	21.77	25.95
NEV	366.00	306.00	66.60	25.60	35.00	45.00	467.60	376.60	14.24	9.33	7.49	11.95	24.16
POS	230.00	170.00	57.95	28.00	35.00	45.00	322.95	243.00	17.94	14.23	10.84	18.52	32.90
PTP	331.77	258.00	50.70	26.91	35.00	45.00	417.47	329.91	12.14	12.47	8.38	13.64	26.54
SDQ	580.00	506.00	190.40	140.86	40.00	45.00	810.40	691.86	23.49	24.37	4.94	6.50	17.13
SJU	430.00	360.00	34.00	22.45	40.00	45.00	504.00	427.45	6.75	12.62	7.94	10.53	17.91
SKB	326.00	242.00	94.00	24.20	35.00	45.00	455.00	311.20	20.66	11.64	7.69	14.46	46.21
SLU	196.00	136.00	84.89	10.39	25.00	45.00	305.89	191.39	27.75	17.70	8.17	23.51	59.83
STT	414.00	344.00	27.50	64.50	40.00	45.00	481.50	453.50	5.71	8.96	8.31	9.92	6.17
STX	408.00	344.00	51.20	64.50	40.00	45.00	499.20	453.50	10.26	8.96	8.01	9.92	10.08

	FARE	FARE	TAXES	TAXES	LIAT FIS	LIAT FIS	TOTAL	TOTAL	TAXES AS A % OF TOTAL FARE/	TAXES AS A % OF TOTAL FARE/	FIS AS A % OF TOTAL FARE	FIS AS A % OF TOTAL FARE	INCREASE / DECREASE % 2011
ORIGIN	2011	2008	2011	2008	2011	2008	2011	2008	2011	2008	2011	2008	OVER 2008
ANU	252.00	192.00	77.20	31.20	35.00	45.00	364.20	268.20	21.20	11.63	9.61	16.78	35.79
AXA	200.00	145.00	47.00	32.00	25.00	45.00	272.00	222.00	17.28	14.41	9.19	20.27	22.52
BGI	392.00	355.00	127.10	84.75	40.00	27.50	559.10	467.25	22.73	18.14	7.15	5.89	19.66
DOM	318.00	258.00	50.86	21.36	35.00	45.00	403.86	324.36	12.59	6.59	8.67	13.87	24.51
GEO	688.00	628.00	130.20	96.20	40.00	45.00	858.20	769.20	15.17	12.51	4.66	5.85	11.57
GND	438.00	378.00	81.33	76.90	40.00	45.00	559.33	499.90	14.54	15.38	7.15	9.00	11.89
NEV	216.00	156.00	82.95	37.60	35.00	45.00	333.95	238.60	24.84	15.76	10.48	18.86	39.96
POS	496.00	436.00	124.85	94.90	40.00	45.00	660.85	575.90	18.89	16.48	6.05	7.81	14.75
PTP	356.04	296.00	82.05	53.91	35.00	45.00	473.09	394.91	17.34	13.65	7.40	11.40	19.80
SDQ	474.00	450.00	185.74	75.25	40.00	45.00	699.74	570.25	26.54	13.20	5.72	7.89	22.71
SKB	232.00	172.00	97.20	24.20	25.00	45.00	354.20	241.20	27.44	10.03	7.06	18.66	46.85
SLU	372.00	312.00	125.09	80.59	40.00	45.00	537.09	437.59	23.29	18.42	7.45	10.28	22.74
STX	250.00	180.00	78.20	31.50	25.00	45.00	353.20	256.50	22.14	12.28	7.08	17.54	37.70
SVD	390.00	330.00	46.50	58.50	40.00	45.00	476.50	433.50	9.76	13.49	8.39	10.38	9.92
SXM	196.00	136.00	71.35	46.35	25.00	45.00	292.35	227.35	24.41	20.39	8.55	19.79	28.59

ORIGIN	POS FARE 2011	FARE 2008	TAXES 2011	TAXES 2008	LIAT FIS 2011	LIAT FIS 2008	TOTAL 2011	TOTAL 2008	TAXES AS A % OF TOTAL FARE/ 2011	TAXES AS A % OF TOTAL FARE/ 2008	FIS AS A % OF TOTAL FARE 2011	FIS AS A % OF TOTAL FARE 2008	INCREASE / DECREASE % 2011 OVER 2008
ANU	376.00	316.00	86.05	59.90	40.00	45.00	502.05	420.90	17.14	14.23	7.97	10.69	19.28
AXA	464.00	454.00	43.45	20.00	40.00	45.00	547.45	519.00	7.94	3.85	7.31	8.67	5.48
BGI	226.00	178.00	94.51	78.70	35.00	27.50	355.51	284.20	26.58	27.69	9.85	9.68	25.09
CUR	366.00	306.00	23.45	35.00	40.00	45.00	429.45	386.00	5.46	9.07	9.31	11.66	11.26
DOM	332.00	272.00	48.35	16.40	40.00	45.00	420.35	333.40	11.50	4.92	9.52	13.50	26.08
EIS	496.00	436.00	50.45	12.00	40.00	45.00	586.45	493.00	8.60	2.43	6.82	9.13	18.96
FDF	356.04	296.00	73.75	35.28	35.00	45.00	464.79	376.28	15.87	9.38	7.53	11.96	23.52
GEO	366.00	230.00	93.35	73.40	40.00	45.00	499.35	348.40	18.69	21.07	8.01	12.92	43.33
GND	206.00	146.00	62.78	53.71	25.00	45.00	293.78	244.71	21.37	21.95	8.51	18.39	20.05
NEV	396.00	336.00	78.05	17.80	40.00	45.00	514.05	398.80	15.18	4.46	7.78	11.28	28.90
PTP	422.01	362.00	66.65	36.91	40.00	45.00	528.66	443.91	12.61	8.31	7.57	10.14	19.09
SDQ	688.00	614.00	216.13	125.65	40.00	45.00	944.13	784.65	22.89	16.01	4.24	5.74	20.32
SJU	492.00	422.00	42.45	33.95	40.00	45.00	574.45	500.95	7.39	6.78	6.96	8.98	14.67
SKB	412.00	352.00	40.00	22.80	40.00	45.00	492.00	419.80	8.13	5.43	8.13	10.72	17.20
SLU	268.00	208.00	113.74	56.55	35.00	45.00	416.74	309.55	27.29	18.27	8.40	14.54	34.63
STT	450.00	380.00	35.95	24.50	40.00	45.00	525.95	449.50	6.84	5.45	7.61	10.01	17.01
STX	450.00	380.00	35.95	24.50	40.00	45.00	525.95	449.50	6.84	5.45	7.61	10.01	17.01
SVD	230.00	170.00	34.95	12.00	35.00	45.00	299.95	227.00	11.65	5.29	11.67	19.82	32.14
SXM	438.00	378.00	67.80	49.35	40.00	45.00	545.80	472.35	12.42	10.45	7.33	9.53	15.55

Index

Abrahams, Eric Anthony, 93
Adams, Sir Grantley, 19–20, 33–36
African, Caribbean and Pacific Group of States (ACP) countries, 132
air access, 183
Air Arabia Egypt, 302
Air Canada, 201, 295
Air Jamaica and Caribbean Airlines
   committee, 327
   losses, 326–327
   profit, 327–328
   and REDjet, 327
airline performance
   Asia, 305
   Europe, 304
   growth projections for 2011, 308
   Latin America, 305–306
   United States, 304–305
airlines, 9/11 attack impact, 185–186
airport safety and security, 183–184, 196
Air Transport Association of America, 305
air transportation
   advocacy, 348–349
   Asia, 305
   aviation fuel, 303
   cargo, 304
   Europe, 304

functional cooperation, 183–184
IATA forecasts, 303–304
international tourism sector, 303
Latin America, 305–306
United States, 304–305
Alexander, Patrick, 92
American Eagle, 324–326
Anderson, Janet, 315
Annan, Kofi, 228
Annual Caribbean Tourism Summit (ACTS), 155
arbitral tribunal, composition, 381–383
Arison, Micky, 186
Arthur, Hugh Anthony, 42
Association of Caribbean States, 151
Astaphan, Dwyer, 217
Astaphan Funding Committee Report
   bilateral agreements, 218
   CARICOM agency, 217–218
   legality issue, 218
   proposed tax, 217
   terms of reference, 218
   US$20 tax justification, 218–222
authority, establishment and functions, 373–374

The Bahamas
   blockade runners, 22

(continues on next page)

Commonwealth, 20
Eleuthera, 20
English Loyalists, 21
gross domestic product (GDP), 25
Lucayans, 20
politics, 23–24
racial issues, 25–28
society, 22–23
tourism growth, 24–25
wrecking, 22
Bahamasair, 328–329, 335–336
Banfield, Harriette, 92
Barbados
air services, 40–41
class stratification, 32
colonial value system, 29–30
cruel and inhumane punishments, 29
hotels, racial discrimination, 40
island's value, 29
land topography, 28
parliament, 28
politicians, 37
reflection, 37–38
slaves, 29
social stratification, 33
tobacco production, 28
tourism administration, 41–43
tourism landmarks. *See* landmarks, Barbados
Barbados Labour Party, 106
Barrow, Errol Walton, 33, 35–38, 152, 245
Barrow, Ruth, 35
Batista, Fulgencio, 62–64
Beckles, Hilary, 28–29, 47, 239
Belfon, Jane, 92
Bell, John, 102
Bereton, Vera Anne, 92
Berman, Laurie, 94
Bermuda

CARICOM, 16
CTO member, 16
location, 17
population, 16
race relations, 17–18
racial discrimination, 19–20
salt trade, 17
school system, 18
standards of living, 18
tourism, 18–19
Bienek, Bernd, 94
Bisignani, Giovanni, 224, 304, 307
Bloomberg, Michael R., 314
Boorstin, Daniel, 2
Boynton, Graham, 315
Brathwaite, Edward, 260
British administrative federal arrangements, 73–74
British West Indian Airways (BWIA), 77, 126, 183, 185
Brown, Dean, 164
budget, authority, 377
Buisseret, David, 250, 251
Bully, Alwyn, 250, 260–262
Burnham, Forbes, 37, 78, 118
Burns, Ian, 336
Burns, Robbie, 335
Bush, McKeeva, 330
Bustamante, Alexander, 46, 75
BWIA. *See* British West Indian Airways (BWIA)
Byer, Patricia, 89, 92

Cameron, David, 3, 315, 316
Canadian market, 200–201
Capital-intensive, 119
Caribbean and Europe air transportation, 138–139
Caribbean Aviation Safety and Security Oversight System, 348

Index 435

Caribbean Commission
  allied colonial powers, 80
  Atlantic Charter, 80–81
  Caribbean Interim Tourism Committee, 81
  tourism, economic sector, 81
Caribbean Community (CARICOM), 71, 78–79, 111, 123
  countries, 421–423
  decision, 222–223
  Multilateral Air Services Agreement, 347
  single market and economy, 290
Caribbean Congress of Labour, 112
Caribbean Conservation Association, 262–264
Caribbean Development Bank, 96, 128–129
Caribbean Forum (CARIFORUM), 281–282
Caribbean Free Trade Association (CARIFTA)
  Caribbean Development Bank views, 128–129
  Caribbean Regional Negotiating Machinery, 128
  Dickenson Bay Agreement, 109
  European Economic Community views, 130
  objectives, 109–110
  tourism control, 118–127. *See also* tourism
  World Bank views, 129–130
Caribbean gateway hubs, 139
Caribbean Hotel Association (CHA)
  CTA and CTRC, 84
  directorate, 84
  hotel committee, 84
Caribbean Plan for Monuments and Sites (CARIMOS)
  international tourism basis, 255
  landmarks and natural features, erosion, 256
  Quito Standards, 255
Caribbean Regional Negotiating Machinery
  agenda points, 287–288
  negotiation, agricultural and merchandizing trade, 278
  research, 278–279
  Youth Entrepreneurship Scheme, Barbados, 278
Caribbean Regional Strategic Plan, 211–212
Caribbean tourism
  air access, 195
  airport safety and security, 196
  CARICOM countries, 345–347
  climate, 176
  critical importance, 343–345
  cruise tourism, economic benefits, 196
  CTO membership, 175
  culture, 176
  ecology and beaches, 176
  effective marketing, 200–203
  First Gulf War, 173–174
  geographical location, 175
  history and language, 175–176
  human resource development, 203–204
  IATA global predictions, 318–319
  information management systems, 196–200
  institutional strengthening and funding, 205
  investment climate and strategies, 194–195
  leadership, 346–347
  product quality, 189–194

(continues on next page)

public and private sector conference, 173
second energy crisis, 173–174
technical and vocational institutions, 347–348
territorial situation, 176
terrorist attacks, 174
tourism potential, poll on, 320–322
UNWTO predictions, 319–320
weaknesses, 176–177
Caribbean tourism arrivals 2008–2011
cruise passenger arrivals, 393, 401, 409, 417
tourist (stop-over) arrivals, 385–386, 394, 402, 410
tourist arrivals by main market, 391–392, 399–400, 407–408, 415–416
tourist arrivals by month, 387–390, 395–398, 403–406, 411–414
Caribbean Tourism Association (CTA), 41, 149–151
Caribbean Tourism Centre (CTC)
agreement, 89
challenges, 89
CTRC. *See* Caribbean Tourism Research and Development Centre (CTRC)
Caribbean Tourism Conference (CTC), 105
Caribbean Tourism Development Company, 157–158
Caribbean tourism industry
aviation policy, 207
cruise tourism, 207–208
growth scenarios, 210–211
human resource development, 209
information management, 208
marketing, 208–209
objectives, 205–206

organization and funding, 209
product, 206–207
profitability and investment, 207
proposed fund, Source and structure, 209–210
sustainable development, 206
Caribbean Tourism Organization (CTO)
Association of Caribbean States, 151
Caribbean Tourism Conference, 155
Caribbean Tourism Development Company, creation, 157–158
1972 CARIFTA report, 149
cruise lines, capacity deployment, 168
CTA, public and private sector division, 149–151
Cuba application for membership, 152–153
economies, 149
forecast, 167
initiative, 154–157
memorandum article, 155–157
policymakers, 149
public and private sectors, relationships, 153–154
Caribbean Tourism Research and Development Centre (CTRC)
action programme, creation, 91–92
Caracas meeting, 104
Caribbean Development Bank, 94
Caribbean tourism, 96
CICATUR system, 93
conference coordination, 103–104
employees, 92–93
European Economic Community, 93–94
governments' ambivalent attitudes, 91
headquarters, 89–90

IAF and, 88
launch, 103–104
OAS and, 93
programme, 90–91
United Nations Development Programme, 94
Caribbean Tourism Strategic Plan, 216
Caribbean Tourist Association (CTA)
budget and staff, 83
directorate, 83
location, 83
membership, 82
official language, 82–83
Caribbean tourist markets
diversification, 132
studies, 132–133
CARICOM. *See* Caribbean Community
CARIFTA. *See* Caribbean Free Trade Association (CARIFTA)
CARIFTA Secretariat report, 1972
Caribbean experience, 117–118
CARIFTA/CARICOM assessment, 111–113
Commonwealth Caribbean, 110
localization, 117
macro strategies, 113
national strategies, 113–115
strategies analysis, 116–117
CARIMOS. *See* Caribbean Plan for Monuments and Sites (CARIMOS)
Carnegie, Ralph, 215–216
Carnival Cruise Lines, 186
Carolyn Cash, 22–23
casino tax, 364
Cave, Maurice, 41
Cayman Airways, 329–331, 335–336
Césaire, Aimé, 260
CHA. *See* Caribbean Hotel Association (CHA)

Chesnut, Mark, 322
Christie, Perry, 25, 329
Churchill, Sir Winston, 23, 80
Clarke, Austin, 260
Clarke, Cecil, 18
Clarke, Shirley, 18
Cole, Lloyd, 102–103
Commission for Unity and Racial Equality (CURE), 18
Commonwealth Caribbean countries, 421
Commonwealth Caribbean states
beet sugar impact, 74
social ills, 75
unemployment, 74
West Indian labour unions emergence, 75
connecting flights, 143
Cook, Thomas, 2
Copa Airlines, 299–300
corporate profit taxes, 364–365
Council for Trade and Economic Development (COTED), 223–224
Cozier, E.L.C., 81
craft, folklore and folk art
experiment, 257
materials, 257
practical guidelines, 256–257
tourism products from, 257–259
Craig, Jerry, 250, 256
Crandall, Robert, 174
Cresser, Hugh, 92
Cromwell, Oliver, 44
cruise lines, 186
Cruise Lines International Association, 160, 163
cruise passenger arrivals, 180, 353–354, 393, 401, 409, 417
cruise passenger taxes, increase in, 214
cruise regulatory authority, 215–216

438 Index

cruise shipping charges, implementation, 378–379
cruise survey, 2000
  bigger ships trends, 360–361
  cruise business sharing, 359
  cruise capacity, 361
  cruise-related expenditures, 361–362
  cruise tourism, region for, 359
  dominance, 360
  North American cruise sector, expansion, 359–360
  port charges and head taxes, 355–356
  purchasing issues, 357
  regional performance, 358–359
  sale items, to cruise lines, 357–358
  tourist and cruise passenger arrivals, 358
cruise tourism
  capacity, 163–164
  CTO forecast, 167–168
  economic benefits, 196
  economic impact comparisons, 167
  Florida Caribbean Cruise Association (FCCA), 161–163
  global cruise expansion, 160
  growth comparisons, 166–167
  land-based and cruise product, comparisons, 159–160
  land-based tourism and, 164–166
  outlook for, 163
  private sector taxes and subsidies, 168–169
  pros and cons, 170–171
  public sector concerns, 169–170
  ships repositioning after 9/11, 164
CTA. *See* Caribbean Tourism Association (CTA)
CTC. *See* Caribbean Tourism Conference (CTC)

CTO. *See* Caribbean Tourism Organization (CTO)
Cuba
  American dominance, 60, 65–66
  Batista, influence of, 62–64
  Cuban Revolutionary Party, 59
  failure, American embargo, 69–70
  independence movement, 59–60
  indigenous tourism, 66
  pre-revolutionary, tourism in, 60–62
  racial dimension, 64–65
  Soviet collapse, impact, 67–69
  US restrictions, 67
Cuba application for membership, 152–153
Cultural Patrimony and Tourism Product, 1983
  CARIMOS, 254–256
  craft, folklore and folk art, 256–257
  culture definition, 251
  literary, performing and visual arts, 259–262
  organizers, 250
  presentations, 250
  seminar recommendations, 262–267
cultural tourism, 248–249
  Caribbean cultural fragility, 246
  Caribbean cultural maturing, 268–270
  concepts, 244–246
  definition, 248–249
  indigenous and foreign cultures, 246–248
Cultural Training Centre, Jamaica, 266
Cunard Line, 186
CURE. *See* Commission for Unity and Racial Equality (CURE)
Curtin, Victor, 174

Damas, Leon, 260
Daniel, Jean, 63

Davis, Philip Brave, 329
Dean, Sir George, 75
de Bermudez, Juan, 16
de Cuellar, Diego Velazquez, 58
de Gaulle, Charles, 76
Demas, William, 173
departure tax, 364
Detzer, David, 63
Dickenson Bay Agreement, 109
Doha Round, 282, 283, 289
Dolara, Peter, 325
Donawa, Martin, 102
Dookeran, Winston, 327, 328
Dorticos, Osvaldo, 64
double-dip recession, 296
draft inter-governmental agreement
   administrative office, 376–377
   amendments to, 384
   arbitral procedure, 383
   arbitral tribunal, composition, 381–383
   authority, establishment and functions, 373–374
   budget, authority, 377
   cruise shipping charges, implementation, 378–379
   denunciation, 384
   depositary, 383
   environmental fund, 380
   governing board, 374–375
   headquarters of authority, 376
   legal capacity, 383
   marine environment protection, 379–380
   parties, 384
   privileges and immunities, 383
   reservations, 383
   settlement of disputes, 380–381
   taxes and charges, determination, 377–378
   terms meaning, 373
   voting in Council, 375
   voting in Governing Board, 376
duty-free importation, 365

Eastern Caribbean Tourist Association (ECTA), 104, 148
economic impact data, 199–200
Economic Partnership Agreement negotiations, 280–283
Economic Partnership Agreements (EPAs), 419
ECTA. *See* Eastern Caribbean Tourist Association (ECTA)
E/D (emigration and disembarkation) cards, 192
EEC. *See* European Economic Community (EEC)
effective marketing
   Canadian market, 200–201
   European market, 201
   intra-Caribbean market, 202
   Japan and Eastern markets, 203
   South American market, 202–203
   US market, 200
Eisenhower, Dwight, 64
Elder, J.D., 250, 256–259
Eleutheran Adventurers, 20
Emissions Trading System, 314
environmental fund, 380
environment as key components, 192–194
EPAs. *See* Economic Partnership Agreements (EPAs)
European Commission negotiators, 419
European Economic Community (EEC), 130, 133, 146
European economic indicators, 297
European market demand study

(continues on next page)

1979 study, 141
1983 update, 142–144
1985 and 1990, forecast for, 135–136
competition to Caribbean, 135
European product preferences, 136
marketing offices, establishment, 137–138
motivation for travel, 134
number of arrivals, 133–134
organization and budget, 137
pricing in Europe, 136
product strengths and weaknesses identification, 134–135
publicity and promotion, 136–137
region knowledge, 134
tour operator, role, 135
visitor profiles, 134
European tour operator, 135, 143
European visitors, 144
excessive foreign ownership, 111

FCCA. *See* Florida Caribbean Cruise Association (FCCA)
FIFA Soccer World Cup 2010, 229, 236
fiscal policies
  casino tax, 364
  corporate profit taxes, 364–365
  departure tax, 364
  duty free importation, 365
  General Consumption Tax, 364
  import duties, 364
  property taxes, 364
  room tax, 364
  structural costs, 365
  tax incentives, 365
Florida Caribbean Cruise Association (FCCA)
  Caribbean countries and cruise industry interaction, 161
  CHA relationship, 163
  cruise industry's economic contribution, 162
  CTA member, 161–162
  and CTRC, CHA, relationship, 162–163
Flynn, Errol, 52
Follett, Barbara, 315
food security
  crops conversion, 274
  economic approaches, 275
  expensive food imports, 274–275
  world's oil supply, 274
foreign direct investment, 121
foreign policy directions
  CARICOM state, 280
  colonial trading relationships, 279
  Commonwealth Caribbean, 279
Free Trade Area of the Americas (FTAA), 282
funding initiative, 2008
  airlines tax, 224
  CARICOM, decision-making body, 223
  COTED, 223–224
  CTO states, tax, 224
  fund contributions, 224

Gabor, Eva, 52
Garvey, Marcus, 46
Gates, Sir Thomas, 16
general consumption tax, 364
global cruise expansion, 160
global tourism performance
  airline performance, 304–306
  air transportation predictions, 306–307
  IATA predictions revision, 307–308
  international trade negotiations, lessons from, 292–303

tourism policies, in traditional
source markets, 311–317
tranquil tourism business environment, 308–311
Griffith, Winfield, 338–339
Gunten, Alex de, 305
Guntley, Carolle, 146
Guttmann, Allen, 231

Harris, Wilson, 260
Hatch, Reverend Andrew, 87
Hearne, John, 30
hemispheric and international negotiations
Caribbean negotiation, 284
Doha Round, suspension, 283–284
world's economic reality, 283
high import content, 111
Hiller, Herbert, 87, 88, 90, 102
Hinds, Patrick, 92
historical architecture
commercial buildings, 252
domestic buildings, 251–252
industrial structures, 252–253
military works, 253–254
public buildings, 254
Hodge, Margaret, 315
Holder, Jean, 89, 92, 177, 249
Holland America Line, 186
Hopkins, Sir Royston, 102
hotels
Atlantis Hotel, 39
Crane Hotel, 39
Fairmont Hamilton Princess Hotel, 19–20
Four Seasons cater, 120
Hamilton Princess Hotel, 19
historic, 50–51
Marine Hotel, 39
ownership of, 52–53

racial discrimination, 40
rates, 111
Ritz-Carlton, 120
Royal Naval Hotel, 38
Howells, Kim, 315
human resource development
competitiveness, 203–204
strategies, 204

IAF. *See* Inter-American Foundation (IAF)
import duties, 364
indigenous and foreign cultures
African origin, 247
clash, 247
"enclave tourism", 247
postcolonial societies, 246–247
social dimensions of globalization, 247–248
information management systems, 196–200
infrastructure, 191–192
Ingraham, Hubert, 174
institutional strengthening and funding, 205
Inter-American Foundation (IAF), 88
International Air Transportation Association, 224, 349
international arrivals *vs.* Caribbean arrivals (1970–2010), 351–353
International Civil Aviation Organization, 184
International Maritime Organization, 170
international sporting events
European Tour Operators Association negative report, 229
FIFA Soccer World Cup, 229
German National Tourist Board, 230
Lastminute.com report, 229

(continues on next page)

Summer Olympics, 229
tourism authorities, counter-arguments, 230
International Tourisme Bourse (ITB), 140
international trade negotiations
  African countries, 301–303
  Brazil, 299–300
  Canada, 295
  Caribbean, 298
  China and India, 300–301
  economic troubles, 293
  Europe, except Germany, 297
  Germany, 297–298
  global economic recession, 292
  Latin America, 298–299
  Russia, 300
  United Kingdom, 295–297
  United States, 293–295
international visitors, 313
intra-Caribbean market, 202
intra-regional carriers 2010 and 2011
  Air Jamaica and Caribbean Airlines, 326–328
  American Eagle, 324–326
  Bahamasair, 328–329, 335–336
  CARICOM countries, 339
  Cayman Airways, 329–331, 335–336
  cruise passengers forecast, 340
  cruise tourism, 339
  LIAT Airline, 331–332
  REDjet, 332–335, 340
  Spanish-speaking Caribbean, 339
  visitor expenditure, 339
intra-regional tourism, 123
ITB. *See* International Tourisme Bourse (ITB)

Jagan, Cheddi, 117
Jamaica

banana trade, by-product, 48–49
diversification out of sugar, 48
government's role, tourism development, 53–54
Great Exhibition of 1891, 51
historic hotels, 50–51
leaders in, 46
modern tourism, beginning, 51–52
Morant Bay Rebellion, 45–46
ownership of hotels, 52–53
political parties, 46
post-emancipation Jamaican society, 45
racial dimension, 54–58
Spanish Town, 44
"staycation" programmes, 55
sugar production, 44
West Indian sugar crisis, 47–48
Japan and Eastern markets, 203
Johnny Walker Professional Golf Tournament, 236
Johnson, Samuel, 2
joint regional marketing programmes, 214

Kelsick, Osmond, 102
Kennedy, John F., 63
King George, 21

Lamming, George, 260
land-based and cruise product
  bargaining chip, 160
  Caribbean hotels, 159–160
  cruise itineraries, 160
  geographical location, 160
  modern cruise ship, 159
land-based tourism
  attractive incentives, 165
  Carnival, cruise line companies, 165
  cruise passengers, 165

discounting, 166
familiarization trip, 166
land-based vacation products, 166
practitioners, 166
landmarks, Barbados
   air services, 40–41
   Atlantis Hotel, 39
   Crane Hotel, 39
   hotels, racial discrimination, 40
   Marine Hotel, 39
   Royal Naval Hotel, 38
   tourism administration, 41–43
land resources, 119
Latin American market, 123–124
Lauder, William, 38
Laulu, Lelei Le, 4
Laville, Maria, 92
leadership, CHA and CTA
   CTA chapters, 102–103
   CTRC, 101–102
Leeward Islands Air Transport (LIAT) Airline, 126
legal capacity, 383
less developed countries (LDCs), 109
Lewis, David, 322
Lewis, Gary, 32
Lewis, Gordon, 31–32, 35, 36, 72
LIAT Airline, 331–332, 424–432
Lister, Terry, 18
Lleo, Manuel Urrutia, 64
Lloyd, Clive, 238
Locke, Gary, 312
Lomé and Cotonou agreements and EPA negotiations
   colonial countries, 280
   critical ACP exports, 280
   impact on tourism, 282–283
   negative consequences, 281–282
   objections, 280
   old trade agreements, 280

Louis, Joe, 52
Ludwig, Daniel, 19
Lufthansa Consulting, 133
Luis Muñoz Marín International Airport, 325
Lutchmedial, Ramesh, 348
Lynch, Noel, 43

Maharaj, Devant, 328
Mais, Roger, 260
Management Information System for Tourism (MIST), 197–198
Manley, Michael, 37, 118, 151, 174, 238
Manley, Norman, 76
Manning, Patrick, 275, 328
marine environment protection, 379–380
market
   performance, 181
   share, 180–181
marketing
   efforts, in Europe, 144–147
   mainland Europe offices, closure, 147
Marshall, Ione, 92
McConney, Emmeline, 39
Mexican Caribbean, 186
MFN. *See* most-favoured-nation treatment (MFN)
Miller, Billie, 43
Miller, Dame Billie, 420
Miller, Luther, 92
MIST. *See* Management Information System for Tourism (MIST)
Mittleholzer, Edgar, 260
Mohamed, Kamaludin, 126
Montas, Eugenio Perez, 250
Montego Bay Convention, 215
Morant Bay Rebellion, 45–46
Morgan, Peter, 40, 89–90, 106

most-favoured-nation treatment (MFN), 288
Mottley, Elombe, 250

Naipaul, V.S., 260
Nassau conference, 174–175
national strategies, CARIFTA
   employment creation, 114–115
   linkages and local inputs, 114
   localization, 113–114
   priority sectors, 114
Niblock, James A., 41
Nicholls, Sir Neville, 129
Nicholson-Doty, Beverly, 340–341
9/11 attack
   benefits to Caribbean tourism, 187
   effects, 216–217
   impact on airlines, 185–186
   impact on cruise lines, 186
   impact on tour operators and wholesalers, 186
   situation before, 182–184
non-Caribbean fiscal policies
   cruise passengers, tax on, 367
   departure tax, 367
   incentives, 366
   investors, 366
   separate room tax, 366–367
   VAT or sales tax, 366

Obama, Barack, 130, 295
Odle, Peter, 102
Office of Trade Negotiations, 278–279
O'Neal, Charles Duncan, 33, 34
Onians, Dick, 3
Osborne, George, 296

Palmer, Audrey, 106–107
Pantin, Martha, 325–326
Parle, Berthia, 102, 155

Parris, Elliott, 250, 260, 261
Payne, Clement, 74
Penn, William, 44
Pepperdine, James, 102–103, 106
Perez, Carlos Andres, 104
Persuad, Avinath, 89
Persuad, Bisnodat, 89
Picaud, Aimeri, 2
Pindling, Lynden, 24
Pomeroy, George S., 39
Poon, Auliana, 92
port charges and head taxes, 355–356
Powell, John, 28
Prescod, Samuel Jackman, 33–34
Prescod, William, 33
Prime, Timothy, 92
Prince William Henry, 38
Pringle, John, 53
Pringle, Rachael, 38
private sector taxes and subsidies, 168–169
property taxes, 364
Prudent, Len, 92
Purnell, James, 315

REDjet
   Air Operating Certificate, 333
   competition, 333
   excitement and controversy, 334
   lowest return fare, 333
   mechanical problems, 334–335
   objections, 335
   other costs, 333
   restarting operations, 336
   taxes, 333
regional airline, 126
regional cooperation, 121
regional integration
   British administrative federal arrangements, 73–74

call for change, 87–88
Caribbean Commission birth, 80–82
CARIFTA and CARICOM, 78–79
CHA birth, 84
Commonwealth Caribbean states, 74–75
CTA birth, 82–83
CTC creation, 88–94
federation, 75–77
government involvement, 86–87
tourism agencies, 79–80
tourism and Caribbean development, 84–86
West India Committee, 72–73
Regional Strategic Tourism Development Plan, 216
regional strategies, CARIFTA
  joint action and common policies, creation, 116
  linkages creation, 115
  widening of markets, 115
regional tourism fund, inability to create
  Astaphan funding committee report, 217–218
  9/11 attack effect, 216–217
  CARICOM decision, 222–223
  cruise passenger taxes, increase in, 214
  cruise regulatory authority, 215–216
  funding initiative, 2008, 223–225
  government contributions, 214
  joint regional marketing programmes, 214
Rhone, Trevor, 261
Richards, Greg, 249
Richards, Larkland, 92
Richards, Pamela, 154–155
Rio Summit Conference, 192–193
Robinson, Nick, 296

Robinson, Rudyard, 92
Rock, Llewyn, 92
Rogers, Woodes, 21
room tax, 364
Roosevelt, Franklin D., 80
Roosevelt, Theodore, 60
Roux, Wallie, 420–421

Sabena, 185
Salkey, Andrew, 260
Sanders, Sir Ronald, 281–282, 345–346, 418–423
Sardinha, Margaret, 92
Saurel, Jean, 93
Seabourne Cruise Line and Costa, 186
Selvon, Samuel, 260
service negotiations
  agricultural subsidies, 284–285
  FTAA negotiations, 287
  negotiators, 286–287
  private sector agencies interaction, 284
  strengths, 285–286
  tariffs reduction, 285
Sethna, Rustum, 92
settlement of disputes, 380–381
Shaw, Audley, 327
Sherlock, Sir Philip, 87
Sherman, Richard, 92
Sinclair, A.C., 51
slave plantation, agricultural legacy, 275
small hotels and local ownership, 120–121
Smith, Edward, 93
Smith, Lydia, 33
Smoot-Hawley Tariffic Act, 19
Sobers, Arley, 97
Sobers, Sir Garfield, 227
Somers, Sir George, 16

South American market, 202–203
Spanish Town, 44
Spinrad, Bernard, 93
sports tourism
   and athletics, 243
   definition, 226–227
   economic impact statistics, 232–233
   existing activities, 234–235
   FIFA Soccer World Cup 2010, 236
   international sporting events, economic impact, 228–231
   marketing reach, 236
   opportunity for Caribbean, 233–236
   seasonal, 233–234
   social development, sports' role, 227–228
   sports/manufacturing linkages, 243
   synergies, 231–232
   Test cricket, direct economic impact, 237–242
Steigenberger Consulting GMBH, 133, 146
Stinson Detroiter seaplane, 19
sugar production
   agriculture and tourism, linkages, 276–277
   cost of production, 276
   environmental considerations, 276
   Inter-American Institute for Cooperation on Agriculture, 277
   new directions for agriculture, 277–278
sustainable tourism development
   Caribbean tourism-dependent states, 178
   definition expansion, 179
   economic survival, 179
   global strategic alliances, 178
   privatization, 178
   resources aggregation, 179
   short-term solutions, 178
   threats to, 178
Swissair, 185
Symonettte, Roland, 24

Tarr, Jasmine, 93
tax incentives, 365
taxes and charges, determination, 377–378
Taylor, Frank, 54
Taylor, Ralph, 102
Test cricket, direct economic impact
   challenges involved, 240–241
   CTO study, 237
   hosting, negative aspects, 241–242
   ICC Cricket World Cup, 2007, 239–242
   positive results, 242
   social cohesion and Caribbean pride, 237–239
tourism
   Caribbean as market, 122–123
   CARIFTA issues, 127
   changing World Bank perspective, 272–273
   colonial education, contribution, 11–12
   critical importance to Caribbean, 343–345
   CTO creation attempt, 104–106
   foreign direct investment, 121
   influencing factors, 127–128
   international tourism, history, 4–5
   land resources, 119
   Latin American market, 123–124
   leadership, 101–103
   modernization, 10–11
   monocrop societies, Caribbean countries, 273–274
   negative views, 2–3

negativity towards, 6–8
product diversification, 124–126
promotional efforts, 5
regional airline, 126
regional cooperation, 121
research, 12–13, 98–99
rise of, 8
small hotels and local ownership, 120–121
sugar industry, 9–10
tourism database, 96–98
tourist markets, 122
training and education, 99–101
West Indian government attitudes, 13
tourism agencies
    CHA, 79
    CTA, 79–80
    CTRC, 79
    NGOs, 79
    pan-Caribbean membership, 80
tourism business environment
    food crisis, looming, 310–311
    IATA and UNWTO, 308–309
    natural disasters, 311
    political unrest, 309
tourism database
    CTRC and CTO programme, 97
    Tourism Satellite Accounts, 98
    tourist accommodation, 97
Tourism Development Fund, 171
tourism performance, 1990 to September 2001
    9/11 attack, 179–180
    business outlook, in July 2001, 181–184
    cruise passenger arrivals, 180
    market performance, 181
    market share, 180–181
    stay-over tourist arrivals, 180
    tourist accommodation, 181

tourism potential, poll on
    BRIC countries, 320–321
    economic performance, 321–322
    recommendations, 321
    2010 World Travel Market poll, 320–321
tourism statistics, 198–199
tourism taxes, selected Caribbean societies
    fiscal incentives, 368, 370
    fiscal policies, 363–365
    long-term viability, 370
    low input cost, 368
    non-Caribbean fiscal policies, 365–367
    non-fiscal incentives, 370
    parameters, 368
    planned incentives, 369
    private sector benefits, 370
    simplification, 369
    user friendliness, 371
    VAT, 370
tourist arrivals (2008–2011)
    by main market, 391–392, 399–400, 407–408, 415–416
    by month, 387–390, 395–398, 403–406, 411–414
tourist (stop-over) arrivals, 385–386, 394, 402, 410
tourist attractions, 190–191
tour operators
    9/11 attack impact, 186
    competition, 135
    European Tour Operators Association negative report, 229
training and education, tourism
    careers guide, 100
    CTRC role, 99–100
    hospitality and vocational training, 99

(continues on next page)

scholarship programmes, 101
teacher workshops, 100
Trott, Harley, 19

UDC. *See* Urban Development Corporation (UDC)
United Airlines, 185
United Nations World Tourism Organization (UNWTO), 5
United States Tour Operators Association, 294
Urban Development Corporation (UDC), 56

Vanderpool-Wallace, Vincent, 93, 155, 157
Venables, Robert, 44
Venezuela, 123–124
visa requirements, 202, 313
Von Hauenschill, Eberhardt, 93

Walcott, Derek, 260, 261
Wedderburn, Carlos Moore, 65

West India Committee
  formation, 72–73
  role, 73
West Indian Labour Congress, 76
West Indian sugar crisis, 47–48
White, Geoffrey O'Byrne, 336
Wilchcombe, Obie, 154–155
Williams, Eric, 9, 78, 81
Williams, Sherman, 92
Wilson, Cynthia, 92, 250
Wilson, Markly, 42
Windstar Cruises, 186
Wint, Colleen, 92
Woodward, Shaun, 315
World Bank perspective, 129–130, 272–273
Worrell, Delisle, 43

Youngman, Michael, 102–103, 294, 295, 298
Young, Sir Mark, 74–75

www.ingramcontent.com/pod-product-compliance
Lightning Source LLC
Chambersburg PA
CBHW052137300426
44115CB00011B/1412